Eyewitness to the Peninsular War and the Battle of Waterloo

Eyewitness to the Peninsular War and the Battle of Waterloo

The Letters and Journals of
Lieutenant Colonel The Honourable
James Hamilton Stanhope,
1803 to 1825
Recording his Service with
Sir John Moore, Sir Thomas Graham and
the Duke of Wellington

Edited by

GARETH GLOVER

Published in association with the
CHEVENING TRUST

Pen & Sword
MILITARY

First published in Great Britain in 2010 by
Pen & Sword Military
An imprint of
Pen & Sword Books Ltd
47 Church Street
Barnsley
South Yorkshire
S70 2AS

ISBN 978 1 84884 392 9

A CIP catalogue record for this book is available from the British Library

Typeset in Ehrhardt
by S L Menzies-Earl

Printed and bound in England
by CPI Antony Rowe

Pen & Sword Books Ltd incorporates the imprints of
Pen & Sword Aviation, Pen & Sword Maritime,
Pen & Sword Military, Wharncliffe Local History, Pen & Sword Select,
Pen & Sword Military Classics, Leo Cooper, Remember When,
Seaforth Publishing and Frontline Publishing

For a complete list of Pen & Sword titles please contact
PEN & SWORD BOOKS LIMITED
47 Church Street, Barnsley, South Yorkshire, S70 2AS, England
E-mail: enquiries@pen-and-sword.co.uk
Website: www.pen-and-sword.co.uk

Contents

Preface

The Stanhopes of Chevening have played a very prominent role in the political and military history of Great Britain since the seventeenth century. Many of the family over the generations have gained renown for their achievements. James Stanhope, the 1st Earl, had a distinguished military career and was one of the foremost generals of his time, capturing Minorca in 1708 and followed this with an influential political career. Charles Stanhope, the 3rd Earl, made a significant contribution to the science of his age and was a political reformist. His daughter Hester Stanhope is probably the most famous and outlandish of the family, living for many years in Syria. Philip Stanhope, the 5th Earl, was renowned as a politician and historian and finally James Richard, the 7th and last Earl, was prominent at the Admiralty during the early years of the Second World War. It is therefore not surprising that other members of the family have been sidelined by history and few glimpses of them remain. But this is an injustice and I hope that this work will bring one such family member, James Hamilton Stanhope, a stepbrother of Hester Stanhope, into the limelight which he so thoroughly deserves.

Lieutenant-Colonel James Stanhope is not known so much for personal exploits, but more for the journals he so faithfully kept. The circles he moved in gave him a unique opportunity to record the conversations of the famous and influential people with whom he worked so closely during many of the great events of the time. This aids our understanding of their reactions to the events unfolding before them and the thought processes leading to their subsequent decisions.

What are now termed the Napoleonic Wars commenced in 1803 after a short peace between France and Britain had failed to hold (really they were a continuation of the Revolutionary Wars fought between 1793 and 1801) and were to last a further twelve years until the final battle at Waterloo in 1815. The French had suffered a very bloody revolution, the king had been executed and anarchy had prevailed. The monarchies of Europe watched events unfold with abject horror; and many feared facing the guillotine themselves. Their armies were mobilized to defeat the French revolutionaries and nearly succeeded, but desperate times bring desperate measures. The French mobilized their entire population for war. Worse still for neighbouring monarchies was that the French saw an opportunity to export their revolution and many ancient thrones were soon being abandoned in flight.

The wars continued, see-sawing back and forth across Central Europe and Italy with no end in sight – until the appearance of a young French artillery officer, named Napoleon Bonaparte. His skills became evident when he recaptured Toulon from the Allies, launching his meteoric rise through the ranks. Developing the latest arts in warfare, combining rapid movement and crushing superiority at the key moment, won him a cluster of spectacular victories in Italy and he became a national hero. The French government was still weak however and feared this young man's popularity and therefore sent him on a very ambitious attempt to disrupt British control of India via Egypt. Although militarily successful, this expedition was effectively imprisoned within Egypt by the Royal Navy. Realizing success was now impossible, Napoleon calmly left the army before defeat loomed, returned to France still a hero and seized effective control in a coup d'état. Napoleon controlled France with an iron will and embarked on a radical overhaul of the state, bringing in strong central government, a reorganized and much enlarged army, and rewriting the law books. He also began a very ambitious territorial expansion, systematically defeating and incorporating neighbouring states to fund his very costly redevelopment of France. By 1802 France and Britain were exhausted and both agreed to a tentative Peace of Amiens, which in fact they saw more as a period of recuperation, before the final overthrow of their arch enemy. It was as the false peace finally collapsed into open warfare again that James Hamilton Stanhope chose to join the armed services.

James Stanhope's life was one of privilege: he came from an illustrious family with connections right at the heart of government. He was very close to his uncle and patron, the Prime Minister William Pitt the Younger, who nurtured his education and undoubtedly helped him in his early military career. He responded with unbounded love for his surrogate father and was at Pitt's bedside when he died, leaving a moving memorial of his final days.

As a third son, with no fortune to inherit, James was sent out to earn a living. He initially chose the Royal Navy, but soon switched to the Army and joined the 1st Foot Guards. Here he learnt his profession with the regiment on home service and when acting as a garrison in Sicily, but after five years of preparation, war finally called him.

James had already met Sir John Moore whilst in Sicily, but via the influence of his sister, Hester, whom John Moore worshipped, he was offered the post of aide de camp and set sail to join the general in Spain. James landed at Oporto and journeyed over the wild mountains of northern Portugal and Spain, reaching the Army and joining Sir John Moore's staff on the eve of the Battle of Corunna. It was not to be a happy experience for James, losing both his brother Charles and Sir John Moore, who so famously died as victory was secured. James was a moving witness to Moore's death and felt the loss of his brother deeply. He participated in the burial of both.

James returned to the social life of London, occasionally taking tours of Wales, Europe not being accessible, and generally enjoying life as if there was no war.

Meanwhile, Sir Arthur Wellesley, later to be known as the Duke of Wellington, commanded a British army in Portugal and sought to support the Spanish nation which had risen in open revolt against Napoleon's attempts to subjugate the country and place his brother Joseph on the Spanish throne. This war, known as the Peninsular War, raged from 1808 until 1814, when the French were finally forced out of Spain. It was probably the time that the British Army came of age and began to be taken seriously by the continental powers. Traditions of this period still resound through every regiment of the Army to this day.

In 1810 James's battalion sailed to help the Spanish forces hold the strategically important port of Cadiz. James was just about to set out on a tour of the Mediterranean with his stepsister Hester, but immediately sailed for Spain where Sir Thomas Graham took him onto his staff. His time on the Isla was spent learning the language and recording the Spanish political machinations of the Cortes which was then sitting there. Soon enough, active operations called again and James is a very important witness to the campaign leading up to the Battle of Barossa in 1811 and the battle itself. Being so close to Graham he is an invaluable eyewitness. He was clearly used by John Fortescue when he wrote his history of this campaign.

Transferring with his general to the main British Army in Spain led by Lord Wellington, James observed the storming of Ciudad Rodrigo and clearly describes the horror on Wellington's face at the carnage of Badajoz and how close he came to failure. James saw the taking of the forts at Salamanca and the manœuvring before the great battle nearby, but unfortunately did not witness the battle itself, feeling honour bound to escort his general home to convalesce.

James returned to the Army as rapidly as humanly possible, and Wellington rewarded him by placing him in the Quarter Master General's Department. He witnessed the abortive siege of Burgos and the horrors of the subsequent retreat into Portugal, but luckily avoided the fate of his new general, Sir Edward Paget, who was captured by marauding French dragoons.

When Sir Thomas returned to Spain, James rejoined him and served with him during the outflanking march that culminated in the Battle of Vitoria, when French influence in Spain was finally crushed. At the subsequent siege of San Sebastian, James received a severe wound, one that was to plague him for the rest of his life, and returned home to recover, ending his Spanish war.

Recalled to the colours in 1814, James sailed with Sir Thomas Graham once more, this time to the Netherlands. James's journal of this campaign is invaluable and his description of the unsuccessful storming of Bergen op Zoom forms the core of Fortescue's history of this inglorious event. His skills as a negotiator were clearly shown as he regained all of the captured soldiers from the fortress for his country's immediate use.

James returned home during the short peace but was recalled to the Army, now at Brussels, to face Napoleon at Waterloo. James fought this campaign as a regimental officer. He describes the hard fighting in Bossu Wood at Quatre Bras and the hours of suffering in squares on the crest of the ridge at Waterloo, standing rigidly whilst being assailed by the hordes of Napoleon's elite cavalry, until they were worn down and finally retired as a spent force. James was a witness to the final defeat of Napoleon's Guard and as such the end of Napoleon's ambitions.

His negotiation skills came to the fore as he was appointed to the staff and secured the fortress of Peronne for the King of France. As peace then finally gained a foothold in Europe, James maintained his army role during the three years of occupation that followed, but also tried unsuccessfully to form a political career.

His military career effectively at an end, James married and put all his efforts into his new family. But fate cruelly snatched his loved ones away all too soon and he eventually succumbed in tragic circumstances at the age of only 36.

The twists and turns of the tragically short life of Lieutenant-Colonel James Hamilton Stanhope can now be read in full for the first time. Working on this book has been a truly bittersweet experience, but one I ultimately consider to have been a real privilege and I only hope that my efforts have done him justice.

I do hope that he can at last claim his rightful place in the Pantheon of celebrated Stanhopes that have so long adorned this country's history.

Chevening House

Chevening Manor has existed since the days of King John when held by an Adam de Chevening. Through a number of changes of ownership it passed to the Lennard family in 1551, who paid £420 for it and eventually became the Lords Dacre. Around 1630 Richard Lennard, Lord Dacre, completed the current three-storey, symmetrical, red-brick house, as designed by Inigo Jones. The Earl of Sussex (Lord Dacre was created Earl of Sussex by Charles II) died in 1715 and his two co-heir daughters, Barbara and Anne Lennard, agreed to sell the house and the 3,466 acres of ground of Chevening to Major-General James Stanhope in 1717 for £28,000. He was made Earl Stanhope the following year. He added the fine brickwork piazzas in 1720.

The house then passed down through seven generations of Stanhopes until the 7th and last Earl, another James, gave the house and gardens to the state on his death in 1967. To preserve the estate the Earl had seen the Chevening Estate Act pass through parliament in 1959 (amended in 1987) by which it was stipulated that the future resident should be the Prime Minister, a Cabinet Minister, the widow or lineal descendant of King George VI, or the spouse, widow or widower of such a descendant. The Earl had hoped that Charles Prince of Wales would take up residence at Chevening and the prince certainly did consider it. However in 1980, following six years of occupancy, Charles renounced any possibility of further residency and since then the house has been used by successive Foreign Secretaries as a country retreat for their families. The Act also allows for its use, if not required by the government, as a country residence for the Canadian High Commissioner or for the Ambassador of the United States of America.

The Board of Trustees of Chevening continue to be responsible for the maintenance and upkeep of the house and a major redevelopment was completed in 1973 to return the roof and attic area, altered by the 3rd Earl, back to its former glory. The upkeep of the property is maintained from the estate and the proceeds of the bequest set up by the last Earl.

Additions and Alterations

The letters and journals used have been transcribed to my best ability exactly as the originals; however I have taken the liberty of making some few minor alterations to aid the reader's enjoyment and understanding. I have altered the spelling of names of people and places to the accepted modern version to aid identification. Where this is doubtful or may cause confusion, I have added notes to explain. I have expanded abbreviations, again to aid the reader's experience.

Where there is a word missing in haste or the writing is impossible to read clearly through smudging, tearing or downright bad handwriting (something James suffered with at times) I have followed established guidelines and included the word within square brackets, if simply omitted, and with a question mark if I am unsure of the exact word. Dating has also been standardized for all letters. Otherwise these letters and journals are a true transcript of the originals.

Any errors within this work are of course my responsibility. I can only crave the reader's forgiveness for any found, as I have done everything humanly possible to check facts. I will be happy to discuss any errors. Readers can contact me through my website: garethglovercollection.com

Acknowledgements

With a book this complex, with numerous different aspects, each of which require expert knowledge to fully understand, I have sought and received help and advice from a great many people, more skilled in their own particular fields than I ever could be. All of this advice has been given freely and with untiring good faith. Many people have devoted hours of their time to helping me, for which I am eternally grateful. There are very many good people in the Napoleonic community, whom I have been privileged to either meet or correspond with across the world – something that is not always self-evident amongst the fiery arguments that always seem to rage.

I will start by stating that I hope that I remember to thank all those who have helped me in varying degrees, but if I make an omission in error I truly hope I may be forgiven for such.

I must begin by thanking Mr Edward Barham, of the Board of Trustees of the Chevening Estate, for originally allowing me to undertake the task of publishing the journals of James Hamilton Stanhope and to Colonel Richard Brook and Kay Thorne, who so kindly allowed my wife Mary and I the rare privilege of visiting the delightful Chevening House, and taking time out of their busy schedules to patiently escort us throughout. I was provided with access to numerous artefacts originally belonging to James and Charles Stanhope, still held at the property, for me to photograph as illustrations for this work. The highlight for myself was the ability to hold and even look through Wellington's own large telescope from the Battle of Waterloo, given to the 4th Earl many years later.

I must also not forget to offer my thanks to Mrs Lela Weavers, Warden at the neighbouring St Botolph's Church, for kindly arranging for Mr Bob Hodges, their historian, to meet us there and escort us throughout the beautiful old church. Bob was extremely kind, spending a long time with us patiently explaining the history of this fine edifice and giving us free access to the numerous monuments to the Stanhope family which again form illustrations to this book.

I have had to liaise with many archivists across the country in an endeavour to track down the correspondence of James Stanhope and must thank a number for their tireless efforts to search out and provide copies of these documents, some being well hidden within huge volumes of family correspondence. I must thank Richard Childs, Archivist at the West Sussex Record Office; Pat Harvey at the Lincolnshire Archives; and particularly Michael Carter, Archivist at the Centre for Kentish Studies at Maidstone, and his staff who cheerfully provided literally dozens of Stanhope family files for us to search over three long days and photocopied numerous letters for me to transcribe at leisure. And although their efforts were eventually in vain, I would also like to thank Jeannie McLean and Mary Young who searched only to confirm that there were no portraits of James at Mellerstain or Scone Palace respectively.

James's regular use of both Spanish and Latin required expert translation, which was kindly undertaken by Mr Pedro Prieto Ramiro, a Spaniard and a retired Latin teacher, a fantastic combination in this case. He has tirelessly corresponded with me to ensure that the translation is as true to the meaning as possible and this book would not be half what it is without his valuable help. I must also thank Andre Dellevoet for his help translating the French texts.

Many fellow military historians have also made significant contributions and or suggestions and all have given great encouragement and support for this project. I thank them all wholeheartedly. I would particularly like to thank the inimitable Mick Crumplin for expert answers on the numerous medical issues I had to raise with him; also, Ian Robertson, Robert Burnham, David Miller, David Bromley for his records on burial sites, Digby Smith, Don Graves, Rod Macarthur, Anthony Gray and Rory Muir for their expert advice.

I thank Jim Lowther for permission to publish the papers I found in the Lowther Archive and Jenny Boyce for permission to publish extracts from N B Penny's article in the *Journal of the Warburg and Courtauld Institutes*.

Finally I particularly thank my beloved wife Mary, who has so tirelessly supported me in this project and helped me greatly, as she always does in everything I do.

Gareth Glover
2010

Chapter 1

Early Life

James Hamilton Stanhope was born to Charles Stanhope, the 3rd Earl Stanhope, and his second wife Louisa Grenville on 7 September 1788. Earl Stanhope had previously married his cousin Lady Hester Pitt, by whom he had three daughters, Hester, Griselda and Lucy; but his happiness was shattered on the sudden death of Lady Hester in 1780. Within six months the earl had married Louisa, a marriage more of convenience than love, providing a mother to his children. However, further children did arrive: Philip, who was known as 'Mahon', the courtesy title of the successor, Charles and lastly our man James Hamilton.

The 3rd Earl was not, as is sometimes stated, an inventor. He was in fact a developer of other people's inventions, taking an idea further than perhaps the inventor had originally conceived, and was very catholic in his endeavours, working in many different fields at the same time. Between this and politics, he had little time for his children.

James grew up in what modern experts would describe as a very dysfunctional family, although there does not appear to have been any physical abuse. Neglect and rigid discipline by their stern, overbearing and permanently distracted father, coupled with the shame he brought on them for his radical anti-war views, seems to have forced each child in turn to flee the parental home.

Hester moved in with her grandmother under the protection of her uncle, William Pitt. Griselda left home and lived at a cottage at Walmer lent by William Pitt, where she fell in love with John Tickell, an army officer[1] who was thought to have prospects. These proved false and Pitt secured him a better appointment. Lucy married a local surgeon, one Thomas Taylor, at the tender age of 16 and Pitt found her husband a lucrative place as Comptroller General at the Customs.

Philip Henry (Mahon) was educated at Chevening by a succession of tutors but his father refused to let him go to university. Hester arranged his escape to Erlanger University in Germany. He then toured Europe with Hester but rejected her 'mothering' and remained estranged from her for the rest of her life. He married Catherine Smith, a daughter of Lord Carrington, had three children but had a strained relationship with all his siblings and even took his father to the Court of Chancery to try to obtain a settlement on an allowance until he inherited, which failed. William Pitt again stepped in and gained two sinecures for him, each worth £1,000 per annum. Philip as heir apparent could not be risked in the front line, but he did for appearance's sake during the invasion threat command the 1st Battalion the Cinque Port Volunteers. He clearly did not take his role seriously as he wrote on 12 October 1803: 'As for my regiment I am persuaded that it does not and cannot stand in need of my presence, for with the assistance of a good adjutant and a very sensible, active major it will be in as great a state of forwardness as any other.' He did however have his portrait painted in the uniform.

James's turn to leave home arrived in 1802 when he and Charles fled Chevening with a Mr Rice, who brought them safely to Pitt and Hester.

Although James's family life was rarely happy, Pitt's influence and wealth did help to promote him in his chosen career. Charles joined the army and at the still tender age of 15 James was enlisted into the Royal Navy in 1803. He did not enjoy the hard sea life and within a year had transferred into the First Regiment of Foot Guards (which would not be known as the Grenadier Guards for another eleven years). James's promotion through the regiment was not meteoric, as he initially was given time to return to school to complete his education.[2]

With the children gone, the earl invited a music teacher, Mrs Walburga Lackner, into Chevening and soon it became clear that the earl's interest was in more than music. On 30 August 1806 a deed of separation was settled and their mother moved out of Chevening permanently, with an income of £1,500 per annum. The children remained loyal to their mother and visited and corresponded regularly. Their father seems to have had no communication directly with his children from this date till his death bed, when he still refused offers of reconciliation.

Chapter 2

Early Days in Service

The early military career of James Hamilton Stanhope is a little blurred, but the general facts can be ascertained. It would appear that in 1803 James was entered as a midshipman in the Royal Navy and served onboard HMS *Iris*, a 32 gun frigate under Captain Clarke. In a short letter to his elder brother he mentions that his ship is bound for Newfoundland again, presumably on convoy duty.

> HMS *Iris*, Spithead 9 May 1803
>
> My dear Mahon
>
> … I coincide what's perfectly with your desire of my going out to Newfoundland once more … We have had a very hot press,[1] everybody was taken, but most released the next day. ... Our squadron is already sailed for Newfoundland and I suppose we shall follow them very soon.[2]

However, the sea life does not seem to have suited him and James was gazetted as an ensign in the 3rd Battalion, 1st Foot Guards,[3] on 26 December 1803. By early 1804, James was staying in London, as a letter to Chevening dated 6 March was sent from 37 St James's Place, a building within Cleveland Court. The reasons for his leaving the Navy are unclear, but before joining his regiment he was given permission to complete his education and was duly enrolled with a tutor, a Mr Richard Harvey of Leatherhead, at serious expense.

> Leatherhead 25 April 1804
>
> … I should be happy to receive Mr Stanhope as a pupil but I am at present so circumstanced as not to have it in my power to admit him before the 1 June.
>
> … I have now four pupils with me, two about fourteen and two considerably younger. Their vacation will be about 21 June. As Mr Stanhope may so shortly be called into active life, I would, if it met your approbation, dedicate the time of their absence entirely to him. My terms are 100 guineas and for those who have remained with me during the vacation, I have had three guineas a week, washing an extra charge.[4]

The 1st and 3rd Battalions of the 1st Guards then formed the 1st Guards Brigade and were stationed at Chatham to protect the vital dockyard in case of invasion by

Napoleon until July 1804, when they moved to an encampment on Barham Down. The brigade remained here until October and then went into barracks at Deal until August 1805. The news that Nelson had forced the combined fleet of Spain and France to seek refuge in Cadiz led to the easing of concern on the coast and the Guards returned to Chatham on 30 August. It should be noted that the troops were stood down from invasion watch well before Nelson's great but costly victory at Trafalgar that October. The Guards Brigade being away from London this long period, it was left to the 2nd Battalion to furnish parties for the funeral of the Duke of Gloucester, Colonel of the 1st Guards, and Lord Nelson, but it is likely that James witnessed these memorable events, not being with his battalion at Chatham.

He was certainly in London with Charles and Hester in January 1806 as they were all present at the death of their 'surrogate father', William Pitt the Younger, who died on 23 January 1806. James recorded the last hours of his patron in great detail and clearly felt his loss deeply; this touching portrait is reproduced as Appendix B to this volume. Hester stated that in one of their last conversations Mr Pitt had spoken to her about Charles and James.

> As for Charles, he is such an excellent young man that one cannot wish him to be otherwise than he is; and Moore is such a perfect officer, that he will give him every information in his profession that he can possibly require. The only apprehension I have is on the score of women, who will perhaps think differently of him from what he thinks of himself: but with James the case is otherwise. He is a young man you must keep under; else you will always see him trying to be a Jolie garcon. For Charles's steadiness, I do not fear; but the little one will one day fall into the hands of men who will gain him over and unsettle his political principles. You can guide him, and so long as he is under your care he is safe.

And, added Lady Hester: 'Mr Pitt was right doctor; for the moment I quitted England he fell into the snares of Lord Bulkeley[5] and his party and instead of being in Mr Canning's place, which he might have been, he became nothing'.[6]

She went on to say on the death of Pitt that several tradesmen applied for settlement of bills.

> So, recollecting an old peer,[7] who had been one of Mr Pitt's particular friends, I sent off James to him to his country seat with a letter, relating the whole business: this person immediately gave James a draft for £2,000 with which he returned, and paid his own and Charles's debts. Well, it was agreed between Charles, James and me, that who ever had the first windfall should pay the £2,000. Charles died: James was not rich enough at any time to do it, and it fell to my lot to pay it … When Coutts wrote me word that my brother James had been very good to me in having given me £1000, he did not know that the civility was not so disinterested as he imagined … James took possession of about five

hundred pounds worth of plate of mine and of my jewels and of Tipoo Sahib's gold powder flask worth £200[8] and of the Cardinal of York's present, which to some persons who wanted a relic of the Stuarts was invaluable. Then there was a portfolio full of fine engravings of Morghen[9] and others that the Duke of Buckingham bought of him: so there was at least as much as he sent me.[10]

After news of Trafalgar, the Neapolitan court was persuaded to resist the French and were duly ousted from the Italian mainland and replaced by Joseph Bonaparte as King. Knowing that the French would now launch an attack on Sicily, Sir John Stuart,[11] who commanded the British forces there, took the initiative, landed on the mainland and defeated a slightly larger French force at Maida but was forced to remove all forces from the mainland by the end of 1806 and Stuart took command of Malta.

Not until the summer of 1806 do we finally find James sailing with his battalion to Sicily,[12] where his brother Charles, then a captain in the 52nd Foot, was already serving as an aide de camp to Sir John Moore,[13] a very close friend of his sister Hester. Orders to prepare for foreign service and to augment their numbers to 120 men per company were received on 8 July and James was allocated to the 6th Company under the command of Lieutenant-Colonel the honourable Edward Capel and the honourable Captain James Macdonald,[14] his fellow ensign being Richard Henry Marsac.

The Guard Brigade marched to Ramsgate on 26 July to embark, being nearly 2,600 men strong, the 3rd Battalion numbering 1,167 men;[15] they were also joined by the 1/52nd, 1/62nd and eight companies of the 95th Rifles. Contrary winds forced the fleet to put into Plymouth on 21 August where the force was further augmented by 1/45th, 1/87th and 2nd King's German Legion Light Dragoons. Fears of attack, following losses in the homeward bound fleet from Quebec, caused the squadron to be detained and the brigade was disembarked on 2 September to encamp on Bickleigh Down.[16] Here the flank companies of the two battalions were formed into a separate corps.

An undated letter from James was sent home from Plymouth, showing all his frustration as they waited to sail to who knows where.

My dearest mother,

I trust you will not take it amiss that you have not heard from me; the only news I could have sent would only have the more perplexed and teased you. I was anxious sincerely to give you the latest accounts of me in this country but by the most unexampled ill fortune with respect to wind, from day to day in anxious expectation we have been waiting to sail. I was also unable (as indeed I now am) to tell you how to direct to me in safety. Perhaps we may be off tomorrow, perhaps not for a week, so my dear mother on the whole I think you had better wait until you hear again. The greatest part of the last fortnight I was in the Isle of Wight with the general, till we came here together, the fleet having passed in the night. I have obtained leave to go out in the *Kingfisher*[17] which is commanded by a son of Lord Hugh Seymour's[18] who was in the cockpit as a midshipman with me, instead of a transport, it is much more comfortable. You may have heard my dear mother that the destination of the expedition is changed & that Sicily (if at all) is not the first object in view, we have a considerable train of battering cannon embarked & everything proper for a siege, a circumstance which I cannot understand & that involves the whole in the darkest veil of mystery. This is certainly a secret & I trust a successful expedition. However we go, and whatever becomes of me, you may depend my dear mother that my affection & duty to you remains unalterable & unimpaired & that I shall always think it the greatest honour to remain your most dutiful and affectionate son, James Hamilton Stanhope

PS I hope Sir Joseph Banks[19] is well. Pray give my most respectful duty to him. If we have a moment's notice, I will write when we sail, at any rate depend on hearing the first opportunity that occurs when I have ought to say. Heaven bless you my dearest mother.
PPS I hope you received my last safe.

Sicily was a dangerous posting, as the locals were just as ferocious to each other as to the French! Charles writing from Messina on 1 September 1806 states:

General Stuart has not yet left us but I believe goes to Malta tomorrow, he is at present in Calabria where the people are in the most shocking state possible, cutting one another's throats and committing daily the most shocking murders. With that also a set of dirty cowards and when the French advanced a party the other day, we had hundreds of them here all armed, that had run away on the report in the greatest fright and not one of them had ever seen the French. At Regia there were 15 people murdered in one night because they were Jacobins, that is to say perhaps had a watch or teaspoon worth stealing.

Charles had already heard that James was likely to join him soon and wrote again of the dangers on the island.

Messina 22 November 1806

… By the Army List I fear James will be with the Guards here, I hope not for your sake and I do not see much good he would derive as I see no great chance of being employed on the Staff …

I have a Maltese bat man who is very good; I have now by the convoy got two owing to a mistake in having sent for one from Malta who came too late after I had procured one here. I trust as they are both very good I shall keep him till the troops come as if James should be amongst them he will I suppose want one, you see I have a magnificent establishment.

The brigade re-embarked on 13 September and sailed on 24 September under Admiral Sir John Duckworth and finally arrived in the Bay of Messina on 2 December 1806. The Guards finally landed at Catania on 4 December with the left wing at Catania and right at Augusta.

Again, there are only a few interesting snippets in James's letters home, but Charles often gave an update on his younger brother's whereabouts in his letters to their mother and these help to paint a clearer picture of the young officer learning his trade on active service.

The first surviving letter from James in Sicily is dated 6 December 1806. His letters ramble on at length about the island, but give no information about himself. However, on 1 January 1807 Charles writes 'I leave this to Messina and return by Catania where I shall see James'. Hamilton in his history of the 1st Guards states that a detachment of two officers and sixty men were sent to Taormina on 8 May; however Charles's letter of 22 February clearly states that James was already at Taormina; Charles also mentions a major expedition being formed.

> I have to return you a thousand thanks … for a joint letter to James & myself which you wrote about a week before which arrived the same day, together with the box which I have not opened but sent on to James at Taormina about thirty miles from this, half way to Catania … I saw Macdonald at Catania, they are living in the same house and I like him more than ever … There is an expedition going to sail from this and the troops are now embarking, it is to be under the orders of Major General James Fraser[20] and consists of 31st, 1st & 2nd Battalions of the 35th, 78th, De Roll's Regiment, Chasseurs Britaniques, a detachment of 2nd Light dragoons, artillery, artificers & Staff, come to at least 5,000 men in all. Major General Wauchope,[21] Brigadier General Stewart[22] and Maule[23] go under Fraser. Mr Percy[24] who came out as extra A.D.C. to General Moore goes as the same to General Fraser. We do not know where they are going but I suspect to Egypt, as I do not think if there was anything to be done they would have sent the regiments I mention.
>
> 23 February 1807
>
> … In addition to the troops I mentioned, a regiment which has been raised in this island and are called the Royal Sicilian Volunteers were embarked. The two battalions of the 35th and Chasseurs are on board and they only wait till the transports with the other troops on board come round.

Charles again writes of the dangers on the island on 8 April 1807:

> There is a circumstance here worth mentioning, within the last six weeks there have been four soldiers hung for murder, which I believe was never known in the British Army before. I hear three of them were privates who had killed a sergeant and one corporal who had shot a private.

> … The corporal was more singular of the kind of case heard as it was for no other reason than because the private was a dirty fellow and he thought the company would be much better without him and he told him so some hours before he committed the horrid murder, telling him to prepare himself for death as he was determined to shoot him before the night.
>
> Alexandria surrendered without opposition on the 17th.[25]

Life on the island was tedious for the Guards officers and many sightseeing visits to temple sites and the mountains were allowed. On 14 April Charles reports that James was still well and enjoying a leave of absence in Catania:

> the general met James on his way to Palermo, he was quite well and he had Mr Macdonald & two officers of the same regiment with him. The Guards when they travel go very much in a thing we call Lettiga,[26] it is used in Italy so I need not describe it, it is carried between two wheels, you may hear them ½ a mile off. The bulls and the harmonious voice of the muleteer, well James' party had one of these things and horses and asses and baggage and provisions, so I hope they will have a pleasant journey.
>
> I expect to hear from him in a few days from Catania as his leave of absence is almost expired.

On 29 April Charles wrote to his sister Hester, enclosing an interesting anecdote of James's character.

> You tell me in your last to look after James so I must tell you how modestly he behaves and how much he is liked, he is a great character at Catania and looked up to by the inhabitants. I heard a thing of him yesterday by accident which gave me so much pleasure as I cannot refrain from mentioning it to you as it shows so good a heart and disposition so different from my other brother.[27] There was a sergeant of the Guards shot by one of the privates at Taormina when James was there, he was a very good man and it is the more distressing as he has left a widow and children. Colonel Anderson[28] was asking a sergeant of the Guards who acts as clerk in the Adjutant General's Office what had become of the poor woman. He said that there had been a subscription among the officers which gave her enough for the present to make her comfortable but that Mr Stanhope had settled £10 a year on her for life and paid the first year in advance. Now, though I have had a great many letters from him, he never made the slightest remark on his having done anything of the kind which in my eyes adds greatly to the merit of the action.

James wrote to Hester himself on 24 May 1807 from Contessa, a village three miles from Messina, explaining how well Charles got on with Sir John Moore, but also with news of the disaster in Egypt.

My dear Hester

… you have heard of the disasters of our troops in Egypt, at least 2,000 have fallen victims to the madness of the administration who sent them and General Wauchope who commanded them. He did a thing unheard of in the annals of war, entering a *town* without summoning it and permitting himself and flower of his army to be shot from the windows. 2 more regiments are just sailed from here to reinforce the remainder at Alexandria, but it is supposed they will evacuate it. A friend of mine, an officer of the 35th, brother to a Captain Joddrell of this regiment, a most amiable and gallant fellow, fell in the second attack of Rosetta and his brother is now deploring his loss in the very next room.[29] The *passage of the Dardanelles* is more disgraceful *if possible* to the persons who *ordered it* than the expedition to Egypt.[30] … The Prince of Hesse[31] with 3,000 men are now in Calabria and the French to the amount of 1,400 are retreating, for we might take Naples in a very short time, but should quickly be obliged to evacuate it again. … I have seen dear Charles lately everyday. He looks very well, is growing fat and is in good spirits. His general and he seem to have a mutual regard for each other and in short nothing can go on better.

Charles wrote home on 25 May giving good news of James but terrible news from Egypt; and more local murders.

I see James now very day, he is looking very well and in good spirits … this has been a pretty business in Egypt, we have lost 1,500 men and I do not think we ought to have lost 50. We were in Alexandria and there was an end of it. I do not find that they were sent there to take the country. If even they chose to take Rosetta why detach such small parties? For poor General Wauchope (old good man) he went quietly into Rosetta without knowing there was an enemy in it and never having taken the means to ascertain whether there was one or not.[32] General Stewart in the second business was astonished one morning to find an army from Cairo between him and Colonel Mclelland's detachment which before he knew anything of it were cut to pieces.[33] General Fox[34] has sent for Sherbrooke[35] and the 21st and 62nd Regiments from this to supply the losses they have sustained. … In my last I mentioned a singular and dreadful circumstance of murders being so common in this army. There have been two since, one in the Guard where one man shot another and the other in the 20th where when confined to the black hole a man took the firelock and shot a man through his leg and the ball unfortunately went through another man also and killed him. He was not in a passion when he did it and no previous quarrel. The man in the Guards is not hung, but flogged and transported for life. Why they forgave him a capital punishment I do not know as it was like the other murders without any cause but a guard at the time he went and took a firelock and shot the man.

James wrote home again to his mother on 24 June stating he was again going on detachment.

> My dearest mother,
>
> I cannot tell you how disappointed in not receiving a letter from you by the last packet. I should have been much more mortified had not chance brought my brother Charles here a few days after, who had received a letter from you saying you were well at bed roses. He had been at Palermos with his general and instead of accompanying him by sea, came here across the country. He remained with me only three days but during that time saw all that was worth seeing here … I have hopes of meeting Charles again soon as he has promised to come and spend a few days with me at Taormina at which place I shall be stationed with a detachment for the whole of next month.

James arrived back in early September and it would seem was posted with a detachment on the Lipari[36] Islands, as again Charles states in a letter from Messina, dated 18 September 1807: 'James is going to the Lipari Islands and is to return in about a week.' However, being very busy, it would appear that James had omitted to write home, as in a letter dated from Messina 30 September 1807 Charles states 'James as I thought on his return from Lipari was extremely grieved by your letter. He has written back as he says a long letter to you.'

This is the last we hear from the brothers in Sicily, as Sir John Moore was ordered to sail with a sizeable force including the 1st Guards in October 1807, initially to Gibraltar with the intention of aiding the Portuguese, who were now threatened by Napoleon's ambition. They arrived too late to stop Junot marching into the country and the Prince Regent and his court sailing to the Brazils. The force returned to England by late December 1807 where Charles soon followed his general in May 1808 on a new and pointless expedition to aid Sweden. James, with the Guards Brigade, landed at Portsmouth and marched to Deal, where they remained stationed peacefully until September 1808.

Chapter 3

Corunna Campaign

Moore's force, returning from Sweden, had arrived at Portsmouth on 20 July, only to receive orders to sail again immediately for Portugal, being sent to reinforce the small army already due to arrive there under Sir Arthur Wellesley, a young and upcoming general who had earned a high reputation whilst serving in India. The government moved to strongly reinforce Wellesley's army and had then decided such a sizeable force should have a more senior commander and quickly despatched three officers senior to Wellesley, including Moore who would inevitably supersede him. This madness duly caused a successful campaign by Wellesley to oust the French from Portugal, including victories at Rolica and Vimiero, to stutter and stall as the more cautious Sir Hew Dalrymple and Sir Harry Burrard subsequently arrived. Eventually the notorious Convention of Cintra, by which Junot's forces were transported home in British ships, caused the recall of all three officers to answer to a government reeling from extremely adverse public reaction.

Charles had sailed to Portugal with Moore but was no longer attached to his staff, as he had recently been gazetted a major in the 50th (West Kent) Regiment of Foot, which regiment he duly joined at Torres Vedras just as the fighting ended. Here he met another new major joining the regiment, one Charles Napier, an old colleague from the 52nd and one of a famous family that seems to have formed the very backbone of the British Army in the Peninsular.

Sir John Moore luckily was not implicated in the Convention of Cintra and was allowed to remain and take command of the expeditionary force now in control of Portugal as Dalrymple, Burrard and Wellesley duly sailed home to face the baying crowds. Moore decided to take his army deep into Spain to aid the Spanish, who sought his support to resist the mighty French Army which Napoleon had now openly sent against them. He was bent upon imposing his brother Joseph as King of Spain, having forced the Bourbon royal family to denounce their throne and having placed them under virtual house arrest in France.

James was gazetted a lieutenant and captain[1] in the 1st Foot Guards on 14 January 1808 whilst on home service. During early 1808 we hear from James on leave of absence in a series of letters detailing a tour of southeast Wales which he undertook with Hester, including Builth Wells, Lanthony Priory, the Black Mountains, Tintern Abbey, Chepstow Castle and Raglan Castle.[2]

Presumably through family connections, it appears that James had been appointed to replace Charles as aide de camp to the commander-in-chief in Ireland, although he had not yet travelled there. Hence he did not sail with his battalion when it eventually sailed on 8 September as part of a corps for Sir John Moore's army in Spain. The 3rd Battalion 1st Guards formed part of a large reinforcement being sent under the command of Sir David Baird totalling some 10,000 men, which landed at La Corunna on 13 October.

However, it would seem that James was unhappy being left behind and through the influence of Hester, who could command any favour of Sir John Moore, permission was granted for him to join his staff as an extra aide de camp with the commander-in-chief's permission, which was duly granted. Moore wrote to Hester from Salamanca, as he drew his forces together, clearly showing that he was far from certain of success. He reported that her beloved Charles would soon be with the army but that James was likely to arrive too late to see anything but the failure of the campaign.

Salamanca 23 November 1808[3]

> … I shall be very glad to receive James if he wishes to come to me as an extra Aide de Camp though I have already too many, I am obliged or should be to take a young Fitzclarence[4] but I have a sincere regard for James & besides can refuse you nothing, but to follow your advice. He must get the Commander in Chief's leave to come to Spain, he may then join me. He will however come too late, I shall already be beaten. I am within 4 marches of the French with only a third of my force and as the Spaniards have been dispersed in all quarters, my junction on the other two thirds is very precarious and when we all join, we still will be very inferior to the enemy. … Charles is not yet arrived, his was one of the best regiments that left Lisbon … We are in a scrape but I hope we shall have spirit to get out of it. … If I extricate myself and those in the army from our present difficulties and if I ever beat the French I shall return to you with satisfaction, but if not it will be better I shall never quit Spain.

News of Sir John Moore's permission to join him seems to have travelled fast for James was at Portsmouth by 6 December seeking a passage to Spain. He wrote a short note from here to his mother.

My dear mother,

> … I delayed my departure [from London] to the last moment I could in hopes of seeing you … I am going A.D.C. to Sir John Moore retaining my position in Ireland till I find myself settled. My horses are embarked this morning and we expect to sail with the first fair wind.

While James hoped for fair winds to carry him swiftly to Portugal, much had changed in the situation of Sir John Moore's army. Napoleon's army, marching south towards

Madrid, seemingly unaware of the presence of Moore's force, had opened his rear to attack. Moore sought to disrupt Napoleon's communications, thereby aiding the Spanish defenders of the capital. He cautiously moved forward, unaware of events near Madrid and sought to catch Marshal Soult's[5] small force in an isolated position. However, the Spanish defence of Madrid proved to be far from desperate and the city fell with ease. Napoleon had now become aware of Moore in his precarious situation, turning his entire army towards him. Napoleon aimed to destroy Moore's force entirely and perhaps thereby force the British government to the negotiating table. Moore, learning of this disastrous turn of events, was forced to order a rapid retreat and only just escaped the trap that had been set for him. Despite a few successful rearguard cavalry actions, the retreat was made at a forced pace, in atrocious weather and with few supplies.

Large numbers of the troops were lost to exhaustion, sickness, malnutrition and excessive drunkenness when large wine stores were unfortunately discovered, but few to enemy action. The cohesion of some units seems to have broken down and much of the army resembled a fleeing mass; but the first sight of the sea and therefore the end of the retreat, the knowledge that there were large supplies stockpiled at Corunna and the news that they would have to give battle to secure a safe embarkation on the fleet of ships that were starting to arrive, rejuvenated their spirits and as if by magic the Army reformed. Charles had endured all the trials and tribulations of this long march across northern Spain and his short journal and letters of this period are reproduced in this volume as Appendix A.

James appears to have landed at Oporto and travelled overland to join Moore[6] but only caught up with the army when it had arrived at La Corunna on 14 January 1809 when he found the army in a terrible condition but now well supplied and eager to do battle with the pursuing French Army which could be seen just a few miles away. James soon joined the staff of Sir John Moore but took time to discover the whereabouts of Charles. The following day the brothers were able to meet; they had always been good friends and this reunion was to become particularly poignant.

On the following morning, the 16 January, the French Army under Marshal Soult advanced and Sir John Moore, who had stationed his troops on the hills overlooking the harbour of La Corunna in defence of his embarkation point, stood ready to defend to the last.

The battle commenced at about two in the afternoon; James spent the day following his general and occasionally riding off at breakneck speed, ignoring the whistling balls to deliver urgent orders to the various formations in the battle line.

Charles Napier later recorded a fine pen portrait of Sir John Moore during the battle, not a little unlike the famous prose of his brother William's *History*.[7]

> Suddenly I heard the gallop of horses, and turning, saw Moore. He came at speed, and pulled up so sharp and close, he seemed to have alighted from the air: man and horse looking at the approaching foe with an intenseness that

seemed to concentrate all feelings in their eyes. The sudden stop of the animal, a cream-coloured one with black tail and mane, had cast the latter streaming forwards, its ears were pushed out like horns, while its eyes flashed fire, and it snorted loudly with expanded nostrils, expressing terror, astonishment and muscular exertion. My first thought was, it will be away like the wind! But then I looked at its rider, and the horse was forgotten. Thrown on its haunches, the animal came sliding and dashing the dirt up with its forefeet, thus bending the general forward almost to its neck; but his head was thrown back, and his look more keenly piercing than I ever before saw it. He glanced to the right and left, and then fixed his eyes intently on the enemy's advancing column, at the same time grasping the reins with both hands, and pressing the horse firmly with his knees. His body thus seemed to deal with the animal while his mind was intent on the enemy, and his aspect was one of searching intenseness beyond the power of words to express …

Charles meanwhile, along with his friend Charles Napier, was fully engaged in commanding the 50th Regiment during severe fighting around the key village of Elvina. Having driven the French from the village in close-quarter combat, the brigade advanced towards the main French line on a nearby hill, only to be attacked by overwhelming forces and pushed back to the village, where they continued to fight, holding on until eventually relieved by the Guards Brigade, including James's battalion. However, during the confused fighting, the 50th had lost many men, including their majors, who were both initially presumed to be dead. Luckily for Charles Napier, this proved to be incorrect, as he was actually wounded and captured, eventually being released in a subsequent prisoner exchange and returned to his regiment. For the unfortunate Charles Banks Stanhope, the rumours proved to be only too true. During the advance whilst leading his men forward towards the French hill, he posed a significant target in his brand new uniform with gleaming silver epaulettes and he had been struck in the chest by a musket ball, expiring instantly.

As the fighting continued, James remained blissfully unaware of the death of his beloved brother and continued to ride across the chaotic battlefield, his first induction into the real horrors of war. First, when returning from carrying a message, he discovered that Sir John Moore had been struck from his horse by a roundshot which had ripped away his left shoulder and exposed the lung, a wound that was inevitably going to be fatal. Soon this was followed by the arrival of the painful news of the loss of his own brother.

There are two versions of how and when James heard of the death of Charles, not surprising in such a chaotic situation, but the general facts agree. George Napier, a fellow aide to Sir John Moore, states that:

At this period [after the 50th had been relieved by the Guards] Captain Stanhope, a brother of the major, and myself were riding towards the 50th in order to make some inquiries respecting our brothers, and I was just at the rear

> of the regiment, when I met some soldiers carrying the body of an officer who was shot through the heart. I jumped from my horse, removed with trembling hands the handkerchief which was over the face, and beheld the pale and ghastly countenance of my valued friend, Charles Stanhope! I had no time to shed a tear to his memory; his poor brother was approaching; I quickly remounted my horse, and meeting him, said 'Come along, we must instantly return to General Hope;'[8] at the same time I seized the bridle of his horse, and turned him round before he had time to recognise the bleeding corpse of his gallant brother. As we went along I told him what had happened, and he bore it as every soldier ought, but could not resist the desire of going to take a last look at poor Charles. To this I could not object, but did not accompany him ...[9]

This version of events seems true and must have occurred towards dusk, and it is possible that there was some delay before Napier plucked up the courage to tell James of the death of Charles. Therefore it is not incompatible with the other witness, Captain John Patterson of the 50th Regiment, who states:

> Soon after nightfall, and when the clash of arms was no longer heard, an internment of the dead took place, and many a poor fellow, who had a few hours before been full of life and strength, was now deposited in his narrow bed. The remains of Major Stanhope were lowered to the grave by his brother officers and comrades, with their sashes. He had worn this day a suit of new uniform, and a pair of bright silver epaulets, in which, with his military cloak around him, upon the same hour as his lamented chief, he was consigned to an honourable tomb.
>
> While we were engaged in the performance of this melancholy duty, the Honourable Captain Stanhope of the Guards, aide de camp to Sir John Moore, rode up, directed by the torch light, to the mournful group. It was the first intimation which he received of his brave relation's fate. Dismounting, and overcome with grief, he took a last farewell, and having obtained his ring, together with a lock of hair, he tore himself away from the heartrending scene ...[10]

James makes it clear in a letter to Lord Lonsdale,[11] that he was present at the burial of his brother exactly as Patterson describes. James must then have also been given the many artefacts of Charles's that now lie at Chevening, taken home as last mementoes for his mother and of course his favourite sister, Hester.

James returned from the burial to the house where Sir John Moore lay mortally wounded and with his fellow aides witnessed his chief's death, in fact his very last words were to James: 'Remember me to your sister'.

Following the costly victory, the army was permitted to embark with only minor hindrance by Soult and this Napoleonic 'Dunkirk' terminated with the successful deliverance of Moore's army. James sailed home with the terrible task before him of informing his family of their loss. He wrote to many family and friends of Charles, giving them a description of his death and the catastrophic effect it had had on Hester in particular.

> To the Duke of Richmond[12]
>
> Montague Square
>
> Monday 30 January 1809
>
> I would have done myself the honour of writing to your Grace before, had I not been employed on the most melancholy, but to me important of duties, that of offering every consolation in my power to a sister who is the object of one's duty & affection & who is now oppressed with the heaviest misfortune that remained in the catalogues of human woes. All who knew my brother & were acquainted with the nobleness, generosity & openness of his soul, his high honour, his zeal for his country's service must truly deplore his loss, but to her the spectator and admirer of his milder virtues & his first & dearest friend, the calamity is doubly severe & more wholly irreparable. It is my only consolation, the only comfort that time & reflection has yet brought me, that if he could have chosen the mode of his death, it would have been (as providence ordained) at the head of his regiment in the point of danger & honour, that of the attack; nor does it bring a slight alleviation of my grief to recollect the sincere & unsought for grief that I saw displayed by the regiment when I saw performed the last sad offices to the departed; all were recalling to their minds his bravery, his humanity & his knowledge of military duties, all felt his loss & every one most feelingly & bitterly deplored it. The day previous to the action, when I first saw him after my landing, he enquired most particularly after your grace and strongly expressed his thanks & gratitude for the favourable light you were pleased to hold him in. The rest of his conversation was divided between anxiety for my dear sister and a wish to have an opportunity of distinguishing himself. I am happy to say that the strength of mind which Hester has exerted on this occasion have tended to support her more than I could have expected, but I dare not hope that any other balm but time can bring peace & tranquillity to her heart. Sincerely thankful to your grace for the kindness you have always bestowed on me, I have the honour to remain, your most obliged & very obedient servant James Stanhope.

A letter written to Lord Lonsdale gives a few more details:

> Montague Square 2 February 1809[13]
>
> Dear Lord Lonsdale
>
> I take the first moment of leisure that occurs, to return you my warmest thanks for your kind enquiries about Hester's health & the solicitude you please to express about myself. I am happy to state that my sister is quite as well as I

could expect, but I well know that the bonds of paternal affection which were so closely interwoven with her happiness could not be torn asunder without a severe pang & that she could not easily forget his open, manly & amiable disposition, which rendered him the greatest treasure of our once more numerous & happy group. Those who knew him can only regret that providence did not allow him to remain longer in that profession to which some say he would have added additional lustre. It is a sincere consolation to us that his death was that which, if permitted, he would himself have chosen, in the post of honour & danger, in the point of attack, to be greeted in the execution of his duty with the loud approbation of the great man whom he so particularly looked up to & whose loss adds another pang to our hearts & to fall regretted by his regiment, which I am rejoiced to perceive in token of their grief have of their own accord gone into mourning. The circumstance of my having seen the last melancholy offices performed to my dear brother's memory seems also in some degree to alleviate my sister's grief.

I should not have neglected my promise of writing to your lordship, but having failed in my attempt to join the army on their march (although for the space of above three weeks I travelled more than 600 miles in pursuit of them) I had no means of communicating with England till the 14th, two days only before the action & then perceived my information could not be interesting. Having arrived in time to witness the last of my brother and General Moore is a compensation for all my anxiety & fatigues. The last expressions of the latter have been naturally gratifying to Hester. A few moments before he expired he said 'Stanhope, remember me to your sister'.[14]

I hope your son is by this time safely arrived at Cottesmore[15] as the cavalry had so many opportunities & did so brilliantly distinguish themselves, he must derive great pleasure from his part of the campaign.[16] I have just seen an officer who escaped through the French army after the action of the 16th. He says they confess 'Qu'ils avaient perdue beaucoup de monde et qu'ils n'avaient jamais supanament ete si bien battus' [That they have lost many men and that they have never been beaten so well] …

Chapter 4

Cadiz

Having returned to Britain James seems to have found new employment caring for his disconsolate sister whose health had suffered. He moved into the 2nd Battalion, which had remained in London for ceremonial duties, and gained a new staff appointment in April 1809.

The commander-in-chief, the Duke of York, had become embroiled via his mistress Mary Anne Clarke, in accusations of corruption and had been forced to resign from his post on 25 March and was replaced by General the Honourable Sir David Dundas, a strict disciplinarian and the architect of the standard British drill.[1] Dundas appears to have initially accepted the members of staff he inherited, but soon a number left and new ones were appointed;[2] amongst them, one James Hamilton Stanhope as aide de camp.

Meanwhile the war continued; Wellesley had returned to Lisbon with large reinforcements on 26 April 1809 to take command of the remnants of the small force left there by Moore when he had advanced into Spain. He had promptly taken the war to the French by launching a swift assault on Oporto, where he successfully defeated the French on 12 May and cleared their forces out of northern Portugal. Returning south Wellesley linked up with the Spanish army of General Cuesta and, despite the numerous difficulties he had to face in attempting to work with his overconfident allies, he did gain a victory at Talavera on 28 July. However, the Spanish failure to provide adequate supplies, and the threat of encirclement by much greater French forces, caused Wellesley to pass to the south of the River Tagus and retire into winter quarters in Portugal, having gained a healthy distrust of any promises made by his Spanish allies.

Whilst enjoying the social life of London, James remained concerned for the health of his sister, who had decided that she could no longer afford to live at Montagu Square and moved to a small house in Wales called Glen Irfon. James visited Hester there but her depression was so severe that Hester finally decided, under medical advice, to travel to warmer climes and she arranged an extended tour of the Mediterranean, starting in Sicily, of which she had heard so much from her brothers. James sought and received permission to join Hester on this grand tour on six months' leave of absence. At this point, James made a decision, apparently trivial but hugely significant for military historians: he began to write a daily journal of his thoughts and occurrences. From this point onward it forms the backbone of this volume, backed by his numerous letters home to friends and family over the next seven years.

They left London on 1 January 1810, proceeding to Portsmouth where the party, which included Doctor Meryon[3] and a Mr Robert Nassau Sutton, waited patiently for a vessel. James sat down to begin his first journal: 'Private Memoranda and Journal from the Beginning of 1810 to the 20 July 1812 when I returned to England', beginning 'My sister Lady Hester being in bad health and determined to go abroad, in hopes of recovering, I obtained leave from Sir David Dundas to accompany her and left London 1st of January 1810.' There were a number of delays as they awaited a ship, as James explained in a letter to his friend Richard Heber,[4] half brother of Reginald Heber:[5]

Southsea Hotel, Portsmouth 30 January 1810

You doubtless think that by this time I have passed the straight 'where Calpe's armed steep'[6] thus to unreginaldize myself. I have approached Mongibello[7] but instead of meeting the wild gales of these climates, I have been boxed up with my sister here in a damp, cold house under the accumulated grievances of cold, disappointment and the Lords Commissioners of the Admiralty. The misconduct of the latter has become more irksome as all our injuries have been accompanied with the highest assurances of regard.

When I last dined with you at the Alfred, I told you that the Admiralty had recommended us to give up the *Unite*[8] and go on board the *Manilla*[9] as being more comfortable from my shipmate Seymour being the captain. When I arrived here (my sister being left in London) I saw all the comforts that he was kindly preparing for her accommodation. The hour of sailing was drawing near and the Admiralty were urging my sister to leave London, the very day after they sent down an order to embark on board the ship 2 generals, their Staff and divers military doctors. You will hardly believe that Ward signed this order first on the Tuesday and on the Wednesday at 2 o'clock wrote to my sister saying that he had just then heard for the first time that Government had found it necessary to turn us out of the *Manilla*, and still will you credit me when you hear that Lord Mulgrave[10] after this declares most solemnly how grieved he is at the event but that the Admiralty never knew of my sister's intention to embark on board the *Manilla* and confesses that he had other ships wherein to send them. We did not want their assistance but merely the civility commonly paid to a woman, that we have not received and I should feel highly indignant if I did not feel convinced that the whole of our mortifications have proceeded more from a bad system than from any other cause. I cannot disguise the ill effects of it, as my sister is much disimproved since she arrived here. God grant us enemies and save us from the friends of Mr. Pitt.

I have so nearly finished my paper that I cannot tell you all that I wish about God's Life of him.[11] The account of the last illness is almost wholly false and the work has a strong and marked bias to the Bishop and Lord C[astlereagh].[12]

Still I like it. The political part appears (to one who is and can be no judge) admirably done and the causes as well as the effects minutely and clearly detailed. Gifford under such tuition cannot be blamed, in such society, God knows how much he is to be pitied!!

We go now as we advance near to the spring strait [sic] to Messina. We sail tomorrow in the *Jason* frigate[13] for Gibraltar from whence you shall hear again.

James recounts in his journal that it was a rough and dangerous passage to Gibraltar.

After waiting some time at Portsmouth for a ship we sailed in the *Jason* Captain King on the 10th of February. We narrowly escaped being wrecked on the shoals of Trafalgar in the tremendous gale of the 5th of March which destroyed so large a part of the fleet at Cadiz. Part of our convoy with the 4th Regiment on board got into Cadiz & some went on shore at Santa Maria. We wore twice on a lee shore and in the middle of the night crossed the shoals, in weathering the cape in 13 fathom water hearing distinctly the sound of the breakers & seeing the glimmering of the white foam which they created. We could not bring up at Gibraltar from the fury of the gale but scudded under Ceuta where in bringing to we drifted with 3 cables ahead. On the 9th of March we anchored at Gibraltar.

At Gibraltar James wrote a longer letter to Richard Heber describing their passage and the latest situation in Spain which did not look good, particularly the failures of the Spanish forces:

Gibraltar 17 March 1810

I fear that from my long absence you will either believe that some accident has befallen us or that I have neglected the promise I made to you over our last bottle. We were detained at Portsmouth some days after I wrote last to you and finally weighed the 14th ulto. Baffling and light winds lengthened our passage considerably and when we at length made Cape Trafalgar, the violent gale in which the Cadiz Squadron has so much suffered, placed us on a lee shore and dispersed the whole of the convoy. We passed the shoals in 14 fathom, but the gales continuing we were obliged to run through the Gut and take refuge under Ceuta,[14] where we have repeatedly drove with 2 anchors ahead; when the gale moderated, we came in here and I landed my sister (I think rather the better for her adventures) on the 10th. The Governor, Colin Campbell,[15] has given us apartments in his house and we are waiting, in patience, for a return chaise to Messina. So much for ourselves, and I am almost ashamed to find 3 pages so employed.

What does Reginald now say to his:

'Go cast thy fetters on the troublous sea
But Spain, the brave the patriot shall be free'[16]

Had I left England with even Anti-Jacobin ideas on the hopes of Spain, I should by now have changed them; and if Mr. Frere[17] had been my idol, the recital of his deeds I every day hear would have inspired me with deep contempt which he deserves. The Junta have perfected their work of folly or treachery by wishing to give Cadiz to the French and had it not been for a rapid and judicious movement of the Duke of Albuquerque, they would have succeeded.[18] As the French had no heavy artillery in Spain and without it any attack on Cadiz would be futile, it became of great importance to save the Spanish arsenal at Seville, and we offered to remove to Cadiz for their own use the whole of it, which was peremptorily rejected and 150 mortars, 300 battering pieces of brass artillery with clothing for 30,000 men furnished by England, fell into their hands; at this same moment when the Spanish troops are without every necessary a soldier requires.

Yesterday we received a total return of all the French troops on this side of the Sierra Morena which on its way to Soult was intercepted and it only amounts (exclusive of 16,000 in Cadiz) to merely 25,000 men. With this force have they overrun and plundered every part of Andalusia. Algeciras, San Roque, Tarifa and other places near here have been laid under contribution by the smallest detachments, the former by 200 men of whom only 16 entered the town, which by the way contains no less than 5,000 patriots who next morning threw up their greasy caps and screamed for independence. Neither my time nor paper will allow me to pursue the nauseating details of weakness and wickedness which darken Spain. Of Frere I have much to tell you but I must leave it till we meet as I cannot commit such infamy to paper, I believe it would blot the whole.

Lord Wellington's army is recovering gradually. The remaining at Badajoz has been defended by no one. No less than 5,000 men have been buried in that ill omened plain.[19] On this you may depend, indeed I have carefully compared everything I have heard of on both sides and I have not allowed my hatred of Spain to outweigh the truth. An officer who came from the army told me they always buried a brigade a month. Indeed I have no reason to change my opinion that Sir John Moore fought for England and Wellesley for himself.[20] These wretched officers who have deluded themselves and their country, these important military diplomats are augmenting in presumption as their prospects diminish and Doyle,[21] Roach, etc. I understand vie with each other in falsehood and folly.

We are not very active here and though I do not wish to libel my host whilst the taste of his wine is on my lips, I think he might by now have secured the occupation of Ceuta to our troops. We have been waiting for nearly a month for the order of the Junta at Cadiz to admit us, it came yesterday, when on being presented, the principal persons of Ceuta have assembled a council of war to decide on the propriety of their obeying it. This is an 'imperium in imperio' [an empire within an empire] to a vengeance. Promptitude and energy may yet succeed but I scarcely know whether to hope or fear. I wrote the numbers of the French on a report given me from high authority but having now obtained the despatches myself I am enabled to give you a correct account of this 1st Corps.

Near Cadiz	18,992
Cavalry round the Country	2,395
Total in Andalusia or on this side of the Sierra Morena	21,992[22]
Detached and on the route	5,619
Total	27,006

Resuming James's journal, we find him visiting Ceuta, before learning of the deployment of his battalion to Spain and his decision to let his sister sail on to Malta without him, as he would join the regiment.

On the 22nd of March I accompanied General Fraser & Captain Heywood[23] of the navy with the 4th Regiment[24] who were destined to garrison Ceuta.[25] During the few days I remained there, the same jealousy & suspicions of our intentions prevailed as we have so often witnessed since and it required a good deal of tact and conciliation to get our troops admitted into the citadel. The sea defences of Ceuta were not nearly as strong as we supposed them to be. On the northern and western sides are several advantageous points of disembarkation possessing speedy cover from the fire of the citadel (which however at this moment had not guns) and the escalade of the latter would in no degree be an impracticable undertaking. With their accustomed military talents, the Spaniards have left all their batteries open to the rear and in the points where the castle guns would sweep the beach they have generally erected traverses to give the enemy immediate cover. As this was the first time I saw their talents in fortification displayed, I confess I was not a little astonished, as although for magnificence of conception, patience of execution & solidity of construction, no people are superior, nevertheless there is always some want of common talent which renders all their labours nugatory if not prejudicial and this is most strongly exemplified than in the construction of their land front.

For to give an idea of the place, there is a channel of communication between the eastern & western bays at A through which boats pass. Had the works of Ceuta ended there they could not be commanded and the canal would add greatly to the defence, or had their line of works been constructed on the ridge B (which has every advantage among other of being a broader part of the isthmus than where they now are constructed) they would be nearly impregnable. In order I suppose to save the expense which a broader front would have occasioned, the Spaniards constructed their works at C of an immense profile with cavaliers of prodigious height, but commanded from B in a most regular shape; for the moment the artificial glacis ends a natural one begins for the benefit of the attackers. The same want of military principles will be more strongly elucidated in the account of Cadiz. With regard to Ceuta I can only say that its safety has much more been owing to the excessive ignorance of the Moors than to any merits of the fortress;[26] for to prove how much it is commanded, there are marks of Moorish shot ½ way down the scarp of the interior ditch. This observation relates to the natural merits, which have been thrown away, for labour and art never perhaps were carried to a higher pitch for the distance, than in erecting the immense works of the land front.

Ceuta.

The old Governor, General Legrand had just been superseded by the Marquis d'Alost, from both of whom I received great civility. Having amused myself for some days I returned to Gibraltar.

2nd of April heard that the battalion of Guards to which I belonged had arrived at Cadiz. I did not hesitate to sacrifice my private feelings & determined to join it, although I had 6 months leave. On the 7th my sister sailed for Malta, on the 10th embarked on board the *Undaunted*,[27] Captain Malling, for Cadiz, foul wind, anchored at Algeciras, returned to Ceuta, got back-strapped as it is termed, when a vessel passes the narrow strait & gets into the Mediterranean, when from the in-draft of water & the funnel through which the wind collected rushes with amazing force, ships frequently are detained during long periods of westerly winds. Remained some days in Tetuan Bay & amused myself in shooting. I saw no gros gibier [big game] but killed a great many partridges and quails.

On the 21st we weighed & in running up under Ape's Hill,[28] though at a considerable distance from the shore, scraped against a pointed sunken rock. It did us no harm, but deranging the order of the dinner with most admired disorder. It is singular that in so bold a coast, such a rock should exist & more so that it should have been unknown in the very portal of the wealthiest sea in Europe.

21st Anchored at Tangier, went on shore and at Mr Green's (the Consul[29]) house, met the Count Ludolf,[30] a remarkably well informed and agreeable Austrian nobleman, son of their Ambassador at the Porte. Being a Jewish festival, all the people of that nation were in their rich dresses sitting at their doors. I never was so struck with the luxuriance of female beauty both as to countenance and figure as in this instance. If there is a Gordian knot in love, no weapon so easily will divide it as a pair of English scissors, which are in high request among the fair Jewesses.

From the deck of the *Undaunted* we could see the smoke of the bombardment of Matagorda.[31] The same evening anchored in Cadiz Bay, lost a man overboard & the *Comus*[32] lost another. On the 22nd beat up the harbour, saw the furious cannonade against Matagorda, on anchoring heard of the death of poor Lefebre,[33] than whom the country did not possess in point of talents as cultivated [a] mind, as well as great military & professional knowledge, a more finished character. Some people have mingled their regrets at his loss with blame for his being unnecessarily exposed, but as Chief Engineer, he was naturally anxious to know in what state of utility to the enemy Matagorda was left in, and after all no one should be blamed for exposure to personal danger, which his own feelings warrants and judgement demands. At midday the fort was evacuated by us and the firing ceased. I accompanied our female passenger Donna Juana Rindon to the house of her friend the Countess Serrea, next morning waited on General Graham who appointed me his A.D.C.

Having seemingly just stepped into a job with General Graham as extra aide de camp, he immediately sat down to write to his friend Richard Heber. The long passage would have been tedious if he had not found female distraction.

Undaunted, off Cadiz 22 April 1810

After I wrote last, we remained till the 7th when we obtained a passage on board the *Cerberus*,[34] but finding that my battalion was arrived at Cadiz[35] I was (most unwillingly) obliged to abandon my Mediterranean prospects and witness her sailing alone. I think she is ere this arrived at her journey's end as the same strong Western blast that has detained us till this time must have expedited her.

The last fortnight has been passed by me in the society of a most agreeable, well informed and (what is more surprising) a very modest Spanish female who with her brother-in-law General Mendozo are also passengers to Cadiz with my old friend Malling. The wind being foul we have passed from Gibraltar to Algeciras, Tarifa, Ceuta, Tetuan and finally Tangier so you can conceive what with society on board and riding and shooting on shore the time has passed rapidly and pleasingly away.

General Graham in the handsomest manner has appointed me as his extra A.D.C. He could not do more as I am still on Sir D. D.'s staff .[36] Fine work here.

The only good news is the occupation of Ceuta by our troops, the 4th Regiment occupies the citadel and as there are no other troops in it with them, I conceive our interests are well secured in that quarter.

James continues his journal with a full description of the situation at Cadiz. The Isla is a term for the Island of Leon, a large area of low-lying marshy land at the southern tip of the peninsula on which Cadiz stands. The majority of the defending forces were stationed here, as it was the most likely route for any attempt by the French to seize Cadiz.

Our time at the Isla was mostly passed in visiting the new works & watching the labour of the enemy; but I will reserve the account of these, till a later period of my stay.

1st May, General Lacy[37] gave a false alarm to see whether the troops were ready, but in order not to distress the inhabitants, it was communicated to them & the principal officers & of course the effect was lost.

At night a few Spaniards made a sally from the advanced battery at the Portazgo[38] against a breast work of the enemy who generally occupied it with a sergeant's picquet. They were received with a volley which killed 3 men and wounded 8, the French then evacuated it leaving a sergeant killed whose head 'Los Valientes' [The Braves] cut off and bore back in triumph.

The 2nd May, the enemy at daylight retook the breastwork. The skirmishing continued all the morning.

There was a grand ceremony in the Iglesia del Carmen in honour of the patriots of the 2nd of May who perished at Madrid.[39] The whole *church* was hung with black with festoons of white and appropriate classical inscriptions, the altar piece being splendidly illuminated. In the front of the altar was a square space covered with black velvet on which was placed a skull as an emblem of the occasion, the whole surrounded by immense tapers. An English officer, a friend of mine, turned round to one of the Guard and asked 'Que cabeza es aquella?' [Who's head is that?] The man thinking the name of head misapplied to those 'chambers desolate & portals foul'[40] answered 'Es Calavera Senor' [It is of a rake Senor[41]]

In the evening, the officer asked with some sign of self-gratulation if people knew whose skull that was & being answered in the negative said, 'I know it was the skull of a Senor Calavera [Rake] who was killed at Madrid'.

The line of redoubts were commenced which afterwards formed the main strength of the Isla. Constant firing took place every day by which immense quantities of ammunition was wasted & no harm done to either party, but the Spaniards like it and call it 'Una demostracion en que nuestras baterias hicieron un fuego terrible con el mayor efecto' [a demonstration in which our batteries delivered a terrible fire with the greatest effect].

On the 3rd we had another general alarm & turn out which ended in more useless fire & smoke.

On the 5th two Spanish lieutenants deserted from the advanced battery, one the officer on duty. At night another general alarm took place & we were on horseback the greatest part of the night. The boy in the fable called wolf too often.

Nothing particular occurred besides the 'acostumbrado fuego' [habitual gunfire] and the military labours of defence, till the 16th of June, when it blowing a gale of wind, a pontoon containing some of the French prisoners unjustly detained after the Convention of Bailen[42] and some detained merchants & civilians, drifted from her anchorage towards the French batteries which immediately opened to protect her and ours commenced a heavy fire against them. The guns at Puntales[43] which pointed at the vessel belonged to us and as we believed she had drifted from the gale, we would not agree to the request of the Spaniards to fire on her. I never saw such exertions as the French officers & men used to get their companions on shore & with a glass[44] one could perceive the joy these poor wretches felt at their unexpected deliverance; meanwhile the boats of our fleet & mortar vessels kept up a heavy fire on the French prison ship which did some execution & many were drowned in the surf. Towards the evening the ship was discovered to be in flames but whether set on fire by the French who by this [time] had evacuated her or by one of our shells was never determined. Afterwards we heard the cause of our navy interfering which at first struck us as unnecessary cruelty. When she drifted Captain Stackpole of the *Tonnant*[45] sent a boat to her which on going alongside was saluted with round shot thrown into her, by which a favourite lieutenant of his was killed and we found out at a subsequent period that she had been cut adrift by the French & did not naturally break from her anchorage.

19th A general alarm at night; the French had advanced 2 or three guns & opened their fire on the white house in front of the Portazgo. One of their shot took off the leg of an artillery officer Lieutenant Cussins[46] as he was stepping out of his tent. The firing continued all the morning.

Colonel Massaredo was very angry at our not destroying the pontoon with hot shot & said 'No importa; iremos nosotros alguna noche y los mataremos mientras duermen' [It doesn't matter; we'll go at night and we'll kill them while they are asleep].

At a party in the evening at the Countess Altamira's, a Spanish lady, was looking at a seal I had of Mr Pitt's head, and on my mentioning the name, a Spanish officer said with a complacent smile at knowing so much of our history, 'Ah Pitt era un general de gran valour' [Ah, Pitt was a very brave general] This reminds me of equal ignorance in Sicily at Count Paterno's, Bendelto Giovanni asked me why so many English visited Etna as we had a burning mountain Hicla or Hecla at home, & before I could answer, Baron Reinach a German & knight of Malta, who had long been resident in Catania corrected him by saying 'Pardon me, Ecla is in Sweden.'

We had a curious exhibition at drawing off some lagoons necessary for the formation of the new canal which was to connect the interior part of the bay with the sea without exposing boats to the enemy's fire in the Cano of Sancti Petri. When the water was partly let off, about 20 fellows quite naked, jumped in with old swords or straightened iron hoops and in a short time threw out a large number of fine fish which confused in the mud came to the top, when these sword in hand fishermen struck them smartly on the back & threw them out with their hands.

On the 24th we had our first races, which attracted the Spaniards by the novelty of the dresses etc. The race course was at the foot of the entrenched camp & the company stood in one of the redoubts in the most panoramic point of view. The general always ended the races with collations & nothing conduced more to keep up the harmony between the two nations, which it was not easy to preserve.

On the 27th, about 2 o'clock, it then blowing hard from the north west, another pontoon drifted from her moorings (being cut away by the prisoners as we found afterwards). Admiral Pickmore[47] sent the boats of the squadron with anchors and cables, on coming near the boats hailed & were beckoned nearer, on coming alongside they were received by a severe fire of musquetry. The ship being high in the water, no ropes & the steps destroyed, it was impossible to board & I believe there were few if any arms in the boats. Our boats were of course obliged to retire having lost 4 officers and 42 men killed & wounded. The ship then drifted under the batteries of the Trocadero[48] which opened a furious cannonade to protect her. After such an act of treachery, the indignation of all parties was not to be restrained. All night did 9 launches, anchored under her stern, pour destruction into this huge vessel which left dry by the tide afforded no shelter. On the morning of the 28th the French landed a great many (though I fear this was a hospital ship), but about 2 o'clock a carcase one of the ships threw, set her on fire. Admiral Valdes[49] commanding the flotilla pulled down to save as many as he could. From some whom he succeeded in saving the carnage on board was represented as dreadful; considering that these prisoners were unjustly detained, one is anxious to draw a veil over all this scene, for though the treachery of the French was unparalleled, our vengeance I think was carried too far. The navy were the sufferers & they revenged their own wrongs. Without being placed in the same situation it is hard to judge of the feelings of others, but in running down a boat filled with wretches escaping & refusing to save a man, proved himself a barbarian. I hated the man ever afterwards as he had the baseness to boast of it.

On the 29th the Regency removed from the Isla to Cadiz, there was a grand procession, but few vivas.

30th The Regency held a court, being Ferdinand's birthday, at which we were all presented. Some of the cavalry were dressed in the old court dresses of the Lancers of the Guard, which had been saved from Madrid & which are the same that were used in the War of the Succession.

The Marquis de Palacios[50] commanded them, the effect was exceedingly picturesque. But two antiques met for the first time for fifty years, one being 94 and the other 88 and they wore the court dresses of the days of their youth. Description can do nothing but I made a rough sketch of them at the time.

The Regency now consists of Castanos (the President),[51] the Bishop of Orense, Saovedra, Escano[52] & Lariszabal for the colonies. Castanos is a friend to the English & a worthy excellent man not disposed to intrigue by nature, but always beset and guided by intriguers, of no military talents and of most indolent habits. His great ability is in facetiousness & there are more good things said by him, than useful actions performed. The Bishop has character and firmness, but as he is bigoted & 'preocupado' [Preoccupied, worried] beyond idea, his virtues have done more harm than the dullness of the two next would ever have accomplished.

The rise of the Regency into power was singular, for at the time that the Duke of Albuquerque by a judicious & spirited disobedience of orders saved Cadiz, the Junta of Cadiz had taken the whole finance into their hands.[53] The army was in the hands of a favourite leader & empty honours were all the Regency possessed at the moment of their nomination. Albuquerque had it more in his power to organise some system of defence, to form some rallying point for the nation than anybody before him and the moment was most propitious. The Regency & Junta alike feared him & he was persuaded to go [as] Ambassador to England and resign the army to Castanos, who being Regent turned it over to Blake,[54] who had not then sufficient power to be ungrateful to his benefactor. From all I have ever heard of Albuquerque, he was a vain & empty man, possessing a mind capable of great actions, but ready to lose among the incense of interested flatterers all the character he had acquired; in England we have many Albuquerques. The Junta (whom he had saved, families, fortunes & commerce from the spoilations of the enemy) afterwards rewarded him with the most outrageous calumnies and all the vulgar bitterness of mercantile insolence & ingratitude. This preying on a fiery & susceptible spirit was the real cause of his death. He wrote just before it a most indignant answer to his enemies.

What a strange spectacle does the Spanish nation now offer, that when her independence is already driven to the utmost verge of her territory 'Et nihil

Old men.

nisi mare et infestiores Romani' [And there is nothing further away, except the sea and the more hostile Romans], that they still amid the delusive dreams of ancient power forget & utterly disregard their danger; talk of reconquering America, when troops are wanting for the ordinary duties of her garrisons at home and already subdivided by force & rebellion, voluntarily split the poor remnant into almost infinite weakness by their own divisions.

4th June. We had all the troops out in honour of the day. At dinner I met Mr Capmany, the author of the Centinela,[55] Dictionary of the Academy etc, and the writer of a patriotic effusion to the Regency on their entry into Cadiz. I asked him if he was the author of it (having no name to it) & he answered with 'Si Senor, es sublime, patetico y elocuente' [Yes Sir, it is sublime, pathetic and eloquent]. I pretended to misunderstand him & said 'You are perhaps a relation?' 'No Senor el mismo autor que ha formado el espiritu publico de la nacion eterna' [No, Sir, the same writer who has shaped the public spirit of the eternal nation]. A good specimen of literary modesty.

A few days afterwards a bag of Cadiz letters was intercepted by the French & many of them published, among them one of Capmany's to a friend I think at Valencia. In this letter, speaking of the Regency he said, 'Poor people who fancied that all the troops around them were for their honour, whilst as for the King in scripture, they were meant to enslave them.' And about the English, 'Que hacian mucha bulla, pero trabajaban solo en limpiar sus dientes y zapatos' [That they made a great noise, but they only worked at cleaning their teeth and shoes].

Poor Capmany was so ashamed of himself as to shut himself up till he thought the affair forgotten.

10th June. I had some interesting conversation with the officer of the French picquet at the Portazgo, who was very angry at the affair of the pontoon & said 'Les espagnols sont des barbares, comment diables puissant les Anglais combattre pour eux' [The Spanish are barbarians, how the devil can the English fight for them?] Talking about Jena, he said 'Ah, les Prussiens sont vraiment braves & ne coupent pas les gorges, je voudrai bien etre contre eux a present' [Ah, the Prussians are really brave hearted and do not cut throats, I would prefer to be against them at present]

He said if Bonaparte arrived, they would take the Isla in two days & mentioned that the Spanish sergeant on guard [who] had given the arms to the prisoners in the pontoon had been made an officer for it & had the Cross of Honour. This was thrown out so much like an invitation to desert that I could not help saying, that seeing the cross on the neck of so many brave men, I was disposed to honour it, & regretted that they should have disgraced it in giving it to a traitor. We parted however good friends.

22nd. The Duke of Orleans[56] arrived and was received with the honours due to an infant of Spain.

30th. The Spanish troops were reviewed by the Duke, who afterwards gave a grand dinner to all the principal general officers. I sat next to a very old Spanish officer who had been apparently deterred [exhumed?] for the occasion, and asked him what news he had from Tarragona 'Nada tenemos, es viento de Levante' [We have nothing, the wind is easterly]. I ventured to suggest that an Easterly wind should not be unfavourable, when he observed in a querulous tone at the idea of my differing from him 'Nunca recibimos noticias con aquel maldito viento' [We never receive the news with that wretched wind!]

July 3rd. The Duke saw the English line out. General Graham supposed the position to be attacked & manoeuvred defensively, Prince Neuwied &

Count Hartopp,[57] who had just arrived from the Austrian army were present. The former a very intelligent, amiable man with a very prepossessing countenance though disfigured with a deep sabre cut. The latter an 'etourdi du premiere ordre' [giddy of the first order] amusing for an hour & insufferable for the rest of the day.

I was at this time taken ill of a fever which confined me three weeks to my bed. When sufficiently recovered I went on board the *Achilles*[58] with Sir Richard King[59] who treated me in the kindest manner & having recovered my strength I returned to the Isla on the 19th of August.

The Bishop of Orense has commenced his duties of President of the Regency[60] and his first edict has been to prohibit short sleeves & white shoes, as I suppose as Johnson[61] said, they excite his amorous propensities.

My friend Dona Juana leaves Cadiz for Ceuta, & I deeply regretted her absence, for though I have since seen many classes of Spanish society in different parts of Spain, I have never met anyone who surpassed her in the characteristic charms & qualities of the Spanish women, who only require a better education and more regard to bienseance [propriety] to be the most delightful creatures in the world; for in point of natural unsophisticated talents, of unforced & inoffensive gaiety of heart, of total absence of mean selfish, envious feelings, for warmth of heart, for elevation & magnanimity of mind, for fortitude under distress, humiliation & danger, for keen feelings of pity & tenderness for others with the most heroic self devotion in their own persons, for the liveliest passions of love & hate, which climate, education & example can give, the Spanish woman is not to be surpassed.[62]

Mrs Spencer Smith[63] also left us for the Friule,[64] a severe loss to our society as her conversation had all the charms of united talent, education & travelling. She wrote a beautiful novel which she allowed her friends to read, *the idea* of which arose from reading in a Spanish History that Abdaraman, the King of Cordoba,[65] declared he had passed fourteen happy days only, in the course of a long & triumphant life. She made this pleasure naturally arise from love & made a wild girl Layla Gibella, the heroine of her tale. These parts much pleased me.

'Du haut d'une terasse ou apercevoit au loin une cascade magesteuse dont le bouillonnement faisait entendre un murmure agreable. Voyez cette eau, disait Talme a son eleve, elle est Claire, elle est brillante comme la cristal, elle embellit cette solitude elle sert a abreuver le voyageur altere elle arrose et rafraichit ces pres et ces champs, mais le ruisseau qu'elle forme, va gonfler la Guadalquivir et ces memes eaux si limpides finissent pas se meler aux flots de l'ocean dont elles prennent toute l'amerturne. C'est l'image de la vie de ceux qui sortant de l'etat puisible ou le sort les avait fait maitre sont entraines par le torrent de l'ambition.

Abdaraman pressoit doucement son amante contre son Coeur. La tete de

> Layla reposait sur son epaule, ce groupe interessant se dessinoit dans les eaux claires et limpides que couloient a leurs pieds. Le prince etait enivre de sa felicite. Ma bien Aime, disait il, considere nos images ainsi reunies, vois comme ils sont reflechies ensemble dans cette onde pure, oh Layla, puissions nous traverser ainsi le songe de la vie. Ah oui, reprit elle, le songe de la vie. Dans la meme instant un leger zephyr prisa la surface de l'eau. Voyez continua elle, en saipirait nos images aussi sont disparus comme les songes'.
>
> [From the heights of a terrace one can notice in the distance a majestic cascade which stirring made you hear an agreeable murmur. See the water, said Talme to his student, she is clear, she is brilliant like a crystal, she beautifies the solitude, she serves to falsely overwhelm the traveller, she sprays and refreshes these meadows and fields, but the stream she forms will inflate the Guadalquivir and those same clear waters end up mingling with the ocean waves of which she takes its bitterness. It is the image of life of those leaving a powerful state where fate has made them master, are trained by the torrent of ambition. Abdaraman presses his lover gently against his heart. The head of Layla rests on his shoulder, that interesting group reflects clearly in the clear and bright waters that runs at their feet. The prince was drunk of his happiness. My true love, he said consider our images so united, see how they reflect together in this pure gulf, oh Layla, I wish we could pass the wave of life like this. Ah yes, she said, the wave of life. In the same moment a light breeze went over the surface of the water, she continued exasperated, our images are also missing like the waves]

In August James wrote to Richard Heber with the latest news. Wellesley's army had been unsuccessfully engaged in trying to break the French siege of Ciudad Rodrigo which fell on 9 July and the French were now beginning the besieging of Almeida.

> 15 August 1810
>
> How melancholy is the fate of poor Lady Sarah Napier and that family at the moment; she escapes a severe loss in one son,[66] to lose another in a stupid manoeuvre of Craufurd's[67] and to have a daughter given over in a decline.[68] I fear she will not be able to support such heavy and accumulated misfortunes.
>
> The last accounts I had from Hester were from Malta 25th June whence she was going to Constantinople and the Greek Islands, having given up Sicily from the existing state of affairs in that country which from letters I have had from Catania is dreadful. The Queen is seen betraying us by everyone but the English Ambassador and General.[69] I believe the threatened invasion is nothing more than a feint to keep our troops there, 10,000 of them would do much and 5,000 would keep the Citadel.

He also wrote to Alexander Murray, Hester's solicitor, explaining that he had been very ill and how much he missed his sister. James clearly liked being on General

Graham's staff, but it would also seem that he had much leisure time and little to occupy it.

Headquarters Isle de Leon, 23 August

My dear Sir,

I am happy to hear from my sister that she is better. From the state of affairs in Sicily, she has judged very properly in not going thither and she is now *probably* in Greece. I need not tell you the grief I feel at being absent from her, but that subject is so painful that I must dismiss it. I have had a very severe fever which kept me in my bed for 3 weeks arising from over exercise in the sun. I am now thanks to the sea air in the bay, and the good table and great kindness of my host Sir Richard King of the *Achilles* quite re-established. We are perfectly quiet here and I pursue precisely the life I did in London, among my books, with society in the evenings. I find Spanish very easy and can now speak it with fluency. The Spanish society is not of the best order, as there is a general and contemptible want of education, excepting & among the very first class of the Madrid refugees; but the natural talents, the liveliness, the quick repartee, and the unassuming good nature of the women make it very pleasant, though I hardly dare say so as the English are swearing this place is a prison, berating the language and never mixing with the people having no means of amusement and being likely to return as wise as they came.

I mean *this in general*, General Graham is everything to me. In his family I sometimes think I am again with Sir John Moore.

Of public news, you must know as much as myself, you have of course seen the intercepted letters, they are authentic and are more valuable than 10 sail of the line. The Spanish troops are improving & the war is still alive. The French though they have 250,000 men are not advancing. They are now for the first time meeting an ignorant people, heretofore they have beaten mercenary armies, corrupt governments, treacherous leaders. But the exertions of this order have been clamped & the majority of the people perceiving that their new government of Spain have never attempted to ameliorate their suffering or restored their long lost liberty are little anxious who is their master, a Joseph or a Ferdinand, still should Lord Wellington keep his ground (of which I have every *just reason to hope* & should be able to keep up the war, I shall begin to entertain a prospect of final success, not (God knows) from our strength but from the weakness of the enemy & the lamentable situation of his finances & the perceived state of the country both as to money & possession. I shall even hope though the Walcheren ministers[70] should still remain (oh shame to England) at the head of affairs. My sister begs you *will write to me when anything about the house*. Pray let me know what *you have done*. I hope at any rate *it is gone* through if he *gives* way. Pray most *kindly, respectfully & affectionately*, remember me to dear grandmamma. When I am rejoined & fever is well with my best regard to your family. Believe me dear Sir most truly yours, James Hamilton Stanhope.

Put your letters under cover Lieutenant General T Graham. I hope you saw the *Isla races extraordinary*[71]

24th 3000 Spaniards sailed last night to destroy a small flotilla in Sanlucar [de Barrameda] but we know [not] yet the results.

James resumes his journal with caustic remarks on the edicts of the Bishop of Orense who now headed the Cortes.

28th August. A fresh edict comes forth from the King Bishop against short sleeves & white shoes and the Spanish women consider it as a *point* of duty to disobey it.

About this time the 4th number of the Espanol came out from England and aided by other circumstances, raised a great ferment against the English, who were generally represented as playing a double part. A curious circumstance fortified our enemies in this idea. In an American paper appeared the appointment of British consuls to their revolted colonies, and on this ground so much abuse was lavished on our government that Mr Wellesley[72] interfered, feeling himself authorised to contradict the statement, its never having been communicated officially to him & of course it was natural to believe that a point of such importance would not occur unnoticed. Afterwards the appointments turned out to have taken place and Mr Wellesley's assertion was considered 'as part of our unworthy policy'.

Lord Liverpool's[73] letter was also severely commented on for said they 'A treaty is binding to the last & nothing but our subjugation can release you from it, but in that letter a power is assumed in the fourth degree of equivocation to release you from your compact, not when Spain is subdued, not when you fear Spain is subdued, or Spain may be subdued, but when you may have reason to fear that Spain may be subdued.'

'Again, Lord Liverpool says that the King of Great Britain *renounces* any claims over the territorial possessions in America & such. Renouncing implies past possession; how and when did he derive his claim?'

29th. Met Don Pasqual Rodriguez, who became a patriot from a singular cause. He was a lawyer and agent for a Spanish grandee whose name I forget. He was ordered by the latter to go to Madrid & marry for him by proxy a certain lady. Meanwhile finding some objection, the grandee wrote to Rodriguez desiring him not; this letter however fell into the hands of the lady, who concealed it, the match took place & the unwilling husband brought the case forward to break the marriage. She was a relation of Godoy's who protected her and Don Pasqual pleaded against her & was banished soon afterwards to Majorca by the indignant & powerful prince. This ill treatment gave him a great disgust of the court & retirement gave him an opportunity of examining further into the constitution of his country than most of those who have started in this soidistant revolution.

I also met General Lopez, who is more what a Spaniard should be than most of his contemporaries, frank & spirited with a just view of the dangers round him and a well organised mind. He died soon afterwards,[74] had he lived he would have been Secretary of War & probably would have contributed much to the benefit of his country. General Graham knows more of him than I do & likes him much, which is not a little in his favour.

I met also Beramendi who was commanding general of the Spanish army at Gerona[75] & who is just *what a Spaniard is*, minding everything but that before him. He would be a general, a musician (& was a very good one), a poet on the breach, an historian of his own deeds, a compound of Caesar & Tyrtaeus,[76] a member of the Cortes, a politician & a reformer. He asked me to translate his history of the siege & sent it me to read. There was some violent abuse in it of Blake; all at once he sent for the book in a great hurry, locked it up & went Commissary General to Estradmadura with this very man whom he flattered afterwards as much as he abused him before.

There was an epigram made on the Regency impromptu.

'La sottise entretient la sante'
Tous ces messieurs vont bien portes
[Foolishness takes care of health,
all these gentlemen will wear well]

When Lucien Bonaparte[77] arrived at Cagliari with a suite of nearly 40 persons, he wished to land, as one of his children was dying, but the Russian minister interposed and said it would be a personal insult to the Emperor, in consequence of which the King [of Sardinia][78] who has great *menagements* with Russia in hopes of her mediating in a general peace, refused him leave. On this Lucien remarked

'Le Ministre Russe a bien marque la chose, mon frère a une tete pour tout, il vent lui-même me persecuter mais jamais il le pemattra des mains d'autria' [The Russian Minister has noticed well the thing, my brother has a head for everything, he wants to prosecute me himself but he will never permit it through the hands of Austria].

The elections for the members of the Cortes were going on. As by the occupation of the capital & almost all the provinces, it was impossible to have a fair representation, but as the meeting of a Cortes was pre-eminently necessary it was determined to elect 'supplentes' for those provinces, who should make way for the real deputy whenever the representation of the country was restored, and these should be elected from only the inhabitants of the place, resident at that moment at Cadiz.

The mode is this, for example of Madrid:

Those at Cadiz entitled to be electors amounted to 800; to be an elector it is required to be a freeholder or house holder or rather house occupier 'viviendo en casa abierta' [Living in a house of which he is the head], of a fair character and never having had connexion with the enemy.

The names of these persons were given in for which a check is given producible on the day of election. The names are then exposed in public and persons are allowed to state opposite them any reasons which may exist against their becoming electors. On the day of election these 800 assemble and each writing down the name he chooses gives it in. The 7 who unite the greatest number by the same ballot choose 3 who draw lots which shall represent provisionally Madrid. *Many* of the best men were excluded by the words of *casa abierta*, for where the parents were living, the sons were not entitled to vote. They left the hall on the day of election without a murmur, saying it was better they should be for *ever excluded*, than disobedience shown to the laws, however absurdly enacted.

With regard to the meeting and proceedings of the Cortes, I have put it all together in my memoranda of their debates[79] which I continued attending till the 24th of October, when Lord Wellington, having retreated to the lines of Lisbon, I became anxious to see what was going on there and obtained leave from the general.

Chapter 5

A Visit to Portugal

James sailed to view the operations of the army under Lord Wellington (a title Wellesley had recently gained), as he had successfully defeated the French at Busaco on 27 September during a fighting retreat against superior forces to the Lines of Torres Vedras. This great project consisting of three lines of fortifications with a total of 108 redoubts in three lines and mounting 447 cannon had been secretly constructed over the previous year by British engineers, aided by 10,000 local labourers. The first line ran some twenty-nine miles across the Lisbon Peninsula from the mouth of the River Sizandre to Alhandra on the Tagus, including a large fortification at Torres Vedras, hence the name. The second and third lines were constructed further back and thus controlled a smaller area of the peninsula, the third really consisting of a final defensive line at a safe point to re-embark the army. These reserve lines were never used as the French never breached the first line and Marshal Massena's army went into winter cantonments in the shadow of the line, seemingly unclear of his next move. This seems to have given the Portuguese over optimistic views of the situation, as they confidently expected Massena to surrender his starving army en masse.

> John Russell,[1] Walpole[2] & myself embarked together on board the *Hardy*,[3] gunboat, and after a miserable passage in a miserable vessel with miserable weather, we landed at Faro, where we dined with the consul and having procured horses, started the same evening. We only reached Loulé, where a Portuguese gentleman entertained us very hospitably who on our drinking success to the Portuguese army said 'Yes, the English by sea & we by land will beat the world.'
>
> From the sea to the great Sierra de Monchique, along the whole of [the] Algarve, is a strip of highly cultivated land, in a rich & populous country, but on ascending the mountain, the traveller must be contented with picturesque alone and where the winding stony path alternately places one on the bare edge of the mountain where rock upon rock is most fantastically piled, and then winding into small glens fed by little mountain streams where the arbitus,[4] the myrtle and the olive relieve the eye from the monotony of the waving cistus,[5] and where the knotty cork tree, flings its huge branches over the path, the only tree which gives shade in this desolate region. These mountains abound in strong positions but too extensive in proportion to the country behind to make them worth defending.

Painting.

At Almodovar we found the Juez de foro, a most extraordinary specimen of Portuguese pride, cruelty, ignorance and vanity. On reading our passport which Mr Crispin insisted on our taking, and coming to the 'muito honoravel' [Very honourable] Lord J Russell, he thought it necessary to give us some idea of his own rank and he began, 'I am the representative de nosso Principe Regente [of our Prince Regent], I have studied at Coimbra, my family is *honoravel* & distinguished, I have orders (pointed to his breast) and a (like a chamberlain's) key for my pocket, but I do not *wear* them as I am thrown away here'. He asked us to walk about the village, which we declined, alleging our being fatigued & wishing to dress ourselves; and asked for some water; on which he said, 'Never mind, see how I am dressed, I beg you will not incommode yourselves' and we could hardly persuade him that our desire arose from personal comfort and not from ceremony.

He said after we were dressed, he would show us an historical picture *which* he had caused to be executed on the approaching surrender of Massena. This wonderful performance was indeed most worthy of being seen, I could not help copying it.

During the night our muleteers ran away and on complaining to the Juez, he summoned a person who had mules, to bring us some, and on the man expostulating, the little gentleman snatched up a long white pole which he said was the Principe Regent's symbol and levelled a furious blow at the head of the poor devil, who escaped by the pole being too big for the room and the historical picture received the blow. He then sent the man to prison in chains, for contempt of his authority; and there he or any other visitors of caprice might remain *without* the hope of redress.

The Alemtejo is too uninteresting a country to be worth describing. I descended the river from Alcacer do Sal to Setubal which has some fine views on the road from Setubal to Aldeia Gallega is exceedingly beautiful, the heights of Palmela being the distinguishing feature. The people at Setubal persisted in believing that Massena had surrendered with 70,000 men.

On the 1st of November I reached Lisbon and on the 2nd arrived at General Hill's[6] quarters at Alhandra, the extreme right of our first line.

On the 3rd went to Pero Negro & stayed at Lord Wellington's headquarters till the 11th during which time everything remaining quiet, I had nothing to do but visit the lines & did nothing else with the exception of going to a great ball given in the palace at Mafra by Lord Wellington to the army on the [Order of the] Bath being given to Marshal Beresford.[7]

It is impossible to give an adequate idea of this wonderful line of defence without entering into long military details. The point that struck me with the greatest astonishment was how first the eye of Lord Wellington could embrace so immense a design; and how his prophetic mind could foresee their primary importance. The possibility of resisting in the Second Line was known to the French as the Duke of Abrantes meant to have occupied it had not the Convention of Cintra taken place. But of the possibility of holding so extensive a range of country as the First [Line] comprises seems never to have entered into the minds of any of them. On the contrary, we were assured that the Portuguese traitor Le Marquis de Lorna told Massena that after passing Busaco, Lisbon was his, as nothing could impede his progress. When Massena came in front of this scarped and unassailable barrier, protected by abbatis; palisades and all the resources of art, with redoubt rising after redoubt as far as the eye could extend, with every valley, plain, or hill, commanded and swept by a powerful range of batteries, he turned to the Marquis and expressed his indignation at having been deceived.

The Marquis excused himself, by saying that nothing of this existed when he was at Lisbon, on which Massena [replied] 'Mais diable, les montagnes y etaient toujours!' [But what the devil, the mountains were always there!]

Indeed I have heard that at first Lord Wellington's own intention was not to have occupied the First Line otherwise than as a kind of outwork to the Second one, but the more it came to be examined, the greater appeared its advantages. The most important one it possessed over the Second Line was the position of Monte Junto which gave the defenders all the advantages of the interior line of operations, by obliging the assailants to concentrate on one side or the other or by remaining on both, to be exposed to certain destruction; thus half the number in defence was equal to any attacking body.

Thus Massena concentrated between Monte Junto & the Tagus, leaving

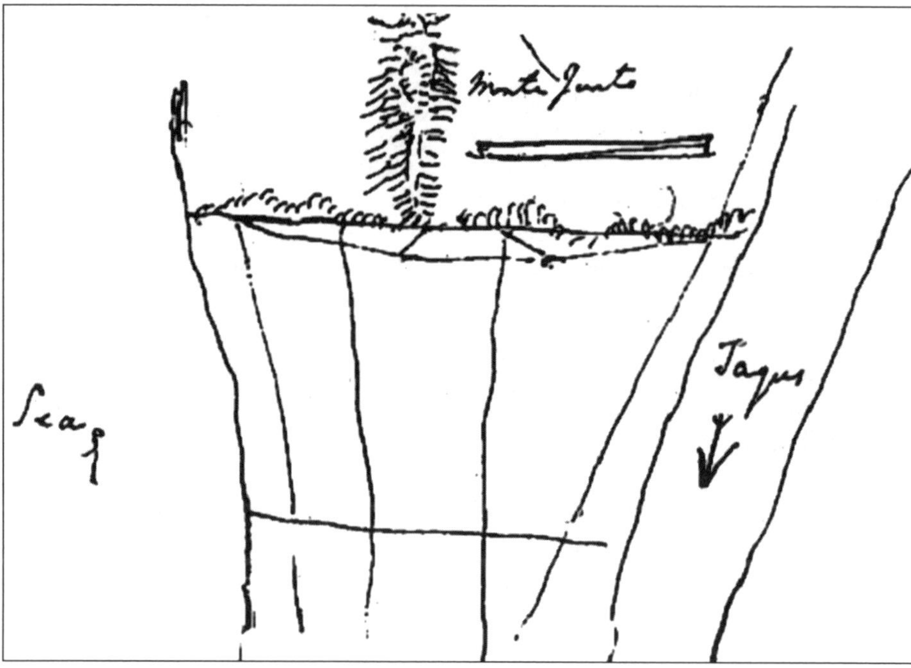

Lines.

only small foraging parties on the other & of course Lord Wellington could dedicate all his attention to that part of the line in his immediate front. The great military perfection of these lines consisted I think in the admirable manner in which every arm is combined and every class of troops beneficially employed. The right, steep by nature when improved by art, became nearly unassailable and was therefore securely guarded by the worst troops; towards the centre were left fields of battle where cavalry could act but where with difficulty [the] enemy's cavalry could arrive & where every quality existed to ensure & improve a victory; direct and good roads of communication are still wanting but I hear they are to be immediately executed. A great property of impregnability also exists in the Second Line, which being of much less extent might be occupied by much fewer troops, therefore supposing the 1st Line to be occupied by 80,000 men, to be driven from it with a loss of 20,000, the remainder would be fully equal to the defence of the second, whilst the enemy whose losses would always be infinitely greater would have gained but little towards his final object, by a dear bought victory.

The 3rd Lines are good for the purpose intended, & for protecting for a short time the embarkation of troops, but had the two lines ever been carried (which I do not believe twice Massena's army could have accomplished), I think the hopes of embarking a large army on such a coast, exposed to such a surf, to have been more flattering than well founded.

I then returned to Lisbon, the mosaics in the Church of St Roque are the things best worth seeing & least seen in this most filthy & stupid town. I went to Cintra, Cuylers [Colares?] etc & was on the point of returning to Cadiz when on the 15th at night I heard the French had retreated. I immediately started again for the army and joined Lord Wellington on the 16th at Alenquer. When he first came into the lines he said 'These fellows will stay here till about the middle of November!!!'

Nothing could exceed the horrible desolation in which the country was left which the enemy had occupied. Here war had played its wildest antics, some villages had been destroyed for fuel, others were unroofed and the tiles replaced at a distance to cover the huts of the encampments; not a living being remained in the houses which had been spared but some sickly soldiers whom they had not the means to convey, or has existence enough to bear it; every street was choked up by masses of putrid straw, intermixed with every class of filth and dead bodies of men & horses in different stages of decay.

Had the enemy been long gone, this might have been accounted for, but this was the state in which they lived. At Alenquer, they threw pieces of meat over the floor of the house which Massena had occupied and which was afterwards headquarters, which attracted such myriads of nauseous flies as to render it almost uninhabitable for their stench.

On the 17th the retreat of the enemy continued. During the two days they left behind about 500 sick and stragglers. As Lord Wellington was riding forward near Cartaxo, he met an officer galloping to the rear who said General Craufurd[8] had found the enemy posted beyond the village and was going to attack them & had sent him for General Grey's Brigade of cavalry.[9] Lord Wellington increased his pace & soon came up to where the enemy were apparently to the amount of two battalions and a few squadrons on the top of a gentle slope with an enclosed country in their rear.

Lord Wellington had not looked long before he saw the bayonets of the head of a column which was intended to be concealed, and immediately ordered Craufurd not to attack, saying that his, was the only division up, that his baggage was between him & the cavalry and that he would only get into a scrape. Next morning Lord Wellington said 'We must be off early or Craufurd will be at them'. And true enough; he just came in time to prevent him attacking with one division, a position which all the army could not have carried. Lord Wellington did not expect the enemy to remain & thought it was only the rearguard protecting their columns in their retreat towards the Zezere & that not above 4 or 5000 men were in his front.

On the 18th General Hill's corps crossed the Tagus and were ordered to make forced marches by Abrantes, to cut off the rearguard on the Zezere. Meanwhile Lord Wellington formed a plan of attack for the 19th.

The Light Division was to cross at a bridge on the right of the causeway & turn & drive away the enemy's battalions commanding the road along which the Guards then were to move. The Highland Brigade on the hill in reserve,

The Zezere.

General Pack[10] was to cross higher up and turn their right. Two guns and two squadrons going to the latter, missing their way, arrived late and Lord Wellington postponed his attack till the 20th by which time Sir W Erskine's[11] Brigade of cavalry had joined Pack & the 5th Division had joined the Guards. During the night information was received that the French had not crossed the Zezere, that troops had been seen returning into Santarem & in the morning the extensive abattis they had formed attested the number of hands they must have employed. The idea of attacking such a position so occupied was abandoned and we afterwards found that they [had] above 15,000 men on the heights. I think that not even the bravery of British troops could have forced them from such a chain of strong ground and a defensible town at top, full of large buildings, convents etc.

The troops were got under cover and Lord Wellington giving me some dispatches I returned to Lisbon and Alcacer do Sal & Beja to Mertola (the ancient Appallonia[12]). The road from Beja is part of the old Roman one which remains in considerable perfection. At Mertola the very extensive remains of the old town prove Appallonia to have been a large place and the ruins of a Roman bridge which the impetuous floods of the Guadiana have swept away, still block up with their huge masses the bed of the river. The cement is so hard (as well as the buttresses of the old castle at Castro Marim) as almost to defy the tools of the artificer. Descended the Guadarama in a boat among most wild & beautiful scenery and obtaining from Colonel Austen at Castro Marim a felucca, I landed at Cadiz on the 29th of November.

Chapter 6

Barossa

James returned to Cadiz and his position on Graham's staff at an interesting period in the defence of the city. The French had reduced the size of their besieging force to bolster the effort to relieve Badajoz, the key to the southern route to Portugal, which had been under siege since 26 January 1811. A joint Spanish and British expedition was therefore planned to transport a large force by sea, which would land to the south and in a surprise attack, storm the French siege lines from the rear, whilst the remaining garrison of Cadiz sortied out and attacked the French in their front. This ambitious project should have been commanded by right of seniority by Sir Thomas Graham, but in a conciliatory act, Graham gave the command to his Spanish counterpart, General La Pena, a diplomatic act that Graham was soon to regret deeply. James is an extremely valuable eyewitness to every turn in this ill-fated expedition, which eventually led to the unlikely and costly British victory of Barossa.

> On my return, Arguelles[1] who had taken so distinguished a lead in the Cortes, asked me to come in the evenings to his house where the most patriotic & the ablest of their friends met every night. The conversation generally turned on the existing politics but sometimes became general. The first time I went, Arguelles spoke with great openness on the difficulties which he everywhere met, not only from his antagonists but from the irresolution, indiscretion or bigotry of his friends and said Mexia by his wildness had done them more harm than all the old councillors of Castile. He complained of the great want of confidence between the executive body & themselves and lamented that they had not delegated that to a committee of their own body which would have preserved a stricter union. I candidly told him that I thought their fault lay in giving all the responsibility without the power to the Regency; and that they treated them like a master who knew his house was going to be attacked and collected his servants for its defence and should thus address them; 'You are responsible for the defence, you shall be all severely punished if you fail, but I know you to be my enemies & therefore I must first tie your hands & you shall have no weapons for fear you should use them against me'.
>
> Arguelles said that all needful power had been given, that Spain was too much subdued to be saved by ordinary measures; that the military part of the Cortes were always calling out *for men & money and not for constitutions.* That

these men were short sighted not to perceive that Spain could only be saved by a general impulse dictated by freedom and animated by renovated enthusiasm, which could only be executed by giving them something to fight for; & to show them some difference between Ferdinand & Joseph. Therefore a good constitution was the best way of getting men & for money, it could only be obtaining [sic] by conciliating America and therefore the long America questions had been most necessary for their defence.

We had a long conversation about the defence of the Isla & the false principles of the Spanish engineers & as he wished to gain some information on the subject, I promised to get some memoranda for him.

I took Robertson's introduction to the club and read some parts I had before mentioned as highly applicable to the present circumstances 'Whether Ferdinand should be secured married to a Bonaparte'.

Padilla's[2] constitution contains these articles.

1stly	That no king shall marry without the consent of the nation.
2ndly	That no foreign troops shall remain in the kingdom.
3rd	That no foreigners should hold any employment in the state.

To my great surprise, Gallegos & several others knew nothing more of Padilla's writings than his address to Toledo and letter to his mother.

Rodrigo complained bitterly of the want of energy. 'Tortosa had only 1 month's provisions and would fall. What but the practise of lowering a boat down makes a man struggle in the water who has fallen overboard; what makes a governor defend himself but the hope of relief.'[3]

But the Spanish maxim is to abandon not protect their fortresses. Los Franceses nos tartan como a una alcachofa, comiendonos hoja a hoja, pero al fin siempre nos comen' [The French treat us as an artichoke, eating us leaf by leaf, but they always eat us in the end].

The debates on the American question continue with the most injurious & indecent heat. The American deputies are doing a great deal of harm to Spain and I believe intentionally, as they consider themselves the elder son & want to get rich by the death of the parent. They ask for South America what is quite inadmissible, a free representation of every class, which would give them the majority over the Europeans and how long would the metropole exist? I have asked them how the Indians and Mestezoes were to be represented? By their own chiefs? Oh no, for men of colour cannot sit in the Cortes and no language but Spanish can be admitted; so then a few whites are to make a nation the tool of their ambition and outvote the representatives of 12,000,000 of their fellow subjects.

The quarrel between the Junta & the Regency is becoming more serious. The Volunteers of Cadiz being ordered to the Isla refused to obey & carried their point.

A curious anecdote is told of the Regents by an officer on Guard who saw it. On a discussion who should command a sortie which began to be spoke of, Agar[4] & Cisgar[5] declared General Graham to be the only proper person, on which Blake [replied] 'that rather than such an insult should be offered to a Spanish army, he would go in person'. Agar remarked 'that would be worst of all' (meaning it is supposed violating the constitution which prohibits a Regent commanding) and on this they were nearly drawing their swords.

The secret sortie became known by every child in the streets. On the 28th of January 1811 the Spanish troops were out at Sancti Petri & General Cruz[6] entered Medina Sidonia, but it was at length determined to embark a corps & march in the rear of the blockading force as the passage of the river in front of the enemy and the operation of laying bridges was considered as too hazardous.

An expedition was prepared of which General La Pena[7] was to have the command. The English part of it (as per margin – Brigade of Guards, 87th, Flank companies 44th,[8] ditto Portuguese 20th, 67th, detachment 95th, 2 squadrons 2nd [KGL] Hussars) embarked on the 17th of February.[9] The Spanish infantry embarked two days before in open boats, a heavy gale of wind came on accompanied with torrents of rain which detained us till the 22nd, when we sailed but the small boats of the Spaniards could not stem the sea & were obliged to return. Their *troops* during this time were suffering the most extraordinary hardships, exposed without cover to this terrible weather with no means of cooking their rations & were eating cold rice & oil with their bread. I expressed my surprise that their infantry was not kept in their quarters on shore till the last moment as in such boats they might have been embarked in a few hours and that their health would be destroyed by this treatment. A Spanish officer of the Staff answered 'No importa, estan bien acostumbrados a padecer' [It doesn't matter, they are well used to suffering]. When we got out the wind increased so rapidly that by the time we were off Tarifa the surf was too considerable to allow the troops to be landed and the naval officers judged it necessary to take us into Algeciras.

24th The troops disembarked, we were obliged to embark the artillery in small boats as the road was impracticable.

On the 25th we marched to Tarifa and by the great exertions of the navy our guns were brought safely round against a strong breeze & the current of the Straits. We were joined at Tarifa by the 28th and a flank battalion under Colonel Brown.[10]

On the 27th the Spaniards arrived, the town of Tarifa has a weak wall, the island is defensible with a little labour. There is a pretty good position in front of Tarifa but it requires a considerable force to occupy it. The town is small & only remarkable for the old castle of Don Gusman el Bueno,[11] and for the beauty of the women who are the handsomest in Spain.

The Spanish order of march was given out, the cavalry including the

English hussars under General Whittingham the Avant guard General Lardizabal;[12] main body Prince of Anglona;[13] the rear Reserve being the English. General Cruz joined the day after we marched and the force then amounted to about 4,000 British & 9,000 Spaniards.[14]

On the 28th we marched; the road having been repaired. About three miles from Tarifa there is a strong pass between the sea & the Sierra del Medio which runs into the sierra above Algeciras, but all these mountains are practicable for infantry. We bivouacked near Facinas,[15] it was impossible to see a sweeter landscape than was there presented from the hill above it, the country being fantastically thrown together in a wild mixture of rocks & woods, of barrenness & cultivation, with the Straits of Gibraltar peeping like a huge lake between two cliffs and the brown rugged masses of the Barbary mountains rising majestically behind.

General La Pena resolved to march at night and on the evening of the 1st of March the army descended into the plain on the road towards Casas Viejas.[16] The Spanish Staff had the sole management of procuring guides & such ones did they provide that the whole column lost their way & we did not arrive till 11 o'clock next day near Casas Viejas, a march of about 12 miles. At the latter place was a picket of 40 cavalry & 80 infantry which might have been cut off, but La Pena insisted on waiting for artillery, so all but the rear guard of 30 men got off, who were rode in upon & taken by the Spanish dragoons who gave them some desperate wounds.[17] So far had we proceeded with the intention of moving on Medina Sidonia; but the Spanish generals here changed their minds & determined to move on Vejer [de la Frontera] (which had been taken possession of by the Regiment of Carmina) and to communicate by Sancti Petri [with?] the corps under General Zayas.[18]

The Spaniards issued the order to move at 11 that night, but General Graham finding they knew nothing of the road, persuaded them to postpone their march till the morning; we were ordered *to follow* the march of their corps at 6 a.m. At mid day they were just moving off & then marched back above a league on the road towards Facinas though Vejer lay before us on a hill about 10 miles off and the road to it over the plain was perfectly evident. General Graham was so convinced that they were taking the wrong road that he galloped to the head of their column and pointed out the straight one to General La Pena & was answered that, that road was impracticable for artillery & that we must move round a lake in our front which would make the march 20 miles.

Having continued some time, they found some peasants & it turned out that the circuitous route was impracticable but that the short & straight road which General Graham had pointed out was a very good one. It became necessary to counter march the whole column. After marching in our new direction some time, we found the Spaniards halted. Again General Graham galloped to the front and found the delay to arise from a natural canal over which was a causeway knee deep in water with some stepping stones & over these (each man taking off his shoes & stockings) did the Spanish army begin to file, the officers being carried over on the shoulders of the men; four and twenty hours would not have passed them. It was already late & General Graham represented the necessity of getting our guns across before dark. They were brought up & Barnard with the 95th as their guard; who marched through locked up as if on parade; a gun stuck in a deep part, the general threw himself into the water & putting his shoulder to the wheel with the assistance of *his Staff* got it out. The Spaniards gradually became ashamed of themselves, the Prince of Anglona went up to his ankles at first and little by little they set a good example & the Spanish troops marched through very well. We arrived at the end of our twelve mile march at midnight & bivouacked in an olive wood near Vejer.

General La Pena proposed another nights' march, but General Graham anxiously represented the necessity of bringing the troops into action fresh and they agreed only to march as far as Conil[19] where ground was to be taken up by the Staff and we were to pursue our march in the morning. We moved at 5 p.m. on the 4th & in spite of their promises, we were kept lagging on all night, coming to a stop every five minutes, then moving a few yards.

5th March. At daylight when General Graham rode to the head of the Spanish column the generals were all in a great dismay at the guides having again lost their road & true enough we saw Santa Ana & the heights above Chiclana[20] in our front instead of Sancti Petri. The whole country round was heath & the Spaniards were going to counter march & look for a road, when General Graham persuaded them to move over the plain.

Little did we know all this time that the enemy were seeing us & that the absurdities of our march & the error of our guides had been accompanied with all the advantages of able manoeuvre & had perplexed the enemy in the extreme. Our patrols towards Chiclana discovered nothing.

Between 9 & 10 o'clock we reached the ridge of Barossa and I there saw the advance guard moving towards Sancti Petri and what appeared to be about 1500 French in line by the Torre Bermeja. The Spaniards soon began sharp shooting & the French regiments moved off by their left covered with their tirailleurs who kept up a warm skirmish in the wood for nearly two hours. When I saw the manner in which these battalions retired I said to General Graham 'that is not like the French'. It was evident that they did not mean to defend the Bermeja heights. In a letter afterwards intercepted from Legentil, Chef des Genie to General Lery[21] at Seville, he expressed himself thus with regard to that part of the action

'Il parait que le Marscal Victor ne fut informe que tard de la vrai direction de l'ennemi. Il arriva a Chiclana le 5 entre 8 et 9 heures du matin suivis des battalion de la 1er et 2eme Divisions. Le plan d'operations a lequel il s'arreta fut d'envoyer sur le champ la division Villatte avec un regiment de cavalrie aux lignes de Sancti Petri avec ordre de laisser arriver l'ennemi de lui resister faiblement pour l'engager a suivre notre mouvement de retraite et de l'attirer ainsi sous le position de Santa Ana ou il ne pouvait manquer a se trouver dans une position extremement desadvantageuse.'[22] [It seems that Marshal Victor was informed late of the true direction of the enemy. He arrived at Chiclana on the 5th between 8 and 9 o'clock in the morning followed by the battalions of the 1st and 2nd Divisions. The plan of operations to which he had held was to send into the field the Division of Villatte[23] with a regiment of cavalry to the lines of Sancti Petri with orders to let the enemy arrive, resist weakly in order to get him to commit to follow our retirement and movement to draw them way from here to the position of Santa Ana where he could not but be in an extremely disadvantageous situation]. So much for the action of which Lardizabal afterwards boasted so much.[24]

About twelve o'clock General La Pena told the general to move with the reserve towards Sancti Petri. We commenced our march through the wood following the track of the Spanish guns. We had not got very far when Colville[25] came after us reporting that heavy columns of the enemy were moving towards the position we had quitted. The general countermarched from the rear. His reasons for so bold but necessary a step are best detailed in his letter to Sir Henry Wellesley, we had left Colonel Brown's and two Spanish Battalions[26] on the hill & the general believed that position to be the key to that of Sancti Petri, as a glance over the sketch proves & he says 'When we *marched* I left General La Pena on the Barossa height,[27] nor did I know of his intention of quitting it & when I countermarched I did so to support troops left for its defence and believing the general to be there in person'.

When we however got clear of the wood, which was impossible to effect in order, some regiments being divided & all looking more like a chain of tirailleurs than a line, we found that those battalions had been obliged to retire and the French columns were formidably posted on the crest of the hill about 900 yards from us & their artillery began to play. Duncan[28] with his 10 guns first got out of the wood with the 95th & Portuguese who skirmished admirably and placing his battery in a very advanced position, poured a most destructive fire on the enemy's masses. It is useless to describe a battle after a dispatch has done it, except to catch points of minutiae which are omitted. The Guards improved their line as they advanced. There was a hollow way between them & the enemy, scarped & difficult of access on reaching the top of it, they were received with a hail storm of shot. Ruffin,[29] when a prisoner told us that he expected to have seen our line turn every instant as he never saw men fall so fast; but still on they pressed & drove with their bayonets three times their numbers from the hill, leaving in a few minutes above 300 men upon the field. At one moment the men began to fire; General Graham, who was riding at their head with his hat off, waving & cheering them on, not being more than 150 paces from the enemy, accompanied by Birch[30] & Nicholas[31] of the engineers, rode along our line as they were firing, striking up their bayonets, crying 'Men, cease firing & charge'.

The rest of his Staff were in different parts of the field, I remained near the left & saw the charge of the 87th. When the action was over Gough[32] gave me the French eagle to present to the general who was standing near examining a severe contusion he had received on his groin, his horse had been severely wounded. We all escaped though all had their horses killed or wounded. Mine was shot through the thigh & I had two balls through my clothes.

The most important feature of this action is the non co-operation of the Spaniards which led to the decision which General Graham assumed of withdrawing from any further operations. A Spanish general officer (I believe Cruz) was close by me when the cannonade began & I begged him to go & report to La Pena the situation that we were in; he went but nobody returned, the Spanish general crossed the bridge at Sancti Petri & then enquired of every one going to the rear the fate of our division. Had the Spaniards moved towards Chiclana (& they were upon the chord) the utter ruin of the French corps was certain, or if General Whittingham had chose to move his cavalry rapidly round their left to have profited by the victory, which our two squadrons of Germans bravely as they conducted themselves were not in numbers to effect, much more advantage might have been reaped. The regiments of Walloon & Ciudad Real who had been attached to us made haste to reach us on finding we were engaged but the action was quite over before they arrived. The real fact therefore stands thus, that an English force only meant as a reserve, harassed with a night march & without food or rest, defeated completely an enemy double in their numbers, fresh in their strength, collected in their front & formidable from their position, whilst at a distance of two or three miles, lay a Spanish army (when joined by Zayas of 12,000 men), not one of whose officers thought it necessary even to see if we were cut to pieces, and that not one musket was fired in our aid, though numbers of their stragglers arrived, who murdered & stripped the wounded French & plundered indiscriminately the baggage of friend & foe. In every part of the field of battle the wounded prisoners were crying out to be protected from their vengeance. I got General Rousseau into a house, but he soon afterwards expired; he had a poodle dog with him in the field that was found 3 days afterwards watching his master's cloak; someone gave him to General Graham to whom the poor animal soon transferred his entire affection.

Our baggage was plundered also & we lay down on the sand for an hour without being able to get anything to satisfy our hunger, having fasted from the middle of the day before. The men were quite exhausted, nothing but their gallant spirit had borne them through so much fatigue & privation, no provisions were at hand as either they were plundered or the muleteers had run away at the beginning of the action. General Graham therefore determined on moving into the Isla at once & ordered it accordingly.

At 2 in the morning General Graham sent me to General La Pena to communicate this, I found him in a house close to Sancti Petri in bed & it was with some difficulty I obtained admittance. As I reported the conversation officially, this was my letter on the subject.

After stating that, 'I was shown into the general's room, where soon were assembled General Lacy,[33] Valcanal etc. on communicating to General La Pena that the British division had retired into the Isla, he expressed his strong regret that you had not earlier acquainted him with your intention as he also would have retired that night, adding "*I cannot remain here without the English*". General Lacy observed how much it was to be regretted that after such brilliant advantages we should abandon them in a manner more resembling the result of defeat than victory, adding "There are no French in Chiclana, a single light battalion would take possession of it." General La Pena asked me whether the British could not remain for the next day, that the *whole might pass together during the ensuing night*. I answered that the division was already in the Isla & that I could not conceive his Excellency would be much pressed in a position protected on both his flanks, with reinforced numbers, the enemy having just experienced a severe defeat, especially as by General Lacy's account there were no French in Chiclana. General La Pena then stated he should write to you, stating his opinion and sent orders at the same time to stop any Spanish troops from going into the Isla (from which a fair conclusion may be drawn that orders had been issued for retiring before).'

The loss on both sides were as follows: the British went into action something less than 4,000 men & they lost 1,241 The French own returns are these: which were intercepted with Legentil's letter.

	Killed, Wounded & Prisoners
1st Division	
General Ruffin, composed of the 9th, 24th, 96th & a battalion of elite	1040
2nd Division	
Laval, of 8th, 45th, 54th, 16th & chasseurs	1104
Cavalry	109
	2253[34]

Loss acknowledged by the enemy.
Remaining by Returns of 22 March – effective

1st Division	2900
2nd Division	3241
Cavalry	500
Remaining	**6641**
Add Killed wounded & prisoners	2253
Total in field 5 March	**8894**[35]

Therefore by the enemy's *own Returns* they had above double our numbers in the field. Their loss against the Spaniards by the same Returns amounted to 299 in killed, wounded & prisoners.[36]

The French meant to have fought again under their position at Puerto Real and had General Graham continued in his cooperation, the whole brunt of the next action would probably have laid also on the British troops who would have been exposed to entire destruction. I however have often wished he had offered it, as I am firmly convinced the Spaniards would not have moved one inch to the front & the onus of the retreat would have rested on them.

General La Pena in his own pamphlet stated that being so near the seat of government, he would have sent to them for ulterior orders. But if the misconduct of the Spanish general was flagrant in the action, ten fold more disgusting was the *ingratitude* and vanity of the whole population of Cadiz. La Pena was declared by a court of enquiry to have deserved well of his country & received the order of Charles 3rd[37] as a reward for having abandoned his allies & lost the brightest moment which had occurred of striking a severe blow & the British troops who had toiled and fought, had bled & conquered for them, were assailed with every species of illiberal abuse which jealousy & hatred and consciousness of their own misconduct could produce. I will not enter into all the details of the paper war which ensued; Frederick Ponsonby[38] wrote anonymously & was answered by General Cruz. I wrote the following letter which made people laugh.

'No alcanzan perezosos honrados triunfos ni Victoria alguna quevedo' [The idle will never achieve either honourable triumphs nor any victory] 'Soy perezoso por naturaleza y no teniendo nada de Gloria he leido con mucho interes los triunfos ajenos, la Guerra venida de las virgenes plumas de su Excelencia el General Cruz etc etc etc y el Senor C. P. que puede tambien ser "*un Excelencia*", per como nada dice el mismo y escribe en castellano, puedo sospechar que no alcanza mas que anadir unas pocas palabras, si mis ideas no son *puestas* en "*terminus militares y topograficos*" como las del General Cruz, tienen una ventaja, son *cortas* y ademas muy en favour de mi General el heroe La Pena.

Supongamos que el Senor C.P. ha visto todo lo que dice cuan poco fue!

Como la columna cerrada del General escapo a su observacion, un hecho que puede originarse de dos cosas, la cortedad de la vista del senor C. P. o la falta de memoria del General. Creo lo primero, porque el senor C. P. (se dice) estuvo muy, muy cerca del enemigo y por consiguiente demasiado lejos del General para verlo.

Cuando lei la carta del General Cruz, no siendo military, pregunte a un official cuyos tres bordados probaban que era un dignisimo jefe y cuyas canas daban demostracion de la experiencia en los campos (de Bailen o de baile que importa) "Que hermosos movimientos!" La columna cerrada debia ser muy fuerte para hacer tanto. Supongo a lo menos de 4000 hombres.

"Setecientos" respondio el valente Viejo. Cedite Romani! Cedite Graeci! Grite en un transporte de verdadero patriotismo. Los trescientos Espartanos no podian comparase con esos!

Pero algunos tontos dicen que el General Cruz hubiera debido maniobrar mas cerca del enemigo Calaveras!!

El Marques de Santa Cruz (sin duda el General actual es su pariente, como el talento military en espana es hereditario y cae siempre sobre los mayorazgos dice en su libro (Vol II P 14/15) "*Que no se permite ningun movimiento en cara o bajo fuego del enemigo*".

Pero es possible que los franceses con sus anteojos hayan visto la columna de los setecientos. Si esto se pudiera verificar, bien podria decir mi General en el lenguaje de los Romanos.

"Aunque con mortal cuidado
dejeis mis sentidos llenos
no me negareis al menos,
Ojos, que me habeis mirado."

En fin no hay duda ninguna que el General Cruz maniobro bajo los mas antiguos y seguros principios y que nada ha impedido los brillantes efectos de sus sabias combinaciones, sino la lastimosa y (como Lacey dice) la "*inesperada* circunstancia de que el enemigo fue batido antes de que llegara. Que dios nos de paciencia para sufrir dignamente tales desgracias!"

Pero el genio mas exquisite para la Guerra es el del *nuestro* La Pena (porque aun nos queda) que con una serenidad sin igual estuvo reconociendo el terreno interesante de Sancti Petri y tomando sabias medidas para una retirada durante el fuego de la batalla y cuando entre los gemidos de los moribundos alzaban los Ingleses los gritos triunfantes de la Victoria.

Por ellos hay un refran diciendo

"Sin pan, carne y Jerez
no combate el Ingles"

Sabemos la entera refutacion de este a los sabios movimientos nocturnos del digno y bien premiado La Pena.

Pero sin broma, como Espanol no temo por mi patria! En el patriotismo del pueblo, aquella clase, tan sufrido, heroico y paciente pongo mis verdaderas y bien fundadas esperanzas. Los rayos del sol de la oppression han hundido sus fuerzas temidas sobre el escudo protector de la libertad de Imprenta.

Amada Espana! Que estos versos te sean profeticos:

"Poco cielo te corona
y en tan breves horizontes
te librara de las penas
quien te guarde de los soles"

SSS Q S M B
Cara Redonda'

[I am naturally lazy and not having anything of glory, I have read with great interest the triumphs of others, the bitter warfare comes from the virgin pens of his Excellency the General Cruz etc etc etc and from Mister C. P., who it is possible is also 'an Excellency', but as nothing is said by himself though he writes in Castilian, I suspect that he only has that simple title. I cannot do less than add a few words; if my ideas are not worded in 'military and topographic terms' as those of General Cruz, they have an advantage, they are brief and in addition very much in favour of my general the hero La Pena.

Let us suppose that Mr C. P. saw everything that he says. How little it was! How the general's close column escaped his observation can only originate from one of two things, the short sightedness of Mr C. P. or lack of memory of the general. I believe the first, because Mr C. P. (it is said) was very, very close to the enemy and consequently too far from the general to see him.

When I read the letter of General Cruz, not being a military man, I asked an officer whose three bars proved that he was a very honourable officer and whose white hairs gave proof of his experience on the battlefield (of Bailen or of the dance, it doesn't matter).

What beautiful movements! The close column had to be very strong to do so much, I suppose at least 4,000 men.

'Seven hundred' the brave old man answered. 'Go back Romans! Go back Greeks!' I shouted, transported by a wave of patriotism. The three hundred Spartans could not compare with these!

But some idiots say that General Cruz must have carried out manoeuvres nearer the enemy, rakes!!

The Marquis of Santa Cruz (the present general is undoubtedly his relative, as the military talent is hereditary in Spain and always falls to the first born) says in his book (Vol II p 14/15) '*that no movement is allowed when facing the enemy or when under his fire*'.

But it is possible that the French with their spy glasses may have seen the column of the seven hundred. If this could be verified, my general could well say in the language of the Romans.

'Though with mortal care
you leave my senses full
you will not deny me at least,
eyes, that you have looked at me.'

Well, there is no doubt that General Cruz carried out manoeuvres under the most ancient and sure principles and that nothing has prevented the brilliant effects of his wise combinations, except the pitiful and (as Lacy says) the 'unexpected circumstance of which the enemy was beaten before he had come'. God give us patience to suffer with dignity such misfortunes!

But the most exquisite genius for the war is that of our La Pena (because we still have to say) that with a serenity without equal, he was reconnoitring Sancti Petri's interesting area and taking wise measures for a retreat during the fire of the battle and when between the groans of the dying, the English raised the triumphant shouts of victory.

For them there is a saying, which says:

'Without bread, meat and sherry
the English do not fight'

We know the complete refutation of this by the wise night movements of the honourable and prize winning La Pena.

But joking apart, being Spanish, I do not fear for my motherland! In the patriotism of the people, that so long suffering class, heroic and patient, I put my real and well founded hopes. The rays of the sun of oppression have sunk his fearful forces under the protective shield of the freedom of the press.

Beloved Spain! I wish these verses to be prophetic for you:

'Little sky crowns you
and in such brief horizons
will save you from *the sorrows*[39]
which defends you from the suns'

Your assured servant, who kisses
your hands Round Face]

The account arrived of Massena's retreat; Mr Wellesley made the following proposition 'To add to Lord Wellington's powers as Captain General of the Spanish army, the temporary rank of Captain General of whatever province, he might enter in the progress in the campaign.' This roused the pride of a nation who in their dangers dream of past security & who for want of a present good commander talk with increased rapture of the Cid & Gran Capitan[40] &

blindly await their fate under the conviction of a fancied invincibility & will not acknowledge the assistance which has kept them from destruction as it would detract from the high idea they have formed of the *Corage Espanol* [Spanish courage].

The most violent discussions have taken place on this question, we have been represented as re-enacting the scenes of French treachery & as wishing to get their army in our power. The nobility were not behind hand, the old intriguing Duchess of Osuna said she wished the last of the English was strangled in the bowels of the last Frenchman & the Duchess of Ajar said that the situation of Spain was like Christ between two thieves & for her part she thought France the honest one.

The most serious opposition arose from a quarter where it was least to be expected, all the liberales with Arguelles at their head (Torrero & Oliveros excepted[41]) violently opposed an appointment they considered insulting to their nation & the Cortes having discussed it for some days got rid of the question by a real Spanish trick, they remitted it for the decision of the Regency, who with cooler feelings & unbiased judgement might decide after they were known to be hostile and had even given in their opinion against it at the bar of the Cortes.

This has shaken my faith in the talents of Arguelles who in the middle of all this brought in a bill for the abolition of torture & the slave trade, one of which does not exist at all & the other in the slightest degree. I believe him to be thoroughly honest & well intentioned & to be qualified to legislate for a nation in peace, but not to assist materially in the deliverance of Spain from her present dangers. I fear what Capmany[42] said will prove true 'You will see Arguelles an exile in a foreign land with an excellent constitution for Spain under his arm of as much use as Plato's Republic.'

One of the most fatal symptoms in this country is that the people are anxious to be deluded as their government can be to delude them and the Spaniards derive as much consolation from the sight of imaginary numbers on paper, as others would from the conviction of effective military strength. To prove this, I met the Duke of Infantado one day coming out of the Minister at War's & he said 'What a nation this is! We have now 8 corps amounting to 180,000 effective men'. He read over the Return in which the Army of Cadiz, including Ballasteros was calculated at 43,000, making him enumerate corps by corps as we knew it existed, we could only make it 22,000 at the highest statement, nevertheless he went off quite pleased with the immense power of Spain. The news arrived of the taking of Figueras by surprise.[43] The joy of the Spaniards knows no bounds 'Puede, pero ahora (said they) que la fortuna nos conduce a destrozar al vil Napoladron' [It is possible (they said) but now fortune drives us on to destroy the vile Napo-thief].

They fired away enough powder to have defended the fortress [for] a month

& never thought more of [it] till they heard of its surrender, when they proved by maximus politicas y militares [political and military maxims] that Rovira[44] had done very wrong to take what he could not preserve. The good doctor himself went from one town of Spain to another like another Peter the hermit,[45] preaching the necessity of sending provisions by which he got nothing, but 'Olla' [a pot] for himself, without bread for his troops.

We were treated with a most extraordinary sermon on the occasion in the cathedral where the Regency & such attended the celebration of high mass. It was a moral, political, military, historical, fiscal, critical & biographical treatise, embracing the past, present & the future, & varying with romantic wildness from Judas Maccabeus[46] to Compigny, from the taking of Jerusalem to the surprise of Figueras, from the banks of the Red Sea to the Ebro & ending with an exhortation of giving all for the Catalans. This was unattended to and if the proverb be true '*que bien come el Catalan si se lo dan*' [How much the Catalan eats, if someone gives it to him]. I fear they would have nothing better than 'La mesa de un hidalgo, poca vianda y mantel largo' [The table of a nobleman has little food and a long tablecloth].

Colonel Juan A.D.C. to Berthier was taken with all his correspondence. His own notes were full of sensible observations & his characters were drawn with boldness. He said of [Marshal] Victor 'Monsieur le Duc est un bon general, mais il s'ennuye beacoup ici et voit les choses un peu en noir.' [The Duke is a good general, but is not happy here and sees things a little black]

A very interesting letter was taken upon him from Legentil on the means of attacking Cadiz, doubting the success of a simple bombardment and stating the Trocadero as the offensive point from which a landing should be made in the rear of the Cortadura. He entered into a very candid & able view of all the evils which had arisen from the siege of Cadiz, by which '*in fact they were themselves blockaded*' & engaged in an operation from which they could neither recede 'without an irreparable loss of time & cannon or hope to prosecute with effect according to their present means'. Their plan of landing in the rear of the Cortadura[47] we were well aware of and General Graham had long pressed the Spanish government to enclose or allow him to enclose it in the rear, but the opinion of a Spanish general of engineers prevailed, who said 'that the guns could not be brought off, if that was executed.' It is difficult to attribute advice of this nature to simple ignorance or folly. When the British troops first arrived at Cadiz, the Isla might have been carried by an adventurous enemy, but General Graham immediately commenced a line of closed redoubts on the 'Cerro de los Martires'[48] which afterwards was improved by several strong redoubts on the inward line of the bay, the great causeway affording several advantageous points. The Cortadura was given to our care and we rendered it very strong & constructed some very formidable redoubts in the rear of Puntales which was likewise greatly improved. The faults of the Spanish line of defence are best explained in the following memoranda of General Graham's which he wrote for the information of my friend Arguelles.

'In order to judge well of the defensive system adopted by the Spanish engineers, it is not necessary to be a military man. The principle of obtaining the greatest security with the smallest number of men must be the best. The first, or most advanced works, of an extensive line, should therefore be *enclosed* works a l'abri d'un coup de main [a shelter against a raid], capable of being defended by a small garrison of say, 200 men, against any assault. They should be as little multiplied as possible & on points which flank the river or the coast, so that their fire may sweep & enfilade the reaches of the river or the beach.

These most advanced works must necessarily be supported by others in the rear or in second line. What would an enemy gain by attempting to break through such a line as this? Unless he is in such force as to be able to besiege several of these advanced works at the same time that he pushes on to attack in the same way the works of the second line, it is impossible he should keep up his communications, he cannot reap any advantage from his attack, which scarcely should create any alarm on our side. He is sure to suffer loss & disgrace in the attempt.

It appears that the system adopted by the Spaniards beginning from the right at Sancti Petri is entirely different. At that point, (one of the most interesting & dangerous, because the river is there narrow & is the only obstacle; whereas everywhere else its course is through marshy intersected grounds that precludes the possibility of the use of any other arm but infantry & that must come forward in small uncoordinated bodies) a plan of an immense front fire instead of a flanking fire has been adopted, the works [which] are close to the river, of course may be destroyed by a superior fire from the enemy's side; they are open in the rear & of course liable to be taken as soon as the enemy can by surprise or open force contrive to cross the river, either there or considerably in the rear. When taken they would afford the enemy great cover & a most formidable artillery, which would make an attack along the narrow isthmus almost impossible to regain it. These works would therefore be immediately converted into a tete du point & the enemy might then bring over an army with cannon, cavalry & such.

Had two strong redoubts, as were proposed been constructed on the sand hills at some distance in the rear, with epaulements [earthen banks] in advance to cover a few field pieces to flank the river & the beach, this valuable post would have been long ago secure with half the number of men now encamped there.

A chain of intermediate & connecting works would however be necessary to secure this point, 3 miles from the 2nd line, from being turned by the enemy crossing the river in the rear of it. These works should be strongly enclosed, towers would be the best, as requiring the fewest men to defend them.

The same observations apply to all the other batteries of the first line. They are generally close to the edge of the river & therefore liable to be boarded from boats & they are open in the rear, therefore liable to be surprised by small bodies of the enemy who might with impunity insult & alarm the whole line, spiking the guns, destroying the carriages & the works themselves, before it could be known where the real attack was meant. It is in the nature of things that such a line should be weak, for there is nothing to satisfy the minds of the soldiers at the different posts that they are in a situation of security. By day the difficulties of the ground will prevent such attacks being made; nothing prevents their being made by night when success to a certain degree would be undoubted, but the gunboats which are still necessary & have been still permitted by the enemy to remain in this river, these might be driven away whenever the enemy chooses. Most, if not all of these batteries might have had wet ditches excavated all round them by the very formation of the rampart & parapet of the works themselves. Fewer works, had they been of this nature, would have answered the purpose, consequently fewer men would have been exposed to harassing duty & a greater reserve would have remained disposable to repel with effect *in daylight* any real or serious attacks that might be undertaken.

The Carraccas,[49] a most valuable point on every consideration to be maintained, might have been long ago impregnable by fortifying as a citadel the presidium, by insulating, by entrenchments, the open batteries at the angles & by barricading & fortifying some of the strongest & most commanding buildings as infantry posts inside, none of all these obvious means have been taken. The Carraccas remain after ten months exposed to a coup de main any night, most of the batteries towards the enemy, being low barbette,[50] giving no protection to the artillery men from grape shot or musketry.

The coast of the harbour in several places has very strong & extensive buildings the Caseria d'Ocio, Lazaretto, Casa Brancas, Cano d'Harrera, Molino de Santa Banos all readily capable of being strongly & quickly fortified. The Spanish engineers seem to prefer making useless lines between some of these as was begun on the coast of Puntales. The chaussee or great road almost all the way from Isla ought to form a line, because it is there & can with little labour be converted into one, having redoubts whenever there are circles on it, like the work lately made in the rear of the Cortadura. The town of Isla should have a connected enceinte to enclose it, taking in as far as the heights of the Torre Alto Observatory, burying ground & such, so as to prevent the possibility of any fatal accident happening by a successful & bold attempt of a few thousand men, who might disembark or penetrate unexpectedly. While Isla remains the seat of government & the place of the Assembly of the Cortes, this is an urgent & indispensable precaution, but Isla is too important for Cadiz not to be made as secure as art can make it. The position altogether should be rendered impregnable by any force, for as long as it is maintained one need not despair of the liberty & independence of Spain being maintained & there can be no more favourable situation meanwhile for the instruction of troops. Were the enemy to come in force, it would require 30,000 men to render Cadiz & Isla perfectly safe, but the enemy must bring two or three times that number against them, therefore their services would not be thrown away.

Much precious time has been lost, it is the more necessary to make up for it by great & well directed exertion.'

The Cortadura was never finished & the front of Cadiz itself though finely constructed as far as the execution is concerned, has a capital fault of being built on the narrowest part of the isthmus, so that a besieging enemy would immediately obtain a greater power of fire than the besieged.

The Isla is its chief defence, General Moreau[51] said that 'Gibralte pour le sec et Cadiz pour l'humide etaient les plus fortes places de l'Europe.' [Gibraltar for the dry, Cadiz for the humid damp were the greatest places in Europe]

Chapter 7

Wellington's Army

It was now clear that the French besieging force was not going to be strong enough to capture Cadiz and a monotonous round of pointless shelling and minor skirmishes no longer held any excitement for the British troops. It is not surprising therefore to see James write joyously of the news that Sir Thomas Graham was to join Wellington's army as second in command.

Much had happened with Wellington's army since James had last seen them, following Massena's retreat from Portugal. The southern force under Marshal Beresford had attempted to besiege Badajoz, which ultimately led to a very bloody stalemate of a victory at Albuera on 16 May and the resurrection of the siege. Meanwhile in the north, Wellington had begun the task of taking the northern frontier fortresses and had blockaded Almeida. Marshal Massena sought to break this blockade and the Battle of Fuentes d'Onoro was fought over three days, which fortunately proved successful for Wellington, although the garrison of Almeida blew up the defences and escaped to the French lines on the night of 10 May, much to his rage. General Graham moved rapidly to join the Army before anything else significant occurred.

> In the latter end of June we to our great joy received orders to go to Portugal, General Graham being appointed Second in Command there. On the Second of July he left Cadiz, for which place he had done all which talents, patience & perseverance could effect & where his only reward had been obloquy, misrepresentation & ingratitude. The Cortes made him after the Battle of Barossa, a Grandee of Spain of the first class by the title of 'Duque del Sierra del Puerco' but as they were vilifying his army & conduct & rewarding La Pena at the same moment, he with spirit, refused it.
>
> Anchored in the Tagus the 9th, whilst we were preparing our field equipment, I saw more of Lisbon, its society and amusements, though the comedy was dull, the play bill is not unamusing.[1]
>
> At the time I arrived the Portuguese government had just performed a trick perfectly in character & indeed I hardly ever found people more consistent in all the weak & bad & base of human nature than the gentry & nobility of Portugal. The Prince of Wales had just sent a present of some salt fish to be distributed gratis among the poor sufferers from the French inroad. The

Portuguese government lodged it in their magazines and opened an office where licences for receiving this present were issued at two dollars each and numbers paid the money, hoping to receive a valuable compensation of food. When they produced their tickets at the magazines, they received about one dollar's worth of fish.

On the prince being told that he was coming out he said 'He won't ___ me will he stink ye'.[2]

I went over the new lines of Almada composed of thirteen redoubts,[3] with each flank resting on the Tagus & covering Porto Brandao. Their object is to prevent the enemy from driving our ships from the Tagus by fire, which the occupation of these heights would have rendered practicable.

I have always thought that had Soult drawn off the army of Andalucia, had abandoned the siege of Cadiz & collected his own force also, with which he besieged Badajoz & with this united corps which had then amounted after masking Badajoz and Elvas to 40,000 men; he had moved into the Alentejo occupying the heights of Almada, driving us from the left bank, he would have enabled Massena to succeed. But, we always have gained much in Spain since Bonaparte left it, by the jealousies of the different French generals always acting from motives of personal ambition without attending to preserve the general chain of public interest.

29th of July we left Lisbon to Vila Franca [de Xira].

30th Cartaxo, 31st Golega. Passing through Santarem I felt more convinced that Lord Wellington could not have carried it, when he meant it in last November.

1st of August Abrantes. Met General Lobo.[4] It is inconceivable how the French did not take this place when they blockaded it for so many months. Even improved as it is, it is hardly to be considered 'a l'abri d'un coup de main' [protected from a raid] and Lobo's garrison only consisted of some wretched militia who could be hardly kept to the common duties of the night.

(The French had a bridge of boats on the Zezere and threw up some redoubts & fortified a church to serve as a tete de pont. Both banks of the Zezere are very strong by nature and against an enemy well posted on either side, it would not be possible to force the passage of the river, which though shallow & fordable in the summer, rises in the winter to a very great height with astonishing rapidity).

In Abrantes the castle is by position the strongest, but there are no wells in it. It is too far from the river to command absolutely, though it might harass the passage or navigation of the Tagus. Otherwise by clearing away part of the town, the castle might be made very strong.

3rd reached Cardigos, about two leagues from Abrantes, pass the Lodes, the banks of which are lofty & defensible but as this road is a very bad one, this position is not likely to become of importance, as the advance of an enemy would always be on the greater roads.

4th Pass through Corticada[5] to Sobreira Formosa (more properly to be termed [unreadable: Fea?]).

As the country from Abrantes is particularly uninteresting, composed of a monotonous succession of mountain & ravine with nothing but the green cistus & a few olives & cork trees on which to repose the eye, the beauty of the village of Corticada became more striking, buried in trees and secluded by surrounding mountains one might fancy its obscurity had secured it from the hand of destruction, which had swept with such unsparing rage over the adjoining country.

5th reached Castelo Branco, 1 league from Sobreira is the famous pass of Taladu, the strongest position on this road against an invading army. It is formed by a precipitous mountain at the foot of which flows a branch of the Ocresa its right rests on that river, its left on the mountains by the Ribiera de Isna;[6] thereby defending the Nova Estrada which runs from Corticada.

6th Remain at Castelo Branco in the Bishop's palace which is a very good house. The gardens are in execrable taste, the trees cut so as to preclude the hope of shade and a number of Episcopal statues glare in every alley. Gold fish swim in marble basins, where fountains should play, but instead 'Swallows roost in Nilus dusty urn'.[7]

James arrived at the front as Wellington tried to impose a blockade on the fortress of Ciudad Rodrigo in an attempt to starve the garrison into surrender; but Marshal Marmont manœuvred his forces very ably to allow a convoy of supplies to gain access to the fortress.

By making a forced march of twelve leagues, we reached Sabugal before daylight on the 8th where headquarters were. 9th moved with them to Casillas de Flores (in Spain) & on the 10th to Fuenteguinaldo.

Lord Wellington had broke up from their cantonments in the hopes of preventing a convoy from entering Ciudad Rodrigo, but he just arrived too late. He again threw his army into cantonments, the Light Division at El Sahugo, Martiago and detachments with the cavalry watching Ciudad Rodrigo; the 1st at Nave de Haver etc, the 4th at St Miguel[8] etc; the 5th at Penaparda etc; the 6th around Sabugal.

The enemy were known to be collecting a large convoy & Count Dorsenne's Army of the North[9] was moving down to assist Marmont[10] in covering it.

11th Rode with Lord Wellington, General Graham etc round Ciudad Rodrigo. Beyond Martiago are two deep & parallel ravines, of Villarejo and Encalado, running from the Sierra de Francia to the Agueda [River], between the two on a lofty point of rock are the remains of an old hold of the Templars now called Lerilla. We gave Ciudad a wide berth & reached Gallegos [de Arganan] at night. It was a long ride, nearly 14 leagues, several of the horses of the escort died of the heat & fatigue. I believe the force under Lord Wellington to be, including General Hill, about 25,000 British infantry & 14,000 Portuguese with about 3,000 British cavalry.

August 29th, rode to the front, a long ride of 14 leagues with Lord C Manners.[11] The day was so hot that both our horses *died* as soon as we came in; I particularly regretted mine as it was a beautiful beast and had been wounded under me at Barossa.

A report is spread that we are going to besiege Ciudad Rodrigo, all the divisions are ordered to learn how to make fascines[12] & to entrench. We began in the rear of Guinaldo. There appears to be great difficulties against a siege.

1st. The time of the year which makes the formation of a bridge very hazardous with a river which swells as rapidly as the Agueda. There is no bridge but the impracticable one of Barca del Puerco.

2nd. There is no covering position beyond the fortress in case of an enemy moving to raise the siege.

3rd. We have no place d'armes to form magazines in or to lodge the heavy artillery in case of failure.

4th. All roads are impracticable for artillery in wet weather which must be expected.

General Graham went to see the Perales del Puerto[13] which he describes as very strong for the road winds up the mountain from Coria, having on its right a rapid descent so that no position could be taken on that side for attack and on the left a number of small hills rising one above the other of inconsiderable breadth to the very top of the sierra, on each of these artillery might be placed to enfilade and flank the road whilst an enemy would from the narrowness of the knolls hardly be able to form his columns at all. This pass is to be turned as a road exists from Coria to Penamacor but of what nature I know not.

James was invited to dinner with Lord Wellington and recorded his conversation on numerous issues, including the defence of Lisbon and Massena's retreat, but perhaps most interestingly on the number of sick and absent officers from his army.

Lord Wellington said at dinner that from the account of the great magazines forming on the frontier he believed Bonaparte was coming in person, but added 'I am damned if he will drive us out'. Went coursing after dinner and Lord Wellington talked a good deal to me. He began talking about the Lines of Almada which he said would be better if taken from Moita to Palmela & that 10,000 men would defend them.[14] That he never could impress sufficiently the necessity of a large naval force in the Tagus, for if the French were capable of a dash, their only way to ruin us, was to send out their Toulon fleet to enter the Tagus and get possession of Lisbon, our fleet and magazines. He talked then about Massena's retreat & the ability of it & said he pretended to throw his columns on the Thomar road when in fact they were on the Leiria one, that he just found it out in time and got all the army that he wanted together at Pombal. He then spoke of the enormous number of sick officers, there being 700 absent and only 1400 present. He said their constitutions must be all broken, he got warm & said 'By God all my generals & officers go home, don't wonder at it, there is no reward in England for service. In France the man gets wealth & dignities but in England a regiment is just as often given to the man who walks about London as the real soldier. Don't wonder at their going, but they ought to have some consideration for their country & profession, I never want to go home!'

September 6th Changed quarters to Naver d'Haver.

14th Heard of the action in Murcia,[15] went over the ground where the Battle of Fuentes was fought. It suggests many reflections; had the French infantry attacked at the same time the cavalry did, I do not see how General Houston could have got from the Poco Velho wood to his second position.[16] There was a ticklish moment when our cavalry was driven in, the Chasseur Britaniques by their firmness and a well directed volley stopped the French. The key of the whole action was the village of Fuentes which lay in a hollow between two hills occupied by the artillery of the contending armies. I think had we occupied the church & higher part of the village and retrenched it as Craufurd did next day, we should have lost many less men, but the highlanders were so impetuous that they pushed into the French part of the village & were taken in flank & rear when separated. I knew Cameron very well who was killed, he was a very good officer but harsh.[17]

Definite news of the supply convoy for Ciudad Rodrigo put the army in motion, but the French were too strong and Wellington's staff were nearly captured.

20th The French convoy left Salamanca, which he had been long expecting, the 1st Division & 6th moved to Espeja, General Anson's cavalry 14th & 16th to ditto with picquets at Carpio [de Azaba]. Lord Wellington had the Light Division at El Sahugo, the 4th & 7th up or nearly so.

24th French convoy came in sight escorted by Dorsenne's Army of the North & Marmont's Army of Portugal, composed of about fifty five thousand infantry & 8,000 cavalry. Of course Lord Wellington could not prevent their entry, but he determined it appeared to make them consume what they brought.

On the 25th at daylight, infantry, cavalry & artillery were seen filing over the bridge of Ciudad Rodrigo, about 14 squadrons made their point at Carpio, the rest moved towards El Bodon. We waited *so long* (the general & Staff) in Carpio that a good many French dragoons had got much nearer the ford of the Azava than we were & we had to gallop for it. It *was* capital sport to see the French dragoons pressing their little horses through the ploughed land on our flanks whilst we were passing them down the road as if they had been standing still. We had hardly crossed when 4 or 5 squadrons of the enemy rashly crossed the ford & entered the wood, where the whole army might have been for all they could know.

In the first open spot they were charged by part of Anson's Brigade[18] & routed, they attempted to reform but a volley from the light infantry company of the 61st decided them on getting back as fast as they could. An Irish colonel they had was dismounted but he would not take quarter but fought desperately till killed.

In the mean time Lord Wellington had gone in the morning to the heights above El Bodon which immediately look over Ciudad Rodrigo. He had with him only two battalions (the 5th & 77th, 2 Portuguese guns & three squadrons of the German Hussars[19]). He soon found against him 8 squadrons, a brigade of guns & a division of infantry. He conducted the retreat of this small body himself to the heights above Guinaldo, in one charge the French cavalry took the guns, the Portuguese behaving remarkably & suffering themselves to be cut down rather than abandon them, but the 5th Regiment charged the French cavalry & retook the guns.[20] This act pleased Lord Wellington more than anything which had happened in his campaigns & he expressed himself in the strongest terms of admiration in General Orders. The hussars made several brilliant charges. The French retired from Carpio but kept increasing their force on their left. Next day about 1 o'clock an immense column was seen from our heights filing from Ciudad Rodrigo towards El Bodon & the head of it had reached the latter 2 leagues off before the rear had left Ciudad Rodrigo. I went over to Lord Wellington to report this, he already knew it; I found him in a fleche thrown up for one of our batteries in the front of Guinaldo, with the 4th Division and Light Division which had just crossed the Agueda and 2 Portuguese Brigades.

He spoke warmly about the skirmish of the day before; I then heard of Charles Manner's escape by a leap from the French Staff whom he went up to, mistaking them for ours when going to change his horse he had left on the same hill an hour before. Lord Wellington said 'It won't do to be bullied out of every position, however the French are strong enough to take this, so I shall be off tonight'. They have now there, 14,000 Guards & 7,000 other infantry and in truth it was a beautiful sight for the sun was getting low and beaming full upon them and at the distance of less than a mile were the French 12 battalions of the Guards in line with long red feathers. Whilst I was with Lord Wellington they all fell in, it was a superb scene; Marmont & Dorsenne slept that night at El Bodon. Lord Wellington then said he should send the orders and told me to take a circuit to the rear, as he had nothing in the valley of the Azava & the French would probably patrol it. A circumstance occurred which proves that he can think of everything great & small at the same moment. He had given me a greyhound a few days before & I had written to Fitzroy Somerset[21] to know its name. As I was getting on my horse Lord Wellington cried out 'Oh, by the way the dog's name is Limbo'. The dog was a great poacher & never stayed with me; he was found several times but was soon finally lost. We retreated in the night by Vilar Major to the other side of the river of that name, the line was too extensive to be occupied with our force & was not a strong one.

The headquarters were at Nave, we were at Bismula,[22] the 5th & 7th Divisions had joined. Towards the evening the enemy felt us at Aldeia da Ponte and were repulsed by the 4th Division, at night the left of the army under General Graham retreated to a position of Rendo with our left flank on the Coa & in the morning the rest of the army drew off & placed themselves on the same height and their right on the Coa, Sabugal & its bridge being in our rear, headquarters at Quadrazais. This was a position just fitted for our numbers, about 30,000 men & where we should have beaten the enemy had they come on, but they did not go further than Aldeia da Ponte and their main body never beyond Vilar Major.

Lord Wellington thus gained his object of making them eat up what they brought, for they drew from Ciudad Rodrigo a week's provision for 60,000 men which is 420,000 rations, equal to 4 months provisions for the garrison. It had however a bad morale effect as it enabled the enemy to say they had driven us from all our positions and taken our entrenched camp (as they called the ditches we had made in the rear of Guinaldo to teach the divisions trench making). Still Lord Wellington's object was a great one and admirably brought to the desired conclusion.

The 28th, the enemy retired, on the 29th broke up for cantonments, moved by Pega, Adao, Vila Mendo to Gata.

30th by Sobral da Serra to Lajeosa [do Mondego].

The army was then cantoned.

Headquarters Regioso & Freineda
1st Division Lajeosa & adjacents
2nd Castello Branco
3rd Alfaiates
4th Nave de Haver
5th Guarda
6th Pinzio
7th moved towards the 2nd
Light Division El Sahugo & Martiago
Anson's cavalry Freixedas
Grey's cavalry Alverca

Lord Wellington in all this operation trusted a good deal to his Belle Etoile [Great Star], for had the French when amounting to 20,000 men in his front that evening began an attack & moved the main body of their army up the valley of the Azava thereby dividing our divisions from the centre & right, he would have found himself in a critical situation, but the French wanted to have all up & Lord Wellington slipped out. He seems always to have known exactly how far he could go with them & when he was to stop trusting to fortune.

2nd of November. The French brought up very secretly some cavalry & 2 brigades of infantry to cover the entry of a new governor (the former having been taken in a ride by Don Julian[23]) and some cattle. The army was ordered up but the enemy had taken such precautions that they threw in the convoy before troops could be assembled to resist them.

I was delighted with Lajeosa from the beauty of the scenery of all the valley of the Mondego and immediately above Lajeosa there is a waterfall at [Cadafaz] Rapa which equals in picturesque beauty anything I ever saw.

22nd of November, we went away for a few days to visit a Portuguese *squire* called Don Pinto de Silva who lives at Real near Mangualde. His hospitality was unbounded, feeding all our horses &c and giving us each day a dinner of pigs, turkeys, geese, all nodding at each other, which would have served an hundred persons. We heard of another convoy & returned but found the division marched, joined it at Bismula.

26th to Nave de Haver, 27th moved headquarters to [La] Alamedilla; convoy did not set off. 30th to Freineda, 1st December to Pinhel. I heard from General Graham that it was owing to the firmness of Mr Wellesley that La Pena has not been reinstated in command.

2nd[24] went to Lord Blantyre's[25] at Escarigo with the general, next day crossed the Turon (a good ford) crossed the Duas Casas by a natural bridge formed by a large stone which might be made a good bridge. Barca de Puerco[26] is situated on the edge of the steepest ravine I ever saw. The 4th [Foot] were to have been here when Brennier escaped, but some misconception between General A. Campbell occasioned their absence. Poor Bevan[27] shot himself in consequence, who commanded the regiment, as excellent an officer & as amiable a man as any in the service. The French came down a track to the right of the road, they lost about 700 either drowned or killed by falls; under the bridge are the massy remnants of a former one, the cement of which is as hard as the stone.

We *went down* by San Felices [de los Gallegos] & Lumbrales, we lost our way, nearly broke our necks & nearly drowned in a ford of the Turon; but at last got home in the dark, wet & tired out.

Chapter 8

Tale of Two Sieges

As the New Year arrived, Wellington was aware that Napoleon was slowly draining troops from Spain to bolster the huge pan-European army with which he planned to invade Russia in the spring of 1812. Meanwhile Wellington planned to seize the key fortresses of Ciudad Rodrigo and Badajoz from beneath the noses of the French marshals. Preparations had been made throughout the early winter months and by January Wellington was ready to attempt to take Ciudad Rodrigo, at a period of the year when supplies were scarce, forcing the French army to disperse. If he was quick enough, the fortress would be his before the French had time to gather and march to its defence. He estimated that he had twenty-five to thirty days.

> It became now evident from the number of gabions[1] &c we were ordered to make & from the great number of wheel carriage assembled that something serious was intended against Ciudad Rodrigo. Some of the objections were removed as Almeida was put in a respectable state of defence. Dorsenne's Army was sent back for the sake of sustenance into Leon & Burgos and Marmont had moved to the south to cooperate with Suchet who though victorious in the Battle of Murviedro[2] was incapable of pursuing his advantages against Valencia without reinforcements; his headquarters were at Toledo. One way or the other the attempt seemed to promise advantages, if they continued their operations in the south, we should regain our northern barrier, if they obstructed us, it would be by giving up their views on the south & there was a possibility with Lord Wellington's good fortune of taking the place and drawing their attention off also. Lord Wellington sent away the 5th & 6th Divisions to get their clothing & continued hunting till the day of the investment which completely deceived Marmont who thought we were quiet for the winter.
>
> On the 4th Sturgeon[3] made a bridge across the Agueda above Gallegos exactly on the plan of Caesar's over the Rhine.[4] On the same day the heavy artillery reached Almeida & a severe frost set in.
>
> On the 6th the 1st Division & headquarters moved to Gallegos [de Arganan] and adjacents; the Light Division to El Bodon; the 3rd Division at Zamarra etc; the 4th at Saelices el Chico.

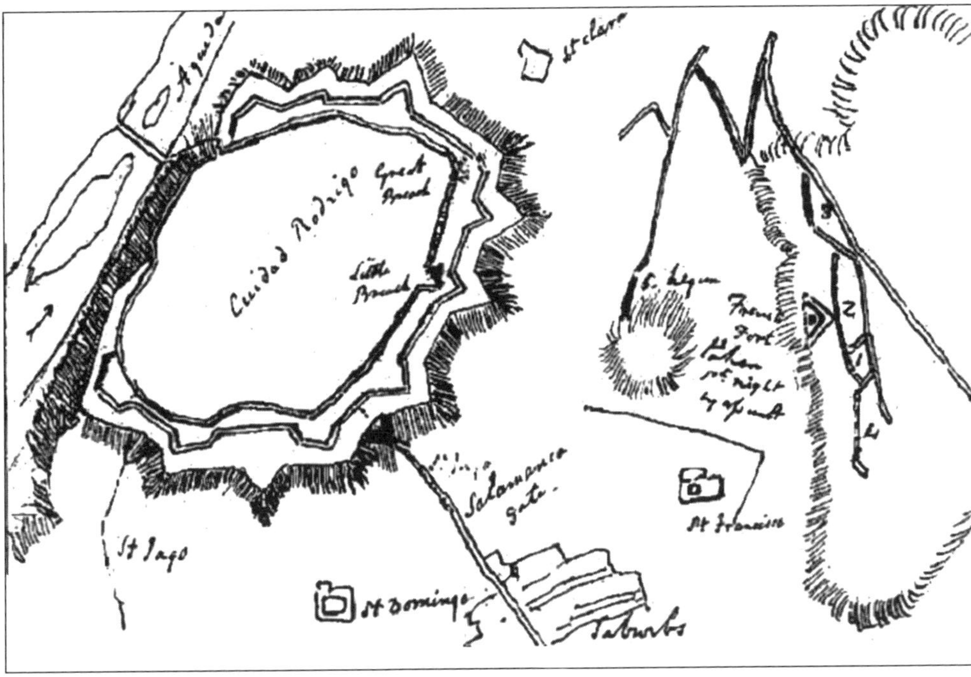

Ciudad Rodrigo.

On the 8th the Light Division invested the town, we heard afterwards that General Brennier[5] thought it was a reconnaissance and had no idea even then of our commencing a siege at such a time of the year.

Ciudad Rodrigo of which is adjoined a rough sketch, is defended by a high, weak rampart revetted with stone, having only in one place opposite the convent of San Francisco, a flank capable of containing a couple of guns. It had besides a fausse bray[6] with salient angles about 12 feet high from the ditch but this was imperfectly covered by the glacis;[7] on the right of the Salamanca gate was a ravelin.[8] Towards the river the slope is very steep, on the side of the Caridad, there is a ravine which covers the approach, but it is highly commanded by the place. The only attackable point therefore was from the Upper [Great] Teson where the French had their second parallel. On it they had now constructed a fort, in the shape of a fleche[9] with a ditch, guard house, palisades, open to the rear for fire from the place, with 3 guns in it. They had two guns in the tower of San Francisco on their right & had occupied Santa Clara which flanked the left, so that it was stronger than when the French attacked it. Had we begun in a regular manner we should have commenced our first parallel where the French did (God knows why there being no fort on the Teson) about 500 yards from it, but that would have cost several days. It was determined therefore to carry the fort by assault which was executed the same evening by Colonel Colborne[10] & with so much skill & gallantry that with a small loss we became masters of the fleche, 3 officers & 47 men surrendering themselves.[11] The party then advanced and remained under the small Teson all night, covering the working party which immediately opened a trench from the fleche to the valley in the rear of the hill where the engineer's park was formed & the first parallel was traced along the edge of the hill. The French in the town were so astonished that they did not open their fire for two hours after we took the fort. In all the enemy had about 50 guns & mortars directed against us & we occupied so small a spot & they got the range so accurately that we lost a great many men by casualties; the first night about 140 including the storm of the fort.[12]

The weather was so cold that it was determined only one division should be on [at] a time for 24 hours, so that each had only one day in four of work & the marches to & from the place. The working parties were from 1,000 to 1,200 men & the covering party was 500, on the 9th the 1st Division came on. The work was carried on with spirit and we began at three batteries and the parallel. The fire of the enemy (especially from San Francisco) was so well directed that our casualties were greater than the preceding day. Poor Ross[13] was killed in the beginning of the night, he had accompanied us from Cadiz & we knew him well & the more each had known, so much did he the more lament his loss on every account.

As the general was passing San Francisco, Hope[14] and myself riding in a line with him, a cannon shot nearly took off our heads, just passing over them.

10th. Relieved by the 4th Division, works continued under the same accurate fire from the enemy.

11th 3rd Division took the duties, ground hard & stony but work continued sharply. French brought a howitzer into the garden of San Francisco, which enfiladed us & occasioned many casualties.

12th Light Division on. We heard of Marmont's being in motion to raise the siege which determined Lord Wellington on breaching from the 1st parallel.

13th 1st Division came on. Battering train arrived in the Park. Casualties fifty, a German officer lost both his legs & likely to do well. He asked immediately if he should have the pension for both! In the evening we surprised & took the Convent of Santa Clara[15] from whence our works had been much incommoded. Began the 2nd parallel.

14th. The enemy kept up a tremendous fire both of cannon & musketry under cover of which some companies came out on their right to call off our attention whilst others penetrated to the second parallel. The 42nd & 24th that were in the trenches showed themselves & they retired. In the mean time General Graham brought forward some men on the flank of San Francisco to drive in their post there which had advanced. During this a cannon shot (a 9pdr) from San Francisco grazed my right leg, passed through my horse & narrowly missed my left knee. This laid me up for 6 weeks & I saw no more of the siege.

The batteries opened 25[16] guns at 5 p.m. of the same day & on the 19th we took it by assault; we lost about 1300 men in the siege[17] and took about 1700. Craufurd[18] was killed and as for myself I never could regret him, being the most tyrannical and uncommandable officer that ever served in any army, but 'De mortuis nil nisi honum' [About the dead, speak nothing except good]. meanwhile I was laid up at Gallegos in a room with three alcoves in it, in the one was I, in another Hope laid up with a fall from his horse, in a third by sufferance rather than see them in the street, a Spanish guerrilla captain & his wife and on a chest of drawers two young sprightly lasses who slept in their clothes, who had come over to get paid for bread. It was always observed that the prettiest were employed to negotiate with the commissaries; these were owed 4,000 dollars. Besides these, outside we had 8 horses and in a nook the mistress of the house who was dying, her husband and a daughter and in the kitchen 4 English servants & the guerrilla's two criados.[19] This is only one instance of how we packed & with all these I used to have my wound dressed & Hope & I used to growl in *concert*. Marmont assembled his army at Salamanca on the 25th and would have relieved the place on the 28th. We had hardly retired the guns to Almeida & withdrawn the bridge, than the most tremendous rain fell which rendered every road impassable and swelled the Agueda to 8 feet above where the top of our bridge would have been. This is one of the instances of the great good fortune which attended the great man at the head of the army.

We got the governor's cook in a droll way, when the assault was given the governor was just going to supper, but run [sic] out to the breach & there being two chimneys, one not lighted, the cook betook him to his natural hiding place; but soon came our officers who took the governor (who had returned to his house) and ate his supper, then the house became filled with soldiers who wanted both fires and on the other being lighted down came Clement. The general heard of it, sent for him, gave him handsome wages & he has had him ever since.

Having ensured that the breaches had been repaired sufficiently to prevent the French seizing it again by a coup de main, for the French had no siege artillery nearby, their siege park having been captured within Ciudad Rodrigo, Wellington turned his army south to face a much bigger challenge, the fortress of Badajoz which guarded the southern route into Spain. James, having recovered sufficiently to ride a horse, joined the long march south.

On the 12th of February orders came to move towards Abrantes. I went with the general's baggage being now able to ride, by Galizes, where no troops were marching. Colborne who was wounded[20] went down with us & G Napier who had lost an arm.[21] If the former ever has an opportunity to show, we shall be astonished at the wonderful talents concealed beneath the shyness of that man.

On the 19th passed the position of [the Serra de] Moita occupied by the French on the 18th of March preceding, right on the Mondego & left on the Alva, on this side it was turned; the whole country has been very picturesque.

20th By Ponte de Mucela, the bridge was repaired both sides excessively strong but the left the strongest. Halted at Foz d'Arouce, it is inconceivable what made the French leave any troops on the left bank of the Coa except to protect their generals sleeping in the village instead of bivouacking. They lost a good many men and an eagle in the river, which was found afterwards.[22] The country quite beautiful.

21st to Espinhal, the country quite beautiful.

23rd reached Tomar, fine town beautifully situated, but the population Jews & Frenchified. The castle & cathedral were built by the Templars in 1168, the former is in ruins & an inscription on the latter says that in 1228 the King of Morocco with 5,000 horse & 100,000 foot destroyed everything outside of it but that the valour of the Grand Master & his garrison obliged him to retreat with loss.[23] The convent was built in 1668 & has the revenue of 30,000 dollars a year. It belongs to the Military Order of Christ and consists only of 28 persons, the head of whom has ex officio the power of Bishop of Tomar. The bridge over the Nabao is very handsome.

We heard of Blake's surrendering his army in Valencia,[24] he has had a good many confided to his care & has lost every one, but none in a manner so apparently treacherous as now. For it is difficult to imagine than simple stupidity and obstinacy could make a general voluntarily shut 18,000 men up in an unfortified city, when he had the whole afternoon of the action he was beaten in, the opportunity of retreat to which Zayas repeatedly pressed him. A curious fact became known by our taking Ciudad Rodrigo, as we found a receipt from the governor to Massena for several eagles he left behind him when *he entered Portugal*. This receipt was returned with a memorandum on Massena taking back the eagles.

On the 27th reached Abrantes. On the 5th of March moved from Abrantes to Elvas where we arrived on the 14th. Great improvements have taken place here but still it is a bad place to defend. Santa Lucia is in want of a ditch & glacis; the whole would require ten thousand men to defend it. Fort La Lippe near Elvas is a model [of] how much art can be united with nature in a small spot uncommanded to make a place impregnable; but I do not think it would hold above 1500 men which is easily masked. An immense sum was spent on it by the general whose name it bears; I never yet saw anything so strong. The battering train is here.

Lord Wellington has been bringing down his army little by little under the idea of getting them clothed at Abrantes and for a long time blinded the enemy.

Having masked his troop movements, Wellington finally launched the siege operations, which were clearly a surprise to the French, giving him the maximum time to seize it before overwhelming numbers of French troops could be collected to force him to retreat. Graham's force was positioned to the east to mask the siege operations.

On the 16th General Hill moved to Merida; the 1st, 6th, 7th Divisions under General Graham crossed the pontoon bridge & moved to the front to Valverde [de Merida] being destined with General Hill as the covering corps of the siege. The 3rd, 4th, 5th & Light Divisions crossed the same day & invested Badajoz.

17th Joined by Le Marchant's Brigade[25] of cavalry & Slade's[26] joined afterwards, rode with General D'Urban[27] over the ground of Albuera; he being Q.M.G. to Beresford of course defends him for his movements on that day and his testimony is a valuable one as he is one of the most sensible men in the army and equally loved & esteemed by all who have the happiness of his acquaintance.

The pros & cons of this action are about as follows. He was obliged to fight, some say he is reproached with having placed the Spaniards in the most exposed spot, but of course the French would have attacked them had they been any where else. Blake was so slow in executing every movement that they were hardly in line in time. Then he ought (they say) to have entrenched himself, or not have fought. Now what struck me on passing the ground was that adopting a hill behind the village as the spot for a reserve with the line appui [in support] on the village & the right entrenched, it would have been much stronger & had the marshal instead of showing his line on the crest of the hill, kept most of it in masses behind it so as to have been able to move to any spot, the French could not have selected the Spaniards; for we lost our men in retaking what they lost, not from want of courage, but of conduct. But in answer to this it is said that the Spaniards were immovable & if put in a mass would never have been deployed.

It is impossible not to admire the able conduct of General Lumley[28] who could keep his cavalry from being defeated, so outnumbered as they were.

The French left 2,200 dead on the hill, Soult said 'Ces bastardes Anglais ne savant pas quand ils sont battus' [These Bastard English don't know when they are beaten]. We moved by Feria on Zafra, [a] fine town capable of holding 10,000 men.

20th through Los Santos [de Maimosa] to Villafranca [de Los Barros].

Intelligence had indicated that up to half of Drouet's[29] corps were at Llerena and according to Oman, a despatch from Drouet to General Reymond had been intercepted on 21 March indicating that four battalions were to arrive at Llerena; therefore Graham anticipated a force in excess of 5,000 men there, which he aimed to surround and capture. During the approach to Llerena a French cavalry patrol ran into Graham and his staff, who were forced to flee and were fired upon by their own jittery troops but luckily no one from the staff was killed.[30] Unfortunately only four battalions were there, amounting to approximately 1,800 men, who were made aware of their danger and escaped into the mountains.

> 25th Moved to Usagre and united the divisions in hopes of surprising a division of 5,000 of the enemy at Llerena. The plan was General Le Marchant's Brigade of cavalry should move round our left of the town and occupy the Guadalcanal road with a troop of horse artillery and a battalion of infantry, whilst General Slade's Brigade of cavalry & Lord Blantyre's[31] Brigade of infantry & horse artillery should turn the right, whilst General Bernewitz's[32] Brigade supported by the Guards were to make their way into the town. The march began in a solid mass and in silence and had arrived within about two miles of Llerena and the Staff with some led horses were about 50 yards from the head of the column, when a few French dragoons galloped over a hill & rode towards us crying out loudly. We turned & rode back to the column; a panic seized Bernewitz's Brigade & the 51st poured a volley at us believing us to be the French cavalry. The Guards were steadied by Campbell crying out 'Remember Talavera'. We soon set things to rights but the surgeon of the 51st was killed & a paymaster & 2 men wounded, the general had a led horse shot. We had been betrayed before and this patrol (which it was said the French general accompanied) was sent out in consequence of information which reached him about midnight of our approach. By daylight we found the enemy all off & their Staff looking at us from the top of the Guadalcanal hill. We have been treated *more* civilly and with more *fine speeches* in Estramadura than anywhere, but without a doubt, the people of all the province are attached to the French, the women particularly so and we had hardly a host who did not send information to them, especially Don Gat de los Bavoirs at Villafranca. The threats of vengeance of the French against the alcaldes & villages were so terrible & unremittingly executed in case of not getting information that no surprise can succeed. They used to ring the bells when we entered by which the enemy always knew in a short time where we were, we stopped this practise. Still at Arroyos Molinos on the other side General Hill found great fidelity.
>
> 25th returned to Usagre.
>
> 27th Valencia de los Torres.
>
> 29th Tried to surprise the enemy with the 6th Division at Usagre but they had information and were off. Here is an inscription to Drusus Caesar,[33] it is a large but wretched town. Llerena is large but melancholy, Zafra is the best town I have been in and Almendralejo the next for society. Soult is collecting & is to move the 31st; it is hoped that he will be too late.

Receiving news of the imminent assault on the breaches of Badajoz, James accompanied Benjamin D'Urban to view the much anticipated event before Marshal Soult arrived with his forces to relieve the fortress. James spent the night very close to Wellington and describes the scene very ably as Wellington heard of the dreadful losses and then suddenly his joy, having heard that victory had been snatched from the jaws of defeat.

> 1st of April, Valencia de las Torres, 3 divisions return to old cantonments round Villafranca. I left the army to see the end of the siege of Badajoz as an amateur, General D'Urban went too. We slept at Talavera [la Real] & next day reached the camp & dined with Lord Wellington who as well as all headquarters were under canvas. The weather was intolerably hot. I went through the trenches, it is astonishing how the troops could have stormed the Picurina [fort] for it is not easy to climb into it now. I believe it was a good deal to my friend Harding[34] who (if he lives, which he tries by all the means he can by getting into fire, not to do) will be an ornament to his country. I found in the fort some pieces of elder with 8 swan shot which the French put in besides the ball. The fire from the castle produces a good many casualties in the trenches, breaches appeared good. Soult entered Llerena the morning of the 4th, he will be at [La] Albuera on the 8th I should think.
>
> On the 5th the breaches were reported practicable but the flank of the bastion of La Trinidad remained. Lord Wellington postponed the assault and began battering it; the wall was old & came down rapidly, so that it was practicable next day. Assault was finally fixed for 10 o'clock in the evening of the 6th.

The plan for the assault on Badajoz was set. The Third Division was to attempt to carry the high castle wall by escalade; The Fourth and Light Divisions were to attempt the breaches; the 5th Division was to make a false attack on Fort Pardaleras but also try an assault on the bastion of San Vincente. The assault on the main breach was repelled with huge losses, not one man getting beyond the chevaux de frise[35] on the crest of the breaches alive. However, against all odds, with most of the defenders sucked into the defence of the breaches, the escalade of the lightly defended castle and that on San Vincente was successful. The castle being secured, the French abandoned their defence and crossed the river to Fort San Christoval, where they were soon forced to surrender. The assault had succeeded, but at horrendous cost, as James records.

> In the morning Lord Wellington with *all* the officers of rank concerned under cover of a stone quarry, made his dispositions (which were very clear and able) and explained everything. When Picton was going away, to whom was entrusted the escalade of the castle, he said laughingly, 'Mind if I don't get into the castle first.'
>
> Lord Wellington derived *a great deal* of information from a French sergeant of miners, who deserted. I never saw a more intelligent fellow, he knew & described all the various mines of the other bastions. The ascent to the castle

is so steep and the wall so high that our best hopes were in the enemy not expecting an attack & being surprised. I remained with Lord Wellington upon a hill where the whole attack was visible; at a little before ten we heard a firing in the direction of General Picton and the garrison beat to arms. At ten the Light & 4th Divisions moved to the assault. They were discovered when still some distance from the breach & such a fire was opened on them as I believe no troops ever were exposed to without turning. When they reached the edge of the ditch, they planted their ladders & descended, then they found water, over which they were obliged to pass on ladders & in which many were drowned; when they got over the troops cheered & run up a ruined ravelin mistaking it for the breach. When they found the breaches they were protected with palisades of sword blades, above 2 thousand men entrenched behind, pouring volleys into the ditch where our divisions were wedged up, incapable of advancing and unwilling to retire. Every species of destruction was showered from the enemy, grape shot from 24pdrs from the flanks of the bastions, barrels of powder, shells tied on cart wheels were rolled down the breaches, showers of hand grenades fell in every direction. The light balls illuminated the scene and a dark red cloud of smoke hung heavily over the scene of slaughter, our men were falling fast. Barnard[36] who commanded the Light Division headed repeated charges with no effect. This scene was the most magnificent I ever witnessed, but the miserable anxiety we all felt for the issue and for our friends rendered those two hours the most painful I ever passed. Report after report came to Lord Wellington that the divisions were annihilating [sic] & could not get in. we had heard the fire & cheering of the 5th Division who were to escalade by the arsenal. Our hopes (such as remained) lay a good deal on them. Lord Wellington who had a flambeau by him never showed in his countenance any alteration from all the reports he received. At last a message came from General Picton to say 'He might be easy as he had carried the castle & had 3,000 men in it.' We gave way to every expression of joy & exultation but not one muscle moved in Lord Wellington's face; he calmly said 'Retire the divisions and let them form ready to attack in the morning.' This however was unnecessary as the garrison finding the 5th Division established & the castle taken, abandoned the breaches & surrendered unarmed in their barracks, Phillipon[37] &c going to San Christoval.

The 5th Division did wonders, but could not be kept together, so that the same spot was taken & retaken many times. They had 30 feet high of wall to escalade, were seen on the glacis and many killed before they could descend the ditch. General Walker[38] did wonders & was desperately wounded. He run [sic] a French artillery man through the body as he was going to fire grape on the scalers.

When I saw afterwards the place where the 3rd Division escaladed my wonder was increased; they were early discovered & the side of the hill was

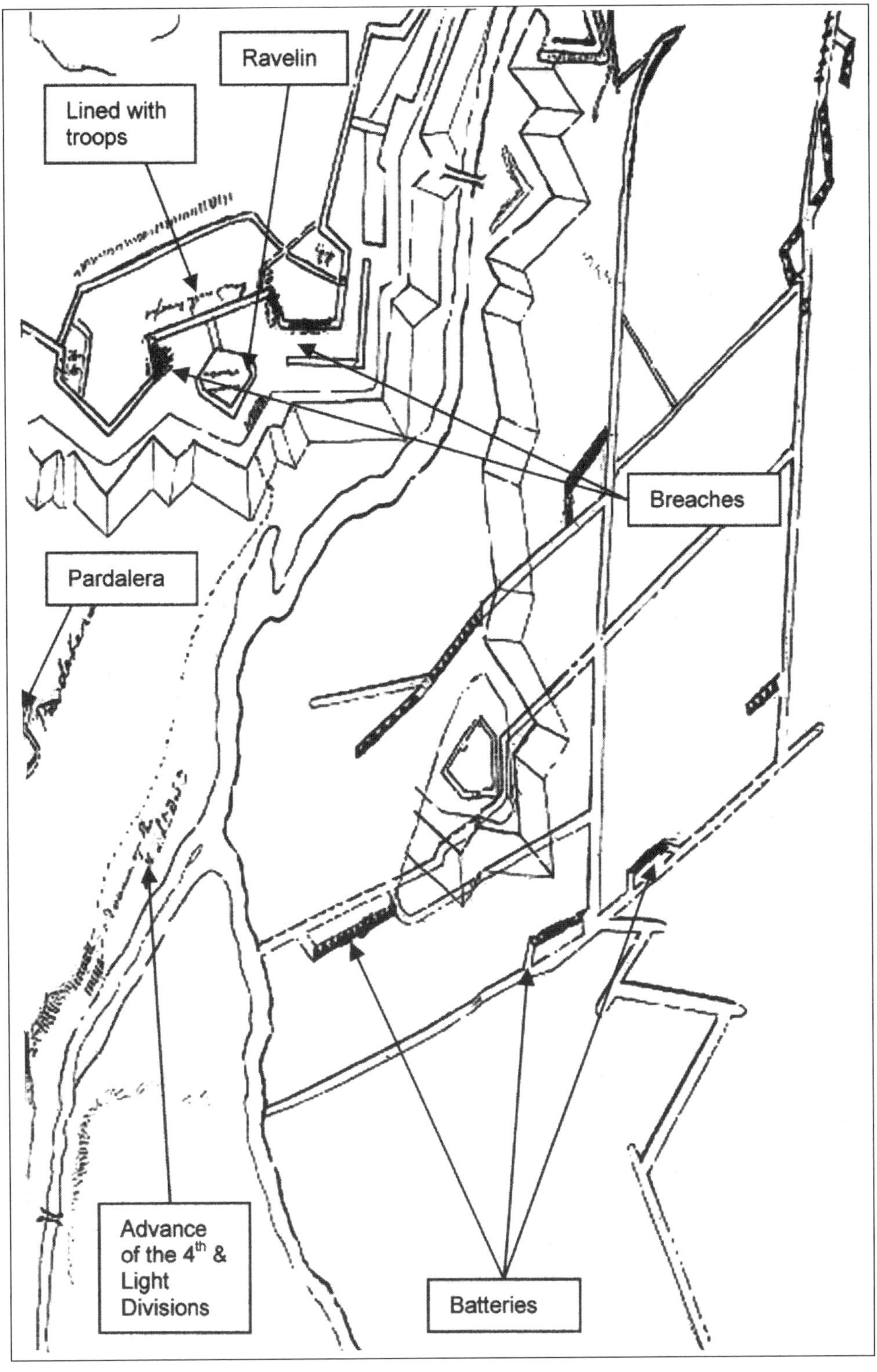
Ravelin
Lined with troops
Breaches
Pardalera
Advance of the 4th & Light Divisions
Batteries

Badajoz.

covered with killed and wounded. The wall had flanks and not above 150 feet long that was practicable. God knows how troops could get in, but they did and put all the enemy to the sword who were in the castle. Soon afterwards a French column came to the gate and an officer spoke in English saying they were part of the 4th Division, who had carried the breach & begged to be admitted. Picton knew the trick, opened the gates & charged out, by which a great number of the enemy were killed. He then shut the gates and waited for the morning. There never was such a scene as the plundering next day by all accounts. I did not see it as I started at 5 o'clock to bear General Graham the news of the surrender. When I returned two days after, I heard more details of what had happened; a Portuguese battalion under Major Hill[39] was ordered to make a false attack against the Pardelera in order to draw off their attention & prevent their firing on our columns. This fort is stronger than the Picurina and cost the French 8 days & 1500 men to reduce it in form. When the regiment approached it, they rushed & leaped [sic] into the ditch, & for some time the men tried to help each other up the scarp but without effect. They had already lost above 100 men when a Frenchman leaning over to fire fell wounded among them. They threatened him with death if he did not show them a way to get into the fort, he purchased his life by showing them a small wicket, through which they forced their way and carried the fort.

Poor Macleod of the 43rd is killed,[40] he is a great loss to the service. Nicholas the engineer who was with us at Cadiz, loved by us all, cannot live. He was shot through the body at the edge of the glacis but determined to show the breach, being appointed to lead the 4th Division, he ordered the men to carry him on till he received several other wounds.

We had 1,035 officers & men killed and 3,789 officers and men wounded, among whom were 306 officers; 72 killed and about 100 missing.[41] The French had about 5,000 men at the beginning and surrendered above 3,500.

The divisions that stormed are in a sad state of disorganisation from the plundering & loss of officers. Lord Wellington fulminates orders & has hardly thanked the troops, so angry is he at the pillage of the poor Spaniards. The French soldiers went leading the English about to where the best wine or the most money was to be found. The sight of the bodies in the ditch is most horrible.

Soult was at Villafranca on the 6th with about 30,000 men, General Hill was at Lobon & General Graham at Albuera. The cessation of the firing made Soult believe we had raised the siege, till some spies confirmed the capture, he retreated the same day. Lord Wellington wished him to come on as there were 18,000 men at Valverde [de Leganes] ready to march & the 3rd Division & 5th were pretty complete.

Chapter 9

The Salamanca Campaign

Whilst the siege of Badajoz was taking place in the south, Marshal Marmont had moved his army westward to blockade Ciudad Rodrigo and pushed cautiously into Portugal. With Badajoz secured and the breaches quickly repaired, Wellington turned his army and marched north again. However, on news of Marmont's sudden retreat, General Graham was given command of the 6th and 7th Divisions and returned south of the Tagus to support General Hill's attempt on the Bridge of Almaraz. Hill successfully surprised and destroyed the bridge, thus forcing any French reinforcements sent to Marmont from the south to make a lengthy diversion.

It is supposed that Lord Wellington would have pursued Soult but all this time Marmont had been in Portugal blockading Ciudad Rodrigo and Almeida & pushing his parties to Castelo Branco & Covilha. Marmont began blockading Rodrigo on the 31st & the place had 40 days provisions. Preparations were making for moving towards the north & the besieging divisions marched on the 11th.

13th came into Elvas, 21st passed Tagus, 25th arrived at Santo Estevao, a league from Sabugal; we found that Marmont had re-crossed the Agueda.

26th moved back to Penamacor & Pedrogao [de Sao Pedro], ordered to the south again, passed through Monsanto which is a very [curious?] fort & village on the apex of a lofty hill, it would be easily repaired. There is a tank for water, 300 men might defend it as long as provisions lasted. It commands an immense view, therefore a telegraph would be most important, couriers might be intercepted from it. I am speaking in the event of a second invasion of Portugal.

30th re-crossed the Tagus, the 6th & 7th Divisions put under the general's command. The 3rd, 4th & 5th sent to Lamego & Sao Joao da Pesqueira to feed from the boats whilst all their means of transport were employed in forming magazines at the latter place.

On the 12th [May] Sir Rowland Hill began his movement from Merida to try to get possession of Almaraz. In order to support the movement the 6th Division was moved to Alegrete & Arronches & General Graham moved to Portalegre.

On the 21st information being received of Drouet's being in motion the general sent me to communicate with General Hill. The road into Spain lays by Porto da Espada, a beautiful village shrouded in trees, about 6 miles from Marvao. About a league beyond this is the frontier which is so singular as to merit description. A high sierra behind which lays Porto da Espada is a barrier and parallel to this runs a ridge or hog's back falling in a steep slope on each side and on the summit rises perpendicularly a natural wall, varying in shape & height, in some places being level with the hill & in others rising to 150 feet. I saw this continue for above 12 miles, in one place there is a gap through which by the side of a small stream which is the boundary line, runs the road. At San Vincente [de Alcantara], 6 leagues I halted to bat and get an account of the Spanish force there, which is worth mentioning, of which I wrote a full account to Arguelles, as it is a proof of the scandalous malversation[1] in the Spanish Army.

There are 1200 rations distributed every day from the town which is only the headquarters of the civil departments, the Marquis de Monsalud's[2] headquarters being at Valencia de Alcantara. That there are effective in the town 80 rank & file; the rest are made of thus:

Un Intendente de excercito
[Army Intendant] }
Un Intendente de Provincia } All drawing
[Provincial Intendant] } as many
Un Contador [Auditor] } rations as
Un Tesorero [Treasurer] } they want.
Un Contador de Maestrazgos }
[Auditor of Military Orders]

A retired general who draws 16 rations, the rest were officers, their servants & a band of forty.

I could not reach Caceres, I already had rode 60 miles on the same horse, the night was dark & I lost the road & after wandering some time got into a wretched cottage where I got a couple of eggs but no bread. I cleaned my horse, gave him some green barley & waited for morning. I got to Caceres early & forwarded a letter on containing the news by a dragoon to Trujillo. Caceres is one of the finest towns in Estramadura but the inhabitants between the French and Ballasteros are quite starving, bread is at 2s 6d a lb; it has been 4 shillings. Many respectable families live on the pastage of the fields. Next day rode to Albuquerque (having my answer from General Hill that all was successfully concluded) 11 leagues, towards night my horse being tired I laid my sword & sabretasche across the horse & walked before him. An eagle passed close over our heads, frightened the horse, which went off kicking at a gallop & left me in the middle of the plains of Estramadura. I ran as long as I could, picking up sword, cloak etc as they successively came off. I met a peasant whom I promised a doubloon (£4) to if he could catch him, as he had gone off towards Valverde [de Merida]; after some time he came back with him. I was most uncivilly treated at Albuquerque for the first time in Spain, because the landlord found me cleaning my horse.

Next day rode by Badajoz believing the general was there, to Montijo 12 leagues. This was immense work for one horse to do, having nothing but green meat the whole time.

With the bridge of Almaraz destroyed, Graham's force could now safely march northward to support Wellington's movements.

26th The general returned from Merida & we began moving to the north. On the 30th we crossed the Tagus & [reached] Castelo Branco next day. We let the divisions go up the old road & we explored a new one by Alpedrinha where the famous wine[3] is made and which ought to be as celebrated for the beauty of its scenery. Its fine woods and magnificent view of the valley of the Zezere and the snow clad Estrella.

4th We went to Fundao, a good town but much pillaged and the 5th to Belmonte, the situation of which is beautiful. I got some trout fishing in the Zezere up by Valhelhas where there is a fine bridge of 4 arches.

It is a singular thing considering the present idleness of the Portuguese that wherever any communication exists and where the rivers permit it, there are numerous and well built bridges.

Crossed the sierra to Bendada a very picturesque but most wretched village. 7th crossed the great sierra by Pena Lobo whence there is a magnificent view over the valley of the Zezere on the one side and that of the Coa on the other. We crossed at Vila do Touro the high [road] from Guarda to Sabugal and crossed the Coa at Rapoula do Coa, sleeping at Ruvina in our old country again. This mountain road is execrable.

11th reached El Bodon. We now prepared to advance, the army was re-divided, the right composed of the 1st, 6th, and 7th Divisions under General Graham with the 14th Light Dragoons. The centre, under Lord Wellington of the 4th, 5th & Light Divisions with a good deal of cavalry, and the left under General Picton composed of the 3rd Division, Pack's & Bradford's Brigades & a good deal of cavalry.

13th Army advanced, bivouacked at Tenebron 4 leagues.

14th Army bivouacked on the banks of the Huebra (3 [leagues]), our headquarters at Tamames.

15th Army on the Rio de la Maya, our headquarters at Villalba de los Llanos (2½ [leagues]).

16th Army on the Zurguen, our headquarters at Palacio Villalones. Skirmished all the morning with some French cavalry.

17th During the night the French evacuated Salamanca & retreated. We entered the town the same day and it is impossible to give an idea of the enthusiastic joy with which we were received by the excellent loyal & good people of Salamanca, who have never under all their hardships & sufferings, been otherwise than true to us & so I may say of the whole province. I like these people the best of any peasantry I ever saw. The French left 800 men in three forts made out of convents, which were in the town but the French pulled down a third of it & many fine colleges to make a glacis. Marmont was going to destroy for the same purpose the superb cathedral which is one of the finest specimens of Moresco Gothic in the world. The whole army bivouacked on the right of the Tormes. The forts command the bridge, so we were obliged to ford the river which was deep.

The engineers began a battery which they said would reduce the forts in 24 hours.

The engineers were being very hopeful. The principal fort of San Vincente was situated on a perpendicular cliff overlooking the River Tormes, the others were smaller but on higher ground, known as San Cayetano and La Merced. Siege operations were soon suspended with the French army drawing close and a period of manœuvre began, not unlike two heavyweight wrestlers sizing each other up, both afraid of making a move that would give his opponent the advantage. The two armies marched and countermarched in parallel for many miles, often close enough to be in full view of each other, as each sought an advantage.

19th The battery opened with 3–18 pdrs & 4–24 pdr howitzers. The fire was directed against the gable end of San Vincente on the first floor of which were mounted several guns. They were soon brought down with the gable end, but the engineers found their ammunition was expended & the fort was as strong as ever.

20th A report arrived that the French army was advancing, our army was moved forward to a position which covered Salamanca, the right towards the Tormes to the front of the village of Villares [de la Reina], Moriscos was at the foot of the right of the hill & Castellanos [de Moriscos] were in front and close at the bottom of the hill. About 5 o'clock the enemy's army moved over the plain and halted about ¾ [of] a cannon shot from our position, occupying the two villages [of Morisco]. Lord Wellington said every now & then 'Damned tempting. I have a great mind to attack um.' A brisk cannonade began on both sides which ceased at sunset. The French seemed to have about 20,000 men & Lord Wellington had above 30,000 on the hill.

The two armies remained tranquil all night, except some skirmishing in the village of Morisco of which the French finally kept possession.

21st The army was under arms an hour before daylight expecting to be attacked, but no such thing occurred. Marmont rode along the front in the day & looked at us & so did Lord Wellington at them, but no firing on either side. We threw up flesches along the position for our artillery, our 18 pdrs &

howitzers were moved into battery.[4] Our position is very strong, but has the disadvantage of being joined on the right by a narrow plateau to a hill too far to be maintained by us in a general action, too near to permit them to occupy it & from which in an action their artillery would have terrible effect. Our position also was intersected on the right with several ravines; but in the event of an enemy gaining the plateau it was possible to throw the right back en potence towards Salamanca on a ridge of hill, but by so doing we should give up the communication with our ford at Santa Marta [de Tormes], in short our part of the position was the most attackable.

The French were considerably reinforced during the night.

23rd The French occupied the distant hill after some skirmishing with several companies of voltigeurs and 2 squadrons of cavalry. Lord Wellington ordered General Graham to dislodge them which he did in person, with General Bernewitz's Brigade in the most gallant manner. The fire was warm & the horse of Hope was killed. I suspect Lord Wellington would have attacked next day from having taken and occupied this hill, but next day we rubbed & rubbed our eyes to see the enemy, but they were all gone; & though our advanced sentries were close together, the armies so singularly near and many officers listening in a very quiet night, they moved off bag, baggage and artillery without being heard. The French did not go far but took up a strong position with their right on Gomecello and their left on Huerta, where there is a good ford over the Tormes. This proved they did not mean to attack our position & put it out of our way to attack them. Much conversation has taken place in the army about this singular incident of two armies being so close & separating without an action & many regrets have been expressed that Lord Wellington did not attack them on the night of the 20th or morning of the 21st when their masses were huddled together and when our columns of attack could have been all concealed behind the hill. The partisans of this side say that Marmont had only 20,000 men (as it was afterwards proved) and that with the plain in his rear and our power of manoeuvring round him, he must have been quite annihilated.[5] I have no doubt all this would have happened had Lord Wellington attacked, but it is judging in an ex post facto manner, for it is very difficult to judge of the number of troops in masses and it was reasonable to believe that Marmont would not expose his army so near except he felt himself strong, for what could bring him to so forward a position, but to attack us. Everything bore the appearance of it and had they attacked us, which Lord Wellington had every reason to believe was their intention, their destruction would have been affected with much less loss. Now their force is ascertained it remains the most unaccountable event that any man should have been mad enough to expose his army as Marmont did and he has good reason to be thankful for his luck. The possibility of defeat should be always taken into consideration and had Lord Wellington been defeated with one bad deep ford in his rear & the enemy commanding the bridge, it would not have been pleasant; still one must regret not having fought. This reminds me of what Lord Wellington said in the lines one day. Looking from Sobral fort at the French encampments, he said 'I could lick those fellows any day but it would cost me 10,000 men and as this is the last army England has, we must take care of it.'

General Bock[6] was sent with his brigade of cavalry across the Tormes to watch the ford of Huerta. During this night the attack was made on Fort Cayatano which failed; poor General Bowes was killed.

25th Before daylight we heard skirmishing across the river and when it became clear we found a large body of the enemy had crossed the river consisting as we afterwards found out, of 3 divisions of infantry & 3 regiments of cavalry. They began cannonading General Bock who had no artillery but who retreated in the most cool and admirable manner.

General Graham was ordered to cross the ford with the 1st & 7th Divisions. The 5th were in reserve at the ford & the left of the line brought to the right ready to act on either side. The enemy occupied Calvarrasa de Abajo but came no further. In the evening they re-crossed the Tormes & so did we. Lord Wellington was convinced they meant to fight and much conversation took place as to the best position. It was determined to throw back our left, fortify a house in the front & put our heavy guns on an island in the Tormes to flank our left.

26th towards the evening we began to fire hot shot against San Vincente at the instigation of Sturgeon,[7] who is always first in all that is able and enterprising. His rope bridge of 100 feet over the broken arch of Alcantara is a monument of talent. The fire continued against the reverse of SanCayetano; its breach was reported practicable on the 27th. The fire of hot shot was renewed with admirable effect and the interior of the building was in flames. The charade was beat; Colonel Waters[8] went to meet their flag of truce and some minutes were allowed for the garrison to decide. The time being expired the firing was renewed & the assault of San Cayetano ordered. That surrendered on our people appearing at the breach; part of the Portuguese began to escalade the San Vincente without resistance when the commandant capitulated on promise of keeping their baggage & being allowed the honours of war. A great scene of confusion now occurred. The Portuguese thought they had taken it by storm; the English pretended to think so, to share in the plunder, order was at length restored but the plundered baggage could not be. In order to protect the French from the indignation of the populace, they were marched out with a guard, which did not answer their ideas of the honours of war. They had no cause to surrender except the account was true that their magazine was in danger. I certainly never saw people in a greater haste to get out. I was in the house of Dona Lorenza de Calvo, a delightful Salamanquina, when the fire began; one of the officers had been often at her house & she rather spoke in his favour, but she cried out 'Vamos a la cathedral para quemar a los Gabachos'[9] [Let's go to the cathedral to burn the French]. The town gave us a splendid ball in which La Calvo shone the brightest. We have had now greater proofs of the esteem of these good people than shouts & rejoicing.

James was certainly struck by the unquestioning support of the people of Salamanca, despite the French army being only a few miles away.

When Marmont was in our front, of course the troops were kept together, there was no wood or water on the hill and every inhabitant of Salamanca with every horse, mule & ass in the town turned out to bring us all we wanted, the higher classes bringing cakes, sweet things & liquers. Marmont retreated on the morning of the 28th, he meant to have fought on the 29th. It was mentioned by Lord Wellington that as an action might be fought an hospital would be wanted. Every class of inhabitant brought their beds & in 24 hours an hospital for 3,000 men was complete in everything. Besides which they clothed gratis some battalions of Don Carlos de Espagna.

29th The army moved and bivouacked on the Orbada, headquarters at [La] Orbada.

30th Right column to Canizal; headquarters & centre Fuentelapena. Heard that Marmont was at Alaejos with 17,000 men; arrangements were made for the army to move at night & to debouch at the same moment in the morning in front of that town. We moved accordingly but the enemy was off, 1st Division with Foy on Toro & the rest on Tordesillas, headquarters at Alaejos.

2nd July General Graham thought that if we moved on Toro we might cross the river and hold both that & Zamora, with the additional advantage of being able to give a hand to Castanos & to D'Urban, who with 800 Portuguese cavalry had advanced on the north bank of the Duero; but Lord Wellington thought that this movement was a feint & therefore made a flank movement on Medina del Campo on the high road from Madrid to Valladolid. Medina del Campo was once a very celebrated town for commerce, wealth and industry, now only for its antiquity though it has some fine houses.

On reconnoitring Tordesillas we had some skirmishing; we found the enemy had not destroyed the bridge but had occupied a fine position in & around the town. Lord Wellington said 'I wish now I had moved on Toro, for I have just passed on their whole army; but the army can't be everywhere & we shall make a better hit next time.'

3rd Lord Wellington ordered the 3rd Division to cross the ford of Pollos, 2 leagues down the river and made a feint of moving columns of attack in hopes that we might make them blow up the bridge. They detached some troops towards Pollos, but saw that our other movements were not in earnest I suppose, for they remained quite quiet.

General Graham was suffering with his sight and James was required to take his request for sick leave to Wellington, who was extremely complimentary of his general. Permission being granted James arranged to escort Graham home, with the promise from Lord Wellington that if he returned he would look after him.

> General Graham had been suffering for many months with his eyes & today has taken the decisive step of going home, for they are so bad as to threaten absolute blindness & his anxiety has shaken his health greatly. I was the bearer of the letter and waited for his answer;
>
> Lord Wellington does not in common express himself warmly but he did in this instance and he said more than I think he ever did before of regret and approbation. I said that if his lordship did not imagine anything would happen, I should like as a mark of respect to attend my general home. He said 'No, I think you have seen the end of it; if he destroys the bridges & throws back his right on the Pisuerga he is safe unless I can cross at Tudela de Duero. I shan't fight him without an advantage nor he me I believe, therefore go and if you choose to come out again I will take care of you. Which department would you like to be in? or what would like to be?' I expressed my gratitude & said the Quarter Master General's Department.
>
> The 4th was spent in preparations for leaving the army.
>
> 5th, not without showing great feeling and amid the universal regrets of every class of the army who flocked to take leave of him, General Graham took a melancholy leave of his old friends.
>
> On the 6th we reached Salamanca; a dreadful accident had just happened. A powder magazine blew up which had destroyed a whole street, nearly a hundred persons were buried in the ruins.[10] We were in the Marquis de Serralva's where Sir John Moore was lodged, a very pleasing person.
>
> 10th reached Barca D'Alva on the Duero where we [went] to get a boat. I sent all my baggage, horses, mules &c to Lisbon as I should want them on my return.
>
> 11th embarked at Sao Sibrao[11] one league below the Barca and on the 12th reached Sao Joao da Pesqueira, but bivouacked near the river, which until three months back was considered the highest point to which boats could ascend, but perseverance accomplished getting them 8 leagues out of the mountainous country, an event of immense importance to the campaign. I cannot describe the magnificence of the trajet down the river, especially immediately above Pesqueira, the deep black stream winding its way through rents or crevices of the mountains which rise perpendicular in craggy masses from its bed, sometimes hardly moving, unstirred by any breeze, for none can reach such gulfs and reflecting the huge peaks which overhang it; and then at once hurrying on, foaming and roaring over all the rocks which impede its progress, whilst thousands of swallows, doves and hawks issue from the caves on the

sides of the rock & screaming, hover between the intruders and the summit. Much labour and money have been with skill expended in making a track way which for some distance is scooped out of the rock. The engineers left a Portuguese flag and an inscription in enormous characters carved on the rock in commemoration of the event. The flag staff only remains & nobody will ever get to it again to replace a flag.

13th reached [Peso de] Regua, 6 leagues from Pesqueira; the falls are still rapid but not so dangerous.

14th got 8 leagues above ½ way to Oporto & bivouacked among some myrtle bushes. The falls below are, when the river is high, the most dangerous; frequently it is impossible to attempt though the people steer to an inch. At all these falls going up, the boats are unloaded & forced up by force of horses. Three years ago a boat was lost with 40 women on it & I recollect in the campaign of Corunna another was lost in the same place.

As we approach Oporto the river widens & finally becomes perfectly beautiful. The richness of every glen, every mountain, crowned with vines, the innumerable villas and quintas scattered on every hill, the dark blue river and the fine sky rendered the journey delightful. We arrived at Oporto and went to the Moraes, the finest house in Oporto[12] though the three brothers who are gold lace makers and Jews live in the entresol.[13] They feed us magnificently and had 8 or 10 places vacant at table for any friends the general might choose to ask. They would never sit down without being requested by the general; this ceremony was very troublesome. One day a note came with several cases of wine saying that the wine company requested his Excellency's permission to give '*that wine to his servants.*' This is the form of making presents and then we had a deputation from them who are the sovereigns of Oporto. General Trant[14] gave us a formal dinner and ball. The Oporto women are very pretty, agreeable and well educated, speak French and are much superior to the Lisbon ladies.

18th embarked in the *Dotterel*,[15] Captain Daniel, for England.

25th made the Lizard and 26th landed at Portsmouth.

Chapter 10

Burgos

Having returned to England with his general, James was horrified to hear that, while he was away from the army, Wellington had fought and won a decisive victory at Salamanca on 22 July, opening the road to Madrid. He arranged to return immediately with Sir Edward Paget, who was going out to replace General Graham as second-in-command and arrived in Spain in early September.

I had not been long in England when an account arrived of the Battle of Salamanca (22 July 1812). It is needless to describe the vexation I felt at having through my own fault been absent; I determined on returning immediately. Sir Edward Paget[1] who was appointed 2nd in command in the room of Sir Thomas Graham offered to take me out with him and we sailed from Portsmouth on the 25th of August in the *Rota* frigate, Captain Somerville.[2]

Landed at Lisbon on the 7th of September, heard the siege of Burgos was continuing and that Soult had evacuated the Andalucias. As General Paget had to fit out, we could not leave Lisbon before the 15th during which I became acquainted with a charming woman, the Countess D'Alverca.

Reached Abrantes on the 18th; Old Lobo,[3] the governor was in high spirits. He declared that Lord Wellington ought to be deprived of his sword for three days, for risking his person so much at Salamanca, as the fate of the peninsula hung on his life.

2nd of October, reached Salamanca. Halted a day and went over the field of battle. I cannot but think that Marmont's movements were very able but with one fault, that he seemed *more intent on reaping the fruits of victory, than obtaining it.* Lord Wellington never shone brighter, or his star ever more favoured him, for he was retreating and would have gone quietly back into Portugal had Marmont kept at arms length. When he saw the French manoeuvring round his right, he said 'This fellow obliges me to lick him'. It was well said of FP[4] of Marmont 'that he manoeuvred till he outmanoeuvred himself.' I am not astonished at the Portuguese being repulsed in the attack of the Arapiles, I do not think British soldiers would have carried it. It is an astonishing thing how Lord Wellington could keep up the pursuit through such a thick wood all night. When the French were defeated, the 1st & Light Divisions which had not been engaged were on their flank. Lord Wellington sent to General Campbell[5] to support the attack, which he did with the light infantry companies. Had a man like General Graham been there who would not have been cowed by the fear of *responsibility* & who possessed a coup d'oeil, by moving both divisions, few of the enemy would have escaped & the loss of the 5th Division had been saved.

4th reached Fuentelapena; the oaths of the constitution were administering and there was a grand 'funcion' [function] of a bull fight and a ball in the evening, which last ended most abruptly. The Alcalde who seemed to superintend our amusements with as rigorous an eye as a Juiz de Foro[6] would a Portuguese village, whilst we were dancing away (but by the way, always with partners whom he chose for one, according to rank and proper old & ugly ones I got). He stopped the ball and said 'Algunos que quieren bailar con honra, que vienen conmigo a mi casa. Vamonos!' [let any who choose to dance with honour, come away to my house. Lets go!] We were astounded at this and asked the cause of the ball being broke up with such admired [sic] disorder. He said that a person was there who should not be & added 'Mi casa no es de los Guzmanes, pero es una casa de honor' [My house is an honourable one though not of the Guzmanes[7]] and off he stomped with about ½ a dozen of the oldest women and the music. They could not dance without men, nor we without music, so after having abused him to our heart's content and had some conversation, we dispersed.

5th Nava del Rey.

6th Crossed the Duero at Tordesillas, we are now entering a new country. General Paget was lodged in the convent where Bonaparte was in 1809,[8] the bridge here is very singular, resembling ½ of one, having a regular slope from the right bank to the left. The ground round it is excessively strong & the town defends the bridge. The same observation applies to Simancas, where we crossed the Pisuerga.

7th reached Valladolid which is superior to Salamanca in the breadth of the streets, the number of arcades against the sun and rain & in the number of good houses but inferior in beauty & public buildings and more than all in the people and in loyalty. Here they are very French and a great number of people, especially women, have accompanied them. They were forming their quotas for enlistment but never did anything. No joy was shown, I hear, when we entered & I saw no civility; we got some good claret, the only good thing I found in the town.

8th recrossed the Pisuerga at Cabezon [de Pisuerga] & reached Duenas.

9th reached Torquemada, instead of going the straight road by Magaz [de Pisuerga], by which we sent the baggage, we went round by Palencia which is a very pretty city both in buildings and situation. It is famous for a manufacture of blankets, it has two stone bridges over the Carrion. On the road from Palencia to Torquemada, the road passes some very extraordinary caverns; they are half way up the side of a nearly perpendicular hill, consisting of cells and communications. By the rains, the earth has been washed from them so as to lay them open. They were the living places of the Christians and if in those days the country was woody, each of them probably had an aperture for light and air. There are several others about the country, but none so remarkable. The people of the country only say 'son de los tiempos de los moros' [They are of the time of the Moors]. Torquemada was a good town but was burnt (to render the name appropriate I suppose) and plundered by the French in 1808, because they were fired on by some peasantry. We went on to Cordovilla [la Real] for the night, which is on the other side of the Pisuerga, which here unites with the Arlanzon, a little higher up the latter the Arlanza runs in.

10th Pampliega which is a nice town on the left bank; this main road is magnificent, but is not laid down in Lopez,[9] whose maps by the way now become so bad as to be absolutely useless, or worse, for they lead one into a thousand scrapes.

On arrival at headquarters, General Paget, accompanied by James, met with Lord Wellington who was overseeing the siege of Burgos. It was not going well because of a severe shortage of siege equipment and a very staunch resistance from the French garrison. Substantial losses and heavy rains had sapped the besieging force of all hope of success. James arrived without an official position and, although he does not mention it, he was appointed a Deputy Assistant Quarter Master General to the 1st Division on this very day and attached to Sir Edward Paget. Wellington was being severely criticized at home for exposing himself to danger too much; James was soon to discover how accurate this criticism was.

11th arrived at headquarters at Villatoro and found Burgos not surrendered. We were quartered at Quintanaduenas. The rains have been so great that off the chaussee every thing is nearly impassable.

Sir Edward Paget who has shown me the greatest marks of esteem and proofs of kindness, asked me whether I should like best to be appointed to the 1st Division or personally to him, had no hesitation in choosing the latter.

When Sir Edward Paget saw Lord Wellington next day, on being asked what they said in England, he replied 'Your lordship has no idea how you are abused for exposing yourself so much.' Lord Wellington said 'I assure you, it is not the case; but there are situations you know, and Salamanca is one where a commander in chief must show himself and act in person.'

Lord Wellington then asked Sir Edward if he would accompany him to see the works, I went too and without any reason we got as well peppered with shot & shell for two hours as anybody could wish. On returning Sir Edward smiled & said 'I thank your lordship for the proof of what you told me before we went out.'

The arrangement of the army is as follows: the 1st Division has the principal part of the siege and is halted or rather *bogged* between the castle & Villatoro. The 6th Division which has charge of the siege on the other side is in quarters at Hospital del Rey. The 5th Division is hutted below the covering position beyond Hurones. The 7th Division on the right of the Calzada near Rubena.

A great person who *ought* to have known the position, took Sir Edward Paget & me to show it & could not find it.[10] We did afterwards and one could as easily miss Wrotham Hill.[11] The Spaniards are quartered at Vivar del Cid where 'El Campador' is said to have been born. At Atapuerca,[12] on this position was fought a famous battle between the Kings of Leon & Castille.

James visited the siege trenches and soon concluded that they were doomed to failure and was not surprised when the final assault failed. He was not afraid to apportion the reasons for failure and criticize those involved.

I visited the trenches, they are the very devil, for if one is not drowned or choked in mud in the first bayau, one is nearly sure of being shot in the first line if above 5 feet high. I never saw anything like it, if you held up a cap you had two or three balls through it at once. At the same time we hardly heard any firing from the French but a pop pop every now & then whilst we were always keeping up a noisy useless fire. Our three poor 18 pounders which were used against the forts at Salamanca & which have been christened *Nelson, Thunder & Lightning,* are all useless but one and when they said *our batteries* were to open, *30 guns* of the enemy opened to *three* and smashed guns and artillery men together. Still, everybody here *at headquarters* says we are to take it by mining, but among the troops there is much dejection & I know Sir Edward never has been able to find out *how* we are to take it. British courage has done much, the great horn work of St Michael should have stood a ten day's attack, but we took it under poor Cocks[13] (who was killed in a sortie & who is a severe loss) by assault. With a battering train we could blow the castle to pieces as their guns on the keep cannot be fired often for fear of shaking it down. The other lines could easily have been breached and what the troops did perform is the best criterior to judge of what they would have done had success been possible, but the misery of the hut encampment, the dreadful deluges of rain, the trenches up to the middle and the want of success, & great loss of the attacks had sadly rebuté [cast down] the troops. There is a want of musket ammunition but there is a convoy expected from Santander. I had never time or opportunity to copy a good plan. I scratched off the above in Fitzroy Somerset's room one day. We had taken & always occupied the *3rd line* where we had so many casualties. It shows what a strong place it is, for an irregular work.

The second line was breached at the angle of the wall where the 3rd line joined and a mine was working on the side next l'Hospital del Rey, we had attempted to storm this line once and had failed. The garrison suffers a great deal from want of wood, a part of them bivouacked in the ditch close to the breach. Nothing occurred but the usual popping till the 16th when our musket ammunition arrived. During the interval I went several times into Burgos, the cathedral of which is well worth seeing, from its antiquity, its solemn appearance and the tombs contained in it. The town is a fine one, but the people are not what they should be.

On the 17th the mine was reported to be ready & the assault was fixed for the same day at 4 p.m. the object which Lord Wellington by his disposition of attack has in view is to establish himself in the 2nd line with the least possible loss. The orders in consequence were that at the same time that, part of the 6th Division were to establish themselves in the chapel under which the mine was formed. The First Division were to assault in three points; the left composed of a detachment of the German Legion under Major Wurmb,[14] were to attack the breach, the centre under Walpole & Crofton[15] were to escalade the line from the shot piles & the right under Percival[16] were to force if possible a stockade & turn the flank of the line, these attacks when completed were to communicate.

The forlorn hope of the centre was of thirty men who were to run in & cover themselves with the shot piles & then on proceeding 50 more in support were to get the same cover and on their proceeding the covering parties of the trenches were to advance; the same nearly in the other attacks. Lord Wellington wished to oppose as few men as possible at once.

On the appointed signal, the whole rushed on & the left & centre soon gained the points [to which] they were ordered. Percival never could get through the stockade & lost a great many men so, but the former when in the line could obtain no cover and were exposed to destructive enfilades from every point, besides which the enemy could bring on any given point a much larger body of men than we had (having only 1300 employed all together) and they did so, for they forced the Germans (poor Wurmb being killed) to abandon the breach & then beat back the Guards. I never saw greater gallantry than that displayed by Burgess,[17] who stood on the parapet waving his hat & cheering his men on till he was killed; one of the Guards was killed in an embrasure of the 1st line. The mine succeeded in part and some of the Portuguese entered the chapel when the French sprung a counter mine which shook it down and buried its occupiers. Thus failed the 2nd assault of the 2nd line & I did not hear after this many people talk of taking Burgos.

19th heard of the French army under Souham[18] advancing from Briviesca. The 6th Division moved during the night to the front & occupied Rubena and the Spaniards were brought forward; two divisions on the right of the latter on a very strong ridge and the others on the left of the ground occupied next day by the 1st Division on the right of the 5th Division. In the evening the enemy drove in our advanced posts from Monasterio [de Rodilla].

On the 20th the 1st Division moved from their ground to the position. The guard of the trenches was taken by Pack and the Portuguese. The 1st Division was bivouacked in a fine wood on the dry slope of the hill above Hurones & was quite in spirits, getting out of the mud of the siege. In the afternoon the French made their appearance on the road to Monasterio and at 3 o'clock 2

Burgos.

divisions of infantry & some cavalry advanced rapidly, driving in our pickets and soon began a sharp firing at the Spaniards in the valley, the whole line of whom began firing volleys at ½ a mile from the top of their hill. In the skirmish at the bottom of the hill, the Spaniards behaved well against some conscripts and took a few prisoners. By the movement of the enemy they presented their flank to us & Lord Wellington galloped up to General Paget saying 'By God, I never saw so impudent [a] thing in my life, do move down and attack them.'

The 1st Division immediately descended the hill in three lines, supported in echelon by the 5th Division & artillery on the left & some cavalry on our right flank. Though the ground was not favourable, it was a beautiful advance & our people seemed to have recovered their spirits. The enemy would not stand, Gardiner[19] pounded them with his guns but the dark prevented pursuit. This trifling event proved next day to be of the most vital importance. The army expected a battle; it was the *21st* the anniversary of Trafalgar.

When news came that Major General Rowland Hill's force at Madrid had been forced to retreat by a superior force led by Marshal Soult,[20] Wellington had to begin a retreat with his wing of the army. Part of the army passed through Burgos at night under the noses of the French garrison without being discovered and a long arduous retreat began.

At two o'clock Lord Wellington heard of General Hill being obliged to retreat before Soult and orders were sent to raise the siege and we were to begin our retreat at sunset, which would have been a most difficult operation, if not impracticable, had the enemy been allowed to occupy in force the wood in our front. Their whole army appeared at sunset but did not advance far; they would have attacked us next day. Including cavalry, Souham[21] had nearly 40,000 men of which the former amounted to 4,000,[22] we had 10,000 effective British & German, about 7,000 Portuguese,[23] about 2,000 cavalry including the Spanish and the Spaniards who were nominally 12,000 but who could not be depended on.

Our orders were to retreat by the chaussee & cross the bridges, the 6th Division was to follow us. As we [were] moving down, it being a fine moonlight night, I mentioned to Sir Edward Paget that I had been very near shot upon the bridges which were closely commanded & enfiladed by the castle and that in such a clear night, I thought we should lose half the column. Lord Wellington was at Villafria [de Burgos] & we stopped going through. Sir Edward said he just came to mention the circumstance; Lord Wellington said 'I don't think they will see you', so off we went. He made the men trail their arms & stopped all the horses till the columns were over; the sketch will show the lines of retreat. They then passed, strange to say, within 250 yards of the fort without being perceived. A party of Spanish cavalry followed us, who went over in a gallop & the French opened a heavy fire on the bridge & Lord Wellington hearing it countermanded the 6th Division & sent them close by Villatoro. We left our 3 guns & some ammunition but brought away our sick & wounded. We assembled in the morning at Buniel & rested till midday when we resumed our march unmolested to Celada del Camino; on the other side of it there is a small rivulet with a bridge and another higher up. The castle at daylight, a feu de joie for their delivery, certainly much owing to their constancy & bravery, but more a great deal to our absolute want of means. We have lost before this cursed place no less than 92 officers and nearly 2,000 men.[24]

23rd the army moved before daylight, the 1st Division in the rear & Halkett's Light German battalions[25] the rear guard. Our Quarter Master

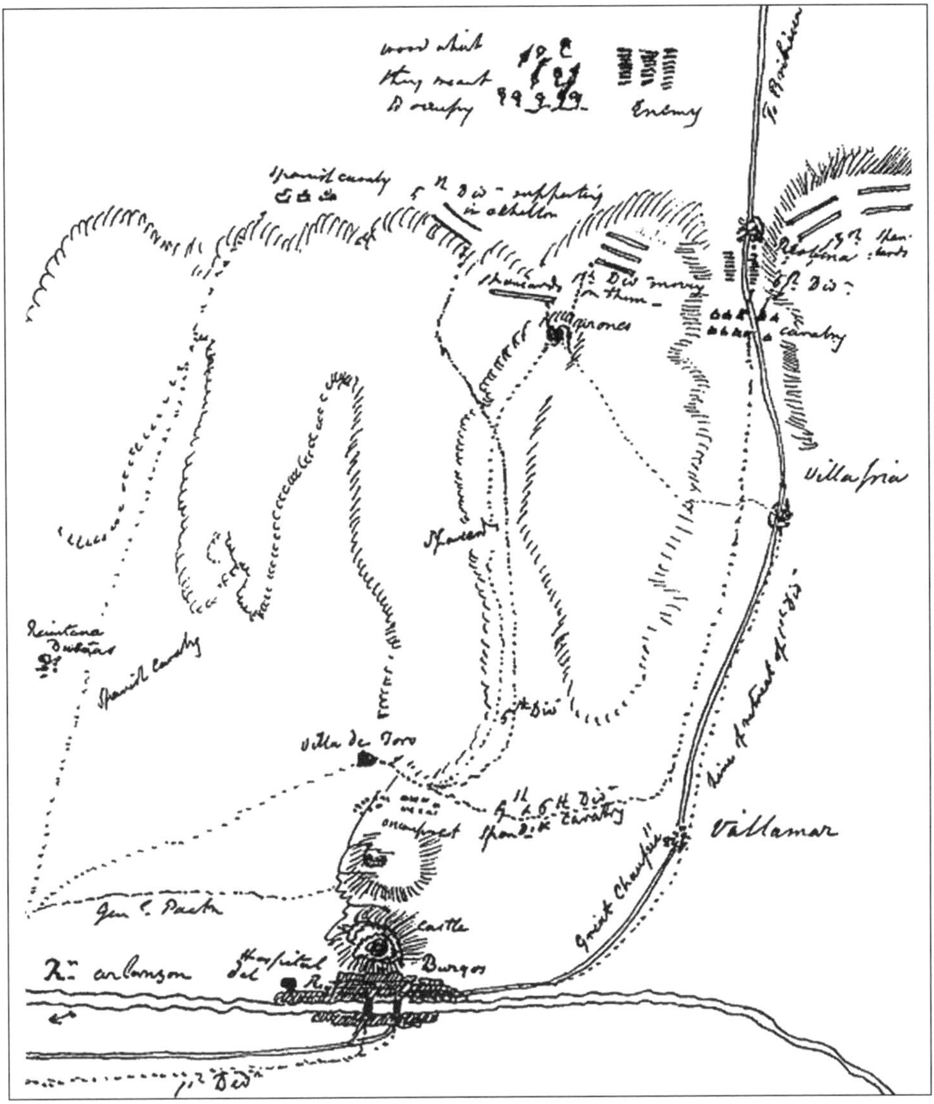

Retreat.

General sent Ponsonby's Brigade,[26] the only strong one we had, by a mountain road where they were no use. A good deal of skirmishing took place in getting over the bridge but the fire of our riflemen protected the retreat of the cavalry. The enemy soon showed a great deal, between 2 & 3,000 in good order especially some of the gendarmes. The enemy crossed the rivulet at the upper bridge which obliged us to retreat. General Anson's Brigade charged with great gallantry but were so outnumbered as to be beaten. Bock's Brigade [of] Heavy Germans (which was a wonderfully fine brigade but were very weak from their losses in action) was sent in support. I never witnessed such clashes and confusion; after some time of their being mixed, the whole were rolled back upon us, the English & French all mingled together cutting & thrusting

> as they came along. Halkett formed his two battalions in squares and charged them to be steady. The French seeing infantry, halted & allowed our men to clear off, when Halkett opened independent firing and the riflemen brought down the enemy as one should partridges. They soon went to the right about & they molested us no more, which was fortunate as this day shook the morale of our cavalry most exceedingly. Lord Wellington's object was only to throw the army over the Arlanzon, a march of 6 leagues, but the Quarter Master General, Gordon, sent us on to Torquemada, there never was so gross a mistake & were then ordered to take up the same ground which they did on the advance, The 6th & 1st Divisions would have been nearly opposite *Cordovilla* [la Real], 5 miles off & out of the way next morning.

James found that the army had no orders to stop and he took it upon himself to order a halt at a good dry encampment, a dangerous decision given Wellington's reputation for arresting officers who dared to interfere with his orders. However, this time James was proven right and received high praise for his actions.

> There was no Quarter Master General or any of the Department in the way. Sir Edward Paget & most of the generals were gone to headquarters at Cordovilla to hear the movements of next day, so I took it on myself to halt the divisions on a dry piece of ground near the town, which was convenient for wood. It was then *9* at night and I sent to headquarters to report what I had done, which was quite approved of. In one of the vineyards near, there were some large vaults of wine which the men found out & the intoxication was dreadful. 24th the army crossed the Carrion, the animals especially those of wheel carriage were so perfectly *abime* [at the abyss] with fatigue that a day's halt became absolutely necessary. This was a favourable place for it, as there was a fine position, the right resting on Duenas & the Pisuerga, & the left extending along a very mountainous ridge parallel to the Carrion to opposite Palencia. Between the two there is the village of Villamuriel [de Cerrato] where there is a bridge & ford. The army formed in columns at the foot of the hill; we were here joined by the 1st Battalion of the 1st Guards 1100 strong,[27] this is no immaterial reinforcement at this moment.
>
> The 6th Division occupied the Convent of St Isidro on the left bank of the Carrion & a little cavalry was left on that side also. It has also struck me that Souham always has manoeuvred on the wrong side of the river; there are practicable though not good roads on that side. *Our* object is to get across the Duero & in the course of that march we have the present position & the Pisuerga itself at Cabezon as positions not to be turned easily by any enemy in our front, but if Souham leaving a body of cavalry to harass our rear and [was] to make forced marches on the other side, marching as well as the French do, it would be very difficult to pass the Pisuerga before him, or if we did (which would not allow a halt here & without a halt we must have left ½ our baggage)

we should be exposed from Cabezon to the Duero to be attacked, which is not Lord Wellington's game or wish I should think.

The 24th we saw the whole French army file over the plain before us, they came down to Palencia and Villamuriel. The 6th Division were retired and the bridges of Tariego [de Cerrato] (a very important point as it afforded a passage to the other side of the Pisuerga, was ordered to be destroyed) besides the bridges of Duenas, Villamuriel and Palencia. The officer ought to have gone to Tariego on the evening of the 24th, but was deterred by hearing that the French were in possession of it (a false report). On the morning of the 25th, 50 men of the 1st Division protected by a squadron of cavalry went with the officer to Tariego; before the move was completed, the French with great gallantry carried the bridge & the cavalry leaving the infantry in the lurch came away, taking away the sergeant of miners & the officer; the rest were taken. The French soon crossed some infantry & more cavalry, Lord Wellington sent me to take 2 battalions of Germans, to cover the retreat of the cavalry & destroy a wooden bridge close to Duenas. I went across, being well mounted, to see what the French were at, and on my return found the bridge fast cutting through; I had hardly passed when the whole went in, a minute more & I must have fallen into the enemy's hands. This was owing to Gordon[28] the ADC who was impatient to see it down, though I had been sent before on purpose.

Wellington sought to halt the French near Palencia along the line of the Rivers Carrion and Pisuerga, but failure to destroy the villages ruined his plans and the retreat continued.

The officer who had charge to see the Palencia bridges destroyed, retreated and the enemy gained them. The bridge by San Isidro [de Duenas] succeeded; we thus had both flanks of the army turned. I do not think I ever saw Lord Wellington so visibly annoyed at anything; fatigue and anxiety had moreover told considerably and he looked very haggard. Lord Wellington moved the 5th, 7th & 1st Division up the hill opposite to Villamuriel as we saw the French army was manoeuvring by our left towards Palencia. Towards the afternoon the French crossed part of a division over the ford at Villamuriel and first the Spaniards were engaged, who crying 'Vamos adelante, carajo, carajo, carajo!' [Let's go forward prick, prick, prick], ran away as hard as they could.

General Barnes' Brigade was moved against them & the French suffered severely. I think we must have lost between 2 and 300 men.

Poor Alava was wounded in attempting to rally the Spaniards *'Dice que cantara major por su herida'* [They say that he will sing better for his wound]. When he was laid up at Rueda afterwards some pretty Spanish women from La Seca kindly brought him some eggs saying *'Dicen que no faltan huevos o van allora a este lugar'* [It is said that these are the eggs missing from Alava who is in this village[29]]. It is worth while to mention Alava's character as he is totally different from any Spaniard I ever saw; he began in the sea service, was ADC to Gravina[30] in the Battle of Trafalgar and afterwards taking to the army was attached to Lord Wellington. His first merit is frankness, he with perfect good taste & good humour tells the truth (or what he believes to be so) to both sides. When the Spaniards are preening themselves and attributing all the victories & hopes of independence to their own exertions, he tells them that they [are] all blind and that if it had not been for Lord Wellington and the heretics, that there would not have been such a thing as a patriot long ago & he equally tells the English of their bullying all other nations, of their haughtiness & their injustice towards the Spaniards in abusing them for want of exertion when they have no means & of discipline when they have neither money nor food. He unites the most amiable manner & the warmest heart with the most romantic bravery. He is popular with the English beyond anything I ever saw; he always says, he owes all his good points to his mother, who had some blood of the moors & from them he says is derived everything that is good in Spain. His kindness of heart so great that whenever he found British officers wounded without quarters, he would give up his own bed or anything to them which their companions did not offer.

In the evening all but the 5th Division moved off the hill and on the morning of the 26th we were all in retreat before 3. All the baggage of the army was sent off earlier & the whole army crossed by one narrow bridge. As long as the river is high the position of Cabezon [de Pisuerga] is unattackable from steep heights which command the bridge, the village serving as an additional defence. We again saw the French army file by us, they bivouacked at Cigales. Orders were sent to destroy the bridges of Valladolid, Simancas, Tordesillas, Toro & Zamora, which were all effected; a happy state we shall leave the communications of this country in. the river keeps full with some rain which fortunately has fallen.

We were all standing by a battery of our guns when a French general & Staff came impertinently near, we treated them with a [round of] shrapnel. The general immediately ordered a brigade of guns forward & gave us some grape, we all laid down but Colonel Robe[31] of the artillery, who thought it decorous I suppose, to stand, in return for which he got a grape shot break his leg. We soon peppered their guns so that they made off, leaving both dead horses & men. Our artillery officers are cool enough, for in the time Marmont was in our front, one of them said whom I met returning with his troop of horse artillery, that he had made *beautiful practise* that morning, and to be sure in a few miles, scattered heads, arms & legs attested the complete truth of his speech.

The 29th, the river began to fall. The 30th the army retreated in two columns, 1st, 6th & 2 Spanish divisions by Tudela de Duero, where we crossed & destroyed the bridge & the rest of the army by ___ [blank in journal, Puente Herrera?]. When everything had passed I rode back into Valladolid to buy some cigars & found all the town ready for the reception of the enemy with the usual signs of rejoicing. The sign of 'Posada de las tres naciones' [Inn of the

Three Nations] had given away to the 'Posada a Napoleon' and I thought it best not to trust myself long in such society.

31st moved opposite Tordesillas; a battery or two were commenced. The French army were all assembled on the other side and they succeeded in repairing the bridge. Headquarters at Rueda; I went over to La Seca to a ball and slept at a curate's house and among some sermons found and brought away this, which if I had not seen it myself in the man's house and acknowledged with complacency by him, I never could have believed [it] to be real.[32]

We remained in position till the 6th, Lord Wellington believing always that the French would cross & attack him. On the 6th, hearing that General Hill would be at Salamanca at the proper time, we moved at night. The day before *the Quarter Master General tried how many people he could employ on the same errand!!*

On the 6th Castrejon [de Trabancos]; 7th Pitiegua; 8th the 1st Division went into cantonments in the front of Salamanca. The 5th & 6th Divisions were encamped on the position, Light Division & 7th in Salamanca, 3rd & 4th at Calvarrasa [de Ariba], General Hill opposite Alba de Tormes which was strongly occupied.

3rd Battalion of 1st Guards joined 1st Division.[33]

Wellington sought to hold the position at Salamanca, hoping to winter in this region of abundance; but the French had other ideas. Forced to retreat because of flanking movements, a further retreat began. This retreat into Portugal, carried out in atrocious weather, rapidly turned the army into a rabble as the commissariat supply system completely collapsed and the troops received virtually no supplies at all. Wellington's infamous private letter to his generals complaining of the breakdown in order was unfortunately published to all. It caused great offence throughout the army and does appear to be completely unfair in its judgement, as Wellington did not realize how poorly the supply system had coped.

On the 13th the French show an inclination to cross near Alba, troops in Salamanca moved that way; 1st, 5th & 6th Divisions came into Salamanca. On the 14th the French begin to cross, on the morning of the 15th the whole of our army was assembled on the position of the Arapiles, the 1st Division occupying a strong hill behind Aldeatejada as a *point d'appui* [fulcrum], here Lord Wellington offered battle. The French consisted of from 70 to 80,000 infantry & about 10,000 cavalry & 200 pieces of cannon. We had of all sorts, 60,000 infantry (40,000 good), 3,500 cavalry & 108 pieces of cannon.[34]They did not like the old ground & began manoeuvring on our communications; Lord Wellington in a moment decided on retreat. Here began the disorder of the retreat; the weather was most dreadful, the men bivouacked up to their knees in water, the wood was so wet it would not burn, the roads so deep that the men were abime! [at the abyss] The provisions were imperfectly served & the troops helped themselves from the pigs in the wood.

Disease was rife in the retreating army and James was no exception, despite his more fortunate circumstances. By pure good luck, General Paget told him to ride ahead to Ciudad Rodrigo in advance of the army, to gain a good billet where he could recover. Paget, who was renowned for his short-sightedness, was captured by French dragoons whilst riding between two divisions of the army and taken off. In his absence, his old friend Lieutenant General William Stewart took command of the division and James, having fully recovered, soon joined him.

> At 12 o'clock the army retreated in 3 columns, crossed the Valmaza.
>
> 16th crossed the Huebra, 17th I had been very ill ever since the 13th with a fever & quinsy[35] and General Paget said 'You see it is all over & we are no longer molested, I insist on you pushing on to Ciudad Rodrigo to get under cover'. I did so; the next day when the surgeon came, he said 'Do you know the news? Sir Edward Paget is taken[36] & Ciudad is to be given up'. I laughed & said both were equally likely; one alas was unfortunately too true. I shall never forget the kindness and I may say, affectionate manner, in which I was treated by that excellent, amiable and able man.
>
> Our horses are near starving, I paid £4 for a bushel of barley & was thought to have a prize; we feed them off spoiled biscuit. The troops are in great want & the roads are covered with dead horses & men. General Stewart is appointed to the 1st Division. On the 23rd being recovered, joined him.

James wrote to his friend Richard Heber, whom he had clearly met again on his last visit to London. James wrote of the recent operations and did not baulk from criticizing Wellington's actions. However, it is interesting to note how positive James was regarding the prospects for the forthcoming campaign of 1813, he saw the results of the retreat to be purely positive. He also shows some empathy for the Spanish people.

> Mangualde, 10 December 1812
>
> When we parted in London I certainly did not expect to be cantoned in the middle of Portugal this winter. I had hopes of sharing in future victories and that expectation certainly occasioned my short stay at home; although I have been disappointed and only arrived in time to witness a bright display of unprofitable gallantry and a repetition of the melancholy scenes unavoidable in every retreat but more prominent in a British one. I by no means regret the determination I have taken as the lesson of the last month is worth an age of pursuit. When one looks back on the campaign, one seeks anxiously for the reason why the tables were so rapidly turned and how it happened that we could hardly keep face before a French army which three weeks before was considered hors de combat for the year.
>
> I think the prime cause and keystone of our reverses was Lord Wellington's entry of Madrid abandoning thereby the pursuit of an army which he could have been right to bring to action, and secondly, when he remained at Madrid some time returning to the chase of an enemy he had released from his fangs.

Of all this I know nothing but from reports, but Burgos I saw, but a rational prospect of success I never could see. With the perfect want of means under which we laboured, we had no right to expect to take the town work: but British soldiers who could storm the Picurina could storm any single line of defence and we carried in a night what should have cost a month's siege. But the fort itself was a triple range of strong and well constructed entrenchments and infinitely stronger than Badajoz. We had but 3 guns and thanks to our engineers they were speedily dismounted and we were besieging one of the strongest places of Spain without guns[37] and with no musquet ammunition. When the latter arrived, we again stormed and lost our most valuable officers in attempting what appears to me impossibilities.

At length the long expected army of relief advances and as usual the Spanish intelligence reduces the force to two thirds of the reality. Lord W[ellington] occupies a strong position in front of Burgos. The French army appears and we see a most numerous body of men reorganised and formidable in their cavalry. They were not collected. Lord W[ellington] heard of Soult's advance and determined on retreat. He had chased them off the night before by moving to attack them. This advantage he possessed and this alone. It is impossible to conceive a situation of more appalling difficulty to an ordinary mind than this retreat presented. The enemy had 4,000 cavalry and we had about 1,200 and these harassed by unceasing duty. The enemy had 40,000 infantry and we had about 10,000 British something like 7,000 Portuguese and the remainder of our force was composed of men whom we suspected and afterwards found could not be relied on.[38]

The Castle of Burgos commanded the high road, the lateral roads were nearly impassable and many [of] the sick and stores were in the front of Burgos.

In one night the whole army was beyond the fort, the 1st Division moved over the bridges within half a musket shot of the fort in a moonlight night without being perceived. The second day the cavalry behaved so ill that nothing but the firmness of two German battalions saved them from a dangerous pursuit. I will not go through the long detail of the retreat but Lord W[ellington] effectually checked and imposed upon the enemy: we halted when and as long as he chose. He effected a retreat over narrow single bridges with a train of baggage unexceeded by all the armies of the east and west without losing a mule and I might have said without the loss of a man, had not the same scenes of intemperance and indiscipline which occasioned the loss of Sir John Moore's army, returned with unabated force.

When we collected at Salamanca our numbers were as you see in the despatch, but he offered them battle and had they attacked him, the result would not have [been] doubtful, but any movement by their left rendered it necessary to retire and when once in retreat no army can stop short of the [one] agreed on. Here the weather which last winter so wonderfully assisted Lord

Wellington, coquetted with the marshals; whilst we wanted rain to swell the Tormes which would have enabled us to hold Salamanca, the sun shone with nearly summer's heat; when we began our retreat over roads of marsh and mud, such torrents of rain fell as hardly ever were experienced before. Here again the indiscipline of the troops made us lose some men and many also sank under the inclemency of the weather.

Yet the heaviest loss and which you know must most deeply have been felt by me was the loss of General Paget. I was taken ill with a fever at Salamanca and the morning he was taken he insisted on my getting on to Ciudad Rodrigo. To this I owe my liberty.

Nothing could be more interesting to a military man than the whole of these operations, the mode Lord W[ellington] took up his positions, the presence of mind, the unshaken firmness, the wonderful nerve he displayed were lessons never to be forgotten.

But allow me to look back to former events and to touch on a string you know vibrates more strongly than any other in my heart, I mean the much censured retreat of Sir John Moore. Though I regret the events and much more the innate cause of them I cannot but feel a satisfaction in perceiving that such things may occur under the command of the greatest general of his day, the favourite of fortune and the un-libelled commander of a large army who besides has the advantage that no perfidious government opposes and no visionary minister clogs him with his aid.

One melancholy fact has been established by this campaign, that the French relying either on a military possession of forts and garrisons or on the terror of future punishment or on the weariness the people feel at this protracted war or conjointly on the whole of these causes, can equally despise the regular army, the guerrillas and the hatred of a nation and can assemble for a considerable time at the extremity of Spain nearly their whole effective force; whilst the only army that could have assisted us remains useless and the only general who united the confidence of the army and the country breaks out in an overt act of unheard of rebellion.[39]

We have also seen that regular Spanish soldiers who for two years have been organising in the Galicias cannot stand against French conscripts who had been 20 days from Bayonne though they have British soldiers by their side as an example.

With regard to our future hopes therefore we can only look to ourselves and I think this retreat will give us great advantage next spring. We shall be able to rest the army as long as Lord W[ellington] likes, whereas in advance we should have been 'a la disposition' of the Marshals. We shall be able to re-clothe and re-discipline the army, we shall be able to form magazines for our future operations. Had we remained forward the whole of our transport would have been employed in feeding us as from hand to mouth and this important operation without which no army can advance in the spring would have been impossible. Against this we have our great disadvantage that for the third time we have abandoned the Spaniards and we shall never be considered otherwise than as birds of passage and we cannot expect vivas from the heart whatever the tongue may utter. It really makes one's heart bleed to think of the poor people of Madrid and Salamanca whom we have left to be tenfold worse plundered and more oppressed in proportion to their attachment to us. I cannot blame the Spaniard for being weary of the war, when sacrifices are so recompensed, and when zeal and kindness so repaid, it must be more than human constancy that does not pray for a cessation of such friendship. I well know that the retreat was necessary and though it justifies our conduct, it cannot remove one's feelings for the poor wretches who are paying for their attachment to us.

If this letter does not put you to sleep, there is no faith in any soporifics.

James resumed his journal as the army reached Portugal and retired into winter quarters for a well earned rest.

On the 11th December 1st Division entered their cantonments at Besin Mangualde. Our headquarters at Mangualde, here is the best country house in Portugal belonging to the Paejo's, brothers of Madame D'Alverca.

This ended this campaign, not certainly within some hundred miles of where I expected it to be when I left England, or I should have stayed the winter. This retreat has been the most dangerous & unpleasant operation we have had, but not unprofitable, as perhaps Lord Wellington never showed his coolness, presence of mind and great qualities so much. Whatever occurred of loss proceeded from the inclemency of the weather & the intemperance of the troops. Lord Wellington was very angry & wrote that harsh and unjust letter which caused so much sensation & which he was more sorry for than anyone when he saw it published. He had meant it as a private letter to the generals, but sending it to them printed with no *private* upon it, many of them put it in General Orders.

Lord Wellington seems to have been rather seduced too far by the surrender of the Retiro & thought everything would fall before him, but a brave man & garrison stopped him pretty short. He had no means for a siege & his two armies were too far apart & too weak to attempt to hold all that country.

In going up, I met at Salamanca a French officer prisoner who said 'Believe me, you are too far forward and will not winter on the Ebro.' The people of Salamanca behaved admirably when we evacuated it; not a reproach, though every sign was there of deep despair and cruel revenge the French took in plundering it for nearly two days.

If Lord Wellington had succeeded in his attack of the 2nd line at Burgos, it would not have made any difference in the campaign, nor do I think he could have stayed so far from his magazines during the winter, even if he had taken it early. But, this year has been glorious, having taken two fortresses & liberated the south of Spain.

Chapter 11

The Great Advance

In February 1813, we find James in reflective mood as he lay in winter quarters and pondered.

February 20th. Whilst I have been quiet here, I have reflected a good deal on the extraordinary difference between the Portuguese & Spaniards, divided as they often are by an invisible boundary or a mountain or a river, but living under the same climate, enjoying the same religion, nourished in the same manner & cultivating the same crops. It is not sufficient to say generally the one is a cringing, fawning & deceitful serf & that the other is haughty, independent, obstinate & repulsive. As for their nobility, in their private stations, I take them to be nearly the same, with some superiority of education resting with the Spanish, but equally proud, bigoted, spoiled & devoid of the feelings of independence which actuate our own nobility. But there is a marked & most important difference in their public conduct & the tenure on which they hold their titles & estates.

The Spanish grandees often have kept the king in check, being possessed of immense wealth & feudal power. Of the way they answer the king numerous instances might be brought. The present Ferdinand once said to the Count D'Altamira (Prince of Benavente) who in size & appearance is very like a baboon 'Que Chico eres Altamira' [How little you are Altamira] 'Si senor, aqui! Pero en mi casa grande como su majestad' [Yes Sir here! But in my house I am as big as your majesty].

But the nobility of Portugal rest on the pleasure of their sovereign, for their titles & estates & unless the prince chances to renew to the son, the honour of the father, it all reverts to the crown. It is therefore customary early to intercede for one of the titles to be bestowed on the son. I never heard it, or could trace that for many, many years, this power has ever been carried into effect, but that it exists is certain and that it must debase the nobility rendering them the mere slaves of the crown is equally evident.

I am inclined to trace in a great measure, the difference between the peasantry of the 2 nations to the magistrates. In Portugal the district is under two officers; one the military governor & the other the Sargento Mor, both appointed by the crown & who possess despotic power and the smallest town and even many large villages have two magistrates and always the last the Capitao Mor & Juez de Foro, who have the same powers. The first has the military arrangements of calling out the militia, registering conscripts &c and the Juez de Foro all the civil jurisdiction & absolute power. He may without any assigned cause (and in every village of Portugal it is practised) throw into prison (constantly next his house) whosoever he chooses & who remain there without the power of making his case known as long as it may please the petty tyrant. Every officer who has been in Portugal can testify that every jail is crowded. They have besides the right of arbitrarily fixing the price of the markets and in many instances (and this very town is one) the Juez puts such a price as renders it impossible to hope for a purchaser & secret agents of his own, purchase at a very inferior rate & retail it at enormous profit. This Juez has set every body against English guineas & receives them as doing a favour, below the value from the peasants & then remits them to Lisbon where he gets 27 shillings for each; and this magistrate is *considered a particularly honest, active & good one*. But this is not the worst, for if the Juez always resided in the same place (the birthplace of his family) he might have some ties of affection, some motives of interest, some causes of fear to force him to be more just, or at any rate more lenient. But these magistrates must be educated at the University of Coimbra. They *cannot be magistrates over their own towns or villages* and *cannot* hold their office in the *same town* for *above three years*. Here then is a rapacious, profligate tyrant, placed at the head of a community with a limited term in which he is to improve his future & where no feelings of affection, fear or hopes of interest can prompt him to relax or perform with mercy the most arbitrary orders he may receive from his government. If I were to recite all the instances of oppression that I know have taken place in Portugal, I could write till the opening of the campaign. Let it be remarked, that though this system renders the peasant the abject slave he is (though certainly still possessing much humanity, kindness of heart & docility of temper; with much patience & fortitude) still it is admirably qualified to bring forth the whole power of a nation. Every house is registered, every horse & cart is known, every corn stack is in their books, & over the whole has the governor a despotic hand. Everybody has seen Portuguese volunteers going to the front; tied together like so many rabbits on a pole and they call them '*Una cadena de voluntarios*' [A chain of Volunteers].

Let us now look at Spain; every district is under a military governor & a corregidor [chief magistrate], both of whom are appointed by the crown with very great power. But the towns and villages, especially the latter (in which being an agricultural country by much the majority of the population is confined) are governed by two alcaldes [combined mayors and chief magistrates] who must be of the same place, who are elected by the others (*fire holders*, every man voting who has a house to himself) and who cannot hold their office above one year. No man who sees all his neighbours about him as rich as himself & in most of these villages there is hardly any difference of fortune and who knows that he is to relapse into the situation of a private individual, will ever much abuse his temporary powers, lest he should injure the person who chosen the next year, might pay him off in kind. They therefore live very peacefully & terminate amicably all the differences of the villagers. This system which renders so happy the state of the Spanish peasant, especially in the province of Salamanca is totally unfit for a state of war. The alcaldes have but little authority and either from love or fear are always prevented from executing their orders. Upon this therefore I mainly found the difference of the two countries both as to the character of the peasantry & the great means which Marshal Beresford has found in the one case and the very little effect that all the Spanish orders have produced in the other.

The 1st Guards were suddenly struck down by a virulent fever and suffered so severely that Wellington was forced to send the regiment to Oporto and left them there to recover whilst the army advanced. James was heavily involved in providing billets for them, having taken up his official position as Deputy Assistant Quarter Master General to the 1st Division.

A very extraordinary sickness has raged here for some time past in the 1st Regiment of Guards.[1] They marched into Viseu 2,100 men, part of whom 1,100 had come from England fine healthy young men from the militia and 1,000 from Cadiz where they had been gradually accustomed to the climate & who were steady soldiers; therefore it was impossible to account for it by any general rule, as the persons who suffered were so different. A man would come to the surgeons and say he was very ill, but unable to explain where; they were carried to hospital and died in 48 hours, the body assuming a yellow hue before death, with black spots coming out after. The other brigade of Guards had a violent typhus fever, against which nature made a long struggle; in this case the pulse was high & the thermometer rose on application to the skin, but in the other brigade, the pulse was almost imperceptible, the flesh clammy & the thermometer *sunk* very low. A curious thing was that no officer, officer's servant or artisan was attacked, everything was done for them. The hospital regulations of the Guards allow great expense & the captains added more, fowls, wine &c were given without effect, quarters were changed, they were released from all duties but they went on dying. The hospital attendants who were taken ill had all the violent symptoms of the other brigade. On the 24th March they were ordered to Oporto & not quite 700 men marched out, 700 had been buried & the rest remained in hospital.[2] I was ordered to Oporto to prepare quarters for them, I took the short way across the mountains and arrived the 2nd night at the Convent of St Christovals[3] which in point of situation and romantic beauty is one of the most striking things in Portugal. It stands out on a jutting isthmus on three sides surrounded with a precipice & brawling torrent, the monks received me most hospitably.

26th I went a little out of my way to see the famous Convent of Arouca,[4] which for wealth & beauty of situation is nearly the most celebrated in the country & one of the few which the war has spared. The scene I have to relate made me deeply regret no French column had come this way. When I entered the convent yard I was astonished at seeing so many people assembled in gay habits, as in celebration of some festival. Presently three young ladies passed whom I thought I recollected & on addressing found I was right as they were the daughters of Senhor Mota, a physician at Lamego at whose house I had been billeted at the end of 1808.[5] Two of them were singularly pretty & the 3rd was an interesting person who sang more admirably than any amateur I ever heard. They were the life & soul of the society at Lamego & I was delighted to meet them again. On asking them the excuse of the fete, they said it was in honour of some ladies who were going to take the veil. I said I was very glad to be in time to see the ceremony, when they burst into tears saying '*We are the victims*!' Soon after I had more opportunity of conversing, I asked if it was possible that they would be going to take such an irrevocable step rather against their will & they said yes, that their father was too poor to support them and that they had used every means to alter his determination in vain; that out of respect to him, they had determined so to self devote themselves. I argued in vain that no one should take a false oath for a father or any one.

I begged here to stay with them as long as they remained in the world and they seemed affected at my wish & gladly consented. During that evening & the next morning they burst into tears whenever anything were touched on which brought their sacrifice to mind. At 12 o'clock they retired to dress themselves in their gayest attire & to fit themselves out for this atrocious sacrifice. They then were brought out hardly able to support themselves before the great gate of the convent which was open & which displayed about 40 nuns in white with the most immovable figures & countenances with tapers in their hands, who formed a lane up to the abbess. Here they were to embrace their parents & friends for the last time & in my life I never witnessed such poignancy of grief. They were then conducted to the church into which we went by another gate, being then separated by iron gates. They were brought up amid the peals of the organ & the chanting of the nuns & were then disrobed of all their finery & clothed in the novice garb; all this time showing every symptom of grief & despair. I was perhaps more affected by having known these poor victims and could not refrain from tears & it was many days before I could get over the impression of this cruel scene. The abbess asked me if I did not admire the ceremony & if it could be performed better & I answered more truly than civilly 'Only by putting in a brigade & taking away the gates'. Old Fray Joachim de Vasconcellos is a bon vivant & a liberal minded monk & I never saw brethren of St Benedict with more hospitality or better cheer.

On the 28th reached Oporto; I spent my time most delightfully here between the Vargellas', Croft & Butler, the Rossi's, Senora Rosa de Fonseca[6] &c; nothing could exceed the kindness & hospitality of those good people or the charms of the society of the Rossi's who were Italians settled in Portugal, possessing all the tact and accomplishments of the former. There were 9 sisters & 3 nieces whom we justly called the muses & graces. Madame Fonseca is the most charming; few women I have met equal her in society; Mr Bankes[7] arrived here who amused us very much by his eccentricities & stories. Soon after he arrived a Captain Smith[8] of the Navy left a card for him & then went on board. It had by chance his *Portsmouth* direction on it in *Governor's Lane* & Bankes fagged his body all day asking for '*La Rua do Gobernador*', or '*La traveisa do Comandante*' [The Street of the Governor or the Side Street of the Mayor] & in short using every synonym of the language in vain. I had great amusement with him at the *Koptky's*, a Danish family in which were 3 maiden sisters, who had a beautiful garden in which almost all our hot house plants were flourishing in the open air. He went round & said '*Ah ici il y a le rose de Japon et voila le te et le café et tous ces plantes en Angleterre sont dans les pots de chambre.*' [Ah here we have the rose of Japan and there the tea and the coffee and all these plants in England are in the chamber pots!] meaning flower pots in rooms.

Avintes, the country house of Mr Vargellas is fitted up like an English country house with beautiful woods & walks looking over the Duero with all the delight of that climate, I never saw a more enjoyable spot. At Sante 3 leagues where we went fishing & caught 14 trout in two days. There is a monster, they say it is a woman, it is about 2 feet & ½ high, of which the head is the full half. The countenance is very stern with bushy eyebrows & a long black head of coarse hair. She has no arms as her wrists proceed straight from the shoulder and her legs & thighs are quite withered up; she is an idiot.

The more I look at the place Sir Edward Paget crossed the Duero, the more inclined I feel to put that passage among Lord Wellington's greatest ideas & most extraordinary actions.[9]

Clearly little happened of consequence whilst the army prepared for the coming campaign in winter quarters and there is a large gap before James's next journal entry. He was very glad to hear that Sir Thomas Graham was back with the army and soon made his way to join his staff again, but now in his role as DAQMG. He was not sorry to leave Stewart; as many others had found, he was difficult to work with, he always had some grand scheme in mind and never wanted to simply follow orders.

On the 2nd of May left Oporto with great regret & much gratitude for the kindness I had received. Reached headquarters the 9th where I found General Graham not looking well, but I am rejoiced to be with him again, especially after Stewart, who is whimsical & plagues himself & every [one] round him for no purpose, who with every particle of zeal that man can possess & with more bravery than any one, is absolutely dangerous to trust, from always having a scheme of his own, which must be better than the orders he receives, which he therefore never obeys.

He also had time to send another letter to Richard Heber describing the possible successes and difficulties of what was clearly going to be a very important campaign.

Headquarters, 13 May 1813

The last letter I wrote to you was at the end of the last campaign. During the winter like Munchausen's horse[10] I have been frozen up in a Beotian[11] land and amid Siberian cold with the exception of the last weeks which I passed in an agreeable manner with my old friends at Oporto. I arrived here on the 9th. My old general had reached it three days before me, looking infinitely better than he did last year. You will be gratified in hearing that I am again to join him and I am to be personally attached to him in my present department as I was to Sir Edward Paget. At all times this would be most desirable but most particularly interesting is it, at the present moment when he is entrusted with a post of great importance in command of the army to the north of the Duero.[12]

You are always so sanguine in England that I suppose you will not be contented without seeing the French armies pushed over the Rhine and the Pyrenees. We have certainly good prospects but how far our hopes will be realised (at least in this part of the world) must depend in a great measure on the improvement of our allies and the confidence which in a military point of view can be placed in them, subjects in no small degree precarious. The great game appears however to be [de]pendent on Germany etc. and I cannot but think that Spain will be won or lost upon the Elbe in preference to the Ebro.

The French army is strong in this country and although our force is in the highest order, we have lost no inconsiderable number of men during the winter by sickness and have received (at least as infantry) no considerable reinforcements. Our cavalry is however good and respectable in numbers and in proportion as we suffered for want of that arm last year, we may hope correspondent advantages from its present state. I suppose we have not less than 6,000.

The French army is 'a portee' [has the range] of the Duero, but whether they will try to defend the line of it remains to be proved. They derive great advantage from the nature of the country, all the towns which command the bridges are on their side and in consequence of that the Duero was no obstacle to the advance of the enemy when we held its line last year in our retreat. I do not believe we could have forced the line of it last year had not Marmont saved Lord Wellington the trouble of trying, by gallantly adventuring first. It is not probable that such an event will reoccur. It appears therefore that the army is to be divided, I think in about equal proportions, that on the north to get the Esla and that on the south the Tormes. This is always a critical movement especially when the enemy have a bridge so near as Zamora which will enable them to throw their whole force against half of ours which must in that case 'rebrousser chemin' [turn back], which in the army on the south of the river would be attended with the disadvantage of having the Tormes in its rear, if it communicates with us on crossing the Esla which of course it must do. Still it is not the object of the French to risk much and perhaps we shall bully them out of the line of the Duero. We may then give a view hallow[13] to the Ebro. There is a considerable Spanish force on foot, I suppose the Galician army would join us. The armies of Murcia and Andalusia (the latter under the Conde de Bisbal[14] is in very high order) will of course move and will always act as a diversion. Suchet appears to have enough on his hands, if Sir John Murray is like Caesar and is a man of many blows as well as of many letters. At any rate we shall have an interesting campaign[15] and that is some comfort!

We gain much by Lord Wellington being supreme and not a little by Soult being off. Jourdan[16] has been bilked so often that he will not wish to change at this period of his military life his earlier habits. We shall be in movement in a few days. If I have time I will write you a line. If I do not, you must forgive it. I need not ask for an answer as I am convinced you will never send one.

I was very near sending you home a most valuable book both as to decency of stile and abstruseness of matter, but I conceived you have certainly got it. *Don Tome Sanchez de Matrimonio*, the learned dissertation de Debitu Conjugali[17] is not to be paralleled and tended much to enliven my winter quarters, as I took the liberty of adding notes critical and historical.

I met at Oporto the other day a very extraordinary young man, Mr. Bankes who is a great friend of Lord Byron and an associate to his Lordship's friend the late Mr. Matthews.[18] I never saw so singular a compound of eccentricity and judgements, of trifling and study, of sound opinions about others and wild speculations about himself, good talents applied to no future object and a most wonderful memory prostituted to old songs and tales of Mother Goose. Do you know him? But why do I ask as till we meet again I have no hopes of being answered. I like the man much for he appears to have an excellent temper, a good heart and a certain degree of freshness and independence in opinions which I do not think the travellers who come to this country generally possess.

On 18 May Wellington issued his final orders for the campaign.

Left headquarters the 19th [May] for Vila Nova de Foz Coa 12 leagues, 20th Torre de Moncorvo, 21st I went to the same gentleman's house who had received me so kindly in 1809[19] & he received me as well now.

22nd Miranda do Douro. Lord Wellington had been for some time moving

> his cavalry round by Oporto on the pretence of getting them forage & he now insensibly moved all the army but a brigade of cavalry & the Light Division under General Graham to the right bank, whilst he remaining in person on the other side still gave the enemy the idea that the main force was there. *He outwitted them completely*.

All was now ready to launch his master stroke. Whilst the French looked to cover Salamanca and defend the myriad rivers running north–south across this part of Spain, Wellington led his army north, crossing the rivers higher up and turning the French right flank. The French would thus be manœuvred out of their defensive lines without any real fighting.

> The divisions assembled thus on the 23rd.
>
> 1st Division Pack & Bock's cavalry at Tabara
> 5th & cavalry to Losilla
> 4th, 6th, 7th & hussars to Carbajales [de Alba]
>
> The Light Division was on the Sant Espiritus River on the 22nd.
>
> 25th reconnoitred the best spot for the pontoon bridge which is just below the Barca de Villalcampo. There is no enemy to guard the important passage of the Esla but a picket of cavalry. On the 30th Lord Wellington arrived at Carbajales. On the 31st the hussars & part of the 7th Division forded the Esla at the ford of Almendra, we lost a good many men drowned from the depth and rapidity of the stream.[20] The French picket remained too long & the hussars caught them all.
>
> 1st of June. Entered Zamora where we were received with great joy. The castle is capable of being made strong but is now useless. The rest of the army had crossed the pontoon bridge.
>
> 2nd June. Headquarters entered Toro with equal acclamation. The 16th Regiment of French Dragoons stayed too long waiting for a contribution and the Hussar Brigade came up. Two squadrons of the 10th charged & took 200 prisoners.[21]
>
> 3rd June army redivided. Left column under General Graham, 1st & 5th Divisions with Anson's & Bock's cavalry. The left of centre column under General Picton of the Light, 3rd & 4th Divisions General Ponsonby's and General D'Urban's cavalry and the right of the centre of the 6th and 7th Divisions with Alten's & the Household cavalry. Sir Rowland Hill crossed the Duero on the 4th and encamped on the [River] Bajoz,[22] the right column towards Torrelobaton; centre & headquarters at [Castillo de] La Mota; left at Villardefrades.
>
> On the 5th the left column entered [Medina de] Rioseco which is a delightful town full of good houses & celebrated justly for the beauty of the women; on dit that the French have taken the best away. The people continue

to be very glad to see us, we are a good force, I suppose not less than 50,000 men in the highest order and spirits. The centre columns & headquarters at Castromonte & the right wing at Torrelobaton.

6th army continues moving left at Villerias [de Campos], headquarters *of it* at [Monte] La Torre, centre columns & headquarters at Ampudia & right towards Duenas. All this time we are insensibly sidling to our left. About this part of the country are an infinity of old frontier castles, some such as Montealegre [de Campos] & [Monte la] Torre, capable of being made good posts.

7th Heard of the French being in force at Palencia & Joseph there in person. Left column on Palencia by Grijota, centre column ditto by another road and right to Duenas. The enemy's infantry had marched & their cavalry only waited to see us. The king had left it the night before, I did not expect they would stand here as the ground was against them.

The 8th the left wing on San Cebrian [de Campos] & crossed the Carrion at Calahorra.[23] The centre moved by Monzon [de Campos] on Amusco where were headquarters & the right also crossed the Carrion. This country is all marshy near the canal of Castilla & is very aguish & unwholesome in the autumn. The houses and villages are dirty & wretched, not like Salamanca & the inhabitants are very Beotian. Got in communication with the Spaniards who had about 12,000 men.

9th Left column & Spaniards moved, former on Santillana [de Campos], the rest of the army halted, this threw us in echelon on the left.

10th left column crossed the Pisuerga at Zarzosa [de Rio Pisuerga], Spaniards Herrera [de Pisuerga]; centre & headquarters Melgar [de Fernamental] & right on high road.

11th left column at Sotresgudo & Villanueva de Odra, Spaniards on our left, centre & headquarters about Castrojeriz, right on high road.

12th the army halted for want of supplies, it is only wonderful that we have got on so far and so fast without being stopped before.

13th country became hilly and the road enters a defile which debouches at [La] Piedra; close to this (at Santa Cruz [del Tozo]) runs the high road from Burgos to Santander, headquarters of our column Villadiego, Spaniards towards Aguilar de Campo. Heard of Burgos being blown up, so that will not stop us this time.[24]

On the 14th left wing moves in two columns towards San Martin de Elines on the Ebro. The *right* road for infantry is by Santa Coloma [del Rudron] & Sargentes [de la Lora], the left by the Santander road as far as the Venta del Pozo & then by Rocamundo, where there is a bridge over which the Spanish column crossed; we remained at Masa.

15th left wing cross the Ebro (here a very insignificant stream but in beautiful scenery), our artillery had to ascend a most tremendous hill believed by the French & country people to be totally impracticable, but with zeal and exertion all was surmounted. We marched by Vallejo, Manzanedo to [Bustillo de] Villarcayo 7 leagues, headquarters of it Quintana [de Valdivieso]. Right column falls in the rear of the centre; both cross at Puente Arenas.

16th centre, right & headquarters about Medina [de Pomar], left wing La Cerca, Spaniards at Quintanilla [de Pienza].

17th the left column preceded the march on the high roads to Vitoria; halt at Lastras de Teza, headquarters at Quincoces [de Yuso].

18th the left column was directed on Osma by one road & the Light Division by another, whilst the rest of the centre and the right moved on Espejo, where the enemy were reported to be in force & strongly posted. On arriving near Osma we found it occupied by some of the enemy. We brought some of Halkett's battalions & some of the 12th Light Dragoons & drove them out, but in our turn were obliged to fall back on seeing a large column debouch on the place. We looked at each other for a long time & at last they began to turn our right with about 2 battalions and sent some force up the hill to our left. They also occupied the village of Karanka. We began a brisk cannonade; part of the 5th Division drove the enemy from it & our right & part of the Guards from our left. They retreated in toto & the Light Division who had got on to Espejo fell in with their rear & took some baggage & prisoners.

19th the centre column moved on the straight road towards Subijana de Alava[25] and the right on Pobes. The left (which by the way had always to get round the flank & thereby marched always over dreadful roads & longer distances) re-passed Berberana & then marched some distance on the great road to Orduna, then crossed by an execrable mountain pass (which we were a long time finding from a thick mist on the mountains) which after crossing the Sierra de Guilijo[26] descends by Jokano into the valley of the Bayas at Zuazo [de Cuartango]. This runs down on Subilana, therefore our army was rather en echelon on our right. The enemy whom we engaged yesterday was posted in an impregnable pass which they were obliged to abandon being turned by one of the centre columns. We find by an intercepted letter that what we engaged was a body going to Bilbao to support Foy and who were highly astonished at seeing us, not hearing we were in that direction.

The 20th, the right and centre of the army halted to allow the other divisions to close up, the 6th Division is left behind to watch Clausel who was sent to look after us at Logrono 'Where the Spanish fleet he could not see as they were not yet in sight'. The left column moved up the river to Murguia on the high road from Bilbao to Vitoria & the Spaniards moved to Orduna & were ordered further. Longa's[27] corps of 5,000 men joined us at Murguia.

Chapter 12

Vitoria[1]

The French army was now in a chosen position on the plains of Vitoria, protected by the line of the River Zadorra. Wellington's and Hill's forces approached this basin from the front whilst Graham's troops arced around the French right wing and attempted to threaten the French line of retreat. The army of Wellington numbered over 80,000 men, the French however, despite numbering only 57,000 men, were so sure of success that large seating areas were constructed for their allies in the Spanish nobility to view the fighting and enjoy the spectacle.

> Reports have arrived which we can depend upon that the enemy's whole army is assembled on the other side of the Zadorra near Vitoria.
>
> On the 21st the army moved forward to attack the enemy. All but the left column was to move at daylight; we being nearer and on an excellent road cooked early & were in motion at 10 o'clock. The general disposition was that the right & centre of the army (with the exception of the 6th Division still left to watch Clausel and the 3rd & 7th who were to move on Trespuentes) were to move by Subijana de Alava & attack the enemy's left & we were to facilitate as much as possible their advance taking care not to go into the plain & being ready for a movement to our left to cut in on the line of retreat towards Villa Real,[2] these roads therefore were early ascertained. The accompanying is a sketch of what passed on the left; I have thrown in the general idea of the right to give some notion of the connection of the action. The Spaniards reached Murguia at 11 & soon after moved to join us. A little before 12 we saw the action (which had begun with Sir Rowland Hill much earlier) & a heavy cannonade towards Subijana.
>
> The enemy seemed in great force about Ariaga, apparently in echelons on a rising ground. In our front we saw a division occupying the hills in front of the village of Abetxuko.
>
> The cannonade had now become furious on the right and the action apparently very warm. The 3rd & 7th Divisions had now crossed the river.
>
> The French seemed to stand very firm at Gometxa, this was a very interesting movement, although by his orders the general was not authorised to move into the plain, he determined on attacking the division in his front & on threatening the communications of the enemy.[3] The brigades of General

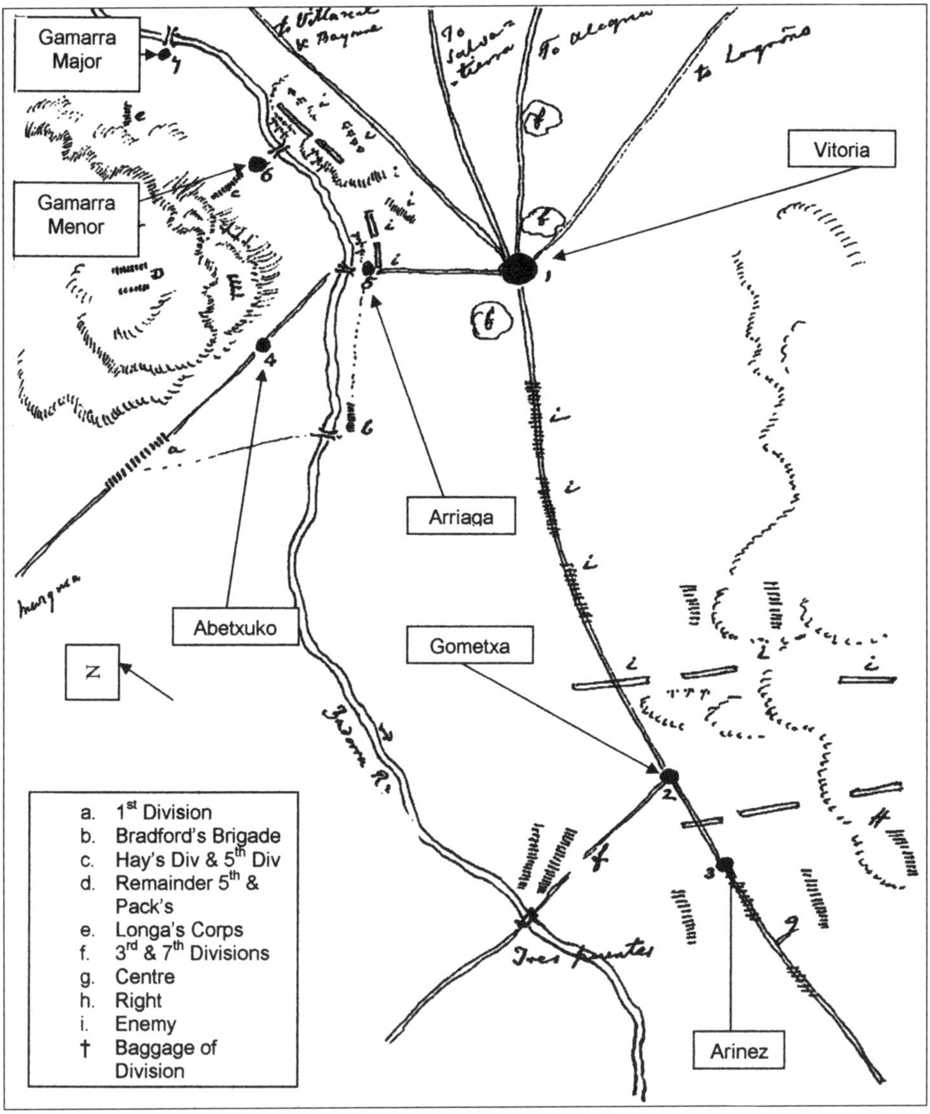

Vitoria.

Hay[4] & General Pack attacked the enemy advantageously posted on the hill & soon obliged him to re-cross the river. *General Graham began his movement at two!!*

Before this his great column had been concealed behind the hill. The enemy evidently never knew that we had such a powerful force at Meczquia.[5] We had hardly appeared all in sight when we saw several columns put themselves in motion towards the bridges we threatened & no small confusion manifest itself round Vitoria; still however, the battle raged hotly on the right. *At 3* General Graham received orders to press the enemy as much as possible; we enquired *'When Lord Wellington gave the order?' and were answered 'About an hour before'*, and thus at *the moment* the commander in chief *wished an order executed*, the *2nd in command intuitively seizes the same idea & executes it of his own accord!* Lord Wellington was exceedingly pleased at this when I saw him soon afterwards.

General Robinson's Brigade[6] which was shortly supported by General Hay's, attacked with great spirit the village of Gamarra Major; the action was most severe, the French resisted most gallantly & after we had driven them over the river repeatedly charged over the bridge to retake it, it was to them of immense importance. We lost nearly 500 men in the village & the enemy a great number more, the bridge was heaped. The enemy attacked with great masses & showed large bodies of troops behind Arriaga, I should think that between the two they had assembled 15,000 men. By this time the enemy were in full retreat, masses of infantry, cavalry & artillery were pressing towards Vitoria. The clouds of dust covered them, but the advance of the British columns were the most beautiful sight which imagination could form.

General Graham now ordered the 1st Division to attack the bridge to the village of Arriaga, which Halkett carried with great gallantry, taking 3 guns. Bradford's Brigade, which had been left in the morning to communicate with the 3rd & 7th Divisions, by a spirited movement of his own head, crossed a bridge & facilitated very much our progress. The 5th Division crossed at Gamarra and we all entered in parallel columns with the rest of the army in pursuit.

Once defeat became inevitable and with their line of retreat under threat, the French army disintegrated as they fled towards the Pyrenees, leaving all their accumulated ill-gotten gains from their years of ravaging Spain and Portugal. The British soldiers, not averse to a little plunder, took great delight in ransacking the hundreds of abandoned carriages left in their flight; many reputedly made their fortune that night. James became fully embroiled in this anarchic melee, but stuck to his duty, rescuing a number of fine ladies from a terrible fate.

I wish I could describe the confusion of the neighbourhood of Vitoria, here several hundred carriages with women *apeure* [frightened] and asking for assistance & protection on every side, there French prisoners to make themselves popular, handing out sacks of silver from the French treasure wagons, there cannon & tumbrils mixed with baggage of all description, the ground covered with arms which the fugitives had thrown away. I took a gallop to the right & seeing an officer getting out of his carriage, put a pistol to his breast & ordered him to surrender, which he did, dropping his hands. As I was getting my horse over a ditch which was between [us], he ran off, mounted a horse which an orderly was holding & galloped away. I pursued & hollered till some dragoons joined me; the French officer rallied some of his men & charged us, fired his pistol in my face, but they got the worst of it, but the blackguard escaped. I soon afterwards met Lord Wellington who was in the highest spirits possible, he said 'Well they have always abused me for want of trophies, I hope we have enough today. You have had hard work on the other side; By God Graham hit it admirably.'

Had the ground been of a nature that our cavalry might have acted, I believe nothing would have escaped, but the numerous woods in which were enemy infantry instantly checked our cavalry till infantry could come up & their columns throwing away arms had the start & speed of our men who had marched so far. Headquarters returned into Vitoria, we all lay together on the floor of a cottage having nothing to eat, for our baggage could not find us in the night. I am too partial to be able to express what I think of General Graham in today's action; the energy with which he pursued the plan he had the manliness to undertake was not more conspicuous than his perfect coolness the whole day. Had it been possible to have carried the bridge of Gamarra earlier, we might have taken more prisoners, but we might also have got into a scrape, for we should have had upon our hands, any number of the retiring army they chose to direct on us.

Longa's people had been engaged at Gamarra Menor; the Spaniards bivouacked close to Vitoria and assisted our *traineurs* [hangers on] to plunder the treasure & baggage. Everything was gone by daylight, valuable maps & pictures, books destroyed and I believe 2 millions of dollars plundered.[7]

22nd Spanish army & Longa moved on Mondragon in pursuit of some of the beaten army & against Foy who had evacuated Bilbao. The rest of the army moved on Salvatierra except the 6th Division. Clausel was within 3 leagues of Vitoria when he heard it was all over.[8]

It is worthwhile to look back at the steps which have led to this brilliant result & to see by what admirable combinations Lord Wellington effected this glorious victory. His first movement of the cavalry & army across the Duero; his gaining the Esla without their knowing it; his turning the Pisuerga, Carrion, Burgos, Pancorbo & the Ebro, the latter by roads which were believed to be impassable, are all admirable. He had already got the left column over the tremendous ground on the north of the Ebro where a small force could have checked us whilst the enemy were expecting us on the great road. It is sufficiently evident how much in the dark they were by the affair at Osma. His dispositions for the action & placing the left wing where it was are not less to be admired. The day before the action a man of the 5th Division deserted, a lawyer like clever fellow and he told exactly the situation of our column, of its strength, to General Rey.[9] When he mentioned it to Jourdan he said 'il ne faut pas croire tous les bêtises de ces gueux la' [we should not believe all the nonsense of these beggars]. This was told by Colonel Brice his A.D.C. who was taken by going up to *our hussars mistaking them for the French*. They say that the king was in person on the left & came in with Jourdan into Vitoria. The latter was giving some orders when the King cried out *'Que faut il faire actuellement monsieur le marechal?'* [What should I do now Marshal?] Some of the soldiers from a passing column answered *'Fini le camp mon roi'* [Quit the field my King].

General Maximilien Foy's force, numbering about 5,000 men, had been ordered by King Joseph to join him at Vitoria and he may well have swayed the outcome of the battle if he had attended to the order promptly. However, Foy not realizing the importance of his order, spread his troops out in various garrisons near the north coast. Spanish forces were to harry Foy, whilst Graham's troops tried to cut them off from France.

The 23rd the 1st Division, Pack's & Bradford's Brigades[10] were ordered over the Sierra de San Adrian, a mountain of very great height to fall on Foy if possible at Villa Franca, the cavalry & artillery were to join us by another road. The road we marched had been the old pavé but unused for a century was totally broken up & worse & steeper than any stairs; such a march I never saw. Our men had not reached their ground before midnight the night before and torrents of rain kept falling both the night & day. On the summit is a very extraordinary place of which this from memory may give an idea.

In the middle of the rock which cannot be less than 80 yards through is a large cavern, lighted from the top, on the one side capacious mangers on the other an inn with a small mill turned by a stream from the rock. From the one side the eye extends over the valley of the Ebro and on the one I have scratched on the view takes in almost to France.[11] It is the boundary of Biscay & on that side there are loop-holed gates which shut. The day was just calculated for such a scene; stormy & wild, heavy white clouds sometimes rested for a moment on the hill & then swept over in all the grandeur of a tempest and the singular effect of the column winding out of this hole detained me a long time. Many of the troops could not get over from fatigue & bivouacked on the summit, the Guards among others; this cave reminds me strongly of Gil Blas.[12]

Our headquarters in Segura, a nice town, the people were vastly astonished to see a column come this way, for it has only been used by smugglers for many years. We have been very well received lately except I hear in Vitoria which is quite French & Orduna worse. There are accounts of Foy's approach from Mondragon.

Foy ordered a convoy of stores to be abandoned, using the troops to hold an important junction until his now near 8,000 troops had passed safely. Graham with his corps arrived just as Foy approached the junction at Tolosa and he tried to sweep Maucune's covering force aside to attack Foy. Maucune however fought well and held Graham off until Foy had safely passed and then withdrew slowly, a rather unsatisfactory day for General Graham.

San Adrian.

On the 24th all the troops which could move, namely Pack, Bradford & Halkett's Brigades marched & just as we approached the high road we saw the French column going by. Bradford's Brigade was moved to head them [off] and we attacked. The French soon found they had to deal with Portuguese and instead of resisting only, drove Bradford off a very steep hill. However, the Germans pursued them sharply along the high road & we drove them out of Villa Franca where they left a great supply of bread &c which had been provided for them. We lost about 100 men & I suppose the enemy about the same. Had the physical force of our men enabled them to get on, I mean the British, we should have made a pretty example of this column, but the fatigues of the last few days have been excessive.

25th marched towards Tolosa, we found the enemy in the front & flanks of the town, well posted on some strong hills.

Bradford's Brigade was ordered to attack them & for several hours the skirmishing continued, the ground being often won by the Portuguese to be lost for want of connection in the wood. Both days however the French have managed their light troops beautifully, at last they entered the town, it was near dark & the general determined to dislodge them. The Germans were ordered

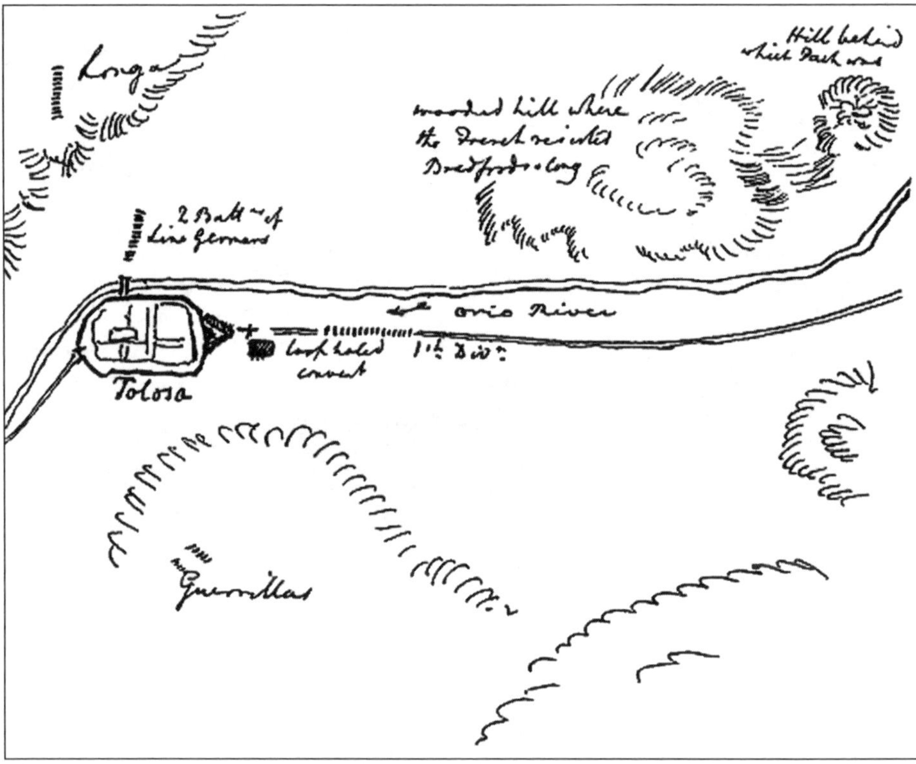

Tolosa.

to attack by the side of the bridge whilst we attacked in front. Tolosa is a walled town, with stockaded gates & barriers on the bridge & loopholed places for infantry, with a small gun over the gate they kept up a heavy fire on the road. General Graham received a severe contusion on his groin, fortunately the ball did not enter, a ball glanced from my shoulder.

The Germans attacked with uncommon gallantry the bridge, cut down the stockades & at the same moment we brought forward a gun & blew open the gates. The French got out of Tolosa as hard as they could but not without leaving some behind, they were of an Italian division & meant to have plundered the town that night, so we were admirably received in Tolosa. They ought to have defended such an exceedingly strong post & it is very extraordinary how we got it so cheaply we lost between 2 & 300 men.

29th 1st Division moved to Hernani, the Spaniards to Irun, the enemy have burnt the bridge. Lord Wellington is going to blockade Pamplona. Longa took the two forts at Pasajes by capitulation with 150 prisoners;[13] Battering train is ordered from Bilbao & preparations are making to besiege San Sebastian.

The people in Biscay as well as the scenery are perfect; the men robust, manly, open hearted people & the women though rather on a large scale are quite beautiful, their long hair hanging down in plaits quite to the ground and their costume is very becoming.

Some of the French officers' wives who were taken at Vitoria pass through on the way to France. General Thiebault's[14] wife told us a good story; he left a colonel in the carriage with her to protect her, soon after the action was turned in our favour, she saw people retiring & said 'mais mon dieu voyez no gens se retirent. Ah non madame ca va tres bien, laissez moi pour ca.' [But my God look at our people withdrawing. Oh no madam it is very well, let me assure you.] Presently more confusion & more troops passing 'mais vraiment nous sommes en danger, absolument la bataille est perdu.' [But we really are in danger, the battle is absolutely lost.] 'Mais madame vous n'etes pas militaire. tranquilles vous, cest un manoueuvre pour tout gagner' [But my lady you are not a soldier. Calm yourself, it is a manœuvre to win everything.] Soon after a charge of English cavalry occurred close by & balls flew about 'mais nous serons pris'. 'Ma foi je pense que oui'. [But we will be taken. Upon my word I think so too.] & so saying, leaped out of the carriage, mounted his horse & left her to her fate.

Sir Thomas Graham was now given the challenge of besieging the fortress of San Sebastian, whilst Wellington prepared the army for the invasion of France.

The French garrison at Getaria evacuate the town & retire into San Sebastian, the commandant executed before his departure one of the most cold-blooded & flagrant acts of treachery that ever disgraced a civilised nation. There was no enemy before the place & the French had lived 5 years in the town; from the guard house he made a mine under the square, placed bags of biscuit & wine over it, left a slow match burning and embarked. Luckily for the inhabitants, a party of guerillas came in & seeing the people taking the provisions, drove them away & left a guard there. In 9 hours after the mine exploded & destroyed about 40 people, he will be hanged when we take the place. Sir George Collier[15] tells me that at Castro [Urdiales] the Italian Division cut off women's breasts & impaled men on gun barrels, *which he & his officers saw*, besides other atrocities too horrible to be mentioned.

San Sebastian seems a strong place and has a castle to take after the town falls. We are to follow Marshal Berwick's[16] foot steps. 1st Division moved on the 5th of July to Oiartzun & the 5th [Division] reached Hernani, the 5th Division is to undertake the siege. The French possessed a convent on a hill (vide plan) which they had once evacuated, but which the Spaniards had foolishly not occupied. On the 14th we opened a battery of four 18 pounders against it with hot shot, but the falling timbers always extinguished the fire we created.

The French constructed a redoubt close to it; on the 17th we brought some field pieces opposite it on the other side of the river, which enfiladed the redoubt & the battery was employed in breaching the convent garden wall which protected the right flank of the redoubt. At 10 o'clock it was attacked by part of General Bradford's Brigade supported by part of General Hay's, whilst

> 3 companies of the 9th [Foot] were to get round by the convent to the breached wall. It was carried with the greatest gallantry but our people went too far (close up to the town) & suffered a good deal. The French then made a weak sortie which we repulsed with shrapnel & the commandant of Getaria received a severe wound of which he afterwards died; too good a death for such a villain!

During the early days of the siege, there was very good news personal for James; he was promoted a brevet major for Vitoria and was therefore appointed an Assistant Quarter Master General, but he remained busy with the siege works and his good luck was not to last long.

> Lord Wellington & the marshal [Beresford] have been at Hernani; they have given me through Lord Wellington's recommendation, my majority for Vitoria & he has appointed me Assistant Quarter Master General. All this time we were working away behind the sand hills at our batteries (as per plan) and on the 20th they opened. The breaching battery of ten 24 pounders at 550 yards from the wall, another of four 24 pounders a little on the right, some howitzers were mounted to enfilade the Mirador [Battery] but they were too far [away]. Our casualties as yet have been very trifling, poor Captain Dubourdieu[17] of the artillery was killed by a shell. The 1st part of the wall came down in sheets but the centre is very tough. On the 22nd the breach was declared practicable, but another breach was commenced on the right of the former. A summons was sent but refused admittance; 23rd a mortar battery opened in the rear of the sand hills.
>
> Attack fixed for the morning of the 24th but when the troops got down there, the houses were discovered to be on fire behind the breach & in consequence it was postponed, a mine had been formed up a drain, *Reid*[18] had found.
>
> On the 25th a little before daylight, the Royals[19] supported by General Hay's Brigade stormed. It was a fine thing to see the countenances of the men by the light of the burning houses. The French opened a murderous fire though they were rather confused at first by the explosion of the mine. The French showered shells on us, one of them stuck under the fascine Lord March,[20] Fletcher[21] & I were sitting on, it broke the small bone of his leg & gave us a good hoist. Meanwhile the Royals reached the top of the breach & found that by taking away the rubbish the French had made a fall of 15 feet. They were so mowed down with the enemy's fire that they rushed back into the trenches; others were pressing on & there was a great crowd. I stood up to wave them back saying the retreat was ordered, when I received a ball which broke my shoulder blade & lodged in my back. I was helped out of the trenches & was obliged to return to England to get cured & so ended my Spanish campaign.

James's wound was quite serious and he sailed home to recuperate, the ball being lodged too deep to remove and therefore causing continual discomfort. He was in England within the month and clearly well enough to write a letter to his good friend Richard Heber from Ryde on 25 August.

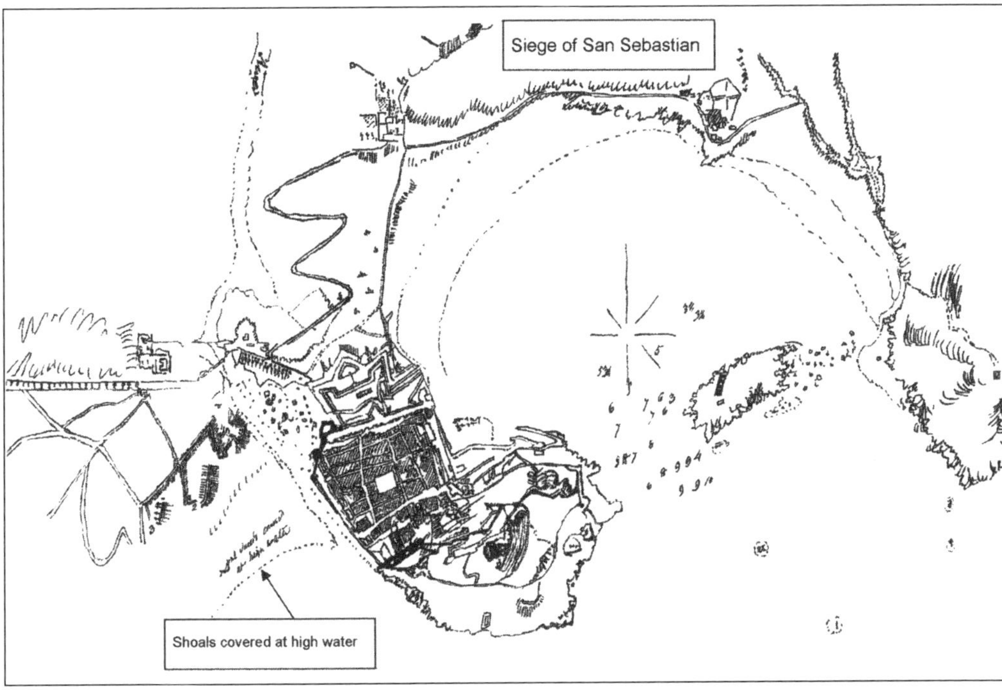

San Sebastian.

… Although you may regret that the papers are not black letter and printed by Aldus,[22] yet I know you still condescend to read them; you therefore may have seen that I was wounded and that I arrived in the *Parthian*[23] at Portsmouth. I meant to have proceeded to town where I should have met you probably before now but Lord Buckingham[24] dissuaded me from jumbling myself and brought me over here with him where I have his own surgeon to attend me, and every comfort. I am going on exceedingly well but the ball remains in my back under the shoulder blade where it probably will reside all my life without molestation. I shall not be any further service this campaign. Have very little pain and sound slumber of 10 hours …

He wrote again to Richard Heber a month later regarding his wound which showed little improvement.

St. James's Place, 28 September 1813

… I cannot tell you how I am, as who shall decide when doctors disagree. How I feel I am, which is as if I had a decayed tooth in my back; but I must have patience. All the surgeons previous to my coming to town thought that the ball would remain quiet and that the wound would heal. Here they foretell bone coming out, some say the ball, some say by one aperture formed by the ball and others by one which is to be formed by them …

Chapter 13

Holland

By the end of 1813 James still found his wound troublesome, but determined to join Sir Thomas Graham again. Following the successful capture of San Sebastian on 31 August 1813, Sir Thomas Graham had gained permission from Wellington to go home to recover his health as it seemed that age and long campaigns had been catching up on his frame. However, the government decided on an expedition to Holland to cooperate with the Russians and Prussians in ousting the French from the Low Countries and Sir Thomas Graham was cajoled into accepting the command of the British force. James joined Graham, now risen to the title of Lord Lynedoch, as AQMG again and resumed his daily journal in December 1813, the 'Journal of our operations in Holland from December 1813 to March 1814'.

Force employed

Brigade of Guards[1]	}	Major General Cooke[2]
2/37th	}	
44th	}	
55th	}	Major General Skerrett[3]
2/69th	}	
Veterans	}	
2/25th	}	
33rd	}	
54th	}	Major General Gibbs[4]
3/56th	}	
2/35th	}	
52nd detachment of	}	
73rd	}	Major General Mackenzie[5]
3/95th detachment of	}	
and the 2nd Hussars [KGL].	}	

We were afterwards joined by the 78th, the 21st, the Royals and 91st under Major General Gore,[6] with the 3rd Hussars and the corps was then divided into two divisions of which Major General Cooke commanded the 1st, composed of Major General Cooke's, Skerrett's and Gore's Brigades; and Major General Mackenzie the remainder.

December 8th. Lord Lynedoch and Staff leave town. Owing to a severe gale of wind the troops could not embark from Ramsgate or Deal till the 12th and on the 13th we sailed.

15th anchored at the Roompot where we found Admiral Young[7] with 11 sail of the line, from him we heard of the enemy having evacuated Breda and Willemstadt, which rendered our operation more easy by obtaining a base on which to rest them. It became however of the highest importance to move to the front and protect these places at least as much so as our small force would admit of, which if all united would not exceed 5,000 effective men, but some of the regiments did not arrive for some days, nor the cavalry or horses for the artillery for nearly a month afterwards.

General Cooke who had been previously sent to the Hague with the Guards, had detached a detachment under Lord Proby[8] to occupy Willemstadt and *Tholen*[9] and to the latter point the troops that arrived with us were directed. Colonel Graham[10] was sent to the Hague with confidential communications relative to the existing state of affairs.

On the 17th the ships moved up to Stavenisse and the troops disembarked; they were cantoned in the neighbourhood for the night,

General Graham went on to Tholen. On our arrival at Sint Maartensdijk, a bourg belonging to the Prince of Orange, we were met by several hundred women, each pair carrying a small triumphal arch of box covered with yellow ribbons. They begged the general to alight and walk through their arches in so pressing a manner that he could not refuse, but no sooner were we all well inside than *Burnham* wood did move, nor could we get out again till we have traversed every dirty street and arrived at the end of the town, not without being considerably incommoded by sheaves of box leaves being thrown upon us and into our faces.

At Tholen we found Lord Proby and Colonel Smyth[11] of the engineers, the latter in the morning had been into Bergen op Zoom with a flag of truce which I confess never appeared to me to answer any useful purpose.

Of course the governor would not listen to any terms, but said 'Il etait prêt pour se mesurer avec les braves Anglais' [He was ready to compete with the brave English]. A further reinforcement was thrown into Bergen op Zoom before daylight on the 18th which it is supposed made their force amount to between two and 3,000 men.

On the 18th the general made a reconnaissance of Bergen op Zoom, we had with us some of the Guards and some Russian hussars belonging to General Benkendorff's[12] corps who personally occupied Breda. I never saw cavalry better mounted or equipped, or indeed finer looking fellows. General Benkendorff had with him 1,200 infantry & 5000 cavalry, principally light troops. As much of our early movements depended on Breda, it is necessary to state the real situation of the place, the name of which is a tower of strength &

the possession of which in winter was a staff of straw. It is a city containing about 12,000 inhabitants with broad & high earth ramparts, not revetted, but on the contrary in almost all places, so sloping that a person might ride up them. In no part was it palisaded, having but few guns & no casements, with broad wet ditches & extensive unarmed & unoccupied outworks. Of course in a severe frost, the outworks so unarmed & unoccupied is a screen to the assailant and the frozen ditch is the best road to attack. To defend it systematically 15 to 18,000 men would be required & to hold it in frost against a coup de main, not less than 8,000 could render it *at all secure*.

When the French evacuated it they had no guns & but little provisions, but on General Benkendorff's entering it he applied to the Dutch government for both and above 50 guns & other '*materiel*' of war were sent. It was but just to suppose then, an officer who dedicates so much care to put his post in a state of defence, is prepared to defend it, we shall see the result.

On the 20th an A.D.C. of General Benkendorff arrived at Tholen giving an account of the French having moved a considerable corps towards Breda from Antwerp chiefly composed of the Imperial Guards & old troops under General Roguet[13] and asking General Graham to move down on the flank of the enemy. The force, small as it was originally intended, was not collected, for the 83rd, 56th, 25th & veterans had not arrived and no cavalry or artillery and the Russian cavalry which had been placed in our front from the beginning proved to us that though they could keep a good look out for themselves; they never considered for a moment that they were sent to cover our cantonments till our cavalry arrived & they several times retired from their posts in front of villages where our infantry were quartered of course in great security [being] so covered, without even sending them word of their retreat. Such protection therefore was not to be relied on; besides which Tholen, a point of great importance and in open weather being an island of considerable natural strength, which preserved our communication with the fleet & covered Zealand could not be abandoned and in the immediate front of Bergen op Zoom could not be occupied by less than 500 men. Willemstadt, the base on which we were to rest all our operations and where all our stores, artillery, troops etc were to land, could not be left without an adequate garrison. These valuable points being so covered, nothing was left for the field and it was therefore impossible for General Graham to listen to Benkendorff's request.

21st An A.D.C. of General Oppen's[14] from General Bulow[15] arrived, who mentioned that the latter occupied Bemmel, Geertruidenberg, Arnhem, Creve Cœur &c. He confirmed the account of the French being before Breda & going to bombard it. He seemed a very amiable man, said he was a man of some property in Westphalia 'et possedait une bonne femme et une bonne famille, mais que dans ces temps out tous des scavans combattaient ce n'etait pas pour lui a penser a soi' [And with a good wife and a good family, but in these times all the scholars were fighting, it was not for him to think of himself].

23rd Another officer arrived from General Benkendorff mentioning he was invested & bombarded. This was a Cossack d'Ordonnance with long lank hair and the most brutal manners, understanding no language but his own. I offered him a chair, he threw it over, a cigar, it went into the fire, schnapps (brandy) it went down his throat & he began to talk exceedingly but unfortunately nobody understood his language. I sent for a dried tongue for him & he pared it with patient attention and I began to hope we had a civilised man to deal with, but alas when I saw that he only pared the rind to select it as the best I gave all hope up, which was speedily confirmed by his taking off a bottle of claret, decanting it down his throat without drawing breath.

General Graham went to Willemstadt to see if any more troops had arrived which might put it in his power to move to assist General Benkendorff. In the meantime a patrol of infantry was ordered down to Roosendaal, who were to spread the report of the advance of 5,000 men & demand rations accordingly. Soon afterwards a patrol of French cavalry came in and on hearing this, returned with the greatest speed. Whether they really believed we were going to move down on their flank or that they found their bombardment ineffectual I know not but they retired from before Breda.

On the 24th the hereditary prince[16] arrived to press our assisting Breda for both Benkendorff & the Dutch government & even our own ambassador thought proper always to conceive that the British corps amounted to 10,000 men & calculated accordingly. Our other regiments which were expected, arrived at Willemstadt with the artillery on the 25th.

On the 25th the headquarters moved to Willemstadt and a general movement takes place to the left occupying Zevenbergen with General Gibbs & leaving the 44th under Colonel Carleton[17] at Tholen as our right. This put the corps more *a portéé* [scope] to assist Benkendorff.

James wrote to his mother explaining their movements since landing in Holland and how he was coping in the extremely cold weather.

Willemstad, 26 December 1813

My dear mother,

I wrote to you from the Roompot before we landed; we had then an intention of moving towards Helvoetsluys, but the news arriving of the evacuation of Breda & Willemstadt by the enemy, determined the general to land on Tholen. The rest of our corps arrived here & we are busily employed in getting in order. Had we been favoured by the winds instead of being so detained by them, we should have probably taken Bergen op Zoom, but the day before we approached it, the enemy threw in considerable reinforcements, which for the present render them secure. About 7,000 French moved on the 19th & invested Breda where General Benkendorff was with his corps, but on hearing of our intended movement or on suspecting it, they retreated again towards Antwerp.

We have today received the very welcome intelligence of the movement of the grand allied army towards Switzerland, on the 20th which country shows the best possible inclinations; the Canton of Berne in particular has re-established the old government under Monsieur de Stieger We have also reason to give credit to the report of the King of Naples having joined the allies[18] & General Neupberg being in command of his advance guard.

Accounts also arrived last night from the headquarters of General Benkendorff that an armistice had been agreed on between the Crown Prince & the King of Denmark.[19]

The people here are very willing & well disposed but not very energetic. The country is plentiful, but the roads execrable & the inhabitants should be web footed to live in such a bog.

The houses are not warm as many of the chimneys have been stopped to avoid paying taxes for them & little else is burnt but peat. The weather is not however very cold, but they promise us some bitter work in January.

I have never rode above thirty miles which does not fatigue one, my shoulder aches as usual, but I think I sleep better considerably than I did in England. I have got a gig which carries my baggage & which I can go in if I am ill & I have ordered a famous fur pelisse from the Hague so I shall be very comfortable. Remember I beg my affections to Sir J[oseph Banks] & the ladies & to Mahon & believe me ever affectionately yours JHS

27th an officer arrived from General Benkendorff with information of General Wintzingerode[20] being in march for Dusseldorf and of his being likely to be called on to join him, in which case it would be necessary for him to evacuate Breda. On this General Taylor[21] was sent to General Bulow's headquarters at Bemmel to urge his advance to save Breda.

On the 30th he returned & brought an account of some troops being already in motion; in the evening an officer arrived from Breda giving information of the French again advancing; their infantry however never came further than Hoogstraten.

On the 31st an officer arrived from Breda stating that General Benkendorff had received his orders & must evacuate Breda. The moment was critical, the frost had set in with severity, the French were near enough to take advantage of any movement & the Prussians could not arrive till the 5th.

James found time to send Richard Heber a long letter, explaining all that had happened to date; it would seem that they did not suffer at the general's table.

Near Willemstad, 1 January 1814

I have not had time to write to you before but I have commenced this huge folio sheet in order to make amends. You will have heard of our having landed at Tholen in consequence of the evacuation of Willemstadt[22] and Breda.[23] We made a reconnaissance on Bergen-op-Zoom the next day but a reinforcement had entered that morning (the 17th). Had the winds not detained us so long in England, I think we should have taken the place by a coup de main, as it [is] of immense size and had at one time but a thousand men in it of all sorts. That day is however gone by. On the 18th the French pushed a strong body supposed to be from 6 to 7,000 men to and invested Breda where (General Benkendorff was with 1,200 Russian infantry and 3,000 cavalry.

After amusing themselves with throwing some shot and shells into the town, they retired on the 21st in consequence we suppose of one of their regiments of hussars being nearly cut to pieces by a regiment of black Prussian hussars towards Tilburg. This occasioned us to draw ourselves more to the left to be *a portee* to move in support of Breda. A garrison has been left in Tholen. Steenbergen is evacuated and our right is at Willemstadt.

In consequence of orders from General Wintzingerode, General Benkendorff evacuates Breda tomorrow moving on Dusseldorf to which point the march of the former is directed. We, although not half equipped, weak in numbers and having a most extensive line to defend, nevertheless send a brigade[24] 'pour le moment' to keep the French out if possible though to one who has never seen these much boasted fortresses, it would be difficult to describe the weakness of these with a small garrison in time of frost. The magnitude of Breda is so great that 12,000 men at least should garrison it for a siege, and frost here is a kind of death to all sorts which levels alike all ranks of systems. From the scarcity of materials hardly any of these works are revetted, thus the slope of the ramparts is so great that one might ride up them and when the wet ditch is frozen over, the works are not so defensible as field entrenchments. Bergen op Zoom is an exception to this. If we can keep Breda for a few days, it will be safe, as Wintzingerode's movement protects Bulow's flank from Macdonald[25] and renders his army disposable. A corps of from 8 to 10,000 men which was blockading Wesel has already been relieved by the Russians and has joined his main body which is occupying the extensive line from Arnhem and Geertruidenberg. I hope therefore we shall be able to do something.

The allied armies moved towards Switzerland on the 20th which has shown the best spirit. Berne has replaced the old Government of 1802 under Monsieur de Stieger[26] but all this I suppose is old news.

You will expect something about the country. I wish I could send you a better account of it. I used to complain of the want of enthusiasm in Spain (I mean the self devotion which comes forward and becomes organised, not good will of which there is plenty both there and here) but the people here are dull and motionless as their canals. Till the Hereditary Prince came here a few days ago, the order for the levy en masse, circulated some days before at the Hague, never had arrived, and since he published it, nobody has been raised. The country is full of young men more than I ever saw in any country but with the exception of some cries of 'Orange boven', some orange ribbons which begin to fade and some triumphal arches which savour too strongly of French prefecture and old drilling to Napoleon's victories, no travellers would know there was such a thing as war, much less that their independence was at stake. They fear the Cossacks and pretty justly more than the French; of the latter I have seen a good many, but must leave the description of them to another time. The weather is very cold but the air is not so searching as in Spain. The hoar frost hangs like snow up on the trees and rarely can you see your neighbour for fog, but I smoke my segar [sic] and am not the worse for it.

My shoulder aches still but I ride 30 miles a day without fatigue and sleep certainly much better, still it remains to be tried how I stand winter operations. I have sent to the Hague for a warm fur pelisse. We have plenty of everything, Burgundy, Champagne, Claret and Curacoa for our friends and a place always for you (I can venture to say) at the general's table if you will come and look at us.

P.S. The fever at Cadiz has killed half my Cortes friends, but the best are still alive.[27]

January 3rd. The frost is broke which puts Breda, etc. in safety. 'On dit'[28] that the Cossacks have taken a French convoy [on route] from Antwerp to Bergen.

General Taylor was sent to General Benkendorff to urge his staying a little longer. He fixed the 2nd as the day of his departure, but promised to commence his movement by driving back the French at Hoogstraten and that he would leave two regiments of cavalry to cover us till ours arrived; but on the 2nd he moved straight off without leaving a man. Great as the risk was, under such critical & indeed imperious circumstances General Graham determined on throwing into Breda General Gibb's Brigade who moved in on the 2nd.

General Vanderplatt & 1,200 Dutch troops remained; the frost broke up for a few days, the Prussians began arriving on the 5th, General Bulow's headquarters on the 7th and Breda was preserved.

Had General Benkendorff left it as he found, without guns & provisions, no one would have feared the French returning to be caught in their own trap and all this unpleasant discussion would have been saved. But he was desirous of getting a name cheaply and to hand over his difficulties to our shoulders, who never had anything properly speaking to do with it. He is a proud, conceited man, more like a Frenchman than anything else, trenchant in his opinions & interfering with everybody else.

On the 7th our cavalry reached us; on the 9th I accompanied General Graham on a visit to General Bulow at Breda when a combined movement was determined on to drive back the enemy from Hoogstraten and if possible to cut them off from Antwerp and then to advance on that place with a view to any ulterior operations which might be found practical. Bulow's general dispositions were very able & detailed, mentioning everything which was to be done by every column in every situation except that of the enemy not being where he expected them. For on the 10th when the movement took place he found himself on the great chaussee as near to Antwerp as the enemy was & he had nothing to do but move on to effect his object; but however, such dispositions were not to be changed & he moved through cross roads to attack the front of the enemy and lost a good many men, the French retreating to Antwerp.

On the 10th the British were collected round Roosendaal and on the 11th at Kalmthout, the Prussian headquarters at Loenhout. At night some Prussian cavalry at Westmalle was surprised & suffered considerably. General Bulow expressing his wish to concentrate more previous to our advance on Antwerp, we made but a short movement on the 12th throwing forward one division to Kapellen & bringing the other from Nispen & Essen to Kalmthout.

I must not omit a characteristic trait of disinterestedness in General Graham who having the rank of full general was senior to Bulow, but in consequence of the latter having the largest corps, he expressed his determination of acceding to his general dispositions.

On the 13th[29] a general advance took place on Antwerp agreeably to a long & detailed order of General Bulow's. The left column of the Prussians under General Borstel[30] was to remain in reserve protecting their communications, whilst the right column under General Thumen[31] supported by the centre under General Oppen was to move along the chaussee on Merksem. We were to move by Ekeren on the flank of that village to assist General Thumen's attack. The 1st Division was left in reserve at Kapellen, Hoevenen, Wilmersdonk &c to watch Lillo.

A small force also had been left at Wouw to watch Bergen op Zoom. The 2nd Division advanced in two columns on Merksem, the left (composed of the 35th, 52nd, 78th & part of the 95th) were already approaching the village when an A.D.C. arrived from General Bulow reporting the village to be in our possession. On advancing a little near[er] several shots were fired at us from the village and the 95th began to return the fire. General Graham & his Staff rode up to our men with our hats off crying out to cease firing for they were the Prussians; we were saluted with a volley & began to think we had been mistaken. It would not have looked well to have retired, being so near. The general ordered the 78th to advance who dashed into the village and at the point of the bayonet soon cleared it, as from the narrow front the enemy could present, the disparity of numbers became of little importance.

The enemy had 1,500 men in the village by the report of the prisoners, principally old troops and the 78th did not muster 500 bayonets; our loss did not amount to above 40 men and the enemy left a general killed & a good many prisoners. As this was going on General Bulow sent to inform General Graham that the object of the reconnaissance being completed and all ulterior operations being impossible, he had determined to retire to protect his communications & protect Breda from Macdonald[32] who was still at Venlo. As soon as we were in full possession of the village General Graham galloped off to General Bulow and to inform of the circumstances in which we were placed thus, decoyed into a village within 900 yards of the glacis of the place garrisoned by 10,000 men and we never had 1,800 in the village and to cause him to wait at any rate till we could make a simultaneous retreat, but the Prussian columns were already in march. Our posts were maintained long enough to retire the wounded & towards the evening were quietly withdrawn and the same night the 2nd Division fell back to Kalmhout leaving the 1st Division as the rear guard.

This strange conduct was afterwards explained; the village of Merskem is long & straggling and General Thumen having taken a few houses reported the post was his, when on seeing our column, which he thought was a French one moving on his flank, he retired again. As we retired afterwards some Prussians of their rear guard mistook us again & had not Major Busche[33] of the 2nd Hussars rode up to them, they probably would have done us some mischief. The only advantages we derived from this trip was obtaining accurate information relative to Antwerp & etc from two Dutch officers, Colonel ____ & Captain Van Gorkum,[34] both engineers in the French service, who deserted from them during the bustle & brought an excellent plan with them. Certainly also the march benefited the young soldiers of which the corps was principally composed and the skirmish gave them confidence and encouragement. Considering the extraordinary severity of the weather our troops suffered but little and even after returning into tranquil cantonments continued healthy.

James wrote to his mother at Clarges Street, Mayfair, regarding the extreme cold and subsequent ice, which had caused him three heavy falls.

Kalmthout 14 January 1814

My dear mother,

We have been so much employed since the 10th in making a reconnaissance on Antwerp that I have not had time to write to you. Circumstances have prevented us from doing anything against the place at present & one of the most prominent reasons is the intensity of the cold which has nearly frozen up the Scheldt & of course renders night work & all military operations difficult & dangerous to the troops. Although we have not attempted any considerable operation, we have derived no small advantage from the trip, as from being within 1200 yards of the works of Antwerp, we have pretty well ascertained the strength of it & in having an opportunity afforded for some of our young troops licking the old ones of the enemy, those indeed who next to the Imperial Guard are counted their best troops. Nothing could exceed the gallantry of the 78th who chased nearly ½ a mile a French column of nearly five times their number, leaving the street covered with the killed & wounded of the enemy, a general was amongst the former.

I have had a good deal of fatigue but am not the worse for it; I have had three severe falls on the ice, which has hurt one of my knees, but which will be well in a few days, one occurred during the fire which gave rise to a report that I was wounded. We are going again into cantonments. Remember me most affectionately to Sir J B[anks] & ladies & believe me in haste, your most affectionate JH Stanhope.

I think I shall go to the Hague in a day or two, to see the lions[35] & amuse myself.

Headquarters were established on the 16th at Oudenbosch and the Guards were sent to Steenbergen & the 2nd Division were centred round Roosendaal; Bulow & the Prussians in Breda & environs.

An incident occurred during this movement as characteristic as it was creditable. As the 78th were advancing the piper began to play, he had scarcely squeezed his pipes when he received a ball which struck him to the ground, but the brave piper still continued his animating notes till the battalion had passed him.

Colonel Macleod[36] who commanded the 78th was early wounded; a beautiful setter which he had & which was slightly wounded at the very beginning, continued running about through the fire looking for its master till a second shot killed it.

James undertook a little tour to the Hague and was struck by the lack of hunger for war amongst the Dutch people to rid themselves of the French.

On the 18th I went on a little tour to the Hague which as far as kindness and hospitality went from the Royal family and society there was very agreeable, but really lamentable when I considered that no one seemed disposed to second with energy the exertions of the two princes, in organising & forming an army and in calling forth the resources of the country; and indeed with the exception of the moving arches at Sint Maartensdijk (which also savoured too much of French education to be quite according to our taste) any traveller might have supposed Holland to have been long buried in profound peace and in the secure possession of that independence which was to ensure them their beloved trade. To this every feeling yielded and whilst the Prussians indignantly exclaimed against those, by whom the state of Brandenburg had been so long observed & humbled, whilst the Austrians seek for atonement against those who so often insulted & spoiled their capital, whilst the Russians breathe nothing but vengeance for unprovoked outrage and whilst the Spaniards deeply feel & keenly avenge the untold horrors which those merciless destroyers have exercised over their land, the Dutch complain bitterly of the douainiers, the suppression of commerce & the diminished goodness & increased prices of sugar, coffee & tobacco. It is the theme of every circle & the burthen of every complaint.

As another movement was in contemplation against Antwerp, which was likely to take place immediately, I returned to headquarters on the 25th. The Duke of Saxe Weimar arrived as Supreme Chief of the Armies in the Netherlands.[37] His Saxon corps was detained by the ice on the Rhine and did not join the Prussian Army till the 10th of next month near Brussels. I do not think in the intermediate time that General Bulow much liked this general without an army. He paid a visit to General Graham accompanied by Prince Frederick of Orange[38] who bears a very high character for gallantry, conduct & amiability.

On the 30th we began our advance by the same roads as the previous one, our headquarters at Kalmthout.

31st General Bulow was anxious to extend his left and to throw General Borstel forward on Malines[39] & Brussels, in consequence of which he moved into the great road from Westmalle to Antwerp and our column took his place on the chaussee, our headquarters at Brecht. General Bulow here received orders to join the army of General Blucher,[40] but on General Taylor & Colonel Smyth going to him, he was persuaded to postpone his movement for a few days which would not at all affect any calculation that might have been entered into dependent on his arrival, for had the order reached him at Breda & his cantonments to the rear of it, several days must have elapsed previous to his being in the advanced position in which this order now found him placed.

1st of February. The Prussians were to move on Deurne by Wijnegem & Schoten, but not to attack that village till the next morning when we were to make a simultaneous movement on Merksem. This was General Bulow's own disposition in consequence of which we moved on Brasschaat towards the evening; when our troops were cantoned & cooking, an A.D.C. of General Bulow arrived, stating he was attacking Deurne and experienced a severe resistance and that he wished us to attack Merksem to distract their attention and forces. It was so late as to be impracticable, we however sent a strong patrol down the road to drive in the French pickets and alarm them. The French however continued in possession of part of Deurne all night and part of it was in flames. Our headquarters was at the foundry in the rear of Brasschaat.

2nd at daylight dispositions were made for the attack on Merksem, the 2nd Division under General Gibbs (General Mackenzie being confined by a severe fall he has experienced on the ice the night before, his horse coming down with him) was to attack, supported by the Guards. General Skerett's Brigade and the flank companies of the 21st moved by Denhorst[41] to take Merksem in flank on the left and General Taylor's Brigade of the 2nd Division was to turn it on the right towards the point of junction of the dyke of Sint Ferdinand. The road where the enemy had their picket was covered with large trees as abbatis, the post altogether might be considered as a very strong one, but the impetuosity of our troops aided a good deal by a thick shower of sleet & snow which fell at the moment, gave us possession of the village with comparatively trifling loss. We took from 150 to 200 prisoners and our loss did not much exceed 100 men; two guns also fell into our hands.

In an attempt to achieve something before the Prussian troops left, a heavy bombardment of Antwerp and the shipping there was commenced but achieved little permanent damage as the siege guns and rockets were ice bound.

The utmost activity was immediately shown by the engineers in forming their batteries and such was their exertions that at 3 o'clock the following day (the 3rd) the following batteries (marked in the sketch)[42] were opened at first with very good effect as we soon saw a large blaze in the arsenal but the enemy succeeded in extinguishing the flames.

The firing was renewed on the 4th & kept up during the 5th with great spirit but unfortunately without producing the desired effect. On the 4th General Bulow informed General Graham of his being obliged to advance and that he could not stay beyond the 6th, we therefore retired our heavy ordnance during the night of the 5th and moved off at sunset on the 6th without molestation. We lost but few men from casualties although the heavy fire that the enemy kept up from an enfilading battery as well as from the dyke & the quantity of vertical fire which proceeded from the town seemed to promise great loss. One shell fell into a house filled with our men & killed & wounded 17 & another took off the legs of two officers who were walking together, a third one who was between them escaping unhurt.

Our failure rose from not having a sufficient weight of vertical fire to keep the enemy from extinguishing the flames we kindled; our battering train was frozen at the embouncher [mouth] of the Scheldt & could not be landed & the ship with the rockets was wind bound at Harwich. We were therefore obliged to collect whatever guns could be found in Holland and they were bad in quality and inadequate in number. Several of the guns burst & the mortars never carried with a correct range with the exception of three napoleons & they had but few shells belonging to them.

Immediately after the abandoning of the bombardment of Antwerp, James wrote accounts to his mother and Richard Heber, but perhaps understandably exaggerated the damage caused to Antwerp.

Merksem, 6 February 1814

My dear mother,

I have not written to you since the middle of last month as either my person has been so employed in our operations or my mind so painfully affected with the sad accounts of poor Lucy's health, that I have not been able to write. I got very bad accounts yesterday as late as the 23rd which make me very anxious.[43]

You will see by the dispatches whenever they arrive what we have been doing here; although from the preparations for extinguishing the fires & from the number of men the enemy have at their disposal, we have failed in burning their fleet, yet I do think that after throwing about 2,000 shells at it, with excellent range among which were 400 [rounds] of the immense Napoleons, their ships cannot remain in a very good state. We set different parts of the arsenal repeatedly on fire but they always extinguished the flames. I think we must have caused them a great loss in men, our attack of this village on the 2nd was beautiful, our troops cheering & behaving like veterans. We took near 300 prisoners and although the French have peppered us most considerably with shot & shell these last 3 days, I do not think we have lost (including the attack of the village) above 200 men.

Show this letter to Sir J Banks, he will like to hear the result to whom I request to be affectionately remembered. I am very well, fatigue only does me good. Believe me my dear mother, ever affectionately yours James Hamilton Stanhope.

Merksem, 6 February 1814

Since I wrote last I went to the Hague from whence I was suddenly recalled by the preparations for the attempt against the enemy's fleet at Antwerp. On the first we arrived at this village and the Prussians near Deurne pushing one division on Lier[44] and Malines. The Prussians (contrary to the General's disposition) attacked Deurne the same evening and experienced a considerable loss, not taking the whole of it till next day. On the morning of the 2nd we attacked the village which in spite of all the abbatis they had made and the opposition of above a 1,000 men strongly posted, was soon carried by the impetuosity of our troops who behaved to admiration. So great were the exertions that were used in the formation of our batteries (animated by knowing that Bulow had received orders to move towards Wintzingerode[45] and would leave us today) that we opened 24 pieces of heavy ordnance principally vertical fire among which were 3 huge Napoleon mortars at 3 o'clock on the 3rd. During that evening, the 4th and 5th we threw at and mostly into the basin above 2,000 shells and 400 of the large ones. We frequently occasioned flames to burst out in different parts, but the enemy always succeeded in extinguishing them, still the mischief we have done there must have been very great. Our loss was not considerable not exceeding I think 200 men. Our heavy guns were removed last night and we retire today to take up positions communicating with the Prussians and protecting Willemstadt and Breda. I think our campaigns are nearly over. Probably by this time the fate of Bonaparte is decided.[46] I think I shall return to England (in case of peace) before I go to Italy, as Hester does not seem certain what she means to do. I have received highly interesting letters from her of 15th July from Latikia.[47] She is quite well and delighted with the people their character, kindness and even her own dangers.

On the 5th General Borstel entered Brussels and General Bulow on the 8th. The morning of the 7th some of the country people went to remove the sandbags from our evacuated batteries & the enemy thinking we were working in them opened a heavy fire to the great discomposure of the boors.

On the 8th our headquarters were at Brecht; on the 10th the 1st Division moved round Roosendaal, General Taylor's Brigade of the 2nd Division at Loenhout and Wuustwezel, the remainder of the division at Groot Zundert & environs; headquarters Groot Zundert.

As campaigning was temporarily at a halt, James received permission to tour Belgium and found the people far superior to the Dutch.

On the 15th I asked leave for a few days to see Brussels; between Lier & Malines I saw the first hill since I have been in the Low Countries. As one goes on the country greatly improves and a number of pretty country houses are scattered over a picturesque (at least comparatively so with Holland) and fertile country, the roads excellent & kept in the best preservation from all intercourse being prohibited during the beginning of a thaw. The towns are clean & well built and the people were intelligent and altogether superior in body & mind to the heavy cold blooded boors of Holland; for even their virtue of cleanliness becomes a vice and a Dutch woman is but a broom which is always dirty itself in keeping the house clean and I believe a muddied officer indoors was more dreaded than a French army without.

Brussels has been so often described for me to say much of it. There is a gallery of fine paintings by celebrated masters but as they have been collected principally from suppressed convents, they generally represent the disgusting scenes of the martyrdom of their respective saints; among them a St Francis protecting the world from the indignation of the Almighty, whilst the virgin is interceding by his side is the finest to my taste. The painted glass, a fine carving of the pulpit in the cathedral are well worthy of notice. The steeple of l'Hotel de Ville is renowned for lightness and elegance. Mr Van der Boght Sauvage was very civil as a cicerone.

On the 17th there was a review of the Saxon troops; their Guards commanded by Prince Bernhard of Weimar,[48] were the finest body of men I ever saw and which no country can have without sacrificing a great deal to show.

On the 18th the Duke of Saxe Weimar sent for me and communicated to me his orders to join the Grand Army, this by withdrawing his force at Lier, disconnected the British corps entirely & left its flank en air. Immediately went to General Graham detailing the conversation and on the 20th at 2 in the morning I received his orders to proceed to the headquarters of the Crown Prince's headquarters [sic] with a letter from him, referring H.R.H. to me for information about the situation of the corps and expressing a wish to be reinforced (on the 19th I rode through the Forest of Soigne which is superb and there is in the museum a flank cut from a white oak which grew in that forest, no less than 97 feet long & 5 broad at one end and two and ½ at the other.

On the 20th started for Liege through Leuven, Tirlemont,[49] Sint Truiden &c; the former is very ancient and the Hotel de Ville is curious. Near Tirlemont is the field of battle of Neerwinden which has been so often drenched with blood.[50] I arrived at Liege about 11 at night and found the Crown Prince had been expected some days but was certainly to arrive next day.

The 21st at a very early hour the municipality were gaily dressed and mounted to meet Bernadotte,[51] all the cooks were in requisition and all preparations made for a general illumination. At 3 o'clock, hearing nothing of him, the maire consented to give me horses to proceed. I reached Aix la Chapelle[52] at midnight & found the preparations had been made every day for some time past and the town was illuminated, but no Crown Prince arrived, but they were quite sure he would be early next day.

James finally caught up with Bernadotte, the Crown Prince of Sweden, at Cologne and had a very long and detailed discussion regarding the war, which James recorded immediately after his interview.

Next morning, 22nd, hearing nothing of him I proceeded to Cologne which I reached at 7 in the evening. I immediately waited on the Crown Prince with whom I had a very interesting conversation which I am enabled to state accurately having taken memoranda of it on leaving him. On being shown into a room where the prince was in conversation with another officer, I delivered him the letter, saying in French 'Your Royal Highness is perhaps already acquainted with the intended advance of the Duke of Saxe Weimar'. The prince said he was. 'Vous venez donc me demander des renforts. J'aurais le plus grand plaisir en les envoyant au General Graham qui est un homme trop estimable, trop Europie.' [You come and ask for reinforcements. I would have the greatest pleasure in sending them to General Graham who is a man too esteemed, too European] (I stared) 'Vous me comprenez qu'il est trop bien connu en Europe que son charactere doit perdre faute des moyens. Je lui enverrais le corps du General Walmoden que est déjà sous la solde de l'Angleterre' [You understand me it is too well known in Europe that he has lost his character for lack of means. I will send him the corps of General Wallmoden[53] which is already in the pay of England].

I then brought forward the subject which was of the greatest importance and which had not been mentioned to any of the other commanders, the probability of the British corps being entirely withdrawn. This led me into the detail of the intended force which was promised, the failure of the militia bill on which those 'hopes' were grounded, the smallness of our corps at present, the extent of our cantonments, the necessity of keeping Tholen & South Beveland to have an eye on Flushing, the considerable numbers of the enemy opposed to us in Antwerp & Bergen op Zoom, the necessity of reinforcing Lord Wellington's army and the inadequacy of the means without breaking up the British corps, which was therefore in the contemplation of our government.[54] I then stated the anxiety which General Graham felt to get hold of Bergen op Zoom as it would facilitate our operations on the other side of the Scheldt, but that he had not a force sufficient to cover and besiege it. The Prince said 'How do you mean to take it, you cannot escalade it?'

I answered that from the small number and bad quality of the garrison, one might hope they might surrender after some days of open trenches.

The prince said 'Have the Dutch no troops? Why does not General Graham apply for some of them?' I answered that they could not be calculated on being few in number and indifferent in quality. The prince repeated his expressions of regard for Sir Thomas Graham & said that had he been pressed he would have sent him a corps besides. I asked him if he had heard of the taking of Soissons by General Wintzingerode and read the account to him. He expressed his approbation of that general having followed *his directions* (which I suspect to be a fetch). On my stating the account of Yorck & Sacken[55] having been beaten, the prince seemed deeply hurt & said 'Y tout comptant nous avons efraye un revers, mais vous autres qui ont sauve l'Espagne ont quelquefois aussi ete obliges de vous retirer, ainsi il ne faut pas desesperer' [All in all we have suffered a reverse, but you who have saved Spain have also sometimes been forced to withdraw, and we must not despair] (raising his voice and becoming very animated 'Mais savez vous monsieur qu'on c'est avance sans ordre y sans methode, bien qu'on pouvait arriver a Paris ca n'etait pas tout. Je leur ai bien dit tout cela et si ils avaient voulu me croire nous aurions a present 250,000 hommes ensemble en bataille range ou devait etre ainsi dans la France toujours, et marcher lentement' [You know Sir, that we have advanced without order nor method, although it is better to arrive in Paris rather than not at all. I have said all this and if they wanted to believe me we would have present 250,000 men together in battle order and would thus have been in France forever and marched quietly].

The prince then went into considerable details about the difference between France & Germany relative to military operations. The want of horses in the former for the artillery etc. he resumed 'Je vois que l'armee allie *se fonde!* Surtout ou aura du eviter un echec ou aura du envoyer des gens dans tous les departmantes pour preparer les esprits et dire. Nous voulons la paix, nous sommes memes plus fatigues de la guerre que la France, mais nous voulons abattre un mechant homme que vous a fait tous malheureux. Nous voudrions etre chez nous revoir nos peres, nos femmes, nos enfants nos Penates. Mais croyez moi, Monsieur Bonaparte *souleve la nation* ou est entre avec le voile a le pillage (qu'on ne peut eviter avec les grandes armees) en recevant un echec vous lui donnez 50,000 hommes de plus et ou sommes nous? Le General Bulow est entre les places fortes, nous n'en avons pas une.' [I see that the allied army certainly diminishes and should avoid a failure or will have to send people into all the departments to prepare the minds and say 'We want peace, we are even more tired of the war than France, but we want to destroy this bad man who has made you very unhappy. We would like to be back with our fathers, our wives, our children our fires'. But believe me, Mr. Bonaparte *raises the nation* or is busy with rape and looting (which cannot be avoided with large armies) while receiving a failure you give him 50,000 men extra men and where are we? General Bulow is between the fortresses, we don't have any.]

(*turning to the officer*) 'Il faut absolument avoir Mastricht. Ou est notre pont? Pas un Le Rhin clarie ses glaces, ou passez? Comment passer? Impossible! Si l'armee allie etrait vraiment battu tous les departments se soulevront sur leur derrieres et ils seront obliges de metre bas les armes. Je ne dis pas que cela doit arriver mais je montre les effets des mauvaises combinaisons'. [We must have Mastricht. Where is our bridge? Not one, the Rhine clears ice, where can we pass? How can we pass? Impossible! If the allied army was really beaten all the departments will rise at their back and they will be forced to lay down their arms. I am not saying that this has to happen but I just show the consequences of bad combinations].

I had stated that Bonaparte had brought his whole force against Blucher and in reference to this, the prince said 'Je ne pense pas que Bonaparte a porte tout son monde sur York et Sachen. Ne serait il pas un erreur impardonable dans le Marechal Prince Schwarzenberg de lui permettre de faire ces manoeuvres on peut toujours gagner une marche en laissant de la cavalrie et les postes avances ou ils etaient. Mais le lendemain ou avec une demonstration ou avec les cefions on decouvre cela et on se met en poursuite. Mais le crisis est venu.' [I do not think Bonaparte focuses all his world on Sacken & Yorck. I would find it to be a mistake in Marshal Prince Schwarzenberg[56] to allow him to make these manoeuvres, one can always win a march by leaving the cavalry and pickets where they are. But the next day either with a demonstration or small probing attacks they discover this and begin a pursuit. But the crisis has already come.]

I said 'Peut etre mon seigneur qu'il est déjàpassé, comme les conferences ont eu lieu'. [Maybe my lord it is already past, the conferences have been held.]

The prince answered 'Mais il n'y a rien que je crains comme la paix, quoi? Permettre cet ambitieux se remettre en force. Quoique en lui tranchant la Belgique ou lui laissera moins fort, mais on devait le detruire et si la guerre continue il est perdu. Je vous repete la consideration que j'ai pour votre General'. [But there is nothing I fear as much as peace, Why? It will enable that ambitious man to regain strength. Either by slicing through Belgium and leaving him less strong, but they must destroy him, and if the war continues he is lost. I repeat to you the respect I have for your general.]

The prince then asked me to dinner, next day I took my leave.

23rd early the major of De Roll's Regiment[57] arrived with the details of the late battles in which Blucher had suffered severely.

At two o'clock I accompanied Mr Thornton[58] & the major to the palace. The Crown Prince talked a good deal about the state of the war nearly in the same style as the day before and speaking of Bonaparte allowing his sick to die at Mayence unattended (one of the circumstances this major mentioned) he said 'Grand Dieu. Quells malheurs cet homme a produit a la France. Il a demoralize l'Europe qui resentira pour 50 ans les effets du corruption qu'il a introduit. Il faut trouver des gouvernements bien sages pour remedier les abus du siècle. La Dannemarc ne peut etre de longue duree si on n'en travaille pas.' [Great God. What a shame this man has produced for France. The demoralizing wind will blow through Europe for 50 years the effects of the corruption he has introduced. We have to find wise governments to remedy the abuses of this century. Denmark could be long term if we do not work] (and this he said at the very time when he was about to take a very large slice from that country) 'Quand on a l'habitude de la luxe, de la bonne chere, de la medisance et pour tout dire de la delation on est long temps a s'en purifier.' [Or when used to the luxury of a good friend, the gossip and all the informers say we are a long time to be purified].

He then returned to the faults of the allies in making unconnected movements and said 'Si Lord Wellington avoit fuit comme cela il aura perdu l'Espagne.' [If Lord Wellington flees like that he will lose Spain.]

He then said that but for his advice to Blucher before the Battle of Leipzig to concentrate, he would have been destroyed 'L'art de la guerre contre cet homme (Bonaparte) consiste dans l'ordre mince dans la poursuite mais restez seulement 24 heures en position et vous devez rapprocher le droite du centre' [The art of war against the man (Bonaparte) is fine order in pursuit, but for only 24 hours remain in position and you must bring the right into the centre] (bringing his right hand in on his chest) 'et mettre la gauche en reserve' [and the left in reserve] (putting his left hand behind him and so remaining like a teapot) 'si non il vous detruira car il a l'habitude des grandes mouvements rapides. Les principles de la guerre sont simples, a la droite' [If not he will destroy you because he is used to large rapid movements. The principles of war are simple, to the right] (acting it all the time) 'a la gauche, en avant en arriere, mais c'est l'affaire d'un general, savoir bien les combiner.' [The left, forward and backward, but it is the business of a general to know how to combine.]

I dined with the prince; the dinner lasted a considerable time, no general conversation ensued but everyone talked with his neighbour. Admiral Gyllenskold[59] (who is said to be very much in the Prince's confidence sat by me) and seems very much pleased with him. He had been very much prejudiced against Sir John Moore by Mr Canning[60] & he said *that from him also* he had been told that Sir John 'Etait toujours un homme impracticable' [Always was an impracticable man] and that in 1807 in a fit of disgust he brought home the expedition from Sicily; having been with that force at the time I found no difficulty in vindicating him from this charge; though it is hardly possible to imagine such a false and base accusation from such a quarter when detection was most certain & Admiral Gyllenskold affirmed it to be so.

After dinner the prince retired into his closet and sent for Mr Thornton & me. He gave me the answer saying that he did not express himself in detail about the reinforcements, leaving me to state & Count Wallmoden would immediately receive orders to march on Holland. Some conversation ensued as to the best point on which to direct them, as to the rank of General Graham & him. On my expressing to him General Graham's regret at not being able to pay personally his respects to him, he said 'Mais mon dieu, cela est impossible. J'irais le plus grand plaisir d'exprimer de bouche les sentimens que j'ai le General Graham non seulement quant au rapport de sa gloire militaire non comme Anglais mais comme Europeen, mais pour ses qualites personelles. Dites lui, je vous prie, que j'irai avec plaisir dix lieues pour rencontrer le digne second de Lord Wellington, voila des bons generaux. Si Lord Wellington etait a la tete des armees allies, Bonaparte serait perdu sans remede, mais j'espere que quatre mois plus tot, ou quatre mois plus tard l'Europe sera sauve, ce sont vous autres en Espagne que l'ont sauves, au moins qu'ici avec quelque bêtise on ne perd le jeu'. [But my God, this is impossible. I would go with the greatest pleasure to the mouth of experience, to utter the sentiments I have for General Graham, not only because of his military glory, not so much as an Englishman but as a European, and for his personal qualities. Tell him, I pray you, that I'll go with pleasure ten leagues to meet the dignified second in command of Lord

Wellington; here we have good generals. If Lord Wellington had been the head of the allied armies, Bonaparte would have been lost without recourse, but I hope that four months earlier or four months later Europe will be saved. It is you people in Spain that were saved, at least here with some stupidity we do not lose the game.]

The Prince then spoke a good deal of his wish to be early informed in the event of our being withdrawn and wished me a good journey.

The impression I derived from what I saw & heard of the Crown Prince is on the whole favourable, that he is penetrating & impenetrable everything proves, for however he may be suspected of interested views towards France, he has never given any just handle for such a charge. I should denominate him a good actor who will act well whatever part may be allotted to him and who will leave an advantageous or unfavourable impression on the mind according to the intrinsic merits or faults of the part which ambition or interests calls on him to perform.

He has been much abused for remaining so long in the north instead of joining the allies on the Rhine; another question arises here, how far the plan adopted by the allies of moving round by Switzerland was conformable to military principles and the peculiar circumstances of the times. If credit can be given to the accounts I everywhere heard of the dismantled or unprovided state of the French fortresses and the disorganised & helpless state of their army after they crossed the Rhine, there can exist but little doubt that a direct & rapid movement across the Rhine would have given the allies Presque sans coup ferir [almost without a fight] the iron barrier of the Netherlands at least and perhaps with a battle Paris, and that their not doing it is more justly to be charged on their own indecision or what is more probable to political circumstances & want of cordial union in the views of the 3 sovereigns than to the non cooperation of the Crown Prince.

With respect to his movement on Denmark, it is not fair to censure it only because it was advantageous to his own interests, but it should first be fairly examined whether that movement abstracted from his own peculiar interests was not pre-eminently useful nay absolutely necessary to the interests of the general cause. We should consider this question in two points of view.

1st what was the cooperation which the allied armies did receive from the Crown Prince & secondly, what assistance they could have received had he acted otherwise.

2nd. The corps of General Bulow part of the Crown Prince's army it is well known was the cause of the evacuation of Holland by the enemy and that corps together with General Wintzingerode's, Woronzov's[61] &c amounting to above 40,000 men, joined Marshal Blucher at the critical moment after his severe check and enabled him to pursue that course which has been since crowned with such glorious & merited success. Therefore, this large part of the Crown

Prince's army entered Paris with the rest of the allies. Exclusive of this, the Saxon corps of the Duke of Saxe Weimar & Thielmann[62] were employed in protecting the communications of the grand army & in keeping garrisons in check. Therefore here again the Crown Prince's releases a certain number of other troops from those duties. Count Walmoden's corps was reforming in Hanover & the Danes were in march; the only force remaining with the Crown Prince when I was at Cologne were the Swedes & I can affirm that in the state of the river at that time, had the salvation of Europe depended on it, not a man could have crossed.

I do not mean to defend the Crown Prince's keeping the Swedes out of fire. The Battle of Dennewitz[63] etc are glaring proofs to the contrary & the voice of his own army attests the facts of an improper & degrading preference being shown to his own troops. Reviewing therefore the question we find that notwithstanding the diversion of the Crown Prince's army against Denmark, that the greatest part of it was present at Paris. It is indeed true that their being so was not owing to him, but that does not weaken the force of my argument that to him was due their being so disposable; by whom disposed is another question.

Now let us suppose that he had pursued his march with the allies and left Davout & the Danes to execute their own plans.

Davout's force reckoned at	30,000 men
The Danes then organised	20,000 men

which is not much to calculate the force of a nation at, for an object at their gates when they can send 10,000 as an auxiliary force for a remote and unpopular one.

The garrison of Magdeburg	16,000
The garrison of Wittenberg	5,000
The garrison of Torgau	6,000
The garrison of Dresden amounted To 22,000 of which suppose	
16,000 effective	16,000
	93,000

here then was a force of 90,000 men left in the rear of the allied armies, besides counting the resources which French activity and genius might have called out & organised under the captivating plea of self preservation; there would have been no reason for Davout not to have united his force with the garrison and to have raised the siege of Dresden and then have operated on the communications of the allies. A powerful testimony may also be brought in favour of the Crown Prince in Lord Wellington's opinion which was communicated in a letter to Sydenham, a copy of which I saw saying that the Crown Prince in a military point of view could have done nothing else than what he did do.

At Cologne I heard an anecdote illustrative of the high opinion the Crown Prince entertained of Lord Wellington. The Emperor of Russia had sent the former a plan of the campaign on which he was requested to comment. The prince in his answer adduced many reasons against leaving the fortresses of Germany detached in their rear adding that he mainly founded his opinion on the practise of the greatest general of the day who before he advanced into Spain took Ciudad Rodrigo & Badajoz & before he invaded France obtained possession of San Sebastian and Pamplona.

On the 26th I reached headquarters at Groot Zundert; in travelling through a country with the rapidity I did, it is difficult to form any just conclusion as to its state of suffering, however I could not help remarking that the country looked very richly cultivated especially between Brussels & Aix la Chapelle, but that the towns apparently had suffered in all of which great numbers of houses were empty. From what enquiries I could make, the price of labour did not appear to me to bear as high a proportion to the price of provisions as it does in England; wages at Liege were next to nothing.

The country people complained much of the Russians, but much more of the French. One man said that the Russians were like a flock of locusts but that the French were like the deserts themselves. At Aix la Chapelle I was told that a person living near the town who had lost two out of three sons in the war and whose remaining one was called for, the exemption being taken off and confined to the only son of a widow, put an end to his existence in order to save his last child by placing him in the exempted situation. Bitter and deep must be the misery which produces such fruits as these.

After he returned to headquarters, things remained very quiet and we do not hear from James until the excitement of the surprise attack on Bergen op Zoom and its ignominious failure. James was intimately involved in the organization of the attack and subsequently played a very significant role in the negotiations that followed and has therefore much of interest to say.

Nothing occurred worth mentioning till the attack on Bergen op Zoom which took place on the 8th of March and it is necessary to give some account of the place and the reasons which dictated the attempt before I relate the causes of its failure. Bergen op Zoom should be garrisoned by 10 or 12,000 men & had but 3,000, consequently the outworks could not be occupied and of course when abandoned they become a screen to the assailants not a defence to the attacked.

The weakest part of the fortification against a siege, where the ditches were deep & the scarp high from the water in them being very low, became the strongest against an escalade during a frost, but in the impenetrable front towards Antwerp, when the ditches were frozen, they formed an easy road protected from the fire of the place by the unoccupied outworks. The scarp of the inmost enceinte was principally *gazon*[64] & therefore easily mounted. It was therefore hoped that the enemy would not expect an escalade on the reputed strong side and the governor afterwards confessed to me that though apprised of our intended attack the day before, he never dreamed of our coming in that quarter. Much confidence also was placed on the bad discipline & small numbers of the garrison and in this only were our expectations deceived as no troops could have behaved better, though the governor told me afterwards that he had formed them out of mere conscripts some months before.

The escalade of Begen op Zoom had often been proposed to General Graham who uniformly resisted making an attempt where there was no alternative but to take or to be taken. But circumstances changed, the allied armies made a great retrograde movement and everything tended to encourage the belief that the French might again return in force to the frontiers of Holland and at this critical moment it was that General Graham received instructions from Lord Bathurst to embark 4,000 men of the line for America whenever the transports should arrive and the Guards for Lord Wellington's army immediately afterwards. Leaving Bergen op Zoom in the possession of the enemy and withdrawing the covering army, Holland was at any moment in the power of an invading army for the right flank on the Scheldt being thus open, Breda (formidable in the summer) Bois le Duc, Gorkum etc became of comparatively small importance but gaining Bergen op Zoom the line of hostile fortifications from Antwerp to Flushing is broken, our naval cooperation brought into the scale & in short on the occupation *depended the existence of Holland*, supposing that we had been withdrawn & the allies had retreated *one of which was certain* & the other but too probable.

When once determined on, General Graham lost no time in carrying it into execution as the continuance of the frost was very precarious and the garrison would probably get intelligence of the movements of the troops. The 1st Division was ordered to move towards Bergen op Zoom on the morning of the 8th and the 2nd [Division] was to look out on Antwerp. The former was divided into four columns; 3 of which (A, B, C) were to be real and the other (D) a false attack; they were as follows.

A.

44th	300 men	} Colonel Carleton
Flank Company 21st	200 men	} though General
Flank company 37th		} Gore & Skerrett
Royals	600 men	} accompanied it.

Charles's epaulettes and spurs.

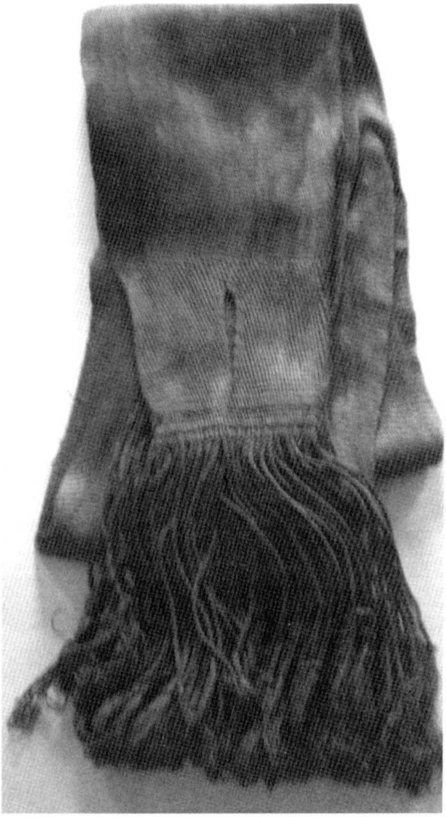

Charles's bloodstained sash.

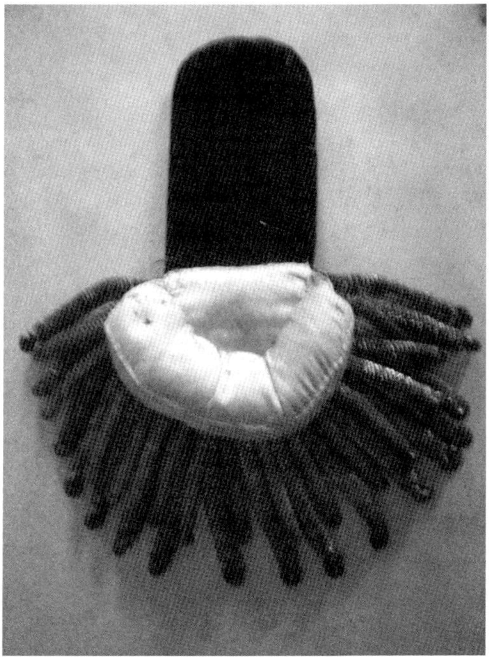

Charles's wing.

Spanish coins from Charles's pockets and links.

Memorial to Charles, Chevening Church.

Sir John Moore.

Death of Moore.

James Stanhope and signature.

Frederica Murray miniature.

James Stanhope miniature.

Hester Stanhope.

Charles Stanhope,
3rd Earl.

Citizen Stanhope,
a cartoon.

William Pitt
the Younger.

William Pitt's writing case.

St Botolph's Church.

Kenwood House.

General O'Donoju.

General Sir
Thomas Graham.

Capture of Paget.

Baron
Wintzingerode.

North entrance, San Adrian tunnel.

San Sebastian, a model.

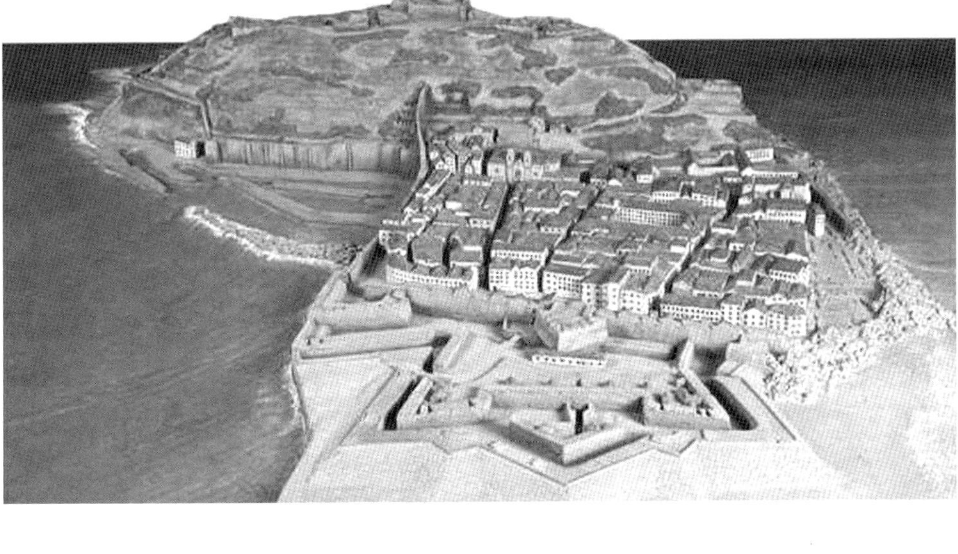

Battle of Waterloo by Sadler.

Guards on the March 1815.

Bois de Boulogne

James's Waterloo Medal.

Wellington's telescope.

Ring of the Wellington Tree.

Chevening House.

Frederica's tomb.

James's inscription.

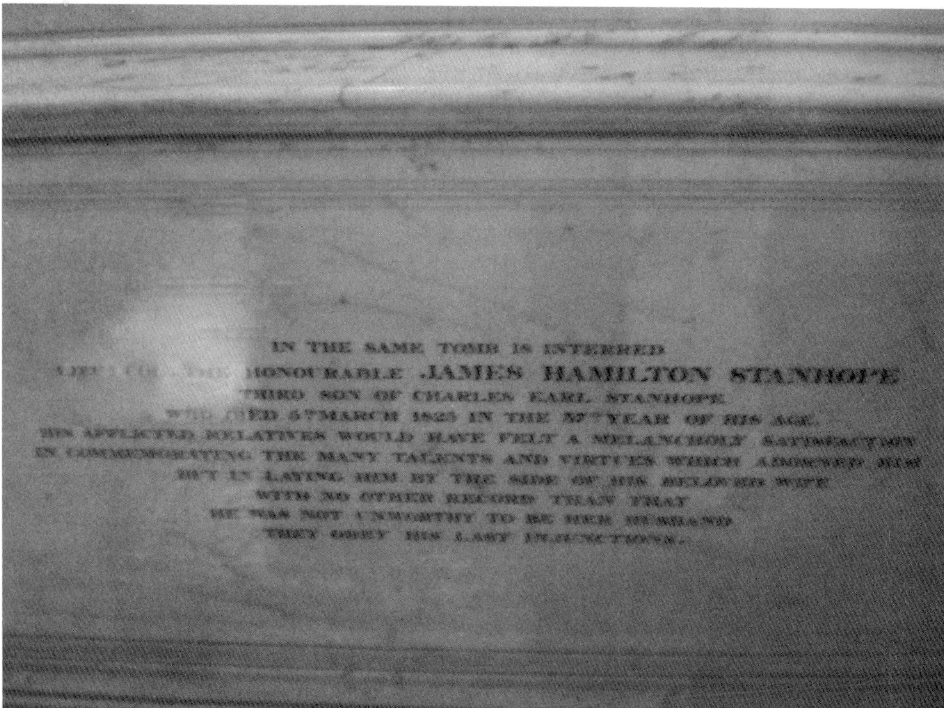

B.		
Brigade of Guards	1,000 men	} Under General Cooke
C.		
55th	250 men	} Lieutenant
69th	350 men	} Colonel
33rd	600 men	} Morice 69th[65]
D.		
91st	400 men	} Lieutenant
21st	100 men	} Colonel
37th	150 men	} Henry 21st[66]

Recapitulation

Attack (A)	1,100
Attack (B)	1,000
Attack (C)	1,200
Attack (D)	650
Total	3,950

The orders issued were that the 4 columns should advance to within cannon shot of the places (specifying their different points) at about 9 o'clock and move to the *attack at ½ past ten* and three watches were set in each column to ensure the accuracy of time. The three real attacks were to *concentrate on the centre* one and they were ordered to *keep together if possible to gain the Antwerp gate and to preserve the ramparts till morning.* The false attack having succeeded in drawing off the enemy's attention which was to be done without risking many men was *to reform* & wait for further orders. *They were meant as the reserve.*

We shall now see how these orders were executed; the false attack (D) began firing at ½ past 9, an hour before the appointed time. Carleton hearing the firing judged it best (as it probably was) to push on, so he entered ½ an hour before his time. When they got near instead of preserving that silence which is peculiarly necessary in night attacks pushed on with loud cheers. Carleton having got in said 'First in Badajoz, first in Bergen op Zoom'. He advanced to the right along the ramparts with the flank companies of the 21st, 37th and 44th amounting to about 250 men. He took a great many prisoners as he cleared the ramparts but with guarding them and with casualties his numbers diminished. Still he thought everything was his and he went to the head of an advancing column of French saying 'Mettez bas les armes' [Lay down your arms] and was shot and bayoneted at the same moment. Meanwhile General

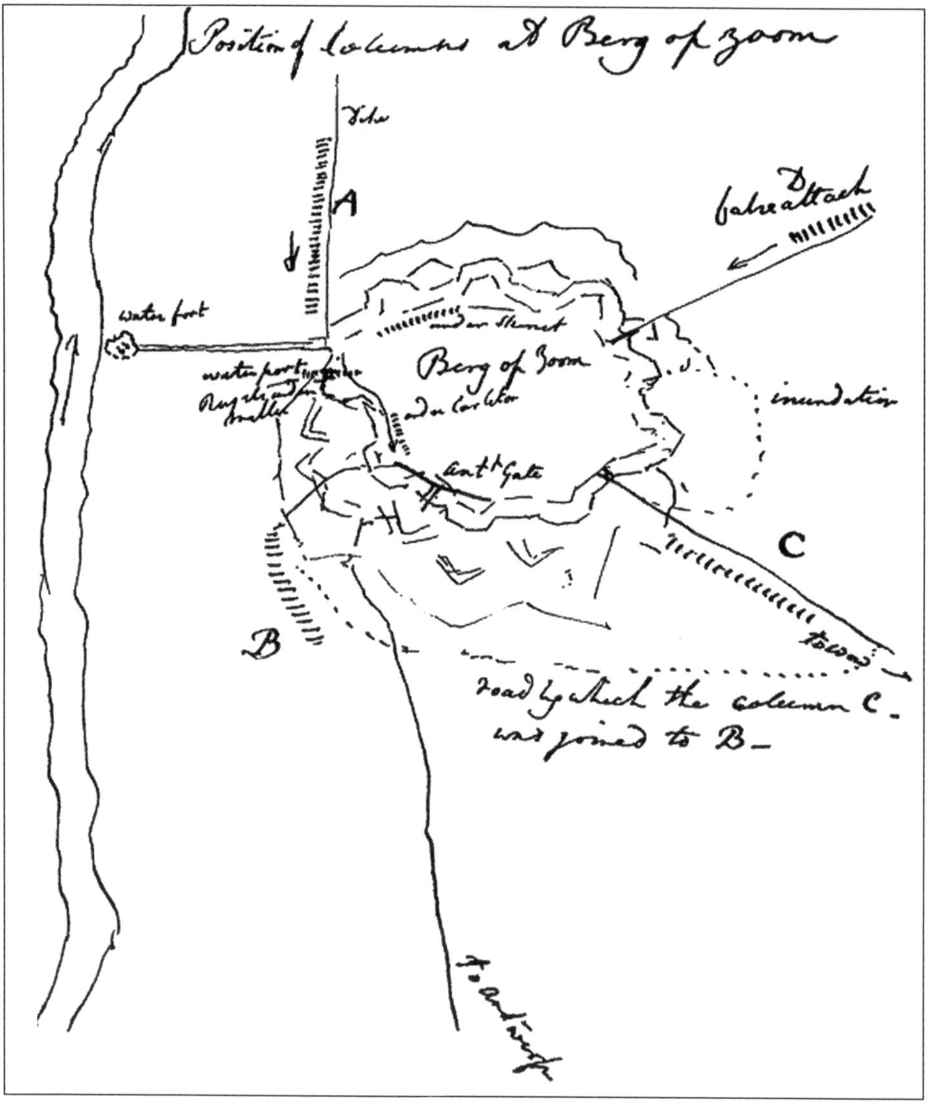

Bergen op Zoom.

Skerrett who during the advance had kept crying out to the troops 'Mind men you are to get out of the ditch to the right', went with the 44th to *the left* (an unaccounted for and incomprehensible fact) and fell into the jaws of a large body of the garrison which were assembled to repulse that attack which was intended as a false one.

The Royals, 600 strong, were left at the *Waterport gate* without orders and they were commanded by a man not qualified to take either any judicious or dashing line of conduct on himself. The Guards meanwhile had been unavoidably delayed in the passage of the ditch, did not arrive on the ramparts till eleven, but they entered with trifling loss. General Cook immediately sent Colonel Clifton[67] and 300 of the 1st Guards to look after Carleton & to secure the Antwerp gate. Carleton had already been overpowered and this reinforcement only arrived in time to share his fate; after a brave resistance the survivors were obliged to surrender.

The column (C) at the beginning of the night when advancing and close to the guns of the place, whether seized by a fear of cavalry or by one of those unaccountable panics which have been known at night among the bravest troops, without the slightest cause or a shot being fired, went to the right about & fled in all directions with the utmost precipitation.

We were all there and galloping among them aided the exertions of their officers sufficiently to rally them at once. No men ever behaved better than these did in protecting the retreat of the Guards; their attack was repulsed with the loss of about 200 men.

Success or failure hung in the balance; ten of the fortress's sixteen bastions were in British hands and nineteen out of twenty-two magazines, but the French rallied and went forward once more, whilst the French cannon swept the streets.

Leaving the left wing of the 55th to withdraw the wounded from the glacis, that column was moved round to the point of entry of the Guards and safely thrown into the town. So after all the disobedience of orders and misfortunes of the night we had still under General Cook the following men:–

The Guards at least	650
The Column C at least	800
The Royals	600
And of Carleton's about	50
	2100

General Graham then sent Colonel Macdonald[68] to bring up the column of reserve which was expected to have been found formed according to orders; a real attack however had been made of course without possessing the means of offence; still as British troops will always execute what they are ordered, some of the 91st etc got over a batardeau[69] into the place, but being cut off from joining the Royals by superior numbers, [not?] knowing of what was going on, they were obliged to retreat into a bastion & surrender in the morning. Therefore instead of 650, Macdonald found 150, all [that was] left of the column of reserve. It was now about one or two in the morning and Sir George Wood[70] commanding the artillery & Colonel Smyth commanding the engineers both came away and officially reported the place was his for all firing had ceased.

The following reinforcements were ordered up:

From Putte, Guards	400
From Wouw, Guards	200

Remainder of Column (blank)	150
Left wing of 55th	100
The 35th Regiment	350
	1300

At about 4 o'clock General Cooke sent to General Graham to know whether he should attempt to clear the streets or only hold the ramparts as the firing was recommenced & they were losing a good many men by shots from the roofs & windows. General Graham left it to himself but announced that reinforcements would arrive in the morning. This answer was not received by General Cooke, when the troops began to retire.

The Royals sent in the morning to General Cooke for support and the 33rd were sent to them. I cannot help thinking that bringing the Royals to join him, instead of detaching to them, was the line General Cooke should have pursued. When the morning came the Royals suffered (as Colonel Muller[71] reported) so much from grape that they retired, some ended in a run when getting under the fire of the sea fort, which they thought was ours, they laid down their arms. The 33rd *afterwards* scrambled over the ramparts *& got off.*

But a little before daylight General Cooke at the suggestion he says of Lord Proby began sending out the Guards & covered their retreat with the 55th and 69th and about 8 o'clock, having thrown himself into a house, Colonel Jones[72] who was taken, was sent to him informing him of the fate of the rest of the column and he then surrendered. Between 6 & 7 o'clock General Graham was moving down with the above mentioned reinforcements when he saw the glacis covered with troops retiring; our sensations may be more easily understood than expressed.

Thus failed the attack on Bergen op Zoom; the attempt was justified by circumstances, the idea was bold & the combinations perfect as the success of throwing into the place a superior body of men to the garrison demonstrated and the failure was caused by events which General Graham could neither foresee or avert.

James now became fully involved in the negotiations over a prisoner exchange and went into the town to discuss the matter; his clever deception was very successful in releasing all the British prisoners. His subsequent record of the French view of the attack is very interesting indeed and shows how close a run thing it was.

On the evening of the 9th Colonel Jones came out with proposals for an exchange of prisoners, in consequence of which I was sent in next morning with a flag of truce & full powers to sign articles for that purpose. As the French had appointed two officers, when I arrived Colonel Jones was added. Knowing the ulterior destination of most of the troops taken to be America, I proposed that they should not serve against France or her allies *'In Europe'* till regularly exchanged. Some manoeuvring was necessary to conceal my reasons & the governor[73] not thinking of trans-Atlantic allies signed it as I wished, our prisoners marched out the same evening. By this he gave us back 1,500 men without exchange although the enemy had a strong interest in getting us out as we should be so many more mouths to feed, it does not diminish the merit of the governor in his treatment of the prisoners. He would examine no letters or papers which I had collected, would set no watch on my actions or confine my steps, as he said he knew 'I should neither act, say or collect anything unworthy of a British officer'. He was an old officer, had served 34 years & had been taken in his youth by us. He said he never was more kindly treated at home than he was by us and was happy in being able to repay it. I dined with him & his family, at dinner he gave the health of General Graham 'Who must be a brave and able man to have made such an attempt which had so nearly succeeded' for at one time he did *not know who were masters of the town*.

The Major de la Place, son & heir to the Duke of Villeroi was equally kind & liberal. In short, as long as warmth of heart, liberality of mind, delicacy of feeling & urbanity of manners, such as used to adorn the French heroes of a better day, continue worthy of admiration so long will every English officer who saw the conduct of the governor, recollect with respect and gratitude the name of General Bizanet, the brave resistance of the night and the friendly hospitality of the morning.

Sir Thomas Graham sent James home with news of the failure at Bergen op Zoom. It was traditional for the bearer of a victory to be given a brevet step in rank, but despite the bad news he carried, it was contrived to give James his lieutenant colonelcy, as Graham's plan was thought to be admirable; it was those who executed the attack who were deemed to have failed.

On the 11th I left headquarters with the evil tidings and reached land on the 13th. I waited on Lord Bathurst and was taken to Carlton House where I had an audience with the Prince [Regent] and explained to him in great detail all that had passed & concluded by expressing my hopes that H.R.H. would not conceive that General Graham had squandered the lives of his men in any rash & impracticable undertaking, but that his reasons for trying it were good, his combinations succeeded and he was not to blame for the failure.

The prince 'By God, so far from blame, I don't think Graham ever deserved more credit for any victory he has ever gained than in the combinations which ended in this failure'.

I then retired & Lord Bathurst remained with the prince; when the former came out, he said he was desired to inform me that 'I might consider myself as a lieutenant colonel but that as no rank ever had been given for bad news he could not set the precedent by giving it at once, but I should have it the first opportunity'.

I begged Lord Bathurst to express my gratitude to H.R.H. but to say that being at the top of the list of the Guards I was so near a lieutenant colonel that the brevet rank was comparatively of little importance except as a public testimony of His R.H.'s approbation of General Graham's conduct '*& as such I should accept it, as the greatest gift he could bestow, but to be so considered it must be done at once*'

I repeated the same sentiments to the Duke of York next day & it was settled that in consideration of General Graham's merit in the plan, it should be treated as a victory & all persons mentioned were promoted & I among the others.

Peace soon returned to Europe and a weary James closed his Peninsula War journal for ever with a simple:

Since I have been in England.

Chapter 14

A Lasting Peace

The Allied armies captured Paris on 31 March and Napoleon was finally persuaded of the futility of continuing the war and signed his abdication on 6 April 1814. The guns finally fell silent on 27 May with the end of the siege of Hamburg; Napoleon made his way to his new kingdom on the island of Elba, where the Allies had placed him in exile with 600 of his Old Guard and King Louis XVIII took the crown of France.

The diplomats of Europe thronged to Vienna as the congress opened on 1 November, in a gloriously vain attempt to gain everybody's agreement to a redefining of Europe's borders. The congress soon fell into chaos; just as we have seen in more recent history, with the Allies turning on each other at the end of the Second World War. The victors wanted heavy reparations including both money and land from those so recently defeated, the great powers all claiming the giant's share and the minnows feeling squeezed from all sides. Secret alliances were formed and outed, causing mutual distrust and enmity amongst so recently firm allies and war seemed to loom again; it was soon to come, but no one could have predicted its source.

Whilst all these political machinations rumbled throughout Europe and continued to fill the broadsheets with the latest rumour or twist in the negotiations, James began to settle into the peacetime role of a Guards officer, mounting regular guard at the regimental mess or at the table of some friend in town. General Graham had returned home and had finally retired to his Scottish home, exhausted by the years of campaigning. James was still officially an extra aide de camp to the commander-in-chief, the Duke of York, but this appears to have been much of an honorary title and he appears to have had few duties to perform.

But James did not come home alone, the wound in his shoulder received at San Sebastian continued to plague him with abscesses and the first glimpse we get of him in London is in a series of short letters from that December when James wrote details of a series of operations performed on his shoulder to Lady Mansfield. Lord and Lady Mansfield[1] suddenly appear as regular correspondents at this time and this may well have been because James had taken a fancy to their 14-year-old daughter Frederica Louisa Murray, who was to become his wife a few years later. The process of searching for the ball and gouging it out without painkillers would have been excruciating and could only be borne for a few minutes at a time.

Half Moon Street[2] Saturday 11 December 1814

My dear Lady Mansfield,[3]

... After I wrote last, I was in such pain with the abscess as to be obliged to take large doses of opium which took away alike the pain and the memory of what passed for some days.[4] On the 6th however the abscess was opened and above a quart of what Crambo[5] should say on the half of it we wipe at best, was discharged, since which I am greatly improved. I have now my natural sleep again and a very good appetite and though rather pulled down am not much the worse for my trials. As yet we can find no trace of the ball, but I have little doubt, this will all finish by its being extracted. The person who attends me, is Mr James Moore,[6] a brother of Sir John's who is a particularly able surgeon and amiable man and who treats me like a friend. He keeps the new wound open and will so until the ball is found.

Half Moon Street, December 1814
I have not written these few days past having been affected with a severe headache proceeding from too great an appetite and no exercise, but I drove out in my mothers' carriage and today I have taken a walk which set me quite to right again. Moore despairs of finding the ball, he probed this morning for the last time (a joyful hearing to me) and explored about 3 inches deep without finding anything. He thinks the wound is going to heal which I anxiously hope may be the case as the ceremony of keeping it open is so painful that I should be glad to get rid of the whole concern at any rate. In the mean time I am stronger and better and sleep well.

December 1814
... On Monday night I was whilst in bed was attacked with a violent pain in my chest and shortness of breathing, that I was obliged to sit up all night and really believed I had a bad chance for the angelic music as I thought the ball must have worked through my ribs but Moore dispelled my fears, it proceeded from the severity of his bandages round my body (for I have been swaddled like an Iroquois child) and that it was the beginning of an inflammation there, in consequence of which he has poured a whole shop into me and has curtailed me of meat, wine, porter and all my good things. I am pretty nearly well of that, got to fish today and shall start with fresh vigour on my old diet tomorrow. I have the most immoderate appetite and begin to fear I shall get *too fat*. I have great hopes of getting rid of Moore in a day or two as the wound is healing fast but I am to stay a week in or about London to see if the abscess reforms and then I shall be liberated.

Half Moon Street, Wednesday [late December 1814?]

My dear mother,

You will I know be happy to hear that I am delivered of part of my plagues. I have been suffering more or less from my wound for some time & last night at 11 it opened of itself from the exercise I had been taking & I came to town this morning & James Moore by probing discovered a hard substance which he wished me to allow him to cut out. This he accordingly did & I have now my enemy in my hand & a more ugly gentleman I never saw. This is the outline of his phiz.

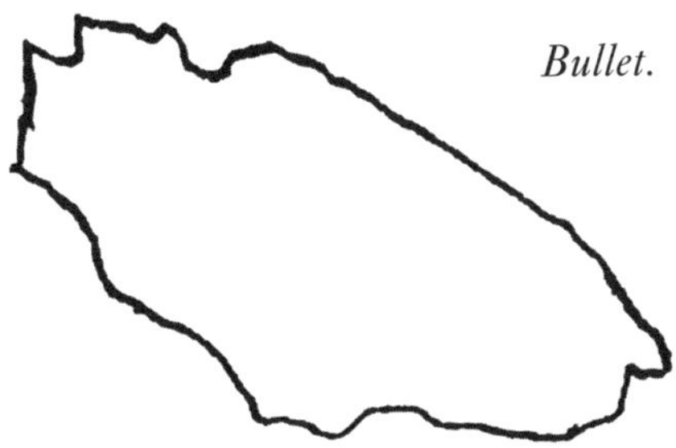

Bullet.

Moore thinks this has been the cause of all my plague & that the ball is lying quiet somewhere or other, but he means to keep the wound open & have a fair probing for some days.

This will prevent my going to Shelley's & consequently I shall not have the pleasure for the present of seeing you but je vous prie de croie a mon amour pour la mere cherie [please believe my love for my dear mother]. Adios ever affectionately yours JHS.

It would appear that the removal of this shard of metal did give some relief, but the wound plagued James every day of his life. He wrote a short note to Lady Mansfield in early January showing that he was healing both in body and spirit, but was extremely frail.

January 8 1815 [Half Moon Street?]

My dear Lady M,

… I am quite stout and my wound is gradually healing. By the way, I weighed a few days ago and found myself 8st 12lbs which is very well for a poor convalescent.

Chapter 15

War Again

The bitter Machiavellian intrigues of the Congress of Vienna raged on into the new year with little sign of any common ground being agreed. But then something happened that shocked the whole world and galvanized the heads of Europe to act as one again.

Napoleon Bonaparte, Emperor of Elba, had remained fully in tune with all the machinations, saw that Louis would renege on his treaty obligations to fund him in his island gaol and, on 26 February 1815, he took perhaps the greatest gamble of his gambling life. Napoleon and his Old Guard sailed from Elba and landed near Cannes and proceeded to march towards Paris.

Louis ordered his vast army to intercept the 'Usurper' but the soldiers simply switched allegiance on his appearance and joined his force, turning the gamble into a virtually bloodless victory parade all the way to the gates of Paris. He arrived on 20 March and regained the vacant throne, Louis having fled for a second time. The Congress broke up, but not before naming Napoleon their enemy and declaring war on him and therefore upon France again. The politicians retired and the generals of Europe were called back to the colours; Wellington who had just started his new career as a politician at Vienna rushed to Belgium, where the force left there after Bergen op Zoom still remained, bolstering the fledgling government of the Kingdom of Netherlands at Brussels which now incorporated Holland and Belgium, always an unhappy mix. Soon the government were looking for any troops available to reinforce Wellington's army in Belgium, a difficult task following their traditional wholesale slashing of defence spending immediately hostilities ended, as the 'Peace Dividend', and the fact that much of Wellington's Peninsular Army was now fighting 'Johnny American'. This pointless war across the Atlantic was rapidly ended by treaty and the troops ordered home. Not all arrived in time, but enough of these troops reached Belgium in the nick of time to bolster Wellington's inexperienced and polyglot army. James set out for Belgium to try and find a new staff appointment under Lord Wellington, presumably with the Duke of York's blessing.

James, like every other soldier, describes how they returned to war. This time there was no glee, more a resigned determination to finish it quickly.

Opening a brand-new leather bound journal, James commenced writing notes which he then reworked into a journal when at Paris later that year.

> The return of Bonaparte broke upon the world like a hurricane, no one who did not witness the mute consternation of London at that period could believe it. None who did will ever forget the impression.
>
> For the first time I went abroad with rather a heavy heart, it seemed as if all was to begin again & that all our former toils & blood & triumphs had been in vain.
>
> However I was not slow in getting off; on the 7th of April I left Dover & after a 38 hour passage in a crowded packet with all the passengers but myself wretchedly sick, arrived safely at Ostend. I set off immediately on my landing for Brussels where I arrived the following morning. I expressed my wish to the Duke to be placed again in the Quarter Master General's Department & he promised not to forget me, but seeing no immediate probability of a vacancy & having completed my equipment & bought a pair of Belgian coach horses & a farm one to carry my baggage, I left Brussels & joined the 3rd Battalion of the 1st Guards at Enghien on the 19th [April].[1]

Six companies of the 2nd Battalion 1st Foot Guards were already stationed in Brussels and were soon joined by the remaining four companies. The 1st Battalion was ordered for foreign service, but as their commander, Colonel Upton, had already received a post as Military Attaché to the Bavarian contingent, the 3rd Battalion was ordered to go instead. The 3rd Battalion duly marched from London on 2 April under the command of Colonel the Honourable William Stuart, reaching Deptford on the 5th, Ramsgate the 9th and Ostend on the 10th, arriving at their destination of Enghien on 14th. The two battalions of the 1st Foot Guards formed together the 1st Brigade of Guards in the 1st Division. Having failed to gain a staff appointment James duly joined his battalion near Enghien. From here, having a good deal of leisure time, James wrote regularly to both his mother and the Mansfields. The first letter in the series was sent to Lady Mansfield.

> Hoves near Enghien, 27 April 1815
>
> … I am just going to start for Brussels and shall leave this letter open to fill up with any news I can pick up. I hope all your good wishes and M[ansfield]'s about myself will be propitiated as I hear by a private friend that my name is gone home as proposed by the Patron as we used to call him in Spain, so I hardly see how I can help being put on the Staff if the Commander in Chief both at home and abroad propose me.[2]
>
> … [The] Prince [of Orange] said [the Belgians are] a more good natured and obliging peasantry, ugly as sin in their persons as Irish, but clean and comfortable at home. They churn everyday for me and select with the most laudable industry their very freshest egg for my breakfast.

The letter continues dated Brussels 28 April: 'Several French officers deserted yesterday in consequence of Bonaparte not allowing them to retire.'

His letter to his mother naturally contains a little more on his own position and how comfortable he was. It would appear that the wound was no longer bothering him.

Hoves near Enghien, 2 May 1815

Does not your ladyship imagine I have great reason to complain when I have not received one line from you since I have left England though I have written two letters containing at least 7 sides each? The day after I wrote last, I joined my battalion here, am quartered in a very pretty and comfortable farm among fresh eggs; pigs, poultry & cows before the house, nightingales in every bush behind it, not a bad cuisine & establishment inside, no aches or cares to molest me, but no letters from you to delight me.

I am frequently in Brussels, there was a concert the other day in which Calalani sung admirably and a ball the next night, given by the Duke of Wellington & very brilliant. I am now going to return to that great city for the second concert & shall be in my farm again tomorrow.

As yet no arrangement has been made towards placing me on the Staff and indeed all the departments are so full and there are so many candidates with superior claims, that I am not very sanguine about it.

Pray let me hear every now & then how Nash[3] is; for I need not further express my hopes of hearing from you. Do you send your letters to Sir H Torrens[4] for I get by that channel my papers every three or four days as regularly as if I was in England.

Remember me most kindly to Sir J[oseph Banks] &c whenever you see them and to General Grenville[5] & lady. I would write to them if there was any news worth communicating, but the misfortune is that when there is a subject, we have no time & when we have time there is no subject. Believe me my dear mother, ever affectionately yours J H Stanhope.

James wrote a more matter of fact letter to Earl Mansfield describing the current situation and preparations in hand.

Hoves near Enghien, 2 May 1815

My dear Mansfield,

To suffer for one's own sins is most just, but it is somewhat hard to pay for others, which I am most likely to do. When I wrote last, I was in the fullest hopes that I should immediately have been placed in the situation I wished and after I wrote to Lady Mansfield from Brussels I was advised from a high quarter to write home for horses. I had the letters in my hand when the answer arrived from Torrens to the letter in which my name, Woodford's & two other names were placed have a positive veto, but the general tenor was so strong against any captains of the Guards who had been honoured with companies from other regiments, being appointed, that though I am not of that number and though there are ten lieutenant colonels with one battalion, this sad bevue [blunder] has stopped my appointment & the whole list from the Horse Guards is in orders, so everything is now filled to choking. Entre nous there is a sad jealousy & bitterness home & abroad at least in the second persons if not in the first; and in the bearer of my letter no great sincerity to me [for] the lists were making out, in which I was omitted, and to this moment since has he [not] communicated to I either my previous offer of service or the Duke's approval. I have written today to both in a very quiet style begging that if I was not included I may not suffer innocently, but if I am, assuring them (which is the real truth) that I will ever cheerfully serve any how or any where & will never bother about it. The old circumstance of the gentleman between two stools is most happily elucidated in my person, but I shall be able to it as comfortably & to make up my mind as cheerfully to the ground as if I had been installed in the more honourable chair. I say this that you may not imagine from my writing four pages about myself that I am either vexed or uncomfortable.

The day I wrote last was concluded by a very brilliant ball, in which were many friends of Lord Lynedoch[6] and very few of mine, so hors des complimens d'usage [beyond the usual compliments], I did not say much and except the gratification of hearing his praises and witnessing the affection & esteem of all classes for him, was not much delighted.

I am going to mount my horse now to return to Brussels from the concert tonight & shall then come back tomorrow; these I think are very gay doings. The Duke of Wellington reviewed us yesterday and was charmed with our appearance. We had about 3,500 bayonets in the field, in the most perfect order. I suspect we do not wait for the 5[th battalion] but with the 4 already here, pursue the line I mentioned very shortly.

The French have collected in our front I understand about 60,000 men but I fancy not that disposable as something considerable must be left as garrisons. To give you an idea of the exertions making to fortify on our side, on the 28th there were 22,000 men at work at Ostend, Nieuport, Ypres, Menin, Mons, Ghent (Citadel at least) are among the first & I believe Tournai; towards the end of the week I mean to go over to see the latter …

So much for this country, I need not say how deeply I have been shocked at our friend's finale, for though I hope it is not a very aggravated case yet it must end in his unhappiness & in his losing the society of those he liked best. I have heard no particulars & know nothing but what the papers tell me; I am convinced no house in London could feel more on that subject than your own.

To you the world; some friends are snatched from one & others voluntarily make a feld de se of one's power of enjoying their friendship & in some instances I question whether the latter does not afflict one more and longer than the first, you know to what I allude.

Many thanks for your letter; I mean to write as often as I can and if you have any charity, pray do the same …

I am quiet, quiet well; remember me with all kindness to all from Lady Mansfield to C & believe me dear Mansfield, ever most affectionately yours. In your next mention having received this letter.

James was now writing regularly, giving details of the war preparations. The next was sent to Lady Mansfield.

Hoves 5 May 1815

I had hardly closed my packet from Brussels when I received yours & Mansfield's of the 25th and return you both my very best thanks for all your news … The Richmonds[7] are at Enghien with General Maitland[8] & we have had cricket matches, collations al fresco etc these three days & which with my ride from Brussels & the enclosed black daub [not present] of my house & the steeple of Hoves near Enghien have filled up my time with a little addition of my travelling companions. I wish you would instruct me how to leave a thing off in time, for this beautiful drawing was at one period not quite so bad, but I went on and effectually finished it. I will not despair but will set to resolutely again.

I have seen a person who left Paris on Sunday & who says Bonaparte is more unpopular than ever since the constitution has been promulgated as the people are sick of them and that the greatest alarm prevails except among the military. The latter have made a new stanza to their old song.

Vive Bonaparte
Let diable a quatre [The devil has four]
Lui a plus de talent [He has more talent]
Que notre heroi 4 [Than our 4 heroes]
Et tous ses descendans [And all their descendants]

Your account of yourselves is the only unsatisfactory part of your letter, but I hope the duties of a champion will not make yourself over exert yourself too much, for it is easier to get into a sick room than out of one. You will certainly laugh at my preaching about taking care of oneself; but now I am a model, for where there is no temptation to set up, it is not very difficult to persuade oneself to go to bed. Both Earl Mansfield & you ask me the same question about enclosing the letters to T[orrens]. In fact he has nothing to do with it, for all letters addressed to him not having 'private' marked are opened by Mr Dighton his under secretary who manages all the A.D.C.'s affairs and who is very happy to be useful. He sends all my letters, papers &c & by coming in the Duke of Wellington's bag, I get them a day sooner than the rest & much safer, especially hereafter when we are further from our communications. Therefore, I think you had better continue to send them, Mr D[ighton] probably got your letter.

I went to Brussels partly in hopes of finding a few cups & saucers & one which I ordered for you. There are to be a dozen, 6 large ones with figures of Cossacks, Bashkirs &c and the same number of coffee cups with Belgian & Dutch costumes. The Brussels china is very pretty & very cheap therefore if you like to give further orders I will get them punctually executed but these are not more than specimens and therefore not coming under the title of commissions, I beg you will accept them. They will be done in ten days and will be sent to the custom house in the river directed to Earl Mansfield, consigned to Mr Rice (the man who escaped with me from C[hevening] & who now is a custom house officer with 700 a year), the same person who were to send you the oranges which I hope are arrived safe.

The Duke of Wellington went on the 4th to meet Blucher half way.[9] There seems to be an idea prevailing that we move in about ten days, in short before the 20th but I do not see what possible authority anybody can have for it. The young prince has established his head quarters at Braine le Comte not far from Hoves. Among our fashionable at Enghien the last few days have been Lady Charlotte Greville[10] & Lady George Seymour.[11] The first certainly is pleasant, but she gives me always so strong an idea of being insincere that I cannot say I altogether like her. Still it is odd that the sister of frank honest F[rederick] B[entinck][12] should be so, but when one considers F[rederick] B[entinck] being brother to the mad skeleton,[13] one can wonder at nothing and indeed I have instances nearer home which still more surprise me.

I must now conclude with best remembrances to Earl Mansfield & all the family, with thanks most gratefully given for you both being such good correspondents, with anxious hopes for the continuance, with fair promises on my part and with the most honest appearances of my being most faithfully yours.

James wrote two long letters on the 14 May regarding various aspects of their preparations for war, including continuous false rumours of the arrival of Bonaparte with the army. The first was written to Lady Mansfield.

Hoves 14 May 1815

How delightfully expeditious is the post! For I get my letters now as punctually as if I were in London & yourselves at S[cone][14] on my return from F[rederick] Ponsonby's.[15] On the 10th I received Earl Mansfield's and yesterday morning got your letter of several dates which is exactly what I wished ...

I heard this morning from T[orrens] confidentially who disdains in the kindest language any idea of its applying to me and has written to the Duke from Duke of York to this effect 'That though H.R.H. meant to preserve the efficiency of the Guards, yet he did not wish to interfere with his discretion regarding any individual and that the officers where wounds might render foot duty difficult to them (among which my name was included) had his permission to be employed on the Staff whenever room could be obtained for them. This so far is very satisfactory and nothing but the full state of the Staff can now prevent it. The augmentation which would bring Cole[16] out might put me on, if he has no private friend. Perhaps Mansfield could sound him there – not from me!!! With all this I do not expect to be put on and therefore cannot be disappointed though by a 'Glorious Reverse', I may be much gratified; this is all most secret.

When I was at Grammont with Lord Hill, we had accounts of Bonaparte's expected arrival at Valenciennes on the 10th and the collection of the French army round Maubeuge in consequence of which all the Hanoverians have been brought up and we are got what we call in hand. I do not think it is Bonaparte's policy to advance but with his daring mind, it is not impossible. It is not quite out of probability that the Duke has made their collection an excuse to get prepared for movement himself, without appearing offensively inclined, in which I am further confirmed by an order for every division to collect 3 times a week & march en masse some hours on the great roads. We formerly marched & exercised in individual battalions. As I long have been accustomed to look for two reasons in everything he does, I think this is probably done to accustom the country people and spies to see many movements of large bodies so that when we really move (of which he never gives 5 hours notice), it will be taken for a common march. The first took place yesterday but I was not at it as the day before as I was cantering along an even road, my horse came down without any assignable cause & fell upon my ankle which is stiff & rather strained, but will be well in a day or two.

If we ever were to believe the Moniteur[17] as to Bonaparte's preparations, it would be enough to frighten us all, but I believe it all to be exaggerated and most of it to be utterly false. I happen to know from good authority that Bonaparte has received letters from whole regiments assuring him of their devotion. Much will depend on the first action, if not everything and I think the Patron will be cautious at first. As for Bonaparte defending Paris & fortifying Montmartre it is nonsense, for no batteries can keep us from shelling & burning it, which the good city would not very easily be brought to acquiesce in.

If we stay quiet I mean to go to Tournai for a day, but shall not return to Brussels unless we wait long enough to allow me to see your china expedited. I have received a letter from A[lexander] A[bercromby] there (who by the way has a pretty good appointment)[18] wishing me to come over, but I was absent when it came and I hardly like to be absent more than a day now the time draws near, so I wished him good luck & told him I could not come.

Your account of the wood[19] is rather triste, but I egotistically am thinking how comfortable it will be when we have next 'the archer sports at noon' there.

I might indeed have included that game in my list of acquisitions as it is most common & popular amusement in this country; the arrows are not unlike the people, big headed, fluent & going straight forward when in high feather but wobbling a good deal when much used in bad seasons ...

The Richmonds are coming over on Wednesday & stay Thursday with General Maitland for a cricket match if we remain undisturbed. I cannot tell you how much use I have derived from your little memorandum book for although there are no materials at present for a journal, it contains the arrangement of the army etc.

Remember me affectionately to Earl Mansfield & all your family, let Chico write one of his impromptus for they are delightful & the first time I have fewer enclosures I will send him a pretty letter.

Adios with all good wishes for your health in your severe campaign, most affectionately yours.

Hoves, 14 May 1815

My dear mother,

I received your first letter on the same day I wrote complaining of not having heard from you and this morning your other two arrived safe. I need not say how rejoiced I am at your having escaped so well, et que vous acter quitte pour l'argent [And note you have left for the money]. As you will perceive by the papers we are still quiet though the French are collecting in our front, but whether to try their hand at offensive measures or simply are preparing to await us it is impossible to say.

The account in the Moniteur of Bonaparte's great means is positive stuff and will hardly be swallowed by the wide mouthed Parisians. Every account on the contrary tends to confirm the belief that he is far from popular with anything but the army.

Time passes in the usual way, well or ill according to the resources each may possess, as there is neither business or society to assist its course. I have been wandering about a good deal seeing neighbouring towns, ancient fields of battle etc, but never remain about [from the regiment] more than a day in the present state of affairs.

Having then nothing to tell you I write principally to say I am well, saving & excepting having strained my ankle slightly from my horse falling on me, but cela se pape un deux jours [This is a pope [sic] in two days]. Whenever you see Sir J[oseph], ladies or the general, remember me affectionately to them as I do not write to any this post. Adios querida madre [Goodbye beloved mother], yours most affectionately JH S

PS Give my best love to Nash when you see her.

He wrote again to Lady Mansfield.

Hoves, 21 May 1815

The night before last I received Lord Mansfield's of the 14th which is an additional proof that you are the best correspondents in the world. Tell him that I do not believe the speculation he mentions of Bonaparte trying to turn our right, as it is by [far] much the strongest part of our line. Taking the line of the Scheldt as far as Dermonde & then the Dender as far as Ath, up to which place it is navigable, Grammont is one of the strongest positions I ever saw & Ath is repaired, a parapet made & wet ditch cut so as to render it very respectable. It is from Ath to the Meuse that is our weakest point, but there is a position I understand at Nivelles which by the way reminds me of a story very creditable to the Orange prince's coup d'oiel. He wrote to the Duke saying he had found out this position & described it and the same post brought a letter from the Duke desiring him to look near Nivelles as he thought by the map there should be a position there.

I am more sanguine than he [the prince] is as to success and nothing has inspired me with better hopes than Fouche's own confession of the disturbed state of France. The people will make a cool selfish calculation how tranquillity is easiest to be purchased, by getting rid of Bonaparte or of the invaders and will act according to the military barometer, therefore it seems of the greatest importance that we should make a good beginning.

The worst news in his letter is the sad account of poor Kenwood, from your account the repairs were of a much more trifling nature & purely voluntary, but this dry rot is a sad enemy, though I believe it exists in a great many houses without being discovered. You will miss your high wood very much in July, except you can fit up the dairy as a collation house & return to [PP?] at night. But at any rate the recommencement of a war & the continuation of the income tax do not form the most agreeable epoch for rebuilding such a house.

The day after I wrote to him, I went with the Richmonds to see Beloeil,[20] a country seat about 8 miles beyond Ath, which the good sort of people here, think is fine & much resembling Versailles; or rather Versailles very much resembling it …

At Ath we found the Duke of Wellington and what was as agreeable a gay luncheon provided for him which we ate. We had a very pleasant day what with the genius of pun 'Old Crambo' and the fright we kindly kept Henry P[ercy?] in from the time we started. I never saw such a coward which is odd for so decided a person; but I believe that the true Cornelias, must have mildness of temper & warm feelings & the rest are all bullies.

I am going to Brussels tomorrow to see the Brunswickers reviewed and shall not return here till Wednesday morning. I anticipate finding a letter from you on my arrival there. I leave this open to be able I hope to egayer [cheer] it a little with some news, you have the organ of patience to a great degree; I am sure to bear such folios of dullness as I have regularly transmitted. I think I shall hear my own fate also, for two divisions are to be formed immediately & if I do not get appointed to one of them, there can be no other chance. I enclose two more performances [etches- not included] which may give you some idea of our animated as well as inanimate beauty. Till tomorrow adios.

Brussels 22nd

I think the Staff to one of the new divisions will be appointed today. I met the Duke last night who was civil but did not enter into the matter. Remember me affectionately to all the family, continue your writing I beg as often as time will permit. Ever faithfully yours

James wrote two weeks later to Lady Mansfield about balls and the latest Brussels society gossip.

Hoves 28 May 1815

Though my last letter to Earl Mansfield was an answer to yours of the 16th I cannot still help thanking you personally for all the interest you take about me & I do hope that you will feel convinced that whether I may or may not have acted in the way most likely to derive success, I have still followed the line of conduct to ensure self approbation though with the large organ of amour proper you proved I possessed, you will doubtless say that never can be wanting to me.

I returned from Brussels last night, having spent a very pleasant evening at the Duke of Wellington's ball and a very agreeable day with some new acquaintances Lady Alvanley & her two daughters,[21] the former whose cyclops figure was in town always before me in every party, I find very entertaining & full of information, the eldest daughter is sensible & sings simply, well & with good taste and the youngest is the same funny rattling thing that her brother would have been had he not been a dandy & member of the cold hearted club.[22] The good Duchess was in a terrible mood at divers flirtations between some of the 'Gentlemen of the Guards' and her numerous chicks, so I did not venture to approach her.

Monsieur 'the shooting baron' & his mad flame were in the same room but the solemn aspect (which woke marvelling like dullness) of the father prevented more than just enough to convince me of the truth of my epithet.[23] But for a further example, suppose a young lady declaring 'If Le B_ was to kick her, she would kiss the shoe'. This is more like papal reverence than Christian humility.

So much for balls, Sir C[harles] S[tuart][24] gives a grand one on the 4th which is understood to be the closing one as the royalties depart for the Hague immediately after and the English families begin to ask whether they had better not follow his regal steps. This looks as if His Majesty thought the campaign was going to begin, people talk of about the 8th being the day; one puts the French army including cavalry & artillery at 250,000, which after all is no very great number …

I am happy to tell you that the Duke has written to W.R.[25] to come on his Staff & I hope it will have the effect of detaching him from a scene which may shake his mind without benefitting her. I should be so happy in a selfish point of view to have him near me again, for with the exception of Maitland with whom I principally live, I do not find the congenial mind which can alone render friendship delightful, though all the older officers are well informed gentleman like men, any of whom would be a blessing to one in the line. This Mansfield will say is a proper Guardsman speech. The more I see of Maitland the more I esteem him. There is a melancholy arising from past misfortunes, which blends with his gaiety and interests whilst the latter amuses. With the most boyish fondness to all sorts of exercises & excelling in them, he reads much & with the most scrupulous attention to his own duties, human or divine, he seems whilst most rigid with himself, to be most indulgent with others. Nothing can exceed his kindness to me & when he was speaking one day of my wound not answering well in bivouacs, he begged me to remember there should be always room in his house if he had one. You may therefore rest satisfied that whatever may happen to me I have a friend at hand.

I wish I could describe what I feel today & my muse would answer my call, for it is the birthday of Mr Pitt & surely never did it dawn over so eventful a period.

Yet sure if ere the spirits of the blest still fondly cherish in the realms of rest, their human passions, he is now employing them (if permitted) on our behalf. Remember me affectionately to Mansfield & all your family … yours faithfully J.H.S

The china will be due on Wednesday

James resumed his journal in early June, noting the reinforcements for the army and the defensive preparations.

From this time till the opening of the campaign, I passed a very quiet but not disagreeable time, in the solitude of the farm house where I was quartered & the society of Brussels where I generally went twice a week. The army was gradually reinforcing and at the end was formed into 6 divisions of infantry & 2 corps. The 1st under the Prince of Orange with its right at Enghien & its left at Nivelles with its headquarters at Braine le Comte; the 2nd under Lord Hill on the Dender with his headquarters at Grammont, the cavalry occupying his front & right. The 5th Division was at Brussels; one brigade only of the 6th had arrived, the rest was [sic] in cantonments. We had about 30,000 British infantry, 7,000 British & old Hanoverian cavalry, about 3,000 more of New Hanoverian[26] & Belgian. We had nearly 20,000 Hanoverian infantry, about 20,000 Belgian & Dutch including the Corps of Prince Frederick and near 8,000 Brunswickers; in all about 80,000 men with about 100 pieces of British artillery & perhaps 30 others. I am not sure I am accurate in this statement but the correct states have been published.

Every exertion was now made to restore the works which the folly of Joseph 2nd[27] had ordered to be dismantled and they soon became a l'abri d'un coup de main. No communication was allowed between the outposts but no hostilities were committed. We were in constant expectation of hearing of the advance of the larger allied armies, but Austria had detached a great part of her force into Italy and the Russians had not approached the Rhine. The Prussians had an army of 120,000 men along the Meuse under Blucher whose headquarters were at Liege. General Seidlitz had the Prussian advance at Charleroi and to him principally was entrusted the charge of sending intelligence of the enemy's movements.

Another letter from James to Lady Mansfield speaks of balls, romances and military preparations. Hester had also written and was proposing he took a leave of absence to visit her in Syria, which he had no intention of accepting, hoping instead to lure his sister home.

Hoves Wednesday morning, 7 June 1815

I received your letter of the 30th on Monday at Brussels but as I was on my horse on my way here I could not write. Sir C. Stuart gave a very gay ball on Saturday night (an odd time) & I dined & spent the next day with the Richmonds, P[28] being in good humour again, for clouds came over her at the cavalry review, of which I should have given you an account, but for our movement next day. It was the finest sight I ever witnessed, about 7,000 horses (in a beautiful meadow with wooded hills all round) and six troops of horse artillery. P got frightened and as fear always confounds, thought the cavalry would ride over her in a carriage & therefore got out & really run into great danger of being galloped over by the Greys, who wondered what the dame might be & they laughed loud.

By the last packet I received a letter from Hester of the 12th of March still from Syria. I have a private reason for once to be glad of the war having sent me here, for she has made out a plan of her remaining this year there and of doing me the honour of the east, believing that such a journey would be attended with every possible advantage to me & solely actuated by anxiety for me, for though she is not every part of Dryden's beautiful description of Lady A[bingdon], she 'is still not humble but humility'[29] whenever my interests are before her and in prosecution of this determination, I think she has written to the Duke of York for leave for a year. Had peace continued there are still so many reasons against such a plan as it is my wish to wean her from the Moors instead of Moslemising myself & it would be hopeless ever to get her from that country if I were to show any willingness of meeting her in her favourite spot, that I should have been compelled to decline it, though it would have been most painful to my feelings & would have had greater effect on hers. You will probably give me more credit for the intention than the power of fulfilling it, but I am convinced I should have been firm. Being again on service of course there is an insuperable obstacle and I wrote yesterday by Sir Hudson Lowe[30] (who was going post to Genoa to command that army) to tell her that she must abandon all hope of seeing me for even should the campaign be short, still public affairs cannot be sufficiently settled to authorise such an absence. So this will be all settled without making her uncomfortable. This is another link to my chain of events, whose public causes have turned out to my private advantage and as I am well persuaded that whatever is right I would hope that all temporary mortifications may turn out the same.

Her letter however afforded me the happiness of knowing she was well, she talks of her being about to start on a long journey without saying where & mysteriously hints at her only being anxious 'for my sharing in the honours that may fall to her lot.' What this may all be heaven only knows but it is provoking to find this fresh impulse given towards adventure at the moment I expected she was returning to the society of beardless men …

I am going in the afternoon to Brussels for a ball the Duke gives this evening which I suspect will be the concluding one.[31] The Richmonds came out to a cricket match on Friday and I think that will [be] the last scene of female society for some time.

I am very sorry the oranges were spoilt for the Maltese ones are particularly good, but I never heard of their reaching England. I directed & sent off the cups & saucers on Monday & have written to Rice about them so I trust you will receive them safe & that they will please you. I find several officers have ordered others & some dandies have them for their canteens, now I find that I've quite enough of soldiers & boon without looking in my tea for them.

Of news there appears to be none, there is an 'on dit' that troops have been moved back from our front & such is the wildness of speculation about La Vendee,[32] that if a commissary which was to be sent sick from Lille, we should say he was sent off in carriages to quell the insurgents.

We have been much amused by Lady Mountnorris's[33] account of our operations especially of the skirmish of Mons which will certainly be handed down in the voracious page of history as a most mysterious circumstance. Had she written a critical disquisition[34] of the qualities & strength of wines, she would have succeeded better, as she has shown great taste in that matter more so than steadiness if reports be true. You see we can make a little scandal at

Brussels and to confirm it, suppose I was to inform you that C[harles] S[tuart] has changed his fine new cane for a very pretty rum sort of bold person, who was more august at Vienna than here. That the young lady who was nearly turned out of the house for a trip has made herself comfortable with the occupation of Barnes.[35] Surely the genius of Dunkin[36] is upon me.

I am very glad to hear of Cole's marriage though people seem to take an odd moment, a [Ulysses?] is gone from here to seek for an Irish Penelope in a boggy Ithaca and poor De Lancey sighs for his Caledonia cottage in the middle of all his prospects of military reputation.[37] I shall leave my remaining page for the chance of a postscript which may well be worth the letter & not be of great value either. With the kindest remembrances to all your family & divers pinches to O & Ito,[38] ever faithfully yours

I send another fancy scrawl, still too black [sketch not included].

8 June Brussels

Ball went off gaily & we went to bed just at the hour when in a few days we shall be enjoying the freshness of a march. I hear there are some movements in our front, for of the extent or object I know not.

Lady D Hamilton[39] is arrived to swell the crowd of English which is enormous. Lady Conyngham's daughter[40] is with her, a blousy with maid beauty. Adios.

A short note in James's journal indicated more rumours that the fighting might start at any time.

On the 9th of June it was known that the corps from Metz was in movement towards the Sambre and that the remaining corps were collecting near Maubeuge.

A few days later we find James writing to Lady Mansfield again, who appears to have become a favourite correspondent. However, his news was not good, his wound was bad and a tumour formed.

Wednesday 14 June 1815

I yesterday received your letter ended on the 7th and am more than commonly thankful for the amusement i[t] afforded as it found me for a wonder much dejected. When you desired me in your last 'not to presume on being free from aches', you as little thought as I did of the approach of another attack. Three days ago I first felt the old symptoms, about the same as when I sent for Doctor Macfarlane at S[cone] and on sending for a surgeon yesterday, he confirmed that a tumour is formed and an abscess probably is forming. If this had happened at any other period I should have been far from complaining for I am convinced I never shall be quite well till the ball comes out and for such an agreeable conclusion I should repine at no means however severe, but just at this moment, a few days before the opening of what promises to be the saving campaign of European liberty & the seal of peace, it is you must confess most grievous. All that I can hope for is that it will form as slow as last time & that I shall be enabled to see part of the campaign at least before I am obliged to lay up. I have one advantage as it is not attended with the loss of appetite I felt at S[cone] and therefore till it comes nearly to a crisis, I shall not feel my strength impaired. That you may not imagine however that I shall do anything imprudent I faithfully promise to obey the doctors & to stop the moment they consider it indispensable. Should it become so shortly, I must go to Brussels where I can have every comfort & good attendance and I shall at any rate have the consolation of feeling that the absence from my duty is not caused by any imprudence of my own & certainly shall repine less at having a situation where little distinction is to be gained, than if I had succeeded in all my wishes & were now in a place to gain all that military ambition could desire. So far my old maxim bears me out & perhaps even this may be a confirmation of it, though not the less so I deeply lament it.

I should apologise for having pursued this subject so long without having taken notice of the event you mention & though no one (I trust you will believe) more sincerely regrets the necessity, none can feel more admiration at the sacrifice; for after all Kenwood is a thing so complete in itself that it would be lamentable not to have it in a good state and it will compensate a great deal for the deprivation of the other. I have often thought how little the poor (I mean those not possessed of a large fortune) know of the situation of the richer part of the community and what enormous demands are made on them which the rest of mankind are never exposed to and there is no greater instance of the disadvantage of too many large houses than in the case of Lord B who with a large rent roll is so eaten up by about seven large houses that he has never been otherwise than distressed. There are many in that situation who go on de pis en pis [from bad to worse], pride preventing them from doing what you [are] about to do and at length being obliged to expatiate themselves to bring affairs about.

We had a very pleasant party from Thursday till Monday at Enghien consisting of the Richmonds and Lady Frances Wederburn-Webster;[41] the Duke of Wellington came over but returned with the latter the same evening it being believed even by him, that Bonaparte was at Maubeuge. We know nothing, there are constant picket skirmishes near Charleroi & in the front of our left outposts; the other night we took 5 of their dragoons & the next they took two Belgians & then they are sent back, which is rather a curious mode of being at peace and a still more extraordinary way of carrying on war.

There is a ball tomorrow night at the Duke of Richmond's but I should not have gone had I been well, for it is by much too near the beginning to be absent.[42]

I heard from Lord L[iverpool] a few days ago, he is going I find to have all the 'sisterhood' at L & he is very busy in forming a general military club,[43] which I do not think will answer & to which there seem many objections, which however I will not bother you with.

I am delighted with your account of Madam Simon.[44] Pray keep her in force till we have done our deeds, for she is too good to be missed ...

It has hardly ceased raining this fortnight & the weather is so cold that I have had a fire & am now writing by the side of one. I hope it will be fine before we move, for this would be desperate work the country being all mud.[45] Remember me affectionately to Earl Mansfield ... I am obliged to conclude as I have an engagement at 2, yours most truly.

Hoves 14 June 1815

My dear mother,

I have not written to you for a considerable time from the same cause which produced your silence; for your first reason, that of having been unwell is not a good one, as that is of all others the time I should be the most anxious to receive your letters; and in the full belief of this I am now writing, as I am sorry to say there is every appearance of my wound breaking out again. A tumour is formed and the surgeons think that matter is collecting. All that now I feel is nothing but that sort of weaning ache I have so often complained of.

It may be a long time before it lays me up & if I can only stand the beginning of the campaign I shall be contented, for I cannot bear the idea of losing what promises to be so brilliant ever of modern times; but of course against a severe illness it would be useless to struggle and you need not therefore be apprehensive of my doing anything imprudent. Of course I shall stick to the army as long as I can hold on and if I then am obliged to go to Brussels to be confined I shall at any rate feel a satisfaction in recollecting that it is not my fault or an illness of my creation. I have only felt it these past few days, so it is not impossible it may yet absorb.

There is every probability of the campaign commencing in [a] very few days, as I believe everything is nearly up. Allow me to hint to you, not to direct your letters to any particular place, but generally 1st Guards & if you send them to Torren's office as I mentioned, they will always come safe.

Remember me affectionately to Sir J Banks & the ladies & tell him 'my tale of woe' as I have not time to write this post. I am rejoiced to hear he is better; tell him I heard from Hester as late as the 12th of March still from Syria, quite well. Ever affectionately yours JHS

We return to James's journal on the eve of the opening of the great campaign.

On the 13th we heard of Bonaparte's arrival on the frontier and on the 15th the enemy drove in the Prussian outposts who retreated to concentrate. The Prince of Orange on the 15th rode round the outposts and found the French withdrawn from our front and returned into Brussels to communicate that and the Prussian retreat[46] to the Duke and at ½ past 5 p.m. on the 15th he received the first intelligence of the real intentions of the enemy. At 7 the orders were issued for the army to be ready to move at a moments notice, but no order for movement was issued till night. Whether the Duke conceived that the enemy's movement on our left was a feigned one and that by a flank march Bonaparte would attempt to turn our right flank and gain Brussels by the Ath road, or whether he imagined the French were not sufficiently prepared to commence the campaign so early; but it is certain the Duke never had the army so little in hand as on the 16th.[47]

The Duchess of Richmond gave a ball the evening of the 15th but I thought it imprudent to be absent, besides which I was very unwell with an abscess beginning to form in my back with every appearance of my old wound breaking out again. The Duke was at the ball & conversed I am told with as much indifference as if the eventful moment had not been at hand. At 3 [a.m.] he was on horseback and in the morning a general movement took place. The Prince of Orange concentrated all he could at 4 Bras [Quatre Bras], consisting of Netherland troops & Brunswickers.[48] The 5th Division moved at night from Brussels and arrived at 4 Bras about 3 o'clock. The 1st Division moved at daylight to Braine le Comte where we were halted for some hours & then moved on to Nivelles. The 2nd was ordered to move also on Braine le Comte from Ath & the cavalry were to halt between it & Steenkirk & feed & then move on again in the evening. We had hardly taken up our ground in the rear of Nivelles at 4 o'clock which had been pointed out for the night when we received the order to move on with all speed as there was a severe action in which the Belgians had suffered considerably. We soon perceived the truth of this, for soon after passing Nivelles we met a good many wounded men going to the rear with ten times their number to take care of them, which did not strike me as a good specimen of the first trial of our allies.

A little farther on I met Colonel Dick of the 79th[49] who was also wounded & who told me they had been rode in upon by the French cavalry & suffered dreadfully.

As far as I can recollect of the ground it was like this: the wood being so thick that it was impossible to see what we were about or where the enemy was in force.

We had hardly arrived opposite the wood when Colonel Abercromby[50] Quarter Master General of the 1st Corps rode up to us in great haste & said 'The French are close to you, a battalion must go into the wood and happen what will you must maintain it'. The 2nd Battalion wheeled into line, entered the wood and in an instant were engaged & we followed also in line. We soon drove the enemy from the wood, but not without confusion from all the

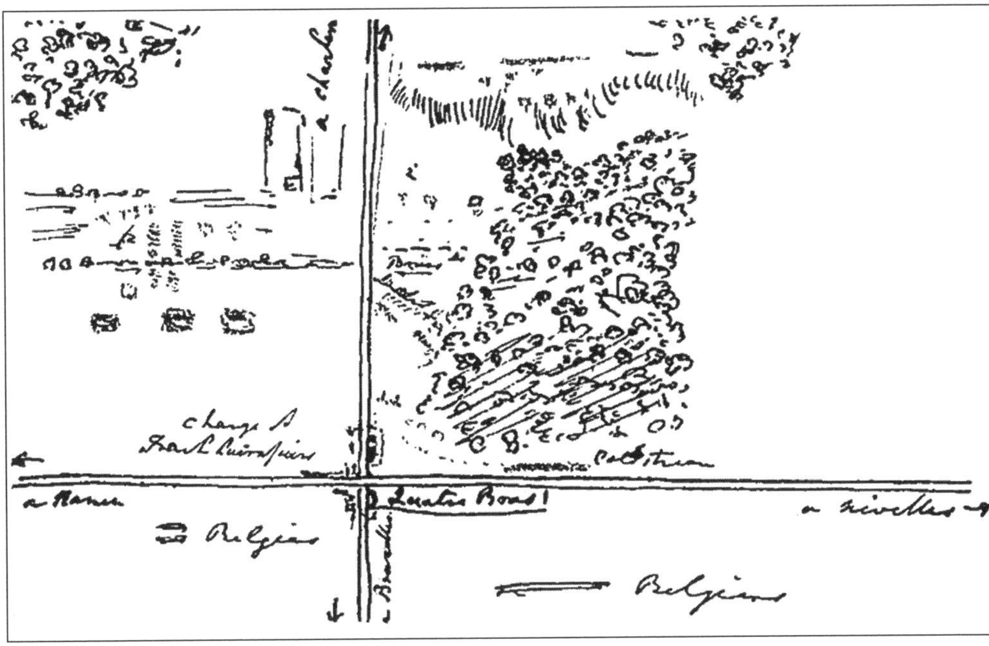

Quatre Bras.

> companies getting mixed in the wood. We suffered severely from the fire of the enemy's grape & round shot from a battery on the hill & still more from partial & I think imprudent attempts to attack it. We should have contented ourselves with maintaining the wood & covering our men. It was an unpleasant sort of battle, for we were very much in air & only supported by one battalion and if the French had moved a strong column round our right we should have been very uncomfortably situated. The enemy's cavalry behaved with great gallantry, some cuirassiers made a splendid charge up the road at two guns where the Duke was standing at the X-ways and in spite of the grape & the fire of ½ a battalion of infantry which were lining the bank, whom they probably had not seen, they *came close* up to the guns, but the fire then was so deadly that they rode into the courtyard of a farm close by where most of them were bayoneted.

James was struck from his horse by a branch when a tree was struck by a cannon ball but luckily he was unhurt.

> In reconsidering this battle there is certainly much truth in Ney's account of it, for our cavalry did not arrive till night having marched 25, 30 & some nearly 40 miles. Till very late we had no support and had the French carried the wood or been able to send a strong column round it, our communication with Nivelles & the advance of our supports would have been cut off.
>
> Two divisions of the French army, of the Guard, were neutralised completely by having first been sent from Ney to assist Bonaparte arriving near Fleurus when the action was decided & returning too late to cooperate in Ney's final attempt on our position.[51]

If Ney had had this addition, he would have outnumbered us so much as to have obliged us to get behind the defile of Genappe; which without cavalry would have been perilous in the extreme. But the great fault which Ney committed was not engaging us the next morning as early as possible so as to impede our retreat which Bonaparte with the victorious army should have been gaining on our right & moving towards our communications. The Prussians sent no report of their defeat & retreat, at least none arrived & it was only by a personal reconnaissance next morning, the Duke ascertained they were gone. Soon afterwards the report arrived, but during this interval, we were in a most critical position, but Ney's inactivity let us depart in quiet. Our brigade suffered a heavy loss, nearly 500 men killed & wounded; I had to deplore many of my best friends, poor Lord Hay,[52] General Maitland's A.D.C., than whom a finer creature could not be seen, Gore[53] whose education & acquirements were beyond what is commonly found & enhanced the esteem his amiable qualities inspired. Poor Miller[54] was a great loss to the service as his whole heart & mind were concentrated in the pursuit of his profession. I met a wounded person in a blanket, on asking the men who it was, he knew my voice & calling me to him, embraced me & bade me an affectionate farewell; passing the colours of the battalion afterwards which were in the rear of the wood, he desired that he might be carried under them & laid hold of them, he felt for the last time. He had been terribly wounded by the lancers & died some days afterwards.

The morning of the 17th summoned us from our clammy beds to perform the last sad offices to Gore & Hay who were buried under an hollow oak on the skirt of the wood. There is nothing more awfully impressive than this sublime service, affecting at all times, at a moment when the bearers feel the decisive hour is not yet come, when the enemy is still marshalled before their eyes & when perhaps before one night has passed, they may themselves require the aid, their affection & piety are now bestowing on their friends.

I took advantage of the pause before we moved to ride over the remainder of the field of battle. The highlanders were cut up from having been too slow in throwing themselves into squares. As I passed the spot where a heap of the French cuirassiers were laying, a figure covered & clotted with blood so that his face was indistinguishable rose up from the heap & with a swift but staggering pace went across the country towards the Guards. I returned & sent 2 drummers after him, but he was too far & the retreat commenced. I never knew who he was or heard of him more, but it was like an apparition, so rising from the mound of dead.

About 9 o'clock the Duke began to retire everything by that time having joined which he required, for Lord Hill was to cover the retreat of the wounded & stores from Nivelles. Whilst the infantry was moving off towards the defile, the Duke kept looking very anxiously towards the front and about

> 10 he said 'Well there is the last of the infantry gone & I don't care now'. Here Ney lost his best chance! We continued our retreat without interruption to the heights of Mont St Jean in the front of that village, having the 3rd Division on our left, the 6th on its left, Hougoumont like a bastion on the front of our right. Lord Hill's Corps at Braine la Leude en potence to the right and the corps of Prince Frederick with the 4th Division watching the great road by Hal.
>
> In the afternoon we heard a cannonade against the cavalry covering our retreat and found afterwards that the Life Guards has distinguished themselves against some of the heavy cavalry which had been too much for our hussars, some of whom came in upon us, rather in too quick time.
>
> Towards the evening we saw the enemy's columns arriving on the opposite hill; they sent some troops forward as if with the intention of occupying the wood of Hougoumont and some cavalry trotted towards the hill to see what was behind it. This obliged us to show some guns (all the columns being concealed behind the hill). After a few shot the enemy desisted and both armies lay on their arms all night & such a night was hardly ever passed before; for the ground was of such a spongy nature that it soon became a bog & torrents of rain fell without intermission till the morning, the wind driving it along with prodigious force & peals of thunder filling up the intervals of the lightnings. We could get no wood that would burn and we were all miserable enough, but the thoughts of the morrow superseded all others. As for myself I had been getting worse every day, could eat nothing, was in wretched spirits at the idea of being obliged to give it up, for my back was now so swelled [sic] I could not button my coat &c this completely overcame me. All my friends & the surgeons had urged me to go to Brussels from the 16th when we marched; I agreed that a board should inspect the wound on the morning of the 18th and determined to go to Brussels that night if the French did not attack. Some of my men got me a little dry wood & some straw & I bought a bottle of champagne from a sutler; I sent my servant (a sort of half Frenchman I had hired as a cook) to get a leg of mutton dressed; he was mounted on my horse & I saw him no more for 3 days. When we arrived on the position the day before, it did not appear so strong as a more accurate observation proved it to be. It was the best sort for English troops, a steep glacis on the French side and a moderate slope on ours, so that all movements might take place without being exposed to the observation or fire of the enemy. The army was in columns at ¼ distance in two lines with cavalry in reserve & powerful batteries of artillery were placed just within the ridge of the hill.

James's battalion remained upon the crest of the position behind the Chateau of Hougoumont for the whole day. The light companies of the two battalions were sent under Lord Saltoun to protect the wood and orchard of Hougoumont where they fought for most of the day. The rest of the brigade stood on the ridge above in line or square depending on the threat throughout the day, but did not move far forward or back. James remained with the battalion commanding his company and was not attached to any Staff as is sometimes stated,[55] and he describes what he saw of the momentous day.

At about 10 o'clock it became evident they meant to attack; the Duke had informed Blucher of his belief of it the night before and at ten, he saw part of the Prussian army filing over a small stream towards Wavre from the left of our position, but we as regimental officers hoped for their assistance, but did not know of it till we saw them.

The hills on which we had seen but small bodies the night before was now black with clustered troops & large masses of infantry and heavy columns began to move slowly over the plain, sometimes concealed by the undulations of the ground & then showing themselves again with increased magnitude & splendour, for gleams of the sun came out & their lancers pennons waved gaily in the wind; a column of infantry was directed against Hougoumont and another against La Haye Sainte. During all this our army was invisible behind the hill & the enemy could see nothing but a few horsemen & spectators amid untrodden & waving grain. It is impossible for a regimental officer to describe a battle, I will only attempt to sketch what I saw.

When the enemy's column was considered within range our artillery crowned the crest of the hill. The 1st shot, the signal of such slaughter was fired from our front, it fell short; the second plunged into the middle of the column and in an instant a blaze burst from the range of the hill, which roared from 100 mouths. Not many minutes elapsed before some round shot coming about us warned us of the French artillery being in position. The men were ordered to lie down, first being formed in echelon of squares, a field officer having the command of each face (I had the right). We heard the action raging hotly at Hougoumont & soon after the roll of musketry from the left announced the main attack on our centre at La Haye Sainte. A number of Staff officers were soon killed & wounded who were at first alone exposed to the cannonade. General Cooke lost his arm, shells began to fall in our squares & though many men were blown up & horribly mangled I never saw such steadiness. As the poor wounded wretches remained in the square it was a horrid sight in cold blood. Soon after a cry of cavalry was heard on the crest of the hill & we saw the artillerymen run from their guns & seek protection in our squares. The men stood up; we advanced a few yards & saw a mass of cuirassiers close to us with thousands of forked pennons waving behind them in all their vanity of colours. From the rain there was no dust & it was a most beautiful sight. The square on the left of the 3rd Division opened their fire first and soon from every square issued a steady well directed & destructive fire. For four hours the cavalry never left our front, sometimes retiring a little under the hill to get into order & then charging afresh with all the fury of despair; it is not possible to exaggerate their bravery. They repeatedly rode in upon & got temporary possession of our guns; the instant our fire drove them back, our brave artillerymen returned & poured fresh volleys of grape into their dense masses till successive charges drove them back into our squares. Thus continued our part of the battle & except a momentary impetuosity on first beating off the cavalry, when our men shouted & wished to charge, they were as cool as if in the park. The French cavalry at length sent skirmishers close up to us to fire pistols into our squares to tease us into a volley at these small game, whilst we saw their great masses below laying wait to charge; but we were as cool as they were & allowed only a few of our good shots to pick these fellows off. When we drove the cavalry from the guns many came up to us & shook their sabres at us in rage & some smashed their swords on the guns they had so often ineffectively taken. The Duke frequently rode by us, Lord Anglesey[56] rode up to us & said 'Well done men, by God we stand on you. If I could only get my fellows to do the same but by God they won't budge; but I'll try again'[57] & he rode and charged ineffectually at the head of a regiment of light cavalry on our left. The heavy cavalry did wonders, but our light cavalry, partly from their being brought up in small isolated attacks instead of a great mass, *in this part of the battle, near us* did very little. When the skirmishers were teasing us, Horace Seymour[58] rode up in a great hurry & said 'God damn you; don't you see there are French. Why don't you fire at them?'; on which Lord Saltoun,[59] who had returned from Hougoumont almost all his men being killed & wounded, answered very coolly 'Why damn you; don't you think we know better when to fire than you do?' and away went our advisor. By this time grape began to thin our ranks and the French infantry approached; they ought to have been there 3 hours before, for by this time we had finished their cavalry. Their first attack we beat off with fire; Maitland who commanded the division on Cooke's wound, one of the bravest, ablest & best informed of our generals, as he is one of the kindest & best of men, began to fear we might lose the artillery in case of a reverse & sent me to find the artillery horses which had departed during our conflict with the cavalry.[60] I passed the cavalry dismounted in a hollow in the rear; nothing could exceed the confusion towards the village of St Jean. During the action with the cavalry, numbers of Belgians had left their places and the whole road was choked with their cavalry of all sorts, wounded on horseback & in blankets, artillery wagons passing & returning. I met the Prince of Orange wounded, Fitzroy Somerset, Elley[61] and as I was returning not having found the horses, I met poor Stables[62] of my own battalion, who had been wounded in my absence with a grape shot through the body. By his looks I saw it was all over, I helped him to an artillery wagon near; he died at a cottage next morning & a sergeant who attended him saw him decently buried.

Napoleon had launched his final gamble, ordering forward his Imperial Guard to smash a hole through the exhausted British line. Wellington, being aware of the danger, called up every reserve unit he could find and formed the troops in lines four rank deep, a precaution against renewed cavalry attacks, and patiently awaited their attack. The French guardsmen, in two huge columns, neared the crest of the ridge despite incurring heavy casualties from artillery fire. For a fleeting moment, success looked within their grasp, then all in an instant changed. The British Guards, who had been lying down for cover, stood up and fired incessant volleys into the column approaching them, destroying the head and the rest turned and fled, the guards in pursuit. The second column was assaulted in flank by the 52nd Foot and took heavy casualties, the column eventually imploding and the remnants fleeing for safety. James returned in time to witness the attack by the 52nd and the general advance launched by Wellington as French morale visibly collapsed and they turned and fled en masse.

> I hastened back to my battalion, but they had advanced. The first regiment I came up to was the 52nd who were on the flank of the grand attack of the Imperial Guard, who advanced beautifully with their officers in their front waving their swords & hats & cheering them on with 'Vive Napoleon'.[63]
>
> A shout burst from the English line and such a shout of victory never can be forgotten when the fire poured in on them on all sides, stopped them as if turned into stone. The front sections fell like cards; they began to show timidity toward the rear & the English line shouted & moved on. Some cavalry (I believe the old Heavy Germans of Bock's in Spain now turned into light cavalry[64]) swept round the flank of the 52nd and the confusion from that moment & rout were complete. Pausing on the top of the next hill for the first time, I saw that it was not all owing to us. I had heard some time an additional firing in the front of our left, but amid such thunder had thought little about it. It was now getting dusk, but the last gleam showed me a sight all description cannot give an idea of. The plain now dimly seen was dark with a mass of mingled combatants and indistinct from the firing which was still partially kept up on the left towards La Belle Alliance, from the wind setting that way & the ground being wet the smoke of the battle hung low on the ground. Through this at speed came gun after gun & squadron after squadron, who with their lances waving seemed as if they were charging on a cloud. To witness such a glorious soul transporting sight, to feel that I had been able to go through the battle & to be grateful at having survived it, was the work of a moment; but the last feeling of that day. I was then with the Coldstream[65] & perfectly exhausted had dismounted from my horse & laid down upon the ground & in a moment was asleep. The Guards were ordered on and when they came to their final bivouac for the night, one of my friends (I believe Major Bowles[66]) missed me & recollected he had seen me lay down. He sent back & after a considerable search I was found still asleep among the dead & the dying, the plunderers &

the plundered. If they [had] not remembered me, some kindly hand would probably have spared me the trouble of awaking again. I remained with the Coldstream all night & next morning rejoined my battalion which was about a mile in front to the left, close to La Belle Alliance.

The morning after the battle, James prepared to take himself to Brussels sick. However, despite his poor health, he was urged to take on a significant role during the advance to Paris.

In the morning of the 19th I prepared to go to Brussels when Sir John Byng,[67] now commanding 1st Corps, urged me so strongly to take if but for a day the duty of Quarter Master General as Abercromby QMG of the 1st Corps & Bradford of the 1st Division[68] were both wounded, that I determined at all risks to attempt it; but it was an arduous undertaking for any one from the ranks with no knowledge of previous arrangements without sufficient horses & with no maps, in my state of health to take such a responsibility, as the charge of the 1st Corps then amounting I suppose to 15,000 men. At Nivelles the same evening I begged him to write to get someone else, but the orders arrived in the middle of the night and it was impossible. The exertion & fatigue began to absorb the abscess, my appetite returned & I was evidently better. In three days I no longer thought of leaving the army & I was rejoiced in being joined by my servant & favourite mare. He had been taken but had escaped in the confusion of the retreat. But I must add a very few thoughts on the general character of this great battle.

On the whole it has been perhaps the severest ever fought by British troops, for although our infantry has been often exposed to more unequal numbers and as destructive a fire, it never was called on to resist the united efforts of such a tremendous cannonade & such a cloud of cavalry at a moment when our artillerymen were driven from their guns & our cavalry were unable to make head against the stream. The contracted limits of the position made the slaughter immense as the cannonade was concentrated, but it was fortunate, for the Dutch & Belgians soon began to disappear and their gaps would have been fatal to us in a more extended position. When the battle began we had two or 3 squares between us & the 3rd Division, before it ended the redcoats were the nearest battalion. The Prince of Orange[69] who has been since praised into believing his countrymen to be heroes, wrote the next morning most anxiously to the Duke 'To know how he could explain or pass over the conduct of the Netherland troops', & the Duke answered 'I shall praise generally and not detail, so nobody will know anything about them'.[70] We appear to have had the least share as all nations equally claim the victory & even the French scarce allow a defeat.

My unbiased opinion is this, as to the real proportion of the victory due to the Prussian & English armies; without the Prussians we should have held our position, we should have made our first advance so as to occupy the field of battle & with that perhaps 100 cannon & many thousand prisoners would have been the trophies of the English victory. The French would have been secure behind the defile of Genappe; our loss was so immense, the little dependence on our Netherland friends so plain, that it would have admitted of a doubt whether we or the enemy had retreated next day. To the Prussians[71] therefore is due the great results of the victory, the sanguinary unrelenting & unceasing pursuit and the total dispersion of the army. So complete was it that our march to Paris was as if through a friends country, not one man of all that mighty army was to be seen. It seemed by the suddenness of their appearance at Ligny & 4 Bras that the earth had disgorged a host to lay it waste and that they had again crept into her womb, so utter the solitude we witnessed. Beyond the limits where the dead marked the pursuit, no trace remained of that boasting & nearly triumphant army.

As it is usual with the unfortunate, Bonaparte has been much blamed for his management of this campaign, & Ney & Grouchy have largely shared in it. I will not enter at length into this question but simply state:

1st That Ney was most to blame at 4 Bras or *whoever directed* the Guard backward & forward without use.[72] That in answer to the attack made on Bonaparte for not having retired before he was entombed by the Prussians round his flank on the 18th; it must be recollected he was an Emperor as well as a general & that if he had retreated, the prestige was gone and his empire must have passed away; & he has been blamed for detaching Grouchy & the latter has been more censured for not having come to his assistance. I will relate the opinions of the Duke of Wellington as I heard him express them on these points for I believe them to be the truth. At a dinner at Grassini's at Paris[73] a Frenchman asked if he might speak frankly to the Duke about the battle, who answered yes, & in answer to several questions said 'It is very easy to fight a battle when it's over. How could Grouchy come to his assistance? He had a superior army in his front, which it was necessary to keep in check; and if he had at last wished to detach, there was no time. I saw the Prussians within four miles of us filing over a stream at 10 in the morning. The impediments were so great that they did not reach us till 7. How then could any detachment of Grouchy who had 3 times the distance to come, have arrived in time?' He was asked what he should have done if he had been Bonaparte, he said 'I think I should have respected the English infantry more after what I must have heard of them in Spain & that I should not have taken the bull by the horns; I should have turned a flank, the right flank. I should have kept the English army occupied by a demonstration to attack or perhaps by slight attacks, whilst I was in fact moving the main body by Hal on Brussels; but if I had determined on attacking as Bonaparte did, *nobody could do more*'.

The French lost much by the destruction of their cavalry against our squares so early, but it was not Bonaparte's fault for he sent frequently to recall them, but once on the plateau they could not be made to retire. The rain was much in our favour for from there being no dust we saw every movement plain & would fire without risk to each other. Nothing daunts the soldier more so much as a charge of cavalry proceeded by a cloud of dust which concealing the force magnifies the peril. Many days elapsed before we knew who had fallen; I had to deplore many of my oldest friends. The country had to mourn Picton, the most intrepid & the sternest soldier we had; for De Lancey who had but one thought, his profession. Few had studied so deeply in theory & fewer still illustrated it so bravely, skilfully & frequently by practise. Frederick Ponsonby who is physically immortal was saved to us;[74] his friends which includes all who know him, could scarce have rejoiced over a battle in which their favourite had fallen. I escaped entirely untouched, one of the 4 out of 14 field officers who marched on the 16th, all the rest being killed or wounded.[75]

The day after the battle, despite taking on the role of Quarter Master General, James found time to send off two very short messages to his mother and Mansfield to confirm his survival from the carnage; that evening he found time to write a much longer letter to Lady Mansfield with a particular account of the battle and one to the Duke of York.

Braine [la Leud] 19 June 1815

My dear mother,

I have only time to tell you that I am safe, not having 30 left out of 400 in the two actions.[76] We never gained such a victory as yesterday; my old wound is very troublesome but I must go on as I am acting as Quarter Master General for the present, Bradford being wounded. Write to Griselda & tell her with my love, I am well & to Sir J[oseph Banks], General Graham & all friends; God bless you, JHS.

Bivouac in front of Braine la Leud [no date, 19 June morning?]

Dear M[ansfiel]d

I have only time to tell you that I am safe after two of the most desperate actions I ever knew, my company have not 30 men left; such a glorious [victory] as yesterday was never seen before and the Guards saved all.

The cavalry behaved infamously, our fatigues have been excessive and I could hardly sit on horseback yesterday, but I must go on as I am desired to act as Q.M.G. to the division, Bradford being wounded.

My health is better than one could have expected. With kindest remembrances to Lady Mansfield and all family, affectionately yours J.H.S.

Nivelles 19 June; Evening

I wrote a few lines this morning from the field of battle to tell you I was safe, but now being again in a house with clean hands and face, I have more time and power of telling you the particulars of the last battle. You will see by the despatches that on the 16th Blucher was somewhat defeated & that the 1st Brigade of Guards (ours) just came up in time to save the Belgians from a complete rout; we suffered amazingly but succeeded in keeping the wood which was the key of everything. But Blucher retiring, we fell back to a position in front of Waterloo where Bonaparte attacked us yesterday with above 100,000 men;[77] we had about 65,000 in position and an immense artillery. The action began with a cannonade such as I believe never was seen before and under its cover about 15,000 cavalry advanced, drove our cavalry fairly off, & then came up to the infantry which was formed in squares, the 2 battalions of Guards in the front thus [see drawing]: with some German & Brunswickers, & never did men behave more magnificently than the French. They charged all the squares, were received as at a field day and repulsed with enormous slaughter, but they never went 400 yards & charged 7 or 8 times in as desperate a manner, particularly the cuirassiers who are nearly annihilated, meanwhile large masses of infantry were coming up.

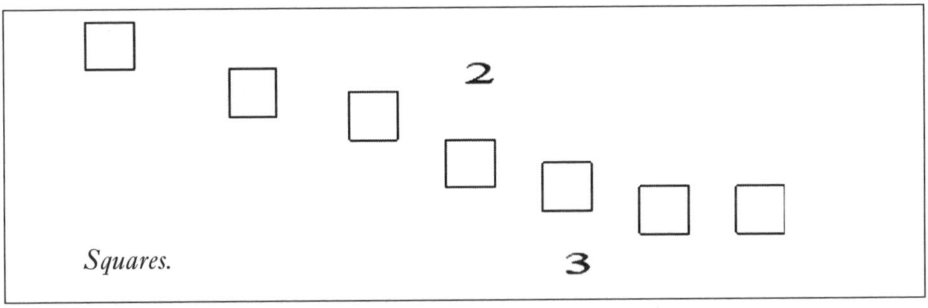

We deployed and charged them, then cavalry came again at us, we formed squares & repulsed them & thus alternately till we were nearly beaten, the French had taken part of our artillery & the English infantry stood exposed to the united efforts of cavalry, infantry & artillery. Lord Uxbridge riding about in the most gallant manner heading everything but lamenting that the cavalry had all deserted him & 'conjuring us to redeem the lost honour', there never was so critical a moment. No retreat was left but through one road blocked up with the baggage & wounded & covered with fugitives of various sorts. The Duke of W[ellington] (over whom providence presided in a most extraordinary manner as he was in the most murderous fire the whole day) thought it nearly desperate but said, 'If the whole artillery can be brought up & the infantry is firm it will all do, for Blucher is coming up.'

Still the attack went on and a slaughter ensued on both sides to which the

French say Leipzig[78] was not equal, and our artillery played with terrible effect, on the infantry advancing [they] retook the guns which were again opened on the enemy. About 7 o'clock they tried their last desperate exertion having fought 7 hours. The Imperial Guard with Bonaparte in person at their head attacked us, the Grenadiers with him, came toward our brigade, the rest to the 52nd, 71st, 95th; we poured in a volley close which mowed down the front ranks, cheered & charged, they wavered, opened & turned round. We pursued them over the plain and at this moment the immense cavalry of the Prussians followed by artillery & columns of infantry as far as the eye could reach, appeared sweeping towards the enemy's right & from that moment no more order was preserved & had we light, the whole army had been annihilated. As it is, most of their artillery and baggage is taken & the field of battle for miles together is covered with their bodies. The Prussians pursued all night & gave no quarter. I can form no idea of their loss or ours, but of the latter I but too deeply feel that it has been dreadful. I never lost so many friends in a campaign as in this 4 days. We have lost I should think 1,500 out of 3,400.[79] I have lost 60 out of 96 and the dreadful number of principal officers killed & wounded exceeds anything we had ever before to lament. Yet recollecting that the battle probably decided the fate of Europe, that this effort was not made by Bonaparte without weakening greatly the army opposed to the Russians & that the effect on the nation will be powerful, and with the proud feeling that the two brigades of Guards were principally conducive to the glorious result, what can one regret? I omitted to say that the steadiness of the other brigade in keeping a wood [Hougoumont], the key of our position, all the morning, was most brilliant & saved us.

The Duke of W[ellington] expressed himself stronger than I ever heard him.

Towards the middle of the action I left the square to bring up artillery & was unable to get back being nearly taken by the cavalry. I got to other parts of the line & fortunately escaped untouched; a ball struck my sword & on the 16th I was knocked off my horse by a cannon shot which struck a bough against me. I was in a good deal of pain yesterday & so beat with fatigue that I could hardly keep my head up, but sleep has banished all and I begin to hope that the battle has frightened away the abscess. In short I shall stay with the army as Sir J Byng now commanding the corps, from everybody being killed or wounded, has desired me to act as Q.M.G. to the division till further orders. I should hope the Duke of W[ellington] will keep me so & then do not you think I shall have reason to be pleased at having remained patient & stuck to my humble duty? The Duke of W[ellington]'s Staff has suffered severely. I am afraid part of this letter is too military & all too badly written to be legible or intelligible, but it is [done]. I have not time to write to Lord Lynedoch so pray remember me to him & tell the particulars. With renewed reminiscences to Lord M[ansfield] & others, ever faithfully yours [Unsigned]

The night before we marched when the orders came I wrote something I shall send when I get my baggage.

To The Duke of York[80]

Nivelles 19 June 1815

Though Y[our] R[oyal] H[ighness] will receive many better accounts of our late battles than I can give you, yet the Guards have in both, so eminently distinguished themselves & so much conduced to the great result, that I cannot deny myself the pleasure of communicating one more testimony.

When the French cavalry attacked us in squares (which they did with the most persevering gallantry, never retiring above 100 or 150 paces & charging again) our men behaved as if they were at a field day, firing by ranks & with the best possible aim. Under a most destructive cannonade & having several shells burst in the middle of us, not a man moved from his place. Our cavalry could not be brought on, and at last we became exposed to the united efforts of all their arms and changed from line to squares, squares from line, as the circumstances of the case required. Of this part, I can give Y[our] R[oyal] H[ighness] a less good account, as I left the square to bring up the artillery horses to the guns the French had taken & we had again got possession of & could not get back for their cavalry; but I reached the right whence I saw the remainder of the action. There was a moment peculiarly critical & where nothing but the extraordinary steadiness of the troops saved the day & the murderous effect of our artillery was not the least cause of our victory. The Duke of W[ellington] exposed himself in the hottest fire the whole day & has lost a number of his Staff. Lord Uxbridge headed every charge & was in the middle of the fire; but was most furious against the cavalry, in whose defence it is however to be said, that they were outnumbered nearly two to one.

The most gratifying event of the whole day was, the desperate attack made about 7 o'clock by the Imperial Guard, headed by Bonaparte in person. The Grenadiers attacked the Guards and had soon cause to find that they would not sup in Brussels, as the Emperor had told them. The arrival of the Prussian cavalry sweeping round the right flank of the enemy, in masses with columns as far as the eye could reach, was a magnificent spectacle. The French were however beaten before, but this was a very pretty finale. The Prussians pursued all night & [I] hear gave no quarter & took most of the artillery which had not fallen into our hands before.

The loss of the Guards, particularly in officers, Y[our] R[oyal] H[ighness] will see by the returns, has been most severe. Poor Stables died this morning as universally regretted as he was by every one loved. I hope Wyndham's[81] wound is not a serious one and I trust the rest of the wounded officers will do well. I fear much however for Miller but have heard nothing of him since the 15th [16th?].

> The steadiness and unconquerable obstinacy with which the Second Brigade held a wood & house in the front of our right excited the admiration of all & saved us, for it was the angle from whence Lord Hill's corps was formed 'en potence'.
>
> I have not mentioned the action of the 15th [16th] though I hope it will also meet Y[our] R[oyal] H[ighness's] approbation, as the First Brigade arrived at the critical moment when the Belgians were giving way. Were it possible for me to add anything to the reputation of Maitland, by stating the gallantry he has shown on both occasions, cheering on with his hat off. I could dwell long on the subject; but I am convinced Y[our] R[oyal] H[ighness] is sufficiently aware of it.
>
> I have fortunately escaped unhurt, though a cannon shot striking a tree knocked me off my horse on the 15th [16th] & I had a ball strike my sword yesterday. I hope Y[our] R[oyal] H[ighness] will forgive this scrawl as I am not a little fatigued. I remain &c J H Stanhope.

James resumed his journal as the army marched towards Paris.

> 19th moved on Nivelles, 20th on Binche, passed field of Malplaquet.[82] The Duke passed the corps who cheered him and such a cheer in such a spot it brought tears into my eyes, & entered Bavay on the 21st.
>
> 22nd Headquarters at Le Cateau [Cambresis], we at Gommegnies I saved a poor woman's cow, whose approaching fate she was lamenting in a most simple & affecting manner.
>
> 23rd we halted, went over to head quarters; the Duke put me in orders as Quarter Master General. I congratulated him on his victory & escape; he said with much feeling in his tone 'Indeed it was wonderful, the finger of God was certainly on me on that day.' Cambrai was taken by escalade.
>
> 24th Bousies, 25th Premont. 26th 1st Division ordered to Caulaincourt, passed the magnificent canal of St Quentin.

The Guards were sent to Peronne whose fortress lay on the bank of the River Somme. The Duke of Wellington summoned the garrison, but being refused ordered an immediate assault. James's version of the assault does not show the engineers in a good light, but some Dutch artillery helped blow down the gates and James was sent forward under a flag of truce to negotiate the terms for the capitulation of Peronne.[83]

> At Caulaincourt I found fresh orders for the Guards to attack Peronne, where the Duke already was. He had summoned it & the governor refused to surrender. The chief engineer insisted on the ditch being shallow as he saw reeds. I examined several peasants & reported to the Duke there was 10 feet [of] water. Fascines were made, the attack ordered & the engineer warned us against the bridge which was mined. We moved on, in went the fascines & after them an engineer, who sank like a float with a bite. There was no entrance that

way, but the light infantry drove the enemy from the suburb & crossed the bridge which was not mined; a gun was brought up & we blew open the gate. The Duke was on the bridge close by me when we were covered with a shower of grape but escaped. Lord Saltoun was knocked over by one which lodged in his purse. I went in to try to negotiate; on seeing my handkerchief they ceased firing at me & I went in alone. Terms were soon settled; in the meantime some Belgian cavalry cut the ropes of the drawbridge & came in with every appearance of violence. On trying to get them out according to the terms of the capitulation, they tried to cut me down & the French governor was obliged to draw in my defence; I never could find out the men though I reported it.

A short note to Lady Mansfield is headed as having been written on 19 June (the morning after the battle) but cannot be, as James refers to Peronne.

Your nice memorandum book with all my journal, etc & 20 Napoleons hopped out of my pocket in the attack of Peronne. Therefore pray send me another for I am in despair at losing it.

At Paris I will write again adieu.

Do not believe when I say I am well, that it is only to calm uneasiness about me, for upon my honour I am as stout & hearty as ever I was saving being a little pulled by work.

When I look back it seems like a dream that I should have been so ill, so cured & am here fifty four miles from la Bonne Ville [Paris]. A hearty cheer will we give when we see Notre Dame. Ever more your dear

27th Billancourt, 28th Conchy [les Pots], 29th Choisy [au Bac] 30th La Chapelle [en Serval].

Conchy [les Pots] 28 June 1815

My dear mother,

I hope you received my letter written the day after the battle acquainting you of my safety, since which I have been too busy to write. I am happy to say the exertion I used on the 18th began my cure & that I have been daily getting better and by the time we get to Paris which I think will be next Sunday I hope not to feel any more inconvenience. We are now fifty four miles only from it and no army against us. We have not seen a French soldier except in their garrisons since we entered. The military are retired to their own homes. The English part of our army behave as well as it is possible for men to do even in their own country, but the Belgians and Prussians plunder.

We had a very pretty affair on the 26th in storming Peronne a very strong place with wet ditches and a garrison of 450 men. It was attacked by the Brigade of Guards and the assault was so well managed that we got the fausse bray without a severe loss. I then summoned the town & went with a flag of truce & the governor capitulated on condition of the garrison retiring chez eux [to them].

We took twenty good guns & considerable stores. It looked a desperate attempt but except a hot fire of grape we received but little mischief.

Had it been well defended it never could have been taken without a considerable siege; I think that it will turn out the last fight. Pour moi je suis satisfait [For me, I am satisfied] with Waterloo, for no earthly consideration, no wealth or honours would I exchange for the delight of having witnessed such a day. I am confirmed on the Staff as Assistant Quarter Master General to the 1st Division. Remember me affectionately to Sir J[oseph] & family and to General G[renville] & Lord G[eorge Russell?], ever affectionately yours, JHS.

1st of July Le Bourget in front of Montmartre, the army took up a position. I went down to Aubervilliers with the 1st Division to relieve the Prussian Corps of Bulow, whose Quarter Master General did not like my visiting the outposts in a red coat & with a white feather & wanted me to change clothes; loopholed & fortified entrance of Le Bourget; heard of Blucher's crossing the Seine

James wrote to Lady Mansfield, giving details of the preparations to drive the French defenders away from Paris.

[Le] Bourget in front of Monmartre 2 July 1815

I never can sufficiently express my gratitude for your kind letter and your solicitude about me. I received it on the 29th, I wrote to Mansfield on the 28th. This far have we got without difficulty & in the utmost order, but since we have entered the Prussian line of march our comforts were materially diminished, havoc having wasted everything in the most wanton manner & the only answer given to remonstrance is that the French did the same in Prussia. I never saw their army in Spain commit ravages more systematically than these fellows. I am now in a beautiful chateau, all the furniture of which is broken, fine glasses smashed, books torn to rags, linens & curtain cut up to adorn the Prussian amazons. The wine vats broke & the wine wasted, all the poultry killed & left in the fields and in short every village is the same. At La Chapelle I was in a notaries and the confusion of the Sybil's leaves were nothing to the disarrangement of his papers. Every inhabitant flies their approach & gradually return when they see the redcoats, hardly knowing their own homes again. We relieved the Prussian 4th Corps (commanded by Bulow whom I knew at Antwerp) yesterday & they have marched by Saint Germain [en Lay] & joined the rest of their army on the other side of the Seine. They are much diminished in numbers (now 65,000) from leaving corps to blockade the fortresses & from having lost nearly 25,000 men in the last battles, mostly on the 16th. We have about 50 [thousand] and the French by the last accounts have about 50 to 60,000 regulars. The National Guard cannot be trusted. Our reception yesterday was very gratifying as the [Prussian] regiments all cheered us with their bands playing 'God Save the King' & crying out 'Brave English'. It is our discipline that most astonishes them & indeed I am nearly as much so, for with most severe marching & not too good supplies, we (the 1st Division at least) have not one complaint. In the several villages we have passed, I have given trifling sums to poor wretches who had crawled back to their desolate cottages, particularly 2 old sisters of about 70 to 80 each to whom I took a great partiality from their resemblance to my old nurse and I never saw people so grateful in my life. In all the towns, the moment the English uniform is seen confidence in the usual occupations are resumed, the Belgians follow, which remember were in the French army and are not too faithful, & every house is shut at the moment. All this makes one justly proud of being an Englishman, for this is no less creditable to us than our fighting.

I had a desperate fatiguing day yesterday in taking up all the posts of the Prussians but stand it perfectly. Have a most outrageous appetite returned & have no inconvenience from the wound except towards the evening. Thanks for your enquiries for the faithful Wheeler.[84] He is the most attached creature, for the joy he expressed when he saw me safe & sound on the 19th when he returned from Brussels to which all the baggage were ordered passes anything I ever saw. The rest of the establishment stands it well, I lost my cook in the bustle but have replaced him with an English groom which in my new capacity is more useful. I have also increased my stud, but a beautiful little pony I had, I gave to my nephew who is just out to join the 4th and who made his beginning on the 18th.[85]

I may now as well tell you something about the front, Monmartre seems to be unattackable, but I think we could gain without much loss the heights of Romainville & then sweep the ridge by Belleville. They have one very strong redoubt but I think we might shell them out of it. I send you an idea of our position for the benefit of any who choose to see it, especially the Laird of L[ynedoch]. We occupy such strong villages that we cannot be attacked, but the Prussians are isolated a good deal and were they beaten we must go behind the Oise. If they could beat us (which they cannot) the Prussian army would be in a nice scrape. In the meantime the Confederation of the Rhine are to arrive in 2 or 3 days to the amount of 25,000; 40 Bavarian called 60 [thousand] about the 6th, the advance of Russians 50,000 about the 8th & the Austrians at Nancy on the 6th. On dit the Royalists have entered Nantes. Davout commands in Paris[86] & is furious, Bonaparte gave back on the 30th & offered to command the army against Blucher 'prenant la responsabilite sur la tete' [taking responsibility at the head] but he was sent out. Meanwhile some negotiation is going on as officers & couriers are going through our posts every hour but I cannot hear what the terms are. I trust in God the thing will be settled so far besides being unwilling to lose any more friends. I should not wish to see Paris exposed to the horrors these villages have endured. It would be madness to hold out for should we even be repulsed, we are but the avant garde of the immense army & on the side of Blucher they have no works. It is a most eventful moment and an awful pause to which however I am indebted for the time to write this. I have not yet found out the number of friends I have lost in the late battles & am afraid to ask. Every moment swells the list, between the English & old Germans (the Legion) we have lost above 13,000. De Lancey alas is dead & his poor wife is quite distracted; still if a person is to fall in the field, more glorious is his tomb on such a spot where the fate of Europe was decided than in any other. Those I most regret are when one's friends fall in petty skirmishers & are only mentioned in a postscript. Frederick Ponsonby is I hear doing well; he was stuck on the ground which is the fashion [of] the lancers. I must conclude for the present, God bless you with most affectionate remembrances to all & pinches extra for O & Ito, ever faithfully yours.

I do admire your spirit, you should be called Cornelia & were I episcopal I would so confirm it.

By the way they say [obliterated] was arrested on Bonaparte's return; I hope he may be well plundered.

Later James wrote in his journal a short but monumental note: 'On the 2nd the convention was signed'.

Whilst at Le Bourget, James wrote a long letter to Lady Spencer giving an in-depth analysis of the campaign and current situation.

Letter to Lady Spencer[87]

Le Bourget, in front of Montmartre. 3rd July 1815

Two things have prevented my writing to you dear Lady Spencer, want of time and ignorance about the state of poor Frederick Ponsonby. But now the war is over as a suspension of hostilities has taken place and as I hear that 'hang it' is quite out of danger, I cannot refrain from giving you an outline of our campaign which I fear you nevertheless consider as an outrageous attack against the just liberties of a people.

Bonaparte's plan appears to have been as able as anything he ever did and was not far from succeeding. The collection of his troops was made in such a manner that either the Duke was lulled into security or, what is more probable, was apprehensive of a false movement and suspected though they assembled near Maubeuge they might attack him on the Ath road.

At any rate the Duke left a ball at Brussels at 2 [am] the army began to collect, marching from their different points at daylight and the 5th Division having marched 25 miles had a severe action in the evening and we having moved something more just arrived to save the wood which was the key of the position which the Belgians had all but lost. We were under every disadvantage, the cavalry having all to move 30 and some 45 miles and therefore they were useless on that day.[88] Had the wood been lost the French army was between our corps and we must have retreated that night.

Blucher's retreat the same night left us in no pleasant position, but the Duke eased us off little by little and expressed his joy when he saw all the infantry gone. We took up the position the Duke will describe in his despatch and endured the most tremendous night troops ever were exposed to, without fires and immersed in all the richness of Belgian mud.

The house [Hougoumont] was the key of the position as it was at the angle on which the potence rested and was defended by the 2nd Brigade of Guards. The whole hill was covered with a formidable artillery and the infantry were in columns ready to form squares: for this was the most singular feature of the battle, at least on the right and centre that it was fought almost entirely in squares, being exposed to the fire of above 250 pieces of artillery and the united efforts of cavalry and infantry. What past [sic] on the left I only know by hearsay, that the heavy cavalry made a most brilliant charge and suffered severely in being led on too far. On our side we were in echelons of squares as I have sketched with my pen most incorrectly[89] but to give a rough idea of it and in two lines supported by cavalry.

Having been pounded by shot and shell till your morning service was about over, we were assailed by a most immense body of cavalry against which our light cavalry made no head and showed a lamentable inferiority of which no one can give a better account than Lord Uxbridge who by the way showed himself one of the calmest and bravest of men.

The reception of the cavalry by our squares was magnificent, though suffering severely from the artillery, every man felt his own security and poured in a fire as destructive as it was well sustained. But the cuirassiers [&] lancers were not to be discouraged and for above an hour they continued never retreating above 200 yards and then charging again, Barnes the Adjutant General waving them on and our men at length learning to despise their power over steady infantry. Frequently the enemy sent in tirailleurs of their cavalry to fire their pistols in our squares hoping that it should fire a volley and that they might charge us with their mass before we could load, but their hopes were disappointed. In the meantime the house and garden had been attacked by a heavy column of infantry, the French cavalry had passed it and were lined on the brow of the hill but nothing shook its defenders and the attacks were successfully and successively repulsed. A heavy column had moved along the high road to the left where supported by an immense cavalry (force), a furious action ensued and two columns of infantry were seen moving over the plain in a concentrating direction, on that front of the line occupied by the 1st Brigade of Guards the 52nd, 71st etc. and some Brunswickers. Here the English infantry did what never was practised before, deploying into line and beating the infantry and then forming four deep to beat the attacks of the cavalry who had been waiting for the moment of our confusion to complete our rout. So stood the battle, when the last desperate effort was made by three columns of Imperial Guards. The Grenadiers of it, accompanied by Bonaparte to the bottom of the hill, came to our share, the right column to that of the 52nd etc. and it is hard to say which was cleaned away the soonest. Our men poured in a fire standing four deep, the men who had fired then went to the fourth rank to load and thus without interruption a destructive hail was kept up against which nothing could stand and the hill was heaped with their dead. Thus long had the army stood, just keeping their ground and where any link breaking, the whole would have been annihilated, for with the superiority of the French cavalry, retreat was out of the question. The first impetus of the French checked, it seems the Duke made up his mind to convert a difficult defence into an attack. Everything advanced and everything before us fled. A French general whom I have met since as a negotiator said that a cry ran through the ranks, 'que la vielle garde fuyait' [that the Old Guard runs away] and that in an instant as if by magic everyone consulted his own safety by flight. Bonaparte told Count Lobau striking his own forehead, 'Il n'y a rien comme l'infanterie anglaise' [There is nothing like the English infantry].

At this time the roar of the Prussian artillery was heard on our left and soon appeared through the smoke which hung heavily on the field what appeared a fresh army springing from the earth and sweeping on in pursuit of the enemy. Of all sights the plain then presented the most magnificent and of all moments that was the proudest and it is useless to attempt to describe it. To give you an idea how well our artillery behaved, I must tell you the French cavalry frequently charged through the guns but could not carry them off, the artillery men ran to the squares for safety and the instant our fire repulsed the enemy, returned to their practice of grape and this was repeated several times.

You will tag me with national vanity if I say that no other army could have kept that hill and stood such attacks but I am well convinced of the fact and that we could not without the Duke who outdid himself and set an example that never was surpassed. How he escaped or indeed how anyone came alive out of that scene of carnage is strange. The field of battle was not large and the killed of both sides could be easily distinguished and I understand above 18,000 French bodies have been buried.

Of our subsequent events I need say nothing as with this exception of our attack on Peronne it has been like a walk through England. These heights on our front were enough to frighten us and I am truly thankful that the business will be settled without the effusion of more blood.

God forbid that I should ever see such a battle again for I hardly dare to ask what friends I have left. Yet it was decisive and we probably should have lost more in several battles to reach this place.

I must now say two words about myself. About two weeks before we moved, another abscess began to form in my back and I suffered so much that I had determined, having got through the 16th, to go to Brussels on the 18th if we had not been attacked. The great exertion of the day commenced my cure and absorption has delivered me for the present of my enemy. I was appointed Assistant Quarter Master General to the 1st Division a day or two after the battle, which I continue.

I fear you can hardly decipher or comprehend this letter. If you can, pray show it to Heber, for I cannot write any more at present.

On the 4th we occupied St Denis, 5th Monmartre & on the 7th the whole army was encamped in the Bois de Boulogne. Much has been said of this convention, it was certainly purely a military one; it was very advantageous to both parties. Blucher against the Duke's advise had hurried on to be the 1st in Paris & would have been attacked next morning by nearly 70,000 men who were in Paris & he had not above 40,000. The Duke meant to have moved the

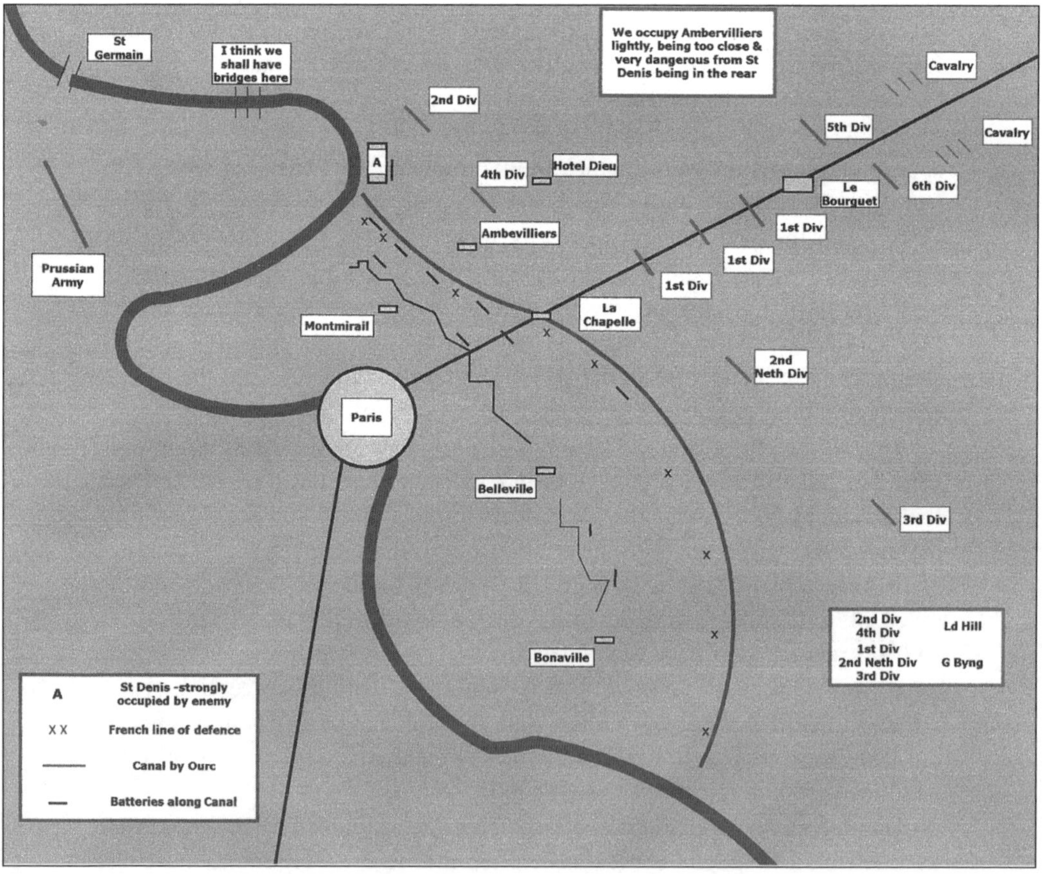

Before Paris (taken from a hand-drawn map by James Stanhope which is now too faint to copy).

English army right to support him and we should have probably arrived in time, but it was foolish to risk anything when the game was our own and if we had waited a few days in position together we might [have] taken Paris without terms & annihilated the army of the Loire. The French saved their capital & we put an end to the possible intrigues of fortune; and thus ended with a pacific march and a coup de plume [stroke of the pen], our shortest & most glorious campaign.

The workload was not onerous at Paris now that peace had arrived and James spent much of his time visiting the 'lions' of the great city or dining and dancing with the great families of Paris. Lady Shelley,[90] a great friend of Wellington, mentions James in her letters, which help build a full picture of our man, who seems to have been liked by all, but loved by none.

At Chateau Montmorenci; Colonel Stanhope, the life and soul of every party, surpassed himself in fun and mirth; and we danced until the small hours of the morning.

What an extraordinary person is Stanhope! If you happen to be in a frivolous mood, he will say foolish things, and will inspire folly in others. If you are in a serious vein, his conversation becomes interesting, and in the highest degree instructive. If you feel sentimental, his wonderful memory will supply poetical images from the finest passages in poetry. ... Without being handsome, Colonel Stanhope is not bad looking but he is never two days alike. He is a charming companion; obliging, good tempered, full of wit; and yet it would be quite impossible to fall in love with him.

Soon after settling in Paris, James wrote to Lady Mansfield of the delights of the fair city, but also shows that military matters were not completely forgotten.

Paris, Wednesday 12 July 1815

I received on Monday your kind letter of the 30th as I was wrapped up with the beauties of the Louvre. Since I have been here I have been in such a bustle seeing everything *a l'Anglais* & asking lots of questions. Today I have been to Les Invalides, where I could not refuse the impulse of my curiosity of asking where such legs had been carried off, those eyes lost 'cet coup de sabre gagne' [the blow of the sword wins] and a vast number were our old Spanish friends. I am delighted with the whole institution which (though inferior in size to it & in architecture to Greenwich) in some points is superior to Chelsea as it furnishes a comfortable retirement to nearly 300 officers, who were setting down to dinner when I went in & a very good one it appeared to be. The columns are all removed from the famous dome under which I was much struck with a beautiful monument with the simple but impressive word of 'Turenne'. I then went to the Palais de Luxembourg where I saw some good Rubens but I think most heterodoxically I fear all his great pictures are vulgar.

There are one or two beautiful ones of David & a whole gallery of Vernet's sea ports, as for the Louvre, I dedicate 2 hours a day to it & examine so many pictures otherwise the eye is bewildered and a headache is acquired instead of pleasure.

Things seem quiet, a squadron two guns (horses harnessed & matches lighted) & 100 men are at each of the multitudinous barriers and under these we beg the free people of Paris to choose their own government! The English are respected & loved by contrast with the Prussians who were going to blow up the Bridge of Jena, pull down the column in the Place Vendome, but for the Duke who [stopped?] that insult to the French nation; now in insult most personal & injurious to our good ally Le Gros. The Duke gave a grand dinner the day before yesterday & all the generals [attended], Blucher's toast was not bad 'May no ministers spoil what we have so gloriously begun'.

The Imperial dandy &c are come but I have not seen them being solely occupied in my own wanderings. I have une Maison de Campagne near the Bois de Boulogne where the division is, where I go early to settle what business there may be and I have une belle quartier here at a Count Castellan's house who is very civil through his maitre d'hotel. They seem so astonished at my wanting nothing, at having no 8 or ten people to dine with me, that their hay & corn are not consumed by my horses. I think they think us great fools for it, but n'importe. I am thinking of sending the faithful Wheeler to England in a short time per mes habits bourgeious [for my bourgeois clothes] previous to my start southward.[91] He shall pay his respects at Ken[wood] if you are not gone. What I should wish would be to get away about the beginning of August into Switzerland if the state of affairs permits & then cross the Simplon before winter. I have bought already a very nice carriage very cheap.

I should now answer your letter; I am very glad you have suppressed the part of my letter about the cavalry. I believe that on the left they behaved admirably, but on the right they might as well have been in England & the cause of it they must explain. I hardly know what I wrote, though you give it so good a character; if it does give a good idea of a battle you were right in showing it to whom you like & I have all confidence in your judgement. I have just heard that every officer & soldier is to have a medal.[92] I wrote to my master stating the want of it, but I believe it was done by the Duke. Every subaltern is to gain two years by the day and all pensions for wounds on that day are to be increasing, thus a lieutenant who would get £70 for his arm will have his 300 when he becomes a general. This is all right, for it certainly was no ordinary a fight; as Barnard[93] says (whom who [sic] met at Lady C[ape]l's 'It was treble distilled essence of war'.

I cannot express to you how shocked I have been in just hearing of poor Merveldt's death[94] which though it does not much surprise me, is no less a subject of deep regret. What will become of her? Whenever you have an opportunity pray express to her what I feel about it.

As for Whitbread's departure[95] I cannot say it is a subject of lamentation. Van will be as astonished at the unaccustomed silence of the house as a cut from the Strand, who arrived at his villa on the Kent road is right glad to miss the 'lumbering of the wheels'.

Grantham is here & departs tonight to bring the Lady.[96] I have commissioned him to inform you all how well I am, fast approaching to the back of a knife. If W[illiam] R[ussell] does not come in time I mean to get Seymour Bathurst[97] as a *compagnon de voyage* & at any rate to have him with us. Apsley[98] talks of going too. I have written to Lady B[athurst] today to assure her that much care should be taken of the former who is a very delightful lad. He is Maitland's A.D.C. & therefore I see much of him. I am astonished you have not yet received the china, pray let Mansfield write to Mr Rice, Albany Road, Kent Road to ask about it, it was to come by the Gravesend packet from Ostend and if nothing is come I must write Brussels …

Another Upton[99] is just come & desires to be rendered to all. He is apparently much vexed at being out of the battle, but if people will go on diplomatic excursions instead of military service what are they to expect? ...

In early August James was writing to Earl Mansfield on a number of matters: the Allied Sovereigns, Napoleon and schooling!

Paris 6 August 1815

My dear Mansfield,

Busy as I always am in this busy town I have been more than commonly so, since I last wrote from having been interested about an old subject in a new form. Some years ago I was amazingly hit with Lancaster's Schools & by contributing what I could afford myself & by laying a tax on the curiosity of others I got much into the vortex of it.

The campaigns of Spain drove it out of my head & when I returned, Lancaster's misconduct & folly gave me a disgust, I believe an unjust one to the system which is certainly not the worse because the founder turns out to be a vain profligate man instead of a simple virtuous one. I heard the other day from Fox the dentist (the secretary) enclosing a host of pamphlets on the subject of the promulgation of knowledge and the proceedings of a society here in prosecution of the same purposes …[100]

But the part of the company at dinner which interested me the most was General Foy[101] & another of our Peninsular enemies. Foy was opposed to us at Tolosa and spoke a great deal about Lord Lynedoch he said nobody doubted that it was by his movement that the Battle of Vitoria was followed by such results and seemed quite au fait of the kindness he showed to the prisoners at

Barossa. Though Foy's character is none of the best, I could not avoid feeling pleasure at hearing him do justice to the great & good qualities of a friend.

Nothing is known as to the proceedings of the sovereigns. The Emperor Alexander had a long audience with the king a few days ago & the latter expressed when he left him the greatest satisfaction at the arrangement which they had made, but what that is I cannot find out. The remonstrance of the king has produced an order from the Emperor of Austria forbidding his officers to feed on the inhabitants and the Prussians now receive money from Paris instead of living at free quarters. The allowance varies from 30 francs to 5 a day in addition to their pay. The plundering to the south of this continues & I told a friend of mine; he feared the French would be driven to an insurrection if it continued. Our movement is still talked of towards the coast, the 1st Division remaining here, but nothing appears definitely settled.

Labedoyere[102] is taken & is now trying and I hear that there is a good intention of shooting him if condemned, but I doubt the nerve of the government.

I have been as you expected equally astonished and disgusted at the absurd respect to Bonaparte & his [audience?]. What an extraordinary circumstance it is that, that man always preserves in every situation & under all misfortunes that ascendancy over the minds of others which first dazzled the world. He seems to consider everyone as a simple tool, which he is to use or abandon according to events without affection or remorse, and he has a satanic pride which looks too like magnanimity. He too might say 'With what compunction & laborious flight we sunk thus, th'ascent were easy then.'[103]

Though St Helena is subject to the disadvantages you mention, I think there is one strong reason to prefer that to any other residence. Though he might be safer at Fort George (but of that you seem to doubt) that at that distance he will be soon forgotten, but if confined within our own shores, every petty riot would be attributed to his intrigues & we should be kept in a perpetual fever. The royalists say [they?] hope you will now put him to death, the others 'Nous esperons que vous ne le laisserez pas échapper' [We hope that you will not let him escape] and all (officers and all) add a mete of insult to the fallen …

I heard one of the French officers at Madame Plesac's take credit to himself for not having shot him during the action 'to have stopped the career of folly by which he was sacrificing the army'. Such is the fate of unsuccessful generals, as I have said before, I think there is some truth in Ney's charges of neutralising troops on the 16th for there the Duke had not his army in hand as usual & was in a terrible scrape; but on the 18th Bonaparte's movements were good enough and there can be no greater proof of it than that he was very near succeeding. The French abuse him for having sacrificed his cavalry before the infantry arrived; there is truth in the remark, but had not their cavalry a fair right to expect success against a motley collection of squares, when most of the guns were in their possession & no cavalry to oppose them? I only speak of our own part of the action. Those very scoundrels who now boast of not having murdered their leader would have been the first to hail the genius of Austerlitz & the miracles of his tactics …

The Granthams come tomorrow & the Alvanleys within a week. I have heard nothing of W Russell except from home and I doubt if he means to have Naples. As to myself I can decide nothing till Bradford comes whose wound is very tedious & until something is settled about the movements of the army …

Nothing can be more flourishing than my health, not an ache of any sort …

James wrote to Lady Mansfield two weeks later.

Paris 24 August 1815

… As for the state of affairs here I see no great difference, as fast as time effaces some misfortune, another more terrible occurs and the public mind is kept at its strongest stretch. The gallant manner in which Labedoyere met his fate has done no good and people talk of misguided zeal, of his being fitted for greater and better actions, of his having been unrelently [sic] pursued to death and a thousand other absurdities; not but that we must all less despise a man who never disguised his attachment to Bonaparte who never took an oath to, or accepted an honour from the King, than a Ney on the infinite cross of greater criminals. I wrote Lord L[iverpool] an account of it, but if he did not mention it, I must tell you that he walked up to the man with his hat off, and a calm countenance & firm step & gave the words '1, 2, 3 feu!' as composedly as if he had been directing an exercise.

The account that was received yesterday of the Spaniards having entered France has also added fuel to the fire. The contribution of 4 millions sterling for the French government in addition to all those of the allies has as you may imagine not rendered him more popular but on the other hand a conversation which he had with the Duke of Orleans had produced a good effect on the minds of those who feel attached to the king but distrustful of the princes and this is a very considerable part of the people. The king stated that the feelings of the country did not allow him to call them to his councils and he could not give him a military command as the French army was in future to be on a different footing. There exists a belief that a treaty has been signed declaratory of the intentions of the allies and that it is to be made public on the fete de St Louis which is tomorrow …

I have succeeded in getting a little Waterloo Croix d'honneur which I enclose & beg you will accept.

There are Russian, Prussian & Austrian orders, distributing in shoals, 'If the heavens were to rain mitres none would fit my head'[104] & I am destined to be as plain as I started. I care nothing about it as I am convinced my real friends will like me as well without a cross as with one as long as one is not so. Affectionately remember me to Mansfield, F[rederica][105] & all, to dear O & Ito tenderest remembrances. I am quite quite well, ever affectionately yours.

A week later he again wrote to Earl Mansfield who had requested information on the state of France. James was now moving in more academic circles.

Paris, 30 August 1815

You ask what is the opinion of the most enlightened class of the country. It is impossible to answer it as this is a chaos in which none quite agree or wholly put confidence in one another. The king by his neutral line has disgusted the old royalists and by being compelled to become the instrument of the extortion of the allies has still further irritated the country against him. His wisest act is that of nationalising the army and making them like our militia which would destroy the esprit de corps and perhaps wean them back to civil life, but as yet this is only on paper. If the King shoots Ney, it may produce good. He is to be tried by [fellow] Marshals, Davout, Moncey,[106] I hear are among the number.

I am convinced the great fault we have committed is having brought Louis in behind, but whose is the blame none can tell, but the Dr.[107] says it is not him and I heard Lord C[astlereagh] equally denies it. We should have entered as enemies, have asked for as many millions as we wanted, have occupied as many fortresses as required for guarantees and then, had the nation chose to call to the throne a pacific king in whom we could trust, we might perhaps relaxed a little in our demands, but we should have left him, instead of which the allies have broken their faith in every way, have brought 500,000 men into France since L[ouis] was restored, have imprisoned and driven away magistrates of his appointment, have taken from him the revenue of his provinces and instead of being known to the French by his beneficence by saving them from the horrors of war, he is considered as the executioner. As for the plundered pictures, it is all very right and they are going fast so you had better come.[108]

I believe Fouche is sincere, nay more, there is every reason to believe he was betraying B[onaparte] and was at the bottom of the insurrection in La Vendee. Anything is preferable to the Voltigeurs du Roi (the old gouty emigres) who maintain Ferdinand [of Spain] is the best king in Europe and that no king can be firm in France if the people is enlightened. They have returned more blind than they were with every folly and prejudice confirmed. I fear with you our officers will not benefit much by Paris. The houses where play and women are combined attract all, and the former makes large gaps in fortunes: l'autre va sans dire! [and the other goes without saying!]

As to myself I like to prostitute myself to about a dozen parties. The Jacobins treat me as a natural colleague from being the son of [the radical

Charles Stanhope], the others with many shrugs and ah ah! at my relationship with Mr. P[it]t. Les savants m'acceuillent avec bonte au rapport de Sir J[oseph] B[anks] [The scholars greet me with pleasure on the mention of Sir Joseph Banks] and between the one and the other, I see a good deal of their society, which is all I wish to do that one may be able to form some opinion for oneself.

I have heard from the Doc, he is for the destruction of all palaces and public edifices but for the preservation of every peasant's cottage, a charming theory but reversed in practice, for the generals live in and preserve the one, the soldiers break into and destroy the other. People are apt over their firesides to talk of destruction and pillage with tranquillity, but if they were to see a specimen they would change their opinion. Nothing can equal the admirable conduct of our army, it has gained the respect of all.

His next letter to Lady Mansfield is full of bitterness, having failed to gain a knighthood, but he seems to have forgotten that he served at the battle as a regimental officer, not on the staff.

Paris, 24 September 1815

... You must have been a good deal surprised at seeing my name not included in the Companions of the Bath, as I was informed of my being one last year and as at *any rate* I have not *less claim now*. I am quite amazed and very angry especially when I find my brother A.D.C. Barclay who never saw a shot fired till the 18th among them and Colquitt a *junior* officer in my own regiment because he commanded the battalion, which had the circumstance been known *I ought* to have commanded.[109] As for the honour, I think nothing of it, but I consider the omission as a positive disgrace. The moment I saw I was not included I went to the Duke's and saw him and stated the case both as to San Sebastian and Waterloo. He desired me to write it down and he would see what could be done ... If I got it, the whole pleasure (if there were any in receiving it) vanishes by being obliged to extort what ought to have been spontaneously given ... My being placed on the Staff was in the same manner extorted by *circumstance* and had there been an officer to do the duty, I might have still been with my company. *That* however *flatters my friends* as I owe no gratitude or thanks for that, except to Byng who desired me to fulfil the duties of the department. I beg you will keep all this quite secret [and] out of Scone.

By October James was writing to Earl Mansfield of the undercurrent of unrest in France at the continuation of the Allied occupation.

Paris, 1 October 1815

My dear Mansfield,

I have to thank you for your letter which arrived with its due punctuality. Everything here is getting hourly more confused & unpleasant & I think we are now those whom the French abuse the most. The Duke found it necessary to write a letter on the subject of the pictures to prove that taking them was not against the Treaty of Paris and nothing can be more satisfactory. Yet I never yet have seen any cause for employing the British to remove them. The fomentation of the public mind are so great that the Prussian army was concentrated near Versailles & during the last night a brigade in the Champs Elysees have been ready to turn out. I do not think we do things in good taste, for it is useless to talk of conciliation now, and any appearance of wishing to convey our points secretly looks only like fear.

The Austrians determined on removing the Venetian horses[110] in the front of the Tuilleries and the king requested they might be taken at night to avoid tumult. The Duke lent them some of our officers of the Staff Corps & some men to assist. When they came about one in the morning the National Guard having no information of their proceedings (which is too extraordinary when the king applied for its taking place at night) resisted and I believe put some of the officers in the guard house. The next night it was attempted but the mob was so great, groaning and crying 'A bas le canaille, vive le roi' [Down with the scoundrels, long live the king] that it was not carried into execution.

Yesterday the Place de Carousel was cleared & a battalion of Austrians placed inside; the horses were then removed without opposition in daylight, as they might have been at first for I hate these midnight deeds.

The French society is now become very unpleasant, for though it is easy to defend the removal of the pictures, it is not quite so clear how to answer the charge of breach of our proclamations of not interfering with the French government & of every man not in arms being our ally. Everything now confirms me in my belief that the act of bringing the king at our heels was the first & greatest fault & that nothing has gone right since.

There still seems a dilemma about signing the treaty which was certainly arranged before the sovereigns went, but no one is bold enough on the side of France to put their name to their own death warrant.[111] There never was such folly to allow the ex ministers a constitutional pretext for retiring & making the first act of the royalist ministers [to] be the most humiliating [one?] to France. Had the king only kept the others till they had done his dirty work, it would have been more politic. I know many here think that the royalist party is gaining ground & indeed we are all chameleons & take the hue of those we live among. Now as the royalists se croient permes [are believed allowed] to abuse us to our faces, I have left them off as it is better not to talk than to be defending a cause not in every point clear, from morning till night. From all that I now see and hear I believe quite the contrary & that the royal cause is more hopeless than ever. Benjamin Constant[112] the other day was in good spirits & I asked him the cause which was really I understand from his having won at play, but he said 'We are more indebted to you than ever, you are doing what nothing else but a miracle could have done, consolidating our parties & uniting our mutual hatred in a general one against you'.

I wish the fortresses were in our hands & we in them, for the smallest recontre might produce an explosion. The former Bonapartists chiefly blame the king for having disbanded the army and having cut off the 'Remaining hand of France'. But even now they say 'Let him refuse such hateful terms & throw himself on his people and let us follow the example of Spain'. I never fail to remind these gentlemen that the Spaniards unsupported by us & the Duke would not have been so successful.

In the meanwhile the weather is getting very bad & our men are suffering from it. There is a report of our going into cantonments near Paris & some in barracks here. I hope there will in that case be a very large army kept round Paris, for otherwise it would be a most dangerous step.

Chapter 16

Family Issues

We have no letters from James for the remainder of 1815 and virtually nothing for 1816, but it is clear that he accompanied the army to Cambrai where they formed a part of the Army of Occupation and then James received a long leave of absence to visit friends in England. He appears to have spent a considerable period at Scone with the Mansfields, hence the lack of letters.

But suddenly, this good life seemed very far away. Whilst visiting England, James had heard that his estranged father was seriously unwell. True to his good nature, James tried to form a reconciliation and offered to see his father a number of times. He immediately wrote to Mahon who was at Vienna on a grand tour with the news.

17 October 1816[1]

Dear Mahon,

I have just returned from Chevening. I had long heard that my father was ill, but it did not seem to be dangerous. The bad accounts we heard yesterday pronounced his illness to be so. I wrote two letters entreating earnestly to see him. He sent me his blessing but declined it. I therefore came away. He has no idea of being in danger and expects soon to be well. His legs are much swelled and now his stomach. I cannot but think you should return home immediately. Madame de L[2] is still there and has complete ascendancy, keeping from him the old servants of the family. By all accounts she and Varley[3] have secured themselves against all reverses of fortune here …

He wrote to Lady Mansfield who had travelled to Paris quoting his touching final appeal to his father.

Cole Harbour 15 December 1816[4]

… 'Though my last entreaties were in vain I could not leave England, your son, the only son in England at home is near you once more. I can add but little to the contents of my last letters but that my most earnest & anxious wishes have been, are and will be to receive from yourself the blessing you sent and to offer whatever comfort or attention may still be in my power to bestow. Though absent from you, I have heard of you and I have waited anxiously but in vain to receive your permission to approach you. I have waited till the reports of your medical attendance allow me to delay no longer. You do not know your son, not even by sight, if you refuse me admittance *now* I have too much reason to fear that in this world we shall not meet again. I therefore once more come near you to implore you to see me, to forget, to forgive and to allow me to attend you, that I may prove the duty and affection of a son.' To this I received thanks for but that the doctors which [entreat] him to be quiet. I hear he is hardly distinguishable from a corpse, that on being moved pulsation ceases and that there is a good deal of water in the membrane round his heart ...

His appeal was in vain and James wrote movingly of his last attempt to see his father before his death on 15 December 1816[5] to Lord Lonsdale.

Cole Harbour Croydon, Wednesday[6] [18 December]

My dear Lord,

From the kind interest you have always shown about me, I am prompted to give you some account of the illness of my father which terminated in his death last Sunday and of his singular will. His disorder was a liver complaint ending in a dropsy and as early as my arrival in town from the north, the physicians began to think badly of his case. I lost no time in going to Chevening at that epoch to entreat him to forget & forgive and to allow me to attend him; he declined. I repeated my request more urgently, he sent me his blessing but refused to see me. On the Thursday before his death I went to Chevening again & represented to him by letter the state he was in and again conjured him to see me, but received the same answer. He persisted in believing he was in no danger and as late as the morning of his death, said he should live for 30 years. An express was sent to me on the event & I went instantly to Chevening to protect the interests of my brother, sealed everything up & removed Madame de Lackner.[7] On the will being opened, he has left £5,000 to her and about 2,000 more to other persons, after deducting which all the rest of his real and personal estate is left to 10 executors & their heirs of whom the principal are Lords Holland[8] & Grantley[9] & Mr Jekyll.[10] I do not understand that the property so left can be considerable. To say I can regret such a father would be hypocrisy but I have the consolation of having done my duty towards him & I fervently pray his God may forgive him as I do. By the marriage settlements my sister becomes entitled to £8,000 on the expiration of one year, till then receiving the interest and I receive £10,000.

Though I have never adverted to the generous hand which rescued my sister from every difficulty, believe me dear Lord Lonsdale, I have not been unmindful or ungrateful for its benefits, but I always conceived it better to be grateful in silence than to distress you by ineffectual acknowledgements, for my sister was the person whom in necessity you assisted, and you could not by any personal favour to myself, have laid me under so lasting an obligation.

I have written to my sister to communicate the event. Life at all times uncertain as this recent event proved, is more so in a land of pestilence, should any thing (which God's avert) happen to my sister before the year expires, I shall consider myself both by duty & inclination responsible for the sum. One debt however I neither can nor wish to be released from, as I shall ever acknowledge it with pleasure, that debt which the memory of your kindness has cherished.

I suppose the funeral will take place next week, after which I shall return to Cambrai from whence I have been absent a very inconvenient time for others. Allow me to congratulate you, Lady Lonsdale etc on the event I hear is to take place and with my best remembrances to all the family.[11]

Believe me, most faithfully yours, J H Stanhope.

P.S. My brother is expected every day from Vienna, my sister Hester was well in September, still on Mount Lebanon but meaning to leave Syria next year for the south of France to meet me for a few months.

We next hear from James, writing to Earl Mansfield, in Paris where he had attended a grand ball and seems to have been in good spirits.

Paris, 15 January 1817

The distress in the country among les paysans unrelieved by the rich is not to be exaggerated, but from all I can collect, the financial difficulties are more feigned than real. It resembles the squeals of a child for fear he should be hurt. The government will succeed in raising their 12,000,000 (without guarantee) in bits and the payment of the contributions will be continued. The military payments have been stopped. The king is going to have 12,000 Swiss but as yet has 2 [thousand]. This step has not produced a good effect anywhere and there are already quarrels of which nothing is said. There is an 'on dit' that 1/5th of the contingent is to be withdrawn. There is another of a quarrel between Portugal and Spain. The former is fitting out an expedition to occupy one side of the Rio de Plata and say it is with Ferdinand's consent, which the Spanish Embassy here denies. 'On dit' and from pretty good authority that the royalists in Mexico have got ahead but at Chile the insurgents are so.[12]

The embassy gave a ball last night but I do not think we assimilate much yet with the natives, but the tone of society is better than when I was here last. Madame de Stael[13] is more odious than ever and her daughter surpasses the mother. There is an Ultra, la Duchess d'Ecave who battles her handsomely and who finished the other night, 'Je vous laisse vos 25 annees des crimes inais laissez vous nos 25 annees des malheurs' [I leave you your 25 years of crimes and you leave us 25 years of misfortunes]. 'Pour le reste', all goes on the same. 'Le Roi mange et les grands ont leurs amours' [The King eats and the mighty have their love affairs]. Talleyrand cuts jokes and praises the ministry 'surtout pour le "budget" qui est inpayable' [especially for the Budget which is unpayable]. The beau monde slide down les Montagnes Russes and real Russian mountains, Kofsolofsky, etc. enchant them by quadrilles. The piece du theatre most in the fashion is called Susanne who comes forth from her bath pursued by a dozen bearded elders. Sir S[idney] S[mith][14] and family attend for philosophical causes as he thinks his anti-terraqueous unsubmergible machine might be of use to her.

A letter to Lord Lonsdale regarding sending mail to Hester reveals his hopes for some further home leave.

Cambrai, 12 September 1817[15]

My dear Lord,

I had already heard from my sister that she had sent you a box, I think by Marseilles. The best channel and that by which letters reach her the most expeditiously is through Vienna. You had better enclose your letter to Sir Robert Liston at Constantinople[16] & send it to the Foreign Office. I shall write very soon & if you prefer sending your letter to me, I shall be happy to forward it. I expect to be in England the 20th in which case prey direct to Half Moon Street …

As James was now in England – the Army of Occupation returned home in November 1818 – we do not find much correspondence to or from him, but we can snatch a few glimpses of major events in his life. James went on half pay in 1818, having developed an interest in politics, although it would be fair to say that he only dabbled and was not firm in his support for his party. One commentator noted him as a 'Wobbly Grenvillite'. He was elected an MP for Buckingham in 1817, for Fowey in 1818 (a 'Rotten Borough' under the control of the Prince Regent) which was overturned on appeal and after a few years out of office, gained the seat of MP for Dartmouth from 1822 till 1825. Indeed Thomas Creevey, the politician and diarist, does not leave a good impression of James's politics, recording:

Dined at Sir Lowry Cole's … That cursed fellow Colonel Stanhope was there amongst others, who I remember was an opposition man 3 years ago, but who now is in parliament and a government lick-spittle. He made up to me cursedly, but I would not touch him.

On a later occasion Creevey caustically states:

I found Master Stanhope there again, and he wanted me to dine with him, but I would do no such thing. He has no talents: he is all pretension and impudence. Colonel Percy is by far the best hand at conversation of the Duke's young men.

Clearly not everyone agreed with the bitter Creevey, but James also had a reputation as a socialite and, despite the continuing problems with his old wound, a light-hearted ditty to Sir Robert Wilmot[17] shows that James's sense of fun was certainly not diminished.

> Longleat 16 November 1818[18]
>
> My dear Wilmot,[19]
>
> I have just received the enclosed letter from Macdonald. If I can be of any further use command me. When shall we two (or as you would classically express it you & me) meet again,
>
> O'er macao tables, sweet champagne.
> In preening mood & merry vein
> Whilst beautys eyes' soft influence rain
> And Standish hollows severs the main
> Nor heeds the Granville's liquid strain
> That might an angel render vain,
> If they should ere (six seven) 'tis plain
> Soup, fish all waiting, as I'm a dinner
> If I finish my verse they will furnish the dinner.
>
> So adieu dear Wilmot, ever yours JHS

Now that Europe was finally at peace and there was no longer any threat of being detained by the French authorities for the length of the war, everyone who could afford it wanted to tour Europe. The Mansfields were no exception. The Earl had already been to Paris in 1816 and in 1819 Frederica Louisa Murray, eldest daughter of the Earl of Mansfield, went on a European tour, with her parents, accomplanied by James Stanhope. Frederica started a journal of the tour which covered Brussels, Baden and Vienna, returning home in early 1820. The journal was started in the beautiful neat handwriting of Frederica but is clearly completed in a very different scrawl, that of James Stanhope. Four years to the day, the Mansfields visited the battlefield but it does not appear that James was then with them. Frederica records her thoughts, beginning at Brussels.[20]

> 18 June 1819
>
> We went to the church of St Michael or St Gudule[21] to hear the Te Deum which is annually sung in commemoration of the Battle of Waterloo. The church was lined with troops; the service was not so impressive as I had expected but the music was good …
>
> We then set off for Waterloo, we passed through the Forest of Soignies and at length arrived at the place of Waterloo. We went into the church[22] where there are a great many monuments to officers who had fallen in the battle. In contemplating these records of the ravages of war and of British bravery, the enthusiasm with which we had entered Waterloo died within us

and gratitude for the lives of those friends who had been spared and the hope that for many years to come no such scenes will occur, feelings which remained …

We then passed a small inn (Quatier General du Duc du Wellington) where he passed the night before the battle. In this house Lord Fitzroy Somerset's arm was amputated. We went to the inn 'Arc Grand du Nivelles' where we dined. We then proceeded to the village of Mont St Jean where we procured a guide; we passed by the farm and stopped on the hill in front of La Hay Sainte. On each side of the road there is a monument, one to the Hanoverians on the left and the other to Sir Alexander Gordon. To the left there is a tree near which Sir Thomas Picton fell; in a field towards Frischermont Sir William Ponsonby was killed. Not far from this to the right of the road is the tree near which the Duke of Wellington is supposed to have remained during the great part of the day, as from thence called the Wellington tree. It was much shattered by balls and many branches were carried off as memorials by travellers and they say it was in a dying state when it was bought by an Englishman for 100 F and carried by him to England. The root still remains and we eagerly collected small pieces of it as relics …

We saw the farm of La Belle Alliance in front of us and near it the farm of Rosomme where Bonaparte was in the morning of the battle at eight o'clock; he then went for a little while to the observatory[23] and from thence to Trimoteau where he remained the whole day. Our guide told us that Decoster[24] who said that he had been taken as guide to Bonaparte was not believed in the country and that a secretary of Bonaparte's had declared when he saw him that he had never been with them. Almost the whole of the field is covered with corn which grows with particular luxuriance, some stalks we pulled up were above 6 foot high. The Chateau of Hougoumont is a sad scene of desolation; the court is filled with the fragments of its walls. The chapel was set on fire but still remains; on the outside the fruit trees were flourishing and the contrast was striking. We went into the garden which is pretty; close to it is a small wood which was a great defence to our troops. After remaining here some time we left this interesting scene which no one who has feelings of an Englishman can witness without the strongest emotions of awe and veneration and of gratitude. The effect it produced on us heightened by this being the anniversary of the day, was such as can neither be described or forgotten.

The party arrived home in early 1820. On the 19 June Sir Joseph Banks died; in his will he left his estate to his wife Dorothea. On her death or remarriage Spring Grove estate and all other possessions would pass to James and Sir Henry Hawley, a relative.

Less than a month later, on 10 July 1820 James and Frederica were married at the Mansion house, Kenwood, by Robert Markham, Archdeacon of York, the marriage being solemnized in the register of St Pancras Church.[25] Frederica was given away by her father as a minor (being under 21 years of age) and his brother, now Earl Stanhope and Lord Cathcart, witnessed it.

The marriage seems to have been a very happy one and blessed with a son, born on 13 May 1821, exactly nine months after the wedding! The boy was named James Banks Stanhope. They lived contentedly at 72 South Audley Street. Another child was conceived in early 1822 and all was happiness and carefree. But then their lives fell apart.

Frederica became ill during the later stages of the pregnancy and although she successfully gave birth to her second child, another boy, both the child and mother succumbed within a few days. James was devastated, he wrote a memoir of Frederica's last days for his remaining son, James, to read in later life; I have added this extremely moving memoir as Appendix D. Frederica died on 14 January 1823, just having turned 23 years of age. On 17 January James commissioned a very poignant marble effigy of his wife with child to be placed in Chevening church, from the famous sculptor Francis Chantrey, for the princely sum of 1,500 guineas plus the costs of transporting and installing it. The monument is both beautiful and haunting; Lady Stanhope reclines on a couch giving the appearance that mother and child are merely sleeping and encourages the hope that they have attained eternal rest in heaven.

The monument was finished by 1827 but James never saw it completed. The loss of Frederica caused him to become depressed and lonely; and as he plunged into his world of despair, his old San Sebastian wound started to plague him again. James often visited Kenwood House with his son. Two years after her death, James was to attend a dinner at Kenwood House, where there were rumours of an impending announcement of marriage.[26] Before dinner James walked out into the adjoining Caen Wood and the alarm was raised when he did not return in time for the meal. The searches became more intense after dinner and in the early hours of the morning, he was found. The following letters give the details:

Kenwood 6 March 1825 2.30 am[27]

My dear Lord Stanhope,

It is with the deepest apprehension that I have to announce to you that your dear brother has destroyed himself. He was found this night in his handkerchief & breeches; your apprehensions may have prepared you for this dreadful misfortune although I shared them and have been in constant anxiety. The blow has taken me as much by surprise as if I had had no previous warning. The formal inquest will be called on Monday, I hope this contact may give me the advantage of your presence for I have been most anxious to prepare Lady Stanhope,[28] have written to Granville[29] to prepare her if possible and in such a way that perhaps the real truth may be concealed from her. I wish I knew of any friend whom I could get to go to her, Lady Mansfield is in such a state of agony & distress that she cannot leave her bed. The fatal act had been long in contemplation for the manner of it showed much thought and determination. He was found suspended in a shed, he had not returned to dinner and we immediately began a search for him in every direction. I went later to see if he had strayed further and on my return heard of the event but even to this hour I [do] not [know] every particular, the agony in which I write render this most horrible calamity most horrid. My apology for this scrawl, God grant us all my dear lord consolation and submission to his will. Your most faithfully Mansfield.

There is also a short account of James's death in the files[30] probably written by Earl Mansfield and kept for his son James Banks.

Account of the Circumstances of the death …

Colonel Stanhope had received a shot at the siege of San Sebastian, that some foreign substance was lodged in the back but whether a ball or not was not known, no probing had reached it but upon different occasions abscesses had formed and pieces of bone and cloth had been brought away.

… Lord M[ansfield] expressed his fear that he should be found in the pond.

Colonel Stanhope had fastened his neck handkerchief to the beam, had taken off his braces & put on his coat again, had fastened these to the neck handkerchief and his other handkerchief to these, had tied small knots so that it should not slip, had then as it is supposed stood on the manger and swung off. His greatcoat was let down so as to pinion his arms.

… he had told a servant a few days before that the pain in his back was excrutiating … Colonel Stanhope had more than once expressed an apprehension which Lord M[ansfield] anticipated, than he admitted that one time or other the ball would be fatal to him, though in what manner at that time neither could have anticipated.

There was an obituary in the local newspaper.

On Saturday night some of the most respectable families in the neighbourhood of Hampstead and Highgate were thrown into great agitation by the intelligence that Colonel Stanhope, brother of Earl Stanhope, had been found hanging from a beam in one of the out-houses, at Caen Wood, the seat of the Earl of Mansfield.

Numerous inquiries were made into the circumstances of the death of the colonel, but no information could be obtained. A Coroner's Jury was summoned with remarkable haste, to meet at ten o'clock yesterday morning, at the Fox-under-the-hill public house, Highgate. The jury, upon being sworn, proceeded to view the premises where the body of the colonel was found suspended. It is an out-house in Caen Wood, at a considerable distance from the family mansion, where cattle are sheltered. The beam from which the body was cut down, was about seven feet from the ground, and there lay across it a pair of braces, by which he had suspended himself. The jury, after inspecting this spot, were conducted to the nearest lodge, where they viewed the body, which was laid out on a bed. The deceased was dressed in a common walking dress, with boots, his top coat was pulled down over the shoulders, his cravat was off, and there was a livid mark on the throat. A silk handkerchief, which he had tied to the braces and fastened round his throat, were exhibited. There was no other mark of violence on the body, than that just described.

The first witness called was William Wright, groom of the Earl of Mansfield. He stated that towards ten o'clock on Saturday night, in consequence of the very great alarm which prevailed in the mansion, he went with several others of the servants to search about the wood; he, as well as the rest, were apprehensive that something might have happened to the colonel. After having searched several places, they went into the shed which the jury had inspected. Witness was the first that entered the shed and he started back on finding the colonel suspended from a beam. Witness's fellow servants cut down the body immediately; the extremities were quite cold. They immediately conveyed the body to the nearest lodge, but life was extinct.

The next witness was J. Wheeler who appeared to be in extreme grief while giving his testimony. He stated that he had been valet to the deceased upwards of seventeen years and had attended upon his master, as usual, on Saturday morning. The family usually dined at seven o'clock and a little before that time the bell rang to dress for dinner. Witness went to attend his master, but was greatly surprised at not finding him, according to custom, about to dress. The deceased was then sought after in various directions, but no intelligence gained of his absence. The dinner passed over without his attendance, when fresh enquiries were made respecting him. There was an arrangement about the purchase of a house, in the disposal of which the colonel was concerned, to be concluded on the Saturday and Earl Mansfield, who was at home, conjectured that the colonel might have gone to town for the purpose of settling the business. For the purpose of ascertaining whether this was the case and from a feeling of uneasiness on the subject, his lordship ordered out the carriage and rode to town; made enquiries at every place in which he thought his relative might have been detained, but returned, without having obtained any tidings about him. The apprehensions of the family increased. Inquiries were made as to the last time he was seen up on the grounds. It was reported, that at about ten minutes after four, he was seen going in a particular direction in the wood. The wood was scoured round, as it was feared the colonel might have been seized with some paroxysm. The deceased had received a wound at the storming of San Sebastian in the Peninsular war. A shot had passed through the thin part of the shoulder blade; that wound had never been cured and occasionally gave him great pain.[31] About two years ago his wife, the eldest daughter of Earl Mansfield, died and his grief at the loss of her was very great. Of late witness had observed that the deceased was very abstracted, was in the habit of sitting a long time, as if in a state of stupor, and then he would suddenly start up, as if from sleep or upon an alarm. Within a few days he had complained very much that he could get no sleep, in consequence of the pain he endured. The deceased was in general very sedate in his manner.

James Alexander, an under gardener in the service of Earl Mansfield, deposed that he was at work in the grounds, when at about 20 minutes past 4 o'clock he observed the deceased going towards the wood, in which the outhouse, where he was afterwards found suspended, was situated. Witness thought that the step of the deceased in going towards this place was remarkably hurried. (it was observed by the jury, who went over the ground, that as the descent towards the place was steep, and in consequence of the late rains very slippery, the hurry of the steps might be accounted for from that fact).

Doctor Gilman of Highgate, stated that he was called in on Saturday night to the house of Earl Mansfield; he found the body of the deceased not quite cold, but life was entirely gone; he took the usual course adopted in cases of that nature, but with no effect. He judged that the body had been suspended several hours, and death was no doubt, caused by suffocation. Witness had attended the family. The deceased had received a shot in the scapula of the left shoulder. Frequent exfoliations of the bone had taken place and there was rather a copious issue. He believed that the spine was affected; in such cases paroxysms of pain might produce temporary derangement. He mentioned one instance, known to some of the jury, of Mr Mitchell, an attorney who, by a fall from a gig, injured a particular nerve, and was frequently taken with a fit of running several yards. The pain and nervous irritation, created by the wound, acted upon by mental causes, might have induced temporary insanity. There was little doubt that the colonel had laboured under considerable nervous irritation.

The coroner summed up the evidence; and the jury returned a verdict to the effect that the deceased had destroyed himself, whilst labouring under a fit of temporary insanity.

The colonel was held in the highest esteem by all in the neighbourhood, who [k]new him, and the unaffected sorrow of the domestics, who gave evidence before the jury, bore testimony to his worth, as a master. He was remarkably pious, although from his early youth in the army, and he paid the highest attention to religious duties. He was in his 39th year,[32] and was Member of Parliament for Dartmouth. We understand that he was about to be married to a young lady, who was on a visit at Caen Wood, at the time the dreadful event took place. The colonel gave up his establishment after the death of his wife, by whom he had one son, who is now living.

> Further Particulars from a Correspondent.
> At the siege of San Sebastian, this gallant officer, (the Honourable Colonel James Hamilton Stanhope) received a grapeshot wound in the spine. Severe as the consequent sufferings were, it was, however, the decided opinion of the eminent surgeons by whom he had been attended, that the ball could not, without imminent risk of fatal consequences, be extracted. Whether by the pressure of an extraneous substance, or by direct lesion of the nerves them selves during the passage of the ball, the result was, that not only the spine was morbidly affected, but the whole nervous system partook of the injury. Occasional determination of blood to the head and of late a temporary access of delirium, were among the results. These were, however, regarded, and probably with justice, as the effects or accompaniments of the processes carried on by nature in the formation of abscesses about the spine. Exfoliation had taken place at different periods and latterly an extreme sensibility to temperature, and an increasing impatience of cold in the extremities, had become a marked symptom. About a fortnight back, after a sharp access of nervous disease connected with the wound, he was deemed convalescent; and was so much restored as to be able to pay a visit to his noble father in law at Caen Wood. On Saturday afternoon, restless in all probability from pain, and the indescribable sensations that come by fits and starts, where the nervous system has sustained a serious injury, he had walked out, and the most probable explanation of the melancholy sequel is that the exposure to the cold had brought on a sudden access of nervous bewilderment and with this that overwhelming and instantaneous desire and resolve of self destruction, of which so many mournful instances are fresh in the recollection of the public. The mournful indeed, as in many cases, the fit is so sudden, and so unprepared for by any precursive signs, as to baffle or preclude precautionary measures. The belief that the act in this instance, the resolve or rather blind impulse of the moment, is strongly supported and confirmed by the circumstance, that in his walk to the shed, in which his body was found suspended, he must have passed three large ponds of water, that might have suggested a more easy and certain mode of destruction; and he had likewise at the time a penknife in his pocket. We have only to add, that the event must have taken places some hours before it was discovered, the body having been found nearly cold.
>
> The Honourable Colonel Stanhope was brother to the present Earl Stanhope, Aide de Camp to General Sir John Moore and General Graham and latterly to the Duke of York, and MP for Dartmouth.

On his death, James did not forget his stepsisters, leaving £1,500 per year to Hester, £500 per year to Griselda as she was married and, as Lucy was dead, £10,000 to Lucy's children, the remainder to his son; to be administered by his guardians Earl Stanhope and Mansfield.

Later in life his son had a simple memorial tablet raised in the Guards Chapel, Wellington Barracks, Birdcage Walk, London, which was unfortunately destroyed by a flying bomb in 1944. However the inscription was recorded as:

Placed by James Banks Stanhope, In memory of his father,
Lieut. Colonel the Hon. James Hamilton Stanhope,
Third son of Charles, Third Earl Stanhope
Born 1788: died 1825

As he had taken his own life, there could be no public funeral and officially no burial on hallowed ground. The only clue to the whereabouts of James's burial is a very small inscription on the reverse (and therefore largely hidden) face of the tomb chest beneath the sculpture of his wife. The inscription reads:

In The Same Tomb is Interred
Lt Col The Honourable James Hamilton Stanhope
Third Son of Charles Earl Stanhope
Who Died 5th March 1825 in the 37th Year of His Age
His Afflicted Relatives Would Have Felt a Melancholy Satisfaction
In Commemorating the Many Talents and Virtues Which Adorned Him
But in Laying By the Side of His Beloved Wife
With No Other Record Than That
He Was Not Unworthy to be Her Husband
They Obey His Last Injunctions

As per his wishes, James was very quietly buried with his wife and the two have been left in peace, rarely visited in the private chapel of the family, which is usually locked. The moving effigy of Frederica is known to only a select few and even those rarely know of the sad story that lies behind the tomb.

It is to be hoped that in the more enlightened age we now live in, the tomb of this unfortunate couple and the poignant story of their shattered young lives will now be better appreciated by all who have the privilege to visit St Botolph's Church at Chevening.

Appendix A

Letters and Journals of Charles Stanhope, Major 50th Foot

On fleeing the family home with James and taking up residence under the care of William Pitt, Charles Stanhope was presented an ensigncy, without purchase on 6 February 1802, by the Duke of York in the 25th (King's Own Borderers) Regiment of Foot, then stationed at Gibraltar. This important fortress was then commanded by the Duke of Kent, a strict disciplinarian who was eventually recalled from his post.

Charles learned the basics of his duties here and quickly advanced by purchase and undoubted influence to become a lieutenant in the 57th (West Middlesex) Regiment on 20 September 1803 and then a captain in the Royal Staff Corps on 17 March 1804. Presumably because of Hester's association with Sir John Moore, an opportunity came to exchange his captaincy into the renowned 52nd (Oxfordshire Light Infantry) Regiment and Charles jumped at the opportunity, being gazetted to the 52nd on 12 June 1804.

Charles then became an aide de camp to Sir John Moore and accompanied his general to Sicily where he served for two years, before returning to Britain.

On 6 February 1808 he gained a majority in the 6th Garrison Battalion which was stationed in Ireland, where he was placed on the staff of the Earl of Harrington,[1] Commander-in-Chief in Ireland and therefore well known to the Duke of Richmond, Lord Lieutenant of Ireland.

Charles however only stayed here a very short period before exchanging as a major into the 50th (West Kent) Foot to which he was gazetted on 23 April 1808. He was allowed to proceed to Sweden on the staff of Sir John Moore again and on his return from this ill fated expedition, he proceeded with Moore to Portugal as part of a reinforcement to Wellesley's small force. However, on arrival in Portugal Charles volunteered to join the first battalion of the regiment as second major,[2] as Major Hill was severely wounded.[3] He marched with the regiment into Spain and with Major Charles Napier, helped keep them going throughout the subsequent retreat to Corunna.

This small journal held at the Centre for Kentish Studies is inscribed in an unknown hand 'The Journal of Campaign of 1808–9 Colonel JH Stanhope'. But this is certainly incorrect, for the information given clearly refers to Major Charles Stanhope, 50th Foot, from May 1808 to his death at the Battle of Corunna.

	Remarks
Left London 27 May 1808 28 May arrived at Yarmouth 4 June Embarked onboard the *Africa*[4] Captain Barrett & sailed.	Colonel Murray QMG was also onboard[5]

11 June Arrived at Gothenburg	
13 June Went to Trolhatten 50 miles	The cataracts are for the extent of about 3 miles & the total fall of water 240 feet. There is a canal & docks from the top to the bottom level. On the opposite side of the River Gota from the one we went. General Moore went to Stockholm on the 12th & returned on the 29th of June[6] and went onboard the admiral's ship.[7]
16 June returned.	
17 June Dislocated my arm[8]	
20 June Went to Jonkoping on the Eastern Lake 110 miles	On the road met flocks of sheep tended only by a dog, the road is beautiful. The two Principal lakes near Gothenburg is the Aspen 10 miles distant & [Wohalls?] about 7 miles.
22 June Returned to Gothenburg	
30 June Embarked on board *Isabella* transport.	
3 July Sailed	
4 July Went onboard the *Audacious*,[9] General Moore, Murray, Captain Grosselin.	Paget, Stewart were onboard.
16 July Landed at Deal and went to London	The convoy sailed from the Downs on 16 July and anchored at Spithead on the 20th
21 July Left London & arrived at Portsmouth the 22nd	
27 July Embarked onboard *Isabella* transport.	Brigadier General Stewart & Billy Gardiner onboard.
31 July Sailed	
21 August Anchored in Mondego Bay	The convoy laid to one day in the harbour of Vigo & a few hours off Oporto
22 August Sailed	The Commodore anchored on the evening of the 20th. The 4th, 28th & 79th Regiments and some artillery were landing on the 22nd when they were countermanded & embarked again by the evening.
24 August Anchored about four leagues South of Peniche	The Battle of Obidos was on the 17th[10] The one at Vimiero on the 21st.
25 August Landed at Maceira	
28 August Joined the 50th Regiment on the ground above Torres Vedras.	

10 September marched into Lisbon	The regiment marched through Bucelas & Santo Antao [de Tojal] & stayed two days at Campo Grande & two nights at the Campo Santa Anna.
Encamped on 13 September	The Reserve were at first in camp on the ground above Santa Anna and afterwards at Monte Santo between Belem & Queluz.
28 October Marched to Sacavem 3 leagues.	The headquarters moved from Lisbon on the 26th.[11]
29 October Vila Franca [de Xira] 3 leagues	
30 October Azambuja 3 leagues	
31 October Santarem 4 leagues	
1 November Halt	Santarem stands on a hill & the plains of Gologa which is beneath are covered by water every winter by the overflow of the Tagus.
2 November Gologa 5 leagues	
3 November Punhente 4 leagues	
4 November Abrantes 2 leagues	
5–8 November Halt	
9 November Gavaio 4 leagues	Crossed the Tagus at Abrantes
10 November Gavaio 4½ leagues	
11 November Sarnadas 4 leagues	Crossed the Tagus at Vila Velha [de Rodao][12]
12 November Castelo Branco 4 leagues	
13 November Halt	
14 November Atalaya 4 leagues	
15 November Covilha 3 leagues	
16 November Belmonte 3 leagues	
17 November Guarda 4 leagues	
18 November Halt	
19 November Castanheiras Amoreira 4 leagues	
20 November Vilar Formoso 2½ leagues Fuentes [de Onoro] 3 leagues	
21 November Ciudad Rodrigo 4 leagues	
22 November Martin del Rio [Yeltes?] 5 leagues	
23 November San Munoz 2 leagues	
24 November Calzada de Don Diego, Barbadillo 5 leagues	
25 November Salamanca 4 leagues	At Salamanca we joined the headquarters.[13]

Total Distance 80 ½ leagues	
12 December Fuente Sauco 6½ leagues[14]	
13 December Aliejos 6 leagues	
14 December Halt	
15 December Toro 6 leagues	
16 December Halt	
17 December Villa Diga 9 leagues	
18 December Halt	
19 December Villarderallaves 4 leagues	
20 December Castroponce 5 leagues	
21 December Arenillas [de Valderaduey] 4 leagues	
22 December Sahagun 3 leagues	
23 December Ordered to march at night with the intention of attacking the enemy at Saldano & Carrion de Coscombes	
24 December Halt[15]	
25 December Valdesaz [de los Oteros] 5½ leagues	
26 December Villamanan 2 leagues	
27 December Halt	
28 December Laguna Dalga 3 leagues	
29 December Halt	
30 December Astorga 6 leagues	
31 December began our retreat & marched all night on the 31st to the 5th, passed through Villafranca [del Bierzo] on the 2nd and arrived at Lugo at 6 in the morning of January 6th.	January 1809
6 January Lugo	
7 January Laid on our arms all night.	
8 January Laid on our arms & march at night. March all night of the 9th & all of the day	
10 January Betanzos	
11 January Corunna[16]	
From Lugo to Corunna 42 leagues.[17]	

Letters of Major the honourable Charles Banks Stanhope

Camp above Lisbon 17 September 1808

… I have not been out of the lines of the regiment since I joined them and have had little opportunity of hearing anything. I think it is impossible but we shall move into quarters in a few days. Lisbon was evacuated the day before yesterday by the French. I do not know the particulars of this disgraceful treaty, but the army are all enraged with Sir H Dalrymple and if old Burrard had allowed them to have followed the enemy force on the 21st not a man could have escaped.[18]

19 September 1808

Sir Arthur Wellesley does not go until tomorrow and as I went over to see General Moore to hear all the news I could for you, I have however heard nothing. He is quite well and begged to be always most kindly remembered to you when I wrote. … I expect my friend, the absent Napier,[19] out everyday which as he has some excellent qualities and a good disposition will make the regiment much more pleasant for me. I know little as yet of the officers but I think in general they are very bad, but the men are fine and I think myself very fortunate being with them. General Moore thinks the same and I am convinced it will be easier to get the next step after doing regimental duty than if I had been on the Staff or in the general's family.

Again, influence had its effect; the 50th Regiment was initially assigned a role remaining in reserve in Portugal; however Sir John Moore arranged for the regiment to reinforce his force in Spain.

Lisbon 16 October 1808[20]

From Sir John Moore to Hester,

… Charles' regiment was in the number of those named to remain in Portugal under Sir H Burrard,[21] this was breaking his heart and so was it mine, but I have at last contrived an arrangement in concert with Sir Harry, who is the most liberal of men, to take the 50th with me and so all is well. The regiments are already marching, his will move in a few days and as soon as I have put everything in train here, I shall push on and get to the head.

But Sir John indicated that there were major difficulties with supplies.

20–22 October 1808,

… We have been delayed by the contractors not being able to supply provisions as soon as they promised. I hope we shall be underway in three or four days.

Charles sat in his camp on a hill writing to his connections at home, including the Duchess of Richmond and of course his dear Hester.

To The Duchess of Richmond[22]

Camp, Monte Santo 3 October 1808

I have not done myself the honour of writing to your grace since my arrival here for bovering [sic] you, as a letter from the top of a hill must be rather a stupid thing at the best, but much more so situated as we are; hearing nothing and not knowing what is to become of us. On my arrival in this country I found a major of my regiment was badly wounded and obtained leave to do duty with the first battalion in his room, which I preferred to any Staff situation. I joined four days after the battle of the 21st and since that we have done nothing. We are rejoiced at our commander in chief being removed.[23] Nothing can exceed the contempt the army have of him and I am sorry to say the one who remains is also not very popular.[24]

I saw Sir Arthur [Wellesley] the day before he embarked and I thought he was looking much better than when I saw him in Ireland. The general officers who were under him have presented him with a piece of plate and the field officers follow their example shortly after to mark their great respect for him.

I have not heard from my sister since I have been here, but I had a letter from James, who filled it with praises of yourself & of the Duke [of Richmond] and he thinks the voice of the latter at certain moments very like to Mr Pitt's. May I beg of you to remember me in the kindest manner to him and to believe me with the greatest esteem, your Grace's most devoted and most obliged, humble servant Charles Stanhope.

To the Duchess of Richmond,

Camp, Monte Santo, 17 October 1808

As I did myself the honour of writing to your Grace but a few days ago, I should not so soon trouble you with another letter, but we have received orders to march into Spain and I can not leave this uninteresting place without addressing you as it [is] so uncertain when I may have another opportunity and shall trust to your kindness to forgive my bovering you with another tiresome epistle. I trust in a short time to making them more interesting, and then I suppose I shall have to apologise for their length.

A great many of the regiments have already marched and we expect to move in three or four days, we are to go into houses every night and march by small columns on the different roads that are tolerable, I do not as yet know the one we are to go. I should at all times feel pleasure in hearing of General Moore being employed in any distinguished command and I think his being employed now is most honourable indeed when I consider the way he was treated on his return from Sweden by some of our ministers. I every day admire him more and I do feel most happy at the idea of his now having a command in which he may show his ability and talents. I received a letter a few days ago from dear Hester dated Builth [Wells] and was quite glad hearing she was something better, James who was there with her gave me an account of the way she passed her time 'doing all the good she could to the poor'. If the prayers of the unhappy reach heaven she will be blessed, but I am in a mistetistical [sic] humour and begging your grace to do me the honour of remembering me most kindly to the Duke shall assure you I remain, your most devoted and very obliged, humble servant Charles Stanhope.

Charles wrote regularly to Hester and these letters chart his movement with his battalion through Spain.

Monte Santo, 26 October 1808

… We got our route sent us this evening, we are to be at Abrantes on 4 of November and we are to halt there until we get orders, I should think but very few days. Colonel Walker[25] who I have mentioned to you is not yet gone. The general sent for him the other day and gave him a dressing [down] about the state of the regiment and then told him he expected them to be much better now they were commanded by another person, and he had just spoke to him before he went that he might know what to expect when he returned if he did not pay more attention, in short he spoke in such a way I do not think we should see the fellow again …

We are at present in a brigade with the 3rd Regiment[26] and under General Disney who came down from Sicily … The frigate that took General Junot to France and is commanded by Captain Percy,[27] brother to my friend,[28] returned yesterday and I heard one of our officers say that he had been with some of the lieutenants who liked Junot very much and said he was the best fellow they ever saw, that he had given every man on board half a guinea and made the captain a present of a very valuable box of jewels and some cases of French wine. Now this appears to me to be damned shabby, I do not think is the custom of the service. … We march on 28th the day after tomorrow and are to be at Abrantes on 4th November.

By now Charles was becoming enamoured of his men and began to believe they were made of the 'right stuff'.

Abrantes, 5 November 1808

We got in here yesterday and except getting wet one day we had a very pleasant march … General Moore did not stop here as he intended but went to Almeida where I believe we shall meet him. We march the day after tomorrow except we are detained by a bridge which was broke and is now repairing which we must pass. We are to go to Castelo Branco in four days and they are long marches. When we get there we shall have our route to Almeida given to us but I believe it will take thirteen days … The stories and old speeches of some of our men along the road, they amuse me very much and I think they are a good humoured set of fellows as I ever saw. They have been in very bad hands or they would be as fine a regiment as any in the army.

Salamanca, 28 November 1808

… We arrived here on 25th but did not come through Almeida as we were at first ordered but had our route changed and when we got to Freineda we turned off and came through Ciudad Rodrigo. General Moore about 16,000 men and we expect General Hope's Division in a few days.

The troops marched and countermarched across Spain in atrocious weather with poor or non-existent supplies. The 50th shared these trials as the army were eventually forced to retreat hurriedly towards La Corunna, where the fleet was expected to be waiting to remove them. At Lugo George Napier records meeting his brother Charles and Charles Stanhope. They were sharing an Irish stew for breakfast and, as he dare not stop whilst carrying orders, his brother ran up and wafted the dish before his nose to tantalize him and then shouted 'You dainty dog, can't eat Irish stew'.

They arrived at Corunna joyful in the knowledge that this marked the end of the terrible marches, but tinged with the fear that the ships would not get to them in time to allow their escape, a veritable Dunkirk. A few days' rest in a large convent with supplies from the depots whilst the ships started to arrive and the men were ready to face Soult's army as it finally approached. The brigade was called into the line facing the village of Elvina, in reality a small group of hovels and a church set in a landscape of rugged rocks pushing through the earth, stone walls, hedges and close winding passages. The French had occupied the village and the 50th were led by their two majors in a headlong bayonet charge which successfully cleared the village temporarily. Many of the French defenders had not found time to evacuate the village and barricaded themselves within the church and continued to fire upon the troops. Captain William Clunes marched his grenadier company close to the church and bravely advanced alone to the doorway, where be bellowed out his demand for their immediate surrender or their imminent destruction to a man. The French made a run for it, many were killed and wounded and even more were captured by Clunes[29] and his company.

But their hard-won success was to be short lived. Advancing upon the hill beyond and attacked in turn by overwhelming numbers, the battalion was forced to relinquish its gains and return to the British line, but not before losing many men including their two majors. Major Charles Napier was seriously wounded and made a prisoner and Major Charles Banks Stanhope died instantly from a ball striking him in the chest.

Patterson records the death of Charles Stanhope saying,

> Among the former [killed] was the Honourable Charles Stanhope, who received a musket ball in the chest, and expired without a struggle. He was a man of dignified appearance, reserved in his deportment, but withal a zealous officer. Having joined the regiment at the outset of this campaign, his career was brief, though splendid. The same round [volley?] of musketry that caused the death of Stanhope, proved fatal to both the officers of the colours, Ensigns Moore and Stewart …[30]

The regiment retired behind the front line to lick its wounds, the Guards taking their post in the front line. James was not made aware of his brother's death until after the battle, when he joined the funeral cortege to bury him with military honours.

Monthly Magazine, March 1809

DIED

> At Corunna in his 24th year, the honourable Major Charles Stanhope. This young man was second son of Earl Stanhope, by his Lady Louisa, the only daughter of Mr Henry Grenville. Several branches of the Stanhope family have been illustrious in arms and have displayed, in various periods of our history, an energy of character and a devotion to their country's cause, which have rendered the name illustrious in the annals of Britain. The youth, whose loss we now deplore, chose at a very early period, the military profession, as that in which he hoped he might be usefully employed. He had been assiduous in forming his character and in attaining a thorough knowledge of the duties attached to several degrees of

military service, through which he had passed. From the high opinion formed of his courage and talents, he was about two or three years since, appointed by General Moore to be one of his aide-de-camps. Nothing could be better adapted to his wishes, he was anxious to be the witness of, and participator in real and active service. He could not bear the idea of being raised step by step in the army, without having, at the same time, the opportunity of proving to his friends and his country, that he was worthy of the rank and honour conferred upon him. It was a source of extreme mortification to Major Stanhope that he returned from Sicily and Sweden, without being able to justify, by his conduct, the expectations which his friends had naturally formed of his character. In Spain he was no longer aide-de-camp, to the General under whom he served and whom he loved with a filial affection, but was appointed with Major Napier, his particular friend, to the command of the fiftieth regiment. Never were men more attached to officers than the soldiers of this regiment to their noble-minded and heroic majors. This body is distinguished by General Hope,[31] as having borne the brunt of the action; and the efforts of the officers and soldiers from its very commencement, claimed the applause of their general, who, witnessing their prowess, and highly approving of the judgment by which their exertions were made, rode up to them, exclaiming 'Well done, my 50th, well done, my majors of the 50th'. To their energy a large portion of the regiment and both the majors sacrificed their lives. The body of Major Napier was not found; but that of Major Stanhope was carried to his tent till the battle was won. His younger brother, Captain James Stanhope, who had shared in the dangers of the day, as aide-de-camp to General Moore, paid the last tribute of respect and sincere affection to the remains of the major. The fatal bullet had passed through the heart of the deceased, and so instantaneous must have been the death of Major Stanhope, that a sense of pain had not torn from his countenance that smile which the bravery of his soldiers and the applause of his commander had excited. At any period, but particularly in times when we may have to contend for our liberties as a nation on our own shores; the death of such a man must be regarded as a public loss: and every lover of his country will deeply lament that so many excellent lives should have been sacrificed to so little purpose. The loss of Major Stanhope to his immediate connections is irreparable: his manners were remarkably mild: his attachments strong; and his heart overflowed with the milk of human kindness. Of his brother, who parted from him at the commencement of the action, and who almost saw him fall, the affliction may be conceived but cannot be described. Well might the unhappy youth exclaim on the occasion 'To lose in one hour the companion of my earliest years, and the kindest protector and best of friends in the gallant Sir John Moore; is almost more than philosophy or human nature can withstand'. Those only can appreciate the affectionate attachment of these brothers, who were witness to their growing years, and who can affirm that in their breasts, were never perceived those emotions of envy, those risings of jealousy so frequently fatal to the happiness of the nearest relations.

Appendix B

Letters by Staff Surgeon John Robert Hulme Discussing the Wound Sustained by General Alava[32]

Freineda 24 April 1813

My dear Sir Thomas [Graham]

I was extremely happy to hear of your safe arrival in Lisbon and this morning had the further pleasure of your letter of the 21st. I am not surprised that your eyes should be more sensible than usual to the sun's glare on the first moment of landing in a very hot part of the country but I would fain hope that as you approach the mountains it will, from custom, become less & less susceptible[33] and I have no doubt of your being enabled to get through this campaign which every one here seems to think will be the last on this side [of] the Pyrenees. Indeed, as the probability is that all our operations will be on the north of the Duero, I should think we shall not suffer so much from the heat as formerly. This however is only conjecture as I believe no one knows anything of the *Lord's* designs. Soday[34] and other great warriors nevertheless have it 'That the left wing under your command and the Lord with the centre and all the cavalry will cross the Duero perhaps in Portugal and by a rapid advance will endeavour to turn the enemies left whilst the Alicante army amuses and occupies Suchet and General Hill makes demonstrations on the Comte d'Erlon's centre & right.'

The cavalry are certainly all drawing toward the Duero but whether with a view to cross or merely for the sake of forage is a question which a few days will decide. From Lord Wellington's conversation I should think he is very anxious to move but I cannot believe that he will have everything ready before ten days or a fortnight. The heavy artillery was at Castelo Branco on the 23rd but some pontoons which he very anxiously looks for, I am told cannot be up for twelve or fifteen days. Hussey's reports[35] of course are the common shaves of the day and I have very little private news to give you. I have not seen Cathcart,[36] I do not know when but I hear of him very often; by all accounts he is very well and very well satisfied with the cavalry. Stanhope I never hear from but I am told he is very well and lately was amusing himself at Oporto. Bouverie[37] has not written to me this some time. You must have heard of poor Jackson's dreadful loss; he is I am told in a state of mind not to be described, how sincerely I feel for him![38] General Castanos[39] arrived a few days ago and has taken up his quarters at Aldea del Obispo. The O'Donaghues,[40] General Wimpffen[41] and the rest of the Spanish Staff are at Fuentes d'Onoro; Alava had a very odd wound in the root of his ___[42] which threatened no very pleasant consequences. In short I had some apprehensions that as he married by proxy and had never slept with his wife, he might possibly be obliged to consummate by proxy also, certainly not 'devoutly to be wished for' by any husband, but however, I recommended him to try the hot baths at Guimaraes and I am happy to say that he has reaped every advantage that could be hoped for, being in all respects *ad munerum veneris aptus*[43] & having practiced at Oporto with great success.[44] He is expected here daily. Lord John Russell came here from La Mancha two or three days ago, he is looking very well. If Lord William [Russell] has come out with you pray remember me kindly to him and tell him I should be very much obliged to him to get my watch which General Kempt left with Geddes[45] and if it is not too much trouble I would thank him to bring it up with him. Hese[46] I am told has not come out with you and from what I hear of Hope I am almost afraid to ask for him. If he has been able to accompany you have the goodness to make my kindest compliments to him and tell him I shall take good care of his horses should he come to Freineda. Calvert[47] and Colville are I presume in good health so I shall not offer *my service* but my best wishes to them. All the Staff here are quite well at present. The Adjutant General however rather disappointed at Sir Charles Stewart's having changed his direction[48] but the QM General's delighted with General Murray who indeed appears a most amiable man. The prince[49] is anxiously expecting letters from his father at Berlin but is quite rejoiced at the turn which the tide of affairs has taken. Gordon [ADC] has gone to Bejar to a wedding but returns on Sunday. Lord Fitzroy & Burgh[50] the steady labouring military secretaries and March[51] as usual going about amusing himself. He is growing very stout and has had an ague this spring. You will be glad to hear that Sturgeon[52] has got the Corps de Guides, Scovell[53] having been appointed to the command of the new cavalry Staff Corps.

I do not recollect any one that you know here or are interested about, so I will not fatigue you with reading. Permit me to remain with the greatest respect, my dear Sir Thomas, ever your most faithful servant Rob Hume.

Appendix C

An Account of the Death of William Pitt, written by James Stanhope[54]

I returned to Downing Street from Norman Cross[55] to which place I had escorted a party of French prisoners, on the night of Lord Wilson's funeral. Mr Pitt was then on his way from Bath to Putney. I heard of his being very ill but had not the slightest idea of the fatal event which shortly took place being so near.

Among the accounts that I heard, the circumstance of Mr Pitt having lost the deep tone and wonderful harmony which characterized his voice both in public & private & that it had become feeble & tremulous, alarmed me the most. My sister remained entirely at Putney[56] from Mr Pitt's arrival till the dinner that was given at Downing St previous to the opening of Parliament. As he was advised to be kept very quiet, and an interview which he had with Lord H__y[57] was productive of considerable evil. I did not go to Putney till Sunday the 19th when I went in the carriage with Hester. When we came within about 300 yards of the house Mr Rose[58] stopped the carriage. We immediately received the most dreadful apprehensions when we perceived him in tears & his manner exhibiting marks of the most poignant grief. He said 'I fear there is danger' & I believe those were his only words. On arriving at the house we found the melancholy intelligence but too true and that apprehensions were entertained for his life, owing to a typhous fever which had succeeded to his state of debility.[59] On the Sunday he however took two eggs beaten up, & on account of their remaining on his stomach, considerable hopes were entertained by Sir W Farquhar.[60] He passed a tolerable night but on the *Monday* evening he grew worse. He passed a bad night and on the Tuesday morning was certainly considerably worse. During these days, a great number of people of all ranks called to enquire after his health. Lord Chatham[61] called on Tuesday morning but by the advice of Sir Walter & Doctors Baillie[62] & Reynolds[63] (who had been sent for on the Monday) was not allowed to see him. The Dukes of Cambridge[64] & Cumberland,[65] besides Canning, Sturges,[66] Steele,[67] Rose etc called on the Tuesday. On Wednesday morning his pulse was at times as high as 130, he was very faint & could not retain any nourishment he took. It was then considered necessary to acquaint Mr Pitt with his danger, which the Bishop of Lincoln[68] did at about 8 on Wednesday morning.

Not being present myself, I can not decidedly state the particulars of the interview, but I understand that the bishop offered to administer the sacrament, which Mr Pitt declined, alleging his unworthiness of receiving it. The bishop prayed with Mr Pitt for some time by his bedside. Mr Pitt received the intelligence of his own danger with unexampled firmness & expressed to the bishop every sentiment worthy of a real Christian. He then stated to the Bishop of Lincoln his last wishes which I need not repeat, their having already appeared in the public prints. Mr Pitt attempted to write himself but was unable. He then dictated to the bishop & afterwards read what the bishop had written aloud & signed it in the presence of three witnesses, two of whom were the bishop & Sir Walter, the other being his own & faithful footman Barlow. After this was concluded Mr Pitt begged to be left alone & he remained composed & apparently asleep for 2 or three hours.

Doctors Baillie & Reynolds arrived about three & gave as their opinion that Mr Pitt could not live about 24 hours. Our own feelings in losing our only protector who had reared us with more than parental care I need not attempt to describe. From Wednesday morning I did not leave his room except for a few minutes till the time of his death, though I did not allow him to see me as I felt myself unequal to the dreadful scene of parting with him & feared (although he was given over) that the exertion on his part might hasten the dreadful event which now appeared inevitable. Hester applied for leave to see him but was refused. Taking however the opportunity of Sir Walter being at dinner, she went into Mr Pitt's room. He though even then wandering a little he immediately recollected her & with his usual angelic mildness wished her future happiness & gave her a most solemn blessing & affectionate farewell. On her leaving the room I entered it & for some time afterwards Mr Pitt continued to speak of her & several times repeated *'Dear soul, I know she loves me! Where is Hester? Is Hester gone?'* In the evening Sir Walter gave him some champagne in hopes of keeping high for a time his wasting & almost subdued strength and as Mr Pitt seemed to feel pain in swallowing it owing to the thrush[69] in his throat, Sir Walter said *'I am sorry Sir to give you pain, do not take it unkind.'* Mr Pitt with that mildness which adorned his private life replied 'I never take anything unkind that is meant for my good'. At three o'clock on Wednesday Colonel Taylor[70] arrived express from H.M. at Windsor & returned with the melancholy of all hopes having ceased. I remained the whole of Wednesday night with Mr Pitt. His mind seemed fixed on the affairs of the country & he expressed his thoughts aloud though sometimes incoherently. He spoke a good deal concerning a private letter from Lord H_y[71] & presently enquired the direction of the wind, then said answering himself 'East, oh that will do, that will bring him quick'. At other times seemed to be in conversation with a messenger & sometimes cried out 'Hear! hear!' as if in the House of Commons. During the time he did not speak he moaned considerably crying 'Oh dear! Oh Lord!' Towards 12 the rattles came in his throat & proclaimed approaching dissolution. Sir Walter, the bishop, Charles & my sister were laying down on their beds overcome with fatigue. At one a Mr Louth arrived from town in a chaise bringing a vial of harts horn oil,[72] a spoonful of which he insisted on Mr Pitt's taking as he had known it recover people in the last agonies. Remonstrance as to its certain inefficacy was useless & on Sir Walter saying that it could be of no detriment, we poured a couple of spoonfuls down Mr Pitt's throat. It produced no effect but a little convulsive cough. In about ½ an hour Mr Louth returned to town. At about half past two Mr Pitt ceased moaning & did not speak or make the slightest sound for some time. As his extremities were then growing chilly, I feared he was dying, but shortly afterwards with a much clearer voice than he spoke in before & in a tone I never shall forget, he exclaimed *'Oh my country, how I leave my country!!!'*. From that time he never spoke or moaned and at half past four expired without groan or struggle, his strength being quite exhausted, his life departed like a candle burning out.

Mr Pitt during his illness frequently enquired after Charles & myself & during his wanderings often repeated our names, in the same manner as he did Hester's after her leaving the room. At 5 I left Putney for Downing Street in Mr Pitt's carriage where with Mr Adams[73] we sealed up his books, papers &c &c. I made these minutes on the *Sunday* & am therefore certain they are correct. James Stanhope.

Appendix D

'The Narrative of my Wife's Last Illness Finished on her Birthday, 15 February 1823'[74]

On Thursday the 9th of January I attended the Duke of York at the consecration of a new church and was out nearly the whole day. When I returned I asked Freddy what she had been doing 'Writing Letters?'

'No something for you which I have long meant to do. Here they are' (giving me some papers) 'You may open them now if you like to see if you approve of their contents, or not as you think best'.

Seeing they were instructions in case of her decease, I said 'I will read them now; you are very right to do so. I was making my will at the same time that our settlements were preparing and I did not think I should die the sooner on that account. Only tell me one thing, have you any fears or presentiment?'

She said 'Of course there is always some risk, but I have no fears or presentiment.'

I read them before her; the perusal of them affected me deeply; for no one could read such angelic sentiments without tears. I kissed her affectionately & thanked her for writing it as I found I had never known her before and that I loved her ten times better than ever I did. I then sealed them up & put them by. I must here mention that on the 7th & 8th she had suffered great agony from the toothache. Granville said he could not allow the pain to go on as it would be detrimental both to herself & the infant and on seeing Parkinson[75] it was decided to take it out. She bore the 2 pulls which were very severe (the tooth breaking the first time) with her usual fortitude.

On the 9th she was particularly well, there was a peculiar calm & serenity of countenance, manner & voice which struck me so much that I told her of it. We passed a most happy evening, but went to bed early. About ½ past 1 in the morning of the 10th she woke me saying she felt unwell & that certain symptoms had appeared. Mrs Smith[76] was to come on the 10th, I sent off immediately for both her & Dr Granville. When they came, they said it might come on or it might be postponed for a day or two. The 10th passed, she being up, but keeping her room. She was in very good spirits, I stayed with her all day but went early to bed for her sake. At about 1 on the morning of the 11th Mrs Smith woke me to tell me that Freddy had been ill since ½ past 11 and that it was time to send for Granville, I did so & I went up to see her. She rejoiced as her pains grew stronger, asked for her chain & locket and put it several times round her neck. When Granville came I retired and at 10 past 2 he gave me the glad tidings of an excellent delivery & a fine boy. Her pulse fell to 60 immediately after; as soon as I could I saw the baby, a beautiful fat child, like his brother in face but stouter. He cried lustily & seemed quite healthy. I then saw Freddy, kissed her and wished her joy; she said she felt quite well. I would not let her talk and left her to write my letters & notes to announce the happy event. Granville was obliged to go some miles out of town and came at a little before 2 and said her face was flushed, that she had a little fever, that it was too soon for fever to come on and that he should change her medicines & send some cooling ones.[77] She asked me if I had finished my letters and hoped I had not mentioned her not being quite so well and repeatedly said she was so glad there was no post on Sunday (next day) for on Monday we should send good accounts. Granville returned at ½ past 5 and finding the fever increased, determined on bleeding her, to which she willingly agreed. She complained of a heaviness in her head & laid in a sort of stupor. Mr Tupper[78] came immediately and took 24oz of blood.[79] They said they never saw blood in a higher state of inflammation, it was yellow and fuzzy. She felt immediately relief & said her head was better. At about 9 Granville & Tupper returned and thought it advisable to take 12 more ounces of blood. Her pulse which had been at 140 now sank to 120. Some remedies were now administered which brought away some faeces of a very bad description which was singular as her bowels had always been open & her stomach in good order. During the night (Dr Granville & myself) determined to call in Dr Baillie & Clerk. In the meantime thirty leeches[80] were put on her stomach as there was a degree of tension & they were afraid it would turn from general to local inflammation. Drs Baillie & Clark[81] came as the leeches had nearly done sucking and the former ordered them to be taken off. They said we had mastered the inflammation but that it was a case of exceeding hazard, that she had youth, a good constitution & a good delivery in her favour, but they would not encourage much hope. I sent for my brother who came & stayed with me without quitting me a moment; I never can do justice to his kindness. His affection, the judgment in his conversation supported me through this dreadful trial.

In the meantime on the Saturday evening the poor baby was affected in the same manner by inflammation in the bowels.[82] He had had all the natural passages the day before and there seemed no reason why he was ill. Mr Tupper since said 'It seemed as if God had but first breathed life into him & withdrew it again'.

Every remedy was resorted to, he was frequently put into hot water, he was relieved by a plentiful motion & seemed better on Sunday morning. A wet nurse was obtained for him, the baby took the breast and slept nearly two hours. My hopes revived, but spasms came on & he became worse. I thought it right to send for a clergyman who baptised the child by the name of Frederick (the Duke of York having kindly consented to be the Godfather of my next child). The baby lingered on and on Sunday evening the poor infant was removed from this world, I trust to that kingdom which we are told is composed of such innocence & purity.

During the time of the violent inflammation Freddy occasionally wandered, had strange & horrible dreams, but always became collected on anyone speaking to her. After the leeches her pulse though still very quick became so low as hardly to be felt, her body was very cold, but she was perfectly collected.

Every means was used to keep her extremities warm, I frequently rubbed her feet. The only relief she seemed to feel was from my laying beside her on the bed. She made me put my arm round her neck & she frequently slept in the position. As her weakness increased she complained of the pains of her bones and particularly of weakness in the back. She asked frequently about the children & expressed a great anxiety to see them. I said that Baillie had positively prohibited it, that she was to be kept quiet & that I could do nothing without the doctor's consent. At 3 o'clock on the Sunday I had sent an express to Lord & Lady Mansfield at Becca[83] & I calculated on their arriving by 10 o'clock or 12 at the latest on Tuesday morning (they would have arrived sooner but the express was somehow several hours too long upon the road). On Monday morning I told her I had received a letter from Lady Mansfield, stating they only meant to remain one night at Becca and would be in town a day sooner, I did this to break their arrival. During all this time I was in a state of alternate hope & fear as the doctors gave their opinions. I tried not to hope & endeavoured to prepare myself but hope still held her place. One of the most painful duties I had to perform was to appear with a calm countenance before my beloved wife, when I had just left the cradle of my dying child.

When the child was first taken ill, she remarked a change in my countenance (which was more on her account) & asked me what was the matter. After this I was wonderfully supported, was always cheerful near her and she never suspected the illness of her child. She several times repeated her written wishes and continued to ask for the children. When Dr Baillie came I proposed that she should see James [Banks] but that we should say the baby was asleep. In the meantime she thought of everything & to prove her filial affection predominated desired Tupper to make her mother consult him about a complaint with which she was troubled. In the evening (Monday 18th) she was put into a hot bath, she was very faint in it but at 10 I laid down beside her & she slept on my breast quite tranquilly till 12. Dr Baillie at 9 on Monday evening told me that as sixteen hours had passed without her being worse, if she could go on so for 12 hours more he should entertain great hopes. Mine revived!!! When she woke at 12 she became restless, everything passed through undigested and I saw a change had taken place. I called up Granville who saw it was hopeless. I went downstairs for a short time to recover myself. During all this time, she fancied she should like different things & we were desired to try everything. She asked for every sort of wine, porter, arrowroot, grapes, figs, but disliked everything when she tasted it. At six she asked for me and when I came said 'Why did not you tell me I was in danger.' I said, 'I meant to have done so whenever I was permitted'.

She desired a clergyman to be sent for and saw James, kissed him repeatedly & implored a blessing on him. She took leave of him with a smile that partook of heaven. She asked to see my brother, shook hands with him & took leave of him. She desired to see Stormont[84] who had gone home with Lady Cathcart;[85] I sent for him, when he came (about 8) she joined our hands and begged I should take care of him & give him advice and begged him to follow my example through life. She again pressed to see the baby, I solemnly promised her she should see him when he woke. She often asked afterwards whether he was awake but never expressed impatience again. The clergyman arrived & we took the Sacrament, Stormont with us. She followed some of the prayers faintly and said Amen to all. I attended the clergyman into the other room & when I returned I found she had written her name (it was all she could do) in the guide to the altar of Bishop Wilson[86] & dated it on Xmas day when we had taken the sacrament together. I told her, her parents were expected that morning. She said 'I shall not see them for all is dim, but I may feel them still.' She told me to take care of myself to have the baby baptized by the name of Frederick William & if I liked to add Pitt. She desired ten guineas which had been left her as a legacy to be laid out in a bracelet like that she had ordered as a present to her mother for her birthday and to be given to Miss Murray. The former only came home on Monday evening. She asked for it, I unpacked it, she called for a candle & examined it minutely but evidently with difficulty & then told me to put it on. I fastened it on the left arm, I said 'I will give it to your mother' she answered in a strong voice, 'not till I am dead.' I told her & I remember I said with a smiling countenance that we were parting but for a time, that we should meet in heaven, that my study should be to live so that I might be worthy of meeting her. If resignation, piety, hope & confidence was ever expressed on any countenance it was stamped on her by a smile which is my comfort when I recall it & which I never can forget. She then said 'Marry', I answered 'I swear that rather than relapse into a state of sin, I will fulfill your wishes', she smiled upon me & appeared quite satisfied. She said 'do not give up your liking for music and keep your fondness for Handel'.

She desired to be remembered to Clanwilliam[87] & to Mr Stanard with 'tell him not to be so violent'. She then said how much I had improved her, that she did not wonder she was unpopular when a girl, that Lord __ was right, that she forgave him & desired me to tell him so with her remembrances. She said soon after 'Do not be too fond of a joke.' I have omitted stating that at intervals I knelt down by her bedside and we prayed together.

She urged me to support myself and to be a comfort to her parents. She complained of a terrible gnawing in her stomach & said it was like the pangs of starvation. As the morning advanced she became more & more anxious for the arrival of her parents & frequently asked what o'clock it was. She desired to be lifted up & there was such a change I thought she was going, but she rallied, it seemed as if filial affection detained her vital spent till her wishes could be fulfilled. She saw James again & remained with her hand in mine & occasionally took Stormont's in the other, looking at Granville, her maid Stewart & Mrs Smith alternately & smiling upon all. She offered to take off her ring; I said 'I will take it by & by', pointing to her wedding ring, she said 'no not that, you must marry'. I answered 'If I ever do, it will be with that ring'.

I then got a Bible & I solemnly swore rather than to return into a state of sin, I would marry and I repeated this oath by her side after her spirit had departed. At about 12 o'clock she asked 'Are they arrived?' I said 'No, but they must be now on this side of the tunnel'. She said 'I wish they would come in time for their sakes for it would be a comfort to them'. And I do not think she spoke afterwards. She asked for a pair of scissors and attempted to cut a lock for me from her forehead, which with my assistance she fulfilled. This I placed in her locket since and I shall wear it till my death. She continued to breath softly & occasionally opened her eyes & a faint smile played on her countenance, but she became weaker, the colour changed and at 20 minutes past one her pure spirit departed & I felt myself alone.

If there is belief in goodness, piety & virtue, in the confidence of a life well spent and of every duty fulfilled, if there is truth in the promises of the Gospel and in the Resurrection of our blessed saviour. I must not permit myself to indulge in selfish regrets, for she must be now enjoying through the merciful intercession of our redeemer, the rewards of her excellent life, in happiness which shall not end. May the Almighty grant me in his great mercy that blessed as I have been by the love of that perfect being, blessed as I am by being the father of our sweet boy, blessed as I ever shall be by the record of her excellence & by the recollection of her virtues, I may bear this severe visitation with proper resignation and that I may so steer through the storms of life as to reach in safety that haven of rest where she is already anchored and to be joined in everlasting happiness with those I have loved & lost.

I wish this paper as well as the last letter of Freddy in case of my decease to be given to my son. I adjure him to study them and on the anniversaries of his mother's birth, marriage & death as well as on mine, to seclude himself for a while to peruse them. If ever he finds himself strongly tempted by sin, if ever his conscience is ill at ease, if ever he feels he is not in a state of grace with God. *I entreat him, I command him* to read the blessed words of his sainted mother and they will *reclaim him. Let him strive to imitate that he may meet her in heaven!!!* If he marries & has offspring I bequeath these papers with the same wishes & prayers to his children & his children's children.

Notes

Chapter 1

1 I can discover nothing about this man.
2 It is stated that his reading and writing were still not proficient when he left Chevening.

Chapter 2

1 Press gang.
2 Centre for Kentish Studies (CFKS henceforth), C473/15.
3 Not to become known as the 'Grenadier Guards' until 1815 in commemoration of their service at the Battle of Waterloo.
4 C473/1–10, CFKS.
5 Thomas James Warren-Bulkeley, 7th Viscount Bulkeley.
6 Charles Meryon, *Memoirs of Lady Hester Stanhope* (London, 1846), p. 76. The memoirs of Hester must be treated with some caution, but it seems true that James spent his life trying to be the life and soul of the party and that his political convictions were not deeply held.
7 This would appear to be Lord Lonsdale from later comments of James's.
8 This item is now at Chevening House.
9 Filippo Morghen came from an Italian artistic family who specialized in drawings of the ruins of classical sites and fantastical images not unlike Gaudi.
10 *Memoirs of Lady Hester Stanhope*, p. 79.
11 Lt-Gen. Sir John Stuart was made a count for his victory at Maida.
12 From a letter addressed HMS *Kingfisher* at Plymouth dated 26 Aug. 1806, indicating he was sailing for 'Foreign service'.
13 Lt-Gen. Sir John Moore, a widely respected general and heavily involved in the development of the Rifle Regiment and Light Infantry training.
14 Later to die at the Storming of Bergen op Zoom in 1814.
15 Hamilton, *History*.
16 Approximately 5 miles north of Plymouth, it is still relatively undeveloped.
17 HMS *Kingfisher*, a sloop of 18 guns.
18 Capt. George Francis Seymour, who had been badly wounded at the Battle of San Domingo aboard the *Northumberland*, where grape damaged his jaw and knocked out some teeth.
19 Sir Joseph Banks (1743–1820), naturalist, botanist and patron of the natural sciences. He took part in Capt. James Cook's first great voyage (1768–71). Banks is credited with the introduction to the Western world of eucalyptus, acacia, mimosa, and the genus named after him, *Banksia*. Approximately 80 species of plants bear his name. Banks was also the leading founder of the African Association, a British organization dedicated to the exploration of Africa, and a member of the Society of Dilettanti, which helped to establish the Royal Academy. In March 1779 Banks married Dorothea Hugesson, and settled in a large house at 32 Soho Square. It continued to be his London residence for the remainder of his life, his country home being Spring Grove, a house with 34 acres along the northern side of the London Road, Isleworth. He was James's grandfather on the maternal side. He eventually left his estate to James after his wife's death to provide him with an independent living.
20 Maj.-Gen. McKenzie Fraser.
21 Maj.-Gen. Patrick Wauchope was to be killed in Egypt in 1807.
22 Brig.-Gen. William Stewart was to make a name for himself as a divisional commander in Spain with Wellington.
23 Capt. Francis Maule, 2nd Foot.
24 Capt. the Hon. Henry Percy, 7th Foot.
25 The British representative in Egypt, Edward Missett, had been urging the government to interfere in a virtual civil war between the mamluks and their Turkish masters. However, their timing was awful and Missett represented it as an easier task than it turned out to be. The portents were not good; the force numbering near 6,000 was scattered by bad weather but Alexandria was easily captured on 20 March 1807 from a hopelessly inadequate Turkish garrison.
26 This was a regular form of transport on Sicily at this time. It looked like a sedan chair but drawn by mules.
27 Charles clearly did not get on with Mahon, whereas James seems to have tried to be on friendly terms with all his siblings.
28 Lt-Col Paul Anderson, Nova Scotia Fencibles, had previously served as an aide de camp to Sir John Moore but was now Assistant Adjutant General in Sicily. Anderson has left a memoir of the death of Sir John Moore at Corunna.
29 The brothers mentioned are Lt and Capt. Henry Edmund Joddrell of the 1st Guards and his brother Thomas Marsden Joddrell who was killed at Rosetta on 8 April 1807. Henry survived the war and died in 1868.
30 Admiral Sir John Duckworth sailed his fleet through the Dardanelles in an attempt to force the Turks to resist the overtures of Napoleon. It failed to achieve anything significant and led to quite heavy British losses from the huge stone cannonballs fired by the Turks.

31 The mercenary Prince of Hesse-Philippsthal led a revolt on the mainland, holding the fortress of Gaeta until June 1806. He was wounded and evacuated and the fortress surrendered.
32 General Wauchope led the 31st Foot and Chasseurs Britaniques to capture Rosetta. He arrived to find the gates open and the city to all appearances unguarded. However, it was a trap and once entangled in the streets they were fired on from every roof and window. Wauchope was killed and the force suffered 460 killed and wounded in total.
33 Stewart commanded the force which went back to retake Rosetta. He detached troops to hold the village of El Hamed which threatened his wing but the Albanian troops landed from a fleet of small boats and their cavalry swarmed around the detachments. Although Stewart got away with the main force, the detachment of around 800 men lost 300 killed and the other 500, who were mostly wounded, were taken prisoner.
34 Gen. Henry Edward Fox commanded the forces on Sicily after the departure of Stuart to Malta, but the *de facto* commander was Sir John Moore, who took over command in July 1807 when Fox returned home on the news of the death of his politician brother.
35 Maj.-Gen. Sir John Coape Sherbrooke was Colonel to the Sicilian Regiment; he later served as second in command at the Battle of Talavera and then became Lieutenant Governor of Nova Scotia.
36 A group of small volcanic islands lying just north of Sicily, including Lipari and Vulcano.

Chapter 3
1 The Guards followed a system of double ranking at this time. To ensure their seniority over similar ranked officers of the line, they were ranked in the army one rank above their regimental rank. Hence James was now a lieutenant in the regiment but ranked a captain in the army.
2 C270 329/2, CFKS.
3 C253/4, CFKS.
4 Because Moore allowed James onto his staff, Cornet George Fitzclarence, 10th Hussars, actually served throughout this campaign as aide de camp to Maj.-Gen. Slade.
5 Marshal Nicolas Jean de Dieu Soult, a very capable soldier who caused Wellington many problems in years to come.
6 We know that James was at Portsmouth on 6 Dec. 1808 and arrived at La Corunna on 14 Jan. 1809 but he does not say how he actually got there. Initially I thought that he had sailed directly to Corunna; however his later journal mentions being at Lamego in Portugal in 1808 and again at Torre de Moncorvo in 1809. Given that James was only in Portugal during the short period of Moore's retreat in 1808/9 these facts can only make sense if James landed at Oporto and rode across country towards Zamora in pursuit of Moore's army, as these places were on the direct route from there. Having heard of the retreat he must then have ridden through the mountains and joined the army at Corunna from some port on the coast such as Vigo where the fleet of transports was, as he states that he 'landed' at Corunna the day before the battle.
7 William Napier, *History of the Peninsular War* (London, 1835).
8 With the wounding of Sir David Baird and Sir John Moore, the command of the army had devolved upon Lt-Gen. Sir John Hope.
9 W C E Napier, *Life of General Sir George Napier* (London, 1884), pp. 71–2.
10 *The Adventures of Captain John Patterson* (London, 1837), pp. 115–16.
11 Lt-Col William Lowther, 1st Earl Lonsdale, 84th Foot, was a family friend (I can find no family link). He was particularly kind to Hester when she left home and continued to show an interest in her throughout her life.
12 West Sussex Record Office, Goodwood Papers 350.
13 Courtesy of The Lowther Archive at Carlisle Archive, D/Lons L1/2/60.
14 These words are confirmed by the memoir of Lt-Col Paul Anderson, 60th Foot, who was Commandant at Headquarters, quoted in Carola Oman's *Sir John Moore* (London,1953), p. 600.
15 The Earl of Lonsdale owned Cottesmore Castle in Rutland.
16 Lt the Hon. Henry Cecil Lowther, 7th Light Dragoons (Hussars), the second son of the Earl of Lonsdale.

Chapter 4
1 He wrote *The Principles of Military Movements chiefly applicable to Infantry* (1788), which for the first time attempted to standardize British tactical movements on the battlefield.
2 Lt-Col Herbert Taylor, 2nd Foot Guards, Lt-Col Arthur Upton, 1st Foot Guards, and Maj. Henry Paget, 7th Light Dragoons, ended their appointments as aides de camp and Lt-Col S Brown of the York Light Infantry Volunteers ended his dual role as aide and secretary to become Assistant Military Secretary. Capt. Lord Arthur Somerset, 91st Foot, and Capt. the Earl of Tyrconnel, 1st Foot Guards, remained as aides and were joined by James Stanhope and Capt. Lord Alexander Gordon, 3rd Foot Guards.
3 Author of *Memoirs of the Lady Hester Stanhope, as Related by Herself in Conversations with her Physician* (London, 1846).
4 Richard Heber (1773–1833), English book-collector and MP. He owned over 150,000 books on his death.
5 Reginald Heber (1783–1826) was the Church of England's Lord Bishop of Calcutta. Now remembered chiefly as a hymn writer.
6 A quote from Reginald Heber's *Europe: Lines on the Present War* (1809), in which he campaigned for the freedom of Spain from the hands of French tyranny. Calpe is the ancient name, possibly Phoenician in origin, of Gibraltar.
7 Mongibello is a Sicilian name for Mount Etna.
8 HMS *Unite* of 40 guns (ex French *Imperieuse*).

9 HMS *Manilla* of 36 guns was a new ship, having been launched at Woolwich in 1809. She was wrecked on the Dutch coast in a gale in 1812.
10 Henry Phipps, 1st Earl Mulgrave, was First Lord of the Admiralty.
11 John Gifford had published *A Political Life of Pitt* in 1809 and was rewarded with a magistrate's appointment.
12 Robert Stewart, 2nd Marquess of Londonderry, Viscount Castlereagh, was Secretary of State for War and the Colonies.
13 HMS *Jason* of 32 guns, captain the Hon. James King.
14 Ceuta was then and is still today a Spanish enclave in North Africa, on the southern coast of the Strait of Gibraltar.
15 Lt-Col Colin Campbell was acting governor of Gibraltar for the Duke of Kent.
16 The closing lines of Heber's *Europe*.
17 John Hookham Frere was minister to the Spanish Junta.
18 The Spanish Junta had failed to organize any serious defence of Seville and had left Cadiz virtually undefended for Soult's forces to simply march in. However, the Duke of Albuquerque reacted quickly and by forced marches arrived with his army just days before the French and manned the defences. The French arrived without heavy guns and they settled down to a formal siege on 5 Feb. which was doomed to failure as the Royal Navy were able to supply reinforcements and supplies without interruption throughout the two-year-long siege.
19 Following the advance into Spain and victory at Talavera, Wellington's army had been threatened with being surrounded and had been forced to cross to the south side of the River Tagus and retire rapidly to Badajoz, which proved a very unhealthy spot. Wellington was forced to remain in this vicinity whilst he carried out protracted discussions with the Portland government at home who wanted his army to protect Andalusia and Cadiz. Wellington argued that his main priority was the defence of Portugal and he eventually won over the government, moving his main force northwards and leaving General Hill with a corps south of the Tagus.
20 An interesting early assessment of Wellesley, one he changed significantly later.
21 Col Charles Doyle, military agent attached to the Spanish army.
22 There is a clear mistake in transcribing the figures here.
23 Capt. Peter Heywood, commanding the 32 gun HMS *Nereus*.
24 The 2nd Battalion of the 4th (King's Own) Foot formed the garrison of Ceuta in 1810. British forces garrisoned the fortress thereby releasing Spanish forces to fight at home.
25 The Spanish allowed a British force under Gen. Sir James Stuart Fraser to garrison Ceuta, 1810–14.
26 Ceuta had been several times unsuccessfully besieged by the Moors, one siege, under Mulai Ismail, lasting 26 years (1694–1720).
27 HMS *Undaunted* of 38 guns.
28 A high hill near Ceuta.
29 James Green was the Consul General to Morocco 1806–17.
30 Count Guglielmo Di Ludolf, later Neapolitan Minister to London.
31 A fort on the mainland facing Cadiz across the bay. The Spanish had originally dismantled it. The British put up a stout defence for 54 days but were eventually forced to abandon it under tremendous artillery fire.
32 HMS *Comus*, 22 guns, Captain the Hon. Joceline Percy.
33 Capt. Charles Lefebre, Royal Engineers, was killed instantly at the defence of Matagorda, being struck in the chest by a 32pdr shot.
34 HMS *Cerberus* 32 guns, Captain Henry Whitby.
35 Six companies of the 2nd Battalion, 1st Foot Guards, had arrived at Cadiz on 24 March 1810 as part of Gen. Graham's force of 5,000 men sent to bolster the defence of the city.
36 Stanhope was still aide de camp to Gen. Sir David Dundas, therefore could only act as an (unofficial) extra aide de camp to Graham at Cadiz.
37 Brig.-Gen. Lacy having lately been appointed Adjutant General of the Spanish troops at Cadiz.
38 Portazgo was a series of bastions built to defend the Ponte Zuazo, the only bridge from the mainland onto the Isle of Leon.
39 The famous uprising at Madrid which ignited the cutthroat guerrilla war against the French invasion that proved so costly to Napoleon's ambitions. Goya famously captured the terrible images of the ensuing French reprisals.
40 From Byron's *Childe Harold's Pilgrimage*.
41 The joke being that Calavera is the Spanish for a rake or dishonourable man.
42 Gen. Dupont's army was surrounded and forced to surrender in one of the most ignominious defeats of French troops throughout the Napoleonic Wars. It proved counterproductive to the Spanish, who thought for a long time afterwards that their armies could match the French in the open field, which proved a very costly error. The convention of Bailen arranged for the French troops to be repatriated to France, but the Spanish reneged on the deal and incarcerated the French troops on hulks in Cadiz harbour and other such desolate spots. Few ever saw France again.
43 Fort Puntales stood on the Cadiz isthmus directly opposite Fort Matagorda.
44 A 'glass' or 'spyglass' was a common term for a telescope.
45 HMS *Tonnant* of 80 guns, the flagship of Admiral Michael de Courcy.
46 I have been unable to identify this officer. Was he Spanish?
47 Vice Admiral Francis Pickmore.
48 The Trocadero Peninsula juts into the Bay of Cadiz. Fort Matagorda stands at its tip.
49 Admiral Cayetano Valdes y Flores had served at Trafalgar.
50 He was Captain General of Andalucia, taking part in the sieges of Gerona and Valencia.

51 Francisco Castanos was famous as the victor over Dupont at Bailen.
52 Antonio de Escano y Garcia was a naval officer and member of the Cortes.
53 The Duke of Albuquerque defied the orders of the Cortes and took his army of 12,000 men into the lines of Cadiz, just before Soult's army arrived.
54 Gen. Joaquin Blake y Joyes.
55 Antonio de Capmany, author of *Centinela contra los Franceses* (Sentry against the French).
56 Louis Philippe, Duke of Orleans, was the cousin of the future King Louis XVIII and eventually became the last king of France.
57 Heinrich Viktor Prinz zu Wied (or Neuweid), had fought with the Austrian Army in 1805 and 1809 and was promoted to major in 1810. He received a two-year leave of absence and, being a virulent enemy of Napoleon, travelled to Spain in 1810/11 to fight the French with Graf Hartopp as travelling companion. Neuweid wrote to his mother regularly but only mentions Hartopp once. He does state that he was a Dutchman in the Austrian service. They were both in Spain as volunteers and held no official position. I thank Leopold Kudrna for this information.
58 HMS *Achilles* of 74 guns had fought at Trafalgar.
59 Capt. Sir Richard King had fought at Trafalgar and was promoted Rear Admiral in 1812 and second in command in the Mediterranean.
60 The Regency, headed by the testy old Bishop Pedro Quevedo of Orense, was extremely conservative.
61 This of course refers to the works of Samuel Johnson (1709–84), author and lexicographer.
62 It would seem that he was smitten!
63 This would be the same Mrs Spenser Smith whom Lord Byron met at Malta in Sept. 1809 and for whom he developed an attachment.
64 Friuli is an area of Italy stretching from Venice northward to the Tyrol.
65 Actually Abd ar-Rahman II, the son of Emir Al-Hakam I. He became Emir of Cordoba in 822 and engaged in nearly continuous warfare against Alfonso II of Asturias, whose southward advance he halted. In 837 he suppressed a revolt of Christians and Jews in Toledo and repulsed an assault by Vikings in 844. Thereafter he constructed a fleet and naval arsenal at Seville to repel future raids.
66 Charles Napier, 50th Foot, had been reported as killed but was actually severely wounded at the Battle of Corunna. He was made prisoner but returned on a prisoner exchange.
67 Capt. William Napier, 43rd Foot, was shot in the hip at the battle on the Coa (24 July 1810), when a superior force under Marshal Ney caught Craufurd's Light Division exposed on the wrong side of the river and they only just escaped. Charles Napier, Craufurd's aide de camp, had two horses killed under him during the same action.
68 Caroline Napier died in 1810.
69 Queen Maria Carolina of Sicily was an arch schemer. Lord William Henry Cavendish-Bentinck, the British Minister, was her chief antagonist, aided by Lt-Gen. Sir John Stuart, Count of Maida. The French under Murat continued preparations to invade the island from the Italian mainland.
70 The British government had promised to launch a second front in northern Europe to aid the Austrians, who had declared war on France. A force of 40,000 men was sent to Walcheren Island as a first step to capturing the fleet at Antwerp, thus denuding Wellington's army of vital reinforcements. Due to mismanagement and sickness, little was achieved, over 4,000 died and many thousands more never fully recovered their health and suffered recurrences of the fever. The Austrians had actually been roundly beaten at Wagram and sued for peace just as the British force arrived at Walcheren.
71 This would have been a report on one of the first horse races the British had set up on the sandy shore of the Isle of Leon. These became a popular local attraction.
72 Henry Wellesley, the youngest brother of Arthur, the future Duke of Wellington, was appointed envoy to Spain in 1809 and retained his position as Ambassador to Spain until 1821. He later became the 1st Baron Cowley.
73 Robert Banks Jenkinson, Lord Hawkesbury, 2nd Earl of Liverpool, was Secretary for War and the Colonies.
74 Such comments show that James revisited his journal and added further notes at a later date.
75 Carlos Beramendi was quarter master at the siege of Gerona in 1809, not the commanding general, who was Mariano Alvarez de Castro. He had been an employee of the Treasury Department; he became Quarter Master General of the Spanish Army at Bailen. He was the author of some important fiscal studies and was a radical liberal in the Cadiz Cortes. He wrote two works on the siege of Gerona 'The Gerundea', a poem, and a 'Historical, military, political and economic journal of the siege', but they were not published.
76 Tyrtaeus was an elegiac poet who led Spartan troops during the Second Messenian War (*c*.650 BC).
77 Lucien was a younger brother of Napoleon and, although he initially supported his brother's rise to power, he soon began to oppose Napoleon's imperial ambitions and went into self-imposed exile in Italy. He later tried to escape to America but was captured by the Royal Navy and was held in England until Napoleon's fall in 1814.
78 Victor Emmanuel I (1759–1824) was the Duke of Savoy, Piedmont, and Aosta, and King of Sardinia 1802–21. The mainland provinces were subjugated by the French but the island of Sardinia remained outside the clutches of Napoleon throughout the war.
79 This memorandum has not been found.

Chapter 5
1 Lord John Russell, a future politician, was then the 18-year-old brother of Capt. Lord George William Russell, 23rd Light Dragoons, a fellow aide de camp to Graham, who presumably had been visiting his brother at Cadiz and now joined James as a travelling companion.

2 Lt and Capt. the Hon. John Walpole, Coldstream Guards.
3 HMS *Hardy* of 14 guns; during Oct. Lt Nops of this vessel was tried for tyranny, reduced and dismissed from his command.
4 Often called the 'Strawberry tree'.
5 A hardy plant found on rocky outcrops in Mediterranean lands.
6 Maj.-Gen. Rowland Hill commanded the 2nd Division.
7 Marshal William Carr Beresford, Portuguese Army, was a major-general in the British Army, who had been given the task of reforming the Portuguese Army from top to bottom. The success of his reforms were clearly shown in the latter years of the Peninsular War, when the Portuguese troops fought with great bravery and were considered equal to British troops.
8 Lt-Gen. Robert Craufurd commanded the Light Division, he was later killed at the storming of Ciudad Rodrigo in 1812.
9 Col. George De Grey, 1st Dragoons, commanded a brigade of cavalry consisting of 3rd Dragoon Guards and 4th Dragoons.
10 Col Denis Pack commanded a Portuguese Brigade consisting of 1st and 16th Line and 4th Cacadores.
11 Maj.-Gen. Sir William Erskine.
12 He is mistaken here. Mertola was known as Myrtilis Iulia in Roman times.

Chapter 6
1 Agustin Arguelles (1776–1844) was a Spanish liberal politician in the Cadiz Cortes who played a large part in the Constitution of 1812.
2 Jose Prudencio Padilla Lopez (1784–1828) who later became an admiral and fought in South America's wars of independence.
3 Governor Alacha defended the city of Tolosa against Marshal Suchet's forces, 16 Dec. 1810–2 Jan. 1811. Alacha was pressurized into surrendering under French threats of 'no quarter' and held captive in France. In his absence he was condemned to death by the Catalan junta.
4 Pedro Agar was a naval commander and member of the Regency.
5 Gabriel Cisgar was the Governor of Carthagena and member of the Regency.
6 Gen. Juan de la Cruz Mourgeon.
7 Manuel la Pena, Captain General of Andalucia; despite having a reputation for incompetence (he had the nickname *Dona Manuela*, the Lady Manuel), La Pena was an ambitious man with a talent for diplomacy.
8 This would appear to be an error on the part of Stanhope. Iit was the 47th Foot that served at Barossa.
9 It is strange that Fortescue in his *History of the British Army* clearly had seen James Hamilton's journal, as he quotes from it occasionally, but differs with Stanhope on all the dates, stating that the British embarked on 19 Feb. and sailed on 21st, landed on 23rd and reached Tarifa on 24th.
10 The eight centre companies of 1/28th had been in garrison at Tarifa whilst Lt-Col John Frederick Brown 28th Foot had arrived from Gibraltar with a flank battalion made up of the light and grenadier companies of 1/9th, 1/28th and 2/82nd.
11 Don Alonso Perez de Guzman el Bueno, 7th Duke of Medina Sidonia, Grandee of Spain (1549–1615) was the commander-in-chief of the Spanish Armada.
12 Gen. Don Joseph Lardizabal.
13 Pedro de Alcantara, Prince of Anglona.
14 Oman and Fortescue both agree that the British numbered approximately 5,000 men, the Spanish probably nearer 10,000.
15 Probably at Venta Facinas on the main road, rather than at Facinas itself, which lies off to the right.
16 Now known as Benalup-Casas Viejas.
17 Oman, echoed by Fortescue, states that the French consisted of two companies of infantry only, that La Pena chose to ignore this force which had retired into a fortified convent, but the French commander bolted and his force was cut up by the KGL squadrons rather than the Spanish cavalry. I choose to believe James Hamilton's version as having more the ring of truth.
18 Gen. Jose Pascual de Zayas y Chacon (1772–1827) commanded the Spanish troops at Sancti Petri which were to sortie in conjunction with the attack on the French rear by La Pena.
19 Conil de la Frontera.
20 Chiclana de la Frontera.
21 Francois Joseph d'Estienne de Chaussegros Lery, Baron of the Empire.
22 There is added to this French text a comment in the margin. 'This division had charge of the whole line from Santa Catalina and Trocadero and therefore had very few disposable troops'.
23 General de Division and Baron of the Empire Eugene Casimir Villatte.
24 It is unlikely that the division of Villatte was merely a decoy. It seems more likely that they were to hold up the Spanish advance as long as possible to allow the other French divisions to launch an attack upon the flank of the Allied force thus held in a bottleneck, but his position was dangerous, with Zayas in his rear, and Villatte retired when the position became untenable.
25 Ensign Frederick Colville, 3rd Foot Guards, was an extra ADC to General Graham.
26 The battalions of Gen. Cruz Murgeon, being those of Ciudad Real and the 4th Walloon Guards.
27 Both Oman and Fortescue state that General Beguine's Brigade of three battalions and Whittingham's cavalry were ordered to strengthen the force on the Barossa heights.

28 Maj. Alexander Duncan, Royal Artillery, had commanded the artillery at Cadiz. He was later killed by an accidental explosion at Seville in 1812. The ten guns came from the batteries of Captains Philip Hughes and William Shenley.
29 General de Division Francois Amable Ruffin, Count of the Empire, died of his wounds 15 May 1811.
30 Capt. John Francis Birch commanded the Royal Engineers at Cadiz.
31 Second Capt. William Nicholas, Royal Engineers.
32 Maj. Hugh Gough commanded the 87th Regiment at Barossa, where it captured the eagle of the 8th Regiment de Ligne; he was promoted a brevet lieutenant-colonel for the action. Lt Edward Keogh of the 87th struck down the French Eagle-Bearer Gillemain, and helped by Sergeant Patrick Masterson seized the eagle, but it was recovered as Keogh was shot through the heart and died instantly. Amidst the melee a savage hand-to-hand fight for the eagle ensued, during which two French officers, two French sergeant-majors and three French private soldiers were killed successively in defence of their standard, and an eighth, Lt Gazan, was severely wounded, finally leaving the prize in the hands of Masterson, the only unhurt British combatant in the small group assailing the standard. Raising the trophy aloft, Masterman was heard to exclaim, 'Bejabers boys, I have the Cuckoo!' Sergeant Patrick Masterson, was commissioned as an Ensign in the 87th for his exploits. The eagle was stolen from the Royal Hospital, Chelsea, in 1852 and has never been recovered.
33 Gen. Luis de Lacy was Captain General of Catalonia.
34 This figure is only slightly different to that of Oman who totals French losses at Barossa as 2,062.
35 Oman estimates the French forces at Barossa as significantly less, at 7,170.
36 Oman states that Villatte lost 317 men out of a force of 2,991.
37 The Royal and Distinguished Spanish Order of Carlos III was established by the King of Spain by means of a Royal Decree of 1771, with the motto *Virtuti et merito*. Its objective was to reward people for their actions in benefit to Spain and the Crown.
38 Lt-Col. the Hon. Frederick Cavendish Ponsonby was Assistant Adjutant General at Cadiz.
39 A play on the meaning of La Pena's name, 'the sorrows'.
40 This refers to two Spanish heroes of yore, Rodrigo Diaz de Vivar, more commonly known as El Cid Campeador (1040–99) and Gonzalo Fernandez de Cordoba, the Great Captain (1453–1515).
41 Munoz Torrero and Gonzales Oliveros were member of the Cortes.
42 Antonio de Capmany (1742–1813) died at Cadiz on 14 Nov. in an epidemic. Having studied humanities and philosophy he joined the Regiment of Dragoons of Merida, but left the army to devote himself to study. He collaborated with Pablo de Olavide in the resettlement of the Sierra Moreno then went to Madrid in 1773 where he entered the literary and political world and became Perpetual Secretary of the Academies of Language and History in 1790. He established himself in Cadiz in 1808 where he ran the journal *Gaceta de la Regencia de Espana e Indias* and later became a deputy in the Cortes for Catalonia.
43 Marshal Suchet's task of taking Tarragona was made somewhat easier by the surprise Spanish capture of Figueras in April 1811. Gen. Campoverde, commanding around 12,000–15,000 men, had been in the vicinity of Tarragona, and could have made Suchet's journey difficult, especially if he had attacked Habert's isolated division and destroyed the siege artillery, but instead Campoverde took two of his divisions northeast in an attempt to help retain Figueras against an inevitable French counterattack. Figueras fell to the French again on 19 Aug. 1811.
44 Alfonso Rovira y Galvez was a representative of Murcia in the Cortes.
45 Peter the Hermit was a priest of Amiens who became a key figure during the First Crusade.
46 Judas Maccabeus (or Judah Maccabee, also spelled Machabeus, or Maccabaeus) was a Kohen and the third son of the Jewish priest Mattathias. He led the Maccabean revolt against the Seleucid Empire (167–160 BC) and is acclaimed as one of the greatest warriors in Jewish history alongside Joshua, Gideon and David.
47 The Cortadura is the thin sandy strip which links the Isla to the city of Cadiz.
48 The Mount of the Martyrs is reputedly where San Servando and St Germain were martyred; the town of San Carlos was established here and renamed San Fernando in 1813.
49 The Carraccas were situated on the eastern end of the Isle of Leon.
50 A barbette was a low bank which cannon or infantry could fire over, therefore only giving limited protection.
51 Gen. Jean Victor Marie Moreau (1763–1813) was a French general who was a contemporary of Napoleon Bonaparte and an arch rival. He was implicated in plots to assasinate Napoleon and was banished to the USA. He returned to fight with the Allies in 1813 but Moreau was mortally wounded in the Battle of Dresden on 27 Aug. 1813, while talking to the Tsar, and died on 2 Sept.

Chapter 7
1 The small bill announcing the play *La Donna di Genio Volubile* is not reproduced as having little interest.
2 This sentence is difficult to interpret but is a correct transcription.
3 These defences on the eastern and southern shores of the Tagus opposite Lisbon are generally overlooked by historians but were as critical to Wellington as the Lines of Torres Vedras. Oman states that the lines on the heights of Almada were some 8,000 yards long, with 86 guns and 17 redoubts connected by a covered way with a garrison of 7,500 men.
4 Actually Brig. John Lobo Brandão de Almeida who was the governor of Abrantes until Dec. 1813.
5 The Valle de Corticada: the village of the name is not to be found today.
6 Isna River.
7 A quote from *Joys of a Garden* by Alexander Pope.
8 Torre de Don Miguel?
9 General Jean Marie Pierre Francois Lepaige Count Dorsenne had recently taken command of the Army of the North

in Spain, replacing Marshal Bessières.
10 Marshal Auguste Frederic Louis Viesse de Marmont, 1st Duke of Ragusa, had taken over from Marshal Massena in July 1810.
11 Maj. Lord Charles S Manners, 10th Light Dragoons.
12 A bundle of sticks bound together, used to fill ditches, strengthen the sides of trenches, etc.
13 A very difficult mountain pass which leads up to a village of the same name.
14 Such a line would have been a very serious and costly endeavour. This would have protected the whole peninsula to the south of Lisbon Bay, but may well have required a bigger troop commitment to hold against a strong French assault. The southern end of the line, ending short of the coast at Palmela, was due to the impassible nature for troops of the area to the south known as the Serra d'Arrabida.
15 This would be the defeat of a force under the Spanish Gen. Freire by Marshal Soult at Goron on 7 Aug.
16 Maj.-Gen. Sir William Houston commanded the 7th Division at the Battle of Fuentes d'Onoro. On the third day of the battle (5 May) his division was forced to march some two miles across relatively open country to a new position on the Freineda road, which was achieved with the support of the Light Division without great loss, despite the enemy cavalry swarming round them.
17 Lt-Col Philip Cameron, 79th Foot, was severely wounded in the village and died of his wounds 13 May 1811.
18 Gen. Wathier advanced with his and Lepic's brigades, half of which he launched in pursuit of the retiring British. Attacked by a squadron each of the 14th and 16th Light Dragoons, and fired on by infantry of the 61st in the woods, the French retreated.
19 Fortescue also includes two squadrons of the 11th Light Dragoons.
20 In an unprecedented act, the 5th Foot fired on the French cavalry then charged them with the bayonet and drove them away.
21 Lt-Col Lord FitzRoy James Henry Somerset, 9th Foot, was Wellington's Military Secretary.
22 Bismula is approximately 7 miles southeast of Nave de Haver.
23 The Spanish guerrilla chief Don Julian Sanchez had led a band of irregulars but in 1811 these were formalized into the 'Lancers of Castile'.
24 James actually wrote 27th, but Lynedoch says 2nd, which seems more likely.
25 Lt-Col Robert Walter Stewart, 11th Lord Blantyre, commanded the 2nd Battalion 42nd Foot.
26 This village is now known as Puerto Seguro.
27 Archie Hunter has written a not completely convincing defence of Bevan entitled *Wellington's Scapegoat* (Barnsley, 2005).

Chapter 8
1 A cylindrical basket or cage of wicker which was filled with earth or stones and used in fortifications as an easily and quickly made form of protection.
2 Fought on 24 Dec. 1811, the French success opened the door for the siege of Valencia.
3 Maj. Henry Sturgeon, Royal Staff Corps, who was eventually killed at Vic Bigorre on 19 March 1814.
4 Julius Caesar built a wooden bridge, reputedly 400 m long, over the Rhine in 55 BC.
5 This was a mistake, Brennier had been governor of Almeida. General de Brigade Jean Leonard Barrie was governor of Ciudad Rodrigo after Gen. Reynaud had been captured by Don Julian.
6 A fausse braie is a low rampart provided with a parapet built forward, parallel and below the main rampart, forming an outer enceinte, used in the 16th and 17th century by engineers as a covered way. Later the work was abandoned because when under bombardment the fragments from the rear wall wounded the defenders, forming what came to be known as a 'shot trap'.
7 The glacis is a broad, gently sloping earthwork or natural slope in front of a fort, separated from the fort proper by a ditch and outworks and so arranged as to be swept with musket or cannon fire, to protect the lower portions of the wall from the direct fire of besieging artillery.
8 A ravelin is an outwork consisting of two faces forming a salient angle at the front and a flank angle to the rear which was usually closed at the gorge. Ravelins were separated from the main body of the place by ditches and functioned to protect curtain walls.
9 A fleche is a projecting, arrow-head-shaped outwork in a fortification.
10 Lt-Col John Colborne, 52nd Foot, famous for his flank attack against the Imperial Guard at Waterloo. Later he became Baron Seaton.
11 Oman agrees with 50 men being captured but makes one less officer than James. Fortescue says 48.
12 Side note by James: They fired during the siege 16,000 shell & 10,000 shot without one being fired by us at the defences, though we fired about 9,000 rounds at the breach.
13 Capt. George Ross, Royal Engineers.
14 Maj. Sir James Archibald Hope of the 26th Foot was senior ADC with Graham at Cadiz and in Spain. He later served as AAG to the 1st Division in the 1813 campaign.
15 Actually the Convent of Santa Cruz which was captured by 300 men of the 5/60th and KGL.
16 Oman and Fortescue say 27 guns, but two were not firing at the breach, so technically James is right.
17 Oman estimates British losses in the whole siege at 1,121.
18 Maj.-Gen. Robert Craufurd commanding the Light Division was severely wounded on the breach and died 24 Jan. He was buried in the breach.
19 Portuguese for an attendant.

20 John Colborne was struck by a musket ball in the right shoulder which then travelled down his arm. He was operated on, but the ball could not be found and he suffered for fifteen months before it was removed in an operation of such agony that he could only bear the surgeon working on it for five minutes per day.
21 George Napier had commanded the forlorn hope of the Light Division at Ciudad Rodrigo. He was severely wounded by grape shot in the right arm which was amputated. He received a pension of £300 for his wound.
22 The Eagle of the 39th French Line Regiment was found in the River Ceira in Portugal, 15 June 1811, and was placed in the Chapel of the Royal Hospital Chelsea.
23 The siege of Tomar was actually in 1190. After a six-day siege in which the gate was forced but the besiegers ousted with terrible loss, the siege ended.
24 Gen. Joachim Blake had attempted to prevent Marshal Suchet's 70,000 strong army from reaching Valencia, but was beaten and he had retreated with 17,000 troops into the city, only to be forced to surrender on 8 Jan. 1812 after a very short bombardment. Blake was to remain a prisoner until the war ended.
25 Maj.-Gen. John Gaspard Le Marchant who was killed soon after at the Battle of Salamanca.
26 Maj.-Gen. John Slade commanded a brigade of cavalry.
27 Lt-Col. Benjamin d'Urban, 2nd West India Regiment, was an Assistant Quarter Master General.
28 Maj.-Gen. William Lumley commanded the British cavalry at Albuera, numbering some 1,100 men; the only other Allied cavalry being Otway's Portuguese (850) and Loy's and Villemur's Spanish cavalry (2,000); a total of approximately 4,000 cavalry. The French army of Soult also numbered some 4,000 cavalry, but the quality was markedly better, as the Portuguese and Spanish cavalry was of very questionable value.
29 General de Division Jean-Baptiste Drouet.
30 Oman states that two members of the staff were killed by this 'friendly fire' incident, quoting D'Urban as his source. But D'Urban does not mention any losses and James's record, as he was on the spot, seems likely to be correct.
31 Lt-Col Robert Lord Blantyre temporarily commanded a brigade in the 1st Division.
32 Maj.-Gen. Johann Heinrich Karl von De Bernewitz, Brunswick Corps, commanded a brigade in the 7th Corps.
33 Drusus Julius Caesar, also referred to as Drusus III (AD 7–33), was a member of a noble family of Ancient Rome. He was a son of Germanicus and Agrippina the Elder. He was brother to Emperor Caligula, nephew to Emperor Claudius.
34 I believe this to be Lt-Col Henry Hardinge, on the staff of the Portuguese Army and mentioned in Wellington's despatch of 27 March relating to the storming of Fort Picurina. James probably knew Hardinge as he was the third son of Henry Hardinge, Rector of Stanhope, in Co. Durham.
35 A huge log chained across the breach and projecting dozens of sharp blades, not unlike a hedgehog.
36 Lt-Col Andrew Francis Barnard, 95th Foot, commanded the Light Division in the assault and somehow escaped serious injury.
37 General de Division Armand Philippon was Governor of Badajoz and used every device to avoid the British capturing the fortress. As the British gained the town, he and the remnants of his garrison retired over the river to Fort San Christoval.
38 Maj.-Gen. George Townsend Walker, 50th Foot, was seriously wounded but survived.
39 Maj. Dudley St Leger Hill, 8th Portuguese Cacadores.
40 Lt-Col Charles Macleod, 43rd Foot, was shot dead at the crest of the breach.
41 These figures are stated with some precision and agree pretty well with Oman's figure for all those lost in the siege, not just on the day of the assault, which cost some 806 killed and 2,855 wounded. French losses are difficult to ascertain but James's figures agree generally with those of Jones and Oman.

Chapter 9
1 Malversation is misconduct in public office.
2 Juan Jose Nieto Aguilar, Marquis of Monsalud, had set up a cavalry regiment with the authorization of King Charles IV and became a member of the Supreme Junta of the Government of Extremadura in 1808. In 1809 he was appointed second chief of the 5th Army, in Aug. 1810 he was elected vice president of the Junta and he was temporarily appointed Captain General of the Army of Extremadura.
3 This light ruby red wine made from select old vineyards was named after Alpedrinha's Cardinal D Jorge da Costa, born in the village of Alpedrinha in 1406. It is still produced today.
4 Mentions of British artillery using field fortifications are very rare, but their use here is confirmed in G. Glover (ed.), *The Letters of 2nd Captain Charles Dansey Royal Artillery 1806–1813* (Godmanchester, 2006).
5 Oman calculates that Marmont had about 30,000 men that morning, but Wellington could have brought 40,000 against him. It would seem that Wellington had read from Marmont's belligerent approach an indication of his willingness to attack Wellington's defensive position head on, in a second Busaco. His failure to attack after a war conference with his more cautious generals saved his army from annihilation.
6 Maj.-Gen. Eberhardt Otto George von Bock. He and his son Lt Lewis von Bock were lost in a shipwreck on the coast of France on 21 Jan. 1814.
7 Maj. Henry Sturgeon, Royal Staff Corps, was killed at Vic Bigorre in 1814.
8 Lt-Col John Waters was Assistant Adjutant General.
9 'Gabacho' is a Spanish synonym for the French with a pejorative nuance, like the English 'frog'.
10 William Warre also mentions this, stating that it was a dump of the explosives found in the forts and was caused by a Spanish officer smoking too near. Two streets were levelled and over a hundred soldiers and inhabitants killed and wounded.

11 I cannot find this on modern maps.
12 The Palácio dos Carrancas built in 1795 is still a major attraction in Oporto. When completed the second storey accommodated the Moraes e Castro family. During the second invasion, it was the official residence of General Soult and, after the flight of the French, it served as the headquarters of the Duke of Wellington.
13 An entresol or mezzanine is an intermediate floor between the main floors of a building.
14 Brig.-Gen. Nicholas Trant of the Portuguese Army was originally a British officer; he was governor of Coimbra and Oporto. Wellington stated that Trant was 'a very good officer, but a drunken dog as ever lived'.
15 HMS *Dotterel* was a cruiser built in 1802.

Chapter 10
1 Lt-Gen. Sir Edward Paget, brother of Henry Paget (more famous under his later titles of Uxbridge and Anglesey) had lost his right arm at the passage of the Douro in 1809 and apparently suffered from very poor sight.
2 HMS *Rota* of 38 guns, Captain Philip Somerville.
3 Brig. João Lobo Brandão de Almeida, Earl of Alhambra, was governor of Abrantes.
4 Possibly Lt-Col Frederick Ponsonby, 12th Light Dragoons, who was mentioned in Wellington's Salamanca despatch.
5 Maj.-Gen. Henry Frederick Campbell, 1st Foot Guards.
6 The *Juez de Foro* was the title of the leading civil official of every Portuguese village, he was judge and mayor rolled into one and held supreme power for the king.
7 The family of Guzmanes was one of the most powerful and influential in Leon.
8 The Convent of Santa Clara, a former palace of Pedro I, was the headquarters of Napoleon at Tordesillas.
9 Lopez's small book of maps of Spain was issued in 1797 and was often used by officers during the Peninsular War.
10 This criticism would appear to be levelled at Col Sir James Willoughby Gordon, who superseded Sir George Murray as Quarter Master General. James is very critical of his incorrect movement orders during the retreat.
11 Wrotham Hill lies 4 miles south of Godalming.
12 The Battle of Atapuerca was fought on 1 Sept. 1054 at the site of Piedrahita in the valley of Atapuerca between the brothers King Garcia Sanchez III of Navarre and King Ferdinand I of Castile and Leon.The Castilians won and King Garcia was killed.
13 Maj. the Hon. Edward Charles Somers Cocks, 79th Foot, had previously been an 'Intelligence Officer' or 'Observing Officer' for Wellington, operating behind enemy lines on a swift horse. His letters have been published as *Intelligence Officer in the Peninsula: Letters and Diaries of Major and Hon Edward Charles Cocks, 1786–1812*.
14 Maj. Adolphus William von Wurmb, 2nd Line Battalion KGL, was killed. Oman incorrectly identifies him as Ernest Wurmb 5th Battalion KGL who was killed at Waterloo.
15 Lt and Capt. the Hon. John Walpole was severely wounded and received a pension of £100 per annum and the Hon. William George Crofton Coldstream Guards was severely wounded and was later killed at Bayonne in 1814.
16 Ensign George Harvey Percival, Coldstream Guards.
17 Ensign Wentworth Noel Burgess, Coldstream Guards.
18 Gen. Joseph Count Souham.
19 Second Capt. Robert William Gardiner, Royal Artillery, had been an aide de camp to Moore; he later commanded a troop of Royal Horse Artillery at Waterloo.
20 Oman states that this force exceeded 60,000 men.
21 General de Division Joseph Comte Souham.
22 Oman calculates the joint armies of Portugal and the North at 53,000 of which 5,500 were cavalry, although Napier and Belmas number the French force between 41,000 and 44,000.
23 Oman numbers Wellington's force of British and Portuguese at 24,000.
24 Oman agrees at 92 officers and 1,972 men killed and wounded during the siege.
25 Col Sir Colin Halkett commanded a brigade in the 7th Division, consisting of the 1st and 2nd Light Battalions KGL.
26 Col William Ponsonby, 5th Dragoon Guards, who was later killed at Waterloo, had taken command of Le Marchant's Brigade after his death at Salamanca.
27 The 1st Battalion 1st Foot Guards had landed at Corunna on 30 Sept. and marched to reinforce the army. Hamilton states the battalion joined the army on 25 Oct. However James clearly shows that they joined on the 24th.
28 Lt-Col the Hon. Alexander Gordon, 3rd Foot Guards, Wellington's senior ADC. See his letters in Rory Muir, *At Wellington's Right Hand* (London, 2003).
29 Gen. Miguel de Alava y Esquivel was the Spanish Representative at Wellington's headquarters. This quote clearly indicates that the women believed that his injury had resulted in the loss of his 'eggs' or testicles. This appears to have been slightly inaccurate, as shown in Staff Surgeon Hume's letter quoted in full as Appendix B. From his expert evidence, it is clear that Alava's wound was to the stem of his penis, not the testicles, and under medical advice, Alava was sent to a prostitute to confirm that the appendage still worked successfully, which reportedly it did.
30 Rear Admiral Federico Carlos Gravina y Nápoli commanded the Spanish fleet at Trafalgar.
31 Lt-Col William Robe, Royal Artillery; because of the shattered state of the leg he was carried on men's shoulders the whole 400 miles to Lisbon over a six-week period. The Royal Military Calendar states that he was shot during a flag of truce, but James clearly shows that this is not true.
32 The 'Sermon which the priest of Chaorna, a little village of the Duke of Medinaceli preached to his parishioners on the day of Saint Bernard, which sermon came to the hands of the king through the said duke' is pasted into Stanhope's journal but I have chosen not to publish it as irrelevant to this work. The sermon is a very long muddle of ideas

punctuated by self-glorification, but shows that the priest's knowledge of the Bible was extremely poor indeed.
33 The 3rd Battalion of 1st Foot Guards had arrived at Salamanca with Hill's corps and joined the 1st Battalion in a brigade commanded by Maj.-Gen. Howard. The 3rd Battalion had marched from Cadiz to Seville at the end of Aug., then to Madrid and on to Salamanca, a distance estimated at 640 miles.
34 Oman agrees that the French army numbered some 90,000 troops, and numbers Wellington's army as just short of 70,000.
35 Quinsy is a complication of tonsillitis, when an abscess forms on the wall of the throat.
36 On 17 Nov. Paget was attempting to close a gap between the 5th and 7th Divisions when he was taken by surprise. Alone, but for a single Spanish orderly, and having lost an arm, he was in no position to defend himself. Wellington put his capture down to his poor eyesight.
37 It is strange that so few guns were made available for the siege of Burgos when there were plenty of heavy guns at Madrid and Ciudad Rodrigo; clearly Wellington had underestimated the strength of Burgos and had made no plans for a formal siege.
38 This statement is slightly misleading, Souham (soon superseded by Soult) had 40,000 and Cafarelli a further 10,000, clearly outnumbering Wellington who had about 35,000.
39 Gen. Francisco Ballesteros attempted a coup on 23 Oct. in protest at the appointment of Wellington as generalissimo of the Spanish army. The coup failed and Ballesteros was arrested and incarcerated at Ceuta.

Chapter 11
1 I have often wondered what this rapid malignant febrile illness was. It appears to have produced both jaundice and petechiae (black spots) and caused dysentery, and often quickly led to death. Advice from Mick Crumplin, the leading expert on medicine and medical services during the Napoleonic Wars, suggests three possible options. The two most likely are a virulent attack of typhus fever or an epidemic of yellow fever caused by mosquitoes at Cadiz where it was evident at this time. A third but less likely option is that of acute hepatitis with sudden irreversible liver failure, jaundice and haemorrhages. This would also be from a virus. Without further evidence it will not be able to fully ascertain which of these was the actual cause.
2 Hamilton confirms this, stating that in April only 785 men were recorded as fit for duty.
3 Sao Cristovao de Lafoes.
4 The convent at Arouca was founded in the 10th century, but the present buildings are from the 17th and 18th centuries.
5 This statement shows that James landed at Oporto in late 1808 and passed here en route to join Moore's army.
6 Vargellas, Croft, Hedges & Butler and Fonseca are all famous port manufacturing houses today.
7 William John Bankes (1786–1855) was a notable explorer, egyptologist and adventurer and travelled through Spain during the war, becoming friendly with Wellington.
8 This is probably Capt. Matthew Smith who commanded HMS *Comus* of 22 guns.
9 Paget had led the force that rowed across the river and captured the seminary, leading to the success of Wellington's victory of Oporto in 1809.
10 Baron Munchausen rode his horse into Russia in the winter, from the *Surprising adventures of the renowned Baron Munchausen, containing singular travels, campaigns, voyages, and adventures* (1811).
11 A district of ancient Greece around Thebes. The inhabitants of Boeotia were satirized as slow and 'yokel-ish' by other Greeks.
12 Gen. Graham was appointed to command the left wing of Wellington's army and was given the task of turning the French defensive lines by marching through reputedly inaccessible country.
13 'View Halloo' is a fox-hunting exclamation indicating that the fox is out in the open and the chase is on.
14 Henry Joseph O'Donnell y Mareschal, Count of La Bisbal, was Captain General of Valencia.
15 Sir John Murray landed a force from Sicily on the eastern coast of Spain to divert troops from Wellington's front, but achieved little.
16 Marshal Jean-Baptiste Jourdan had shared the defeat at Talavera with Victor. He now commanded the army of the centre and as such fought at Vitoria.
17 The Conjugal Debit is the right of husband and wife to carry through between themselves the sexual act.
18 Lord Byron's Cambridge friend, Charles Skinner Matthews, drowned himself in the River Cam.
19 Further evidence of his ride through Portugal from Oporto to join Moore's army in Jan. 1809.
20 Each hussar crossed with an infantryman hanging on to his stirrup and a small number were swept away. The operation is vividly described by Capt. Edwin Griffith, 15th Hussars, in G. Glover (ed.), *From Corunna to Waterloo* (London, 2007).
21 Grant's Hussar Brigade, led by the 10th Hussars, came up with the French rearguard of two regiments of French dragoons at Morales. They charged instantly and the French were broken and fled, with the Hussars in hot pursuit, until formed French infantry stopped the chase. The French 16th Dragoon Regiment had two officers and 208 men captured.
22 James mistakenly wrote Badajoz, but the river here is clearly named Bajoz.
23 Probably Caserio de San Juan de Vecilla.
24 The French abandoned Burgos and blew it up on 13 June.
25 A tiny village of 44 inhabitants 14 km west of Vitoria, it rarely appears on maps.
26 Actually the Sierra de Gillarte.
27 Francisco Anchia y Urquiza, nicknamed Longa after his native village, was a famous guerrilla leader, who by 1814 was a lieutenant-general in the Spanish Army.

Chapter 12
1 Many British accounts then and now persist in spelling this place Vittoria, however the Spanish spelling with one 't' has been consistent over two hundred years.
2 Comparing old and modern maps, Villa Real stood in the vicinity of Urretxu.
3 This is a very interesting statement in that Stanhope assures us that Graham was only authorized to sweep round the French right and threaten their lines of communication, thus forcing the French to retire, but instead chose to attempt to enter the plains of Vitoria and thus physically cut the French line of retreat.
4 Lt-Gen. Sir James Leith Hay commanded a brigade in the 5th Division.
5 I cannot discover any such place on the maps.
6 Maj.-Gen. Sir Frederick P Robinson.
7 The dollar coin was worth 8 reales, hence the term 'pieces of eight'. The coin was worth about 4s 6d sterling; therefore 2 million dollars was worth £450,000 in 1813, which in modern terms would be worth approximately £26 million!
8 Bertrand Comte Clausel commanded the Army of the North which was hurrying to join Joseph at Vitoria. It did not arrive in time, but escaped the Allied pursuit.
9 General de Division Louis Emmanuel Rey.
10 Maj.-Gen. Sir Thomas Bradford commanded a Portuguese Brigade.
11 This describes the extraordinary San Adrian Tunnel which has been in use since at least the 11th century as part of the 'Way of St James'. Formed naturally by water action it passes through the mountain and holds a hermitage within. It passes from just north of Zalduondo towards Zegama and can still be used, but no longer forms part of the 'Way of St James' which was moved to the lower flatter coastal route over a century ago.
12 'Gil Blas' refers to the picaresque novel by Lesage actually entitled *Histoire de Gil Blas de Santillane* which was published in twelve small books from 1715 to 1735.
13 A useful little success, gaining the harbour of Pasajes (spelt Passages by the British) for supplies to land near to the siege of San Sebastian.
14 General de Division Paul Charles Francois Adrien Henri Dieudonne Thiebault.
15 Commodore Sir George Ralph Collier (1774–1824) was in command of a force of twelve vessels off the Spanish coast, which he commanded from his flagship, the 32-gun HMS *Porcupine*. He and his squadron supported Wellington and Sir Thomas Graham in the capture of San Sebastian and the blockade of Bayonne.
16 In 1719 San Sebastian was captured, for the first time, by a strong French army under the command of the Duke of Berwick. Two thousand French soldiers occupied the town until 25 Aug. 1721, when it was evacuated after the Peace of the Hague.
17 Second Capt. Saumarez Dubourdieu, Royal Artillery, died of a severe wound received in the siege on 22 July 1813.
18 First Lt William Reid, Royal Engineers.
19 The 1st Foot or Royal Scots Regiment were known as the 'Royals'.
20 Capt. Charles Lennon, the Earl of March, 52nd Foot.
21 Lt-Col Richard Fletcher, Royal Engineers, was slightly wounded but then killed during the final storming of San Sebastian on 31 Aug.
22 Aldus Manutius (1449–1515) printed Dante's works in 1501. His beautiful italic typeface and presentation of the author's work without heavy commentary were revolutionary and copies of his books have always been highly sought after.
23 HMS *Parthian*, Captain James Henry Garrety.
24 Richard Temple Nugent Brydges Chandos Grenville, 1st Duke of Buckingham and Chando

Chapter 13
1 Consisting of 800 of the 1st Guards and a detachment of 800 from the 2nd and 3rd Guards combined.
2 Maj.-Gen. Sir George Cooke who commanded the Guards at Waterloo where he lost his right arm.
3 Maj.-Gen. John Byne Skerrett was killed later at the storming of Bergen op Zoom.
4 Maj.-Gen. Sir Samuel Gibbs.
5 Maj.-Gen. Kenneth Mackenzie.
6 Actually Brig.-Gen. Arthur Gore.
7 Admiral Sir George Young.
8 Lt-Col John Lord Proby, 1st Foot Guards, commanded the Brigade of Guards for Cooke who now commanded the corps.
9 A fortified port very close to Bergen op Zoom
10 Col John Graham of Fintry, a kinsman of Sir Thomas, was aide de camp and military secretary.
11 Lt-Col James Carmichael Smyth, Royal Engineers.
12 Russian Gen. Count Alexander von Benckendorff (1781– 1844).
13 Lt-Gen. Count Francis Roguet was an experienced soldier, having joined the army in 1789, and had fought in Italy, Germany, Poland, Spain and Russia. He died in 1846.
14 Prussian Gen. Adolf Friedrich von Oppen.
15 Prussian Gen. Friedrich Wilhelm Freiherr von Bulow, Graf von Dennewitz (1755–1816) who commanded a corps at Waterloo.
16 Gen. Willem Frederik George Lodewijk van Oranje-Nassau, Prince of Orange (1792–1849), became King Willem II in 1840.

17 Lt-Col the Hon. George Carleton, 44th Foot, was killed at Bergen op Zoom.
18 Joachim Murat, king of mainland Naples, signed a treaty with Austria on 11 Jan.
19 Bernadotte the Crown Prince of Sweden had signed the Treaty of Kiel on 14 Jan. 1814, by which peace with Denmark was concluded. The Danish King Frederik ceded to the King of Sweden and his successors the Kingdom of Norway. Denmark received 1 million riksdaler and the province of Pomerania as compensation.
20 Russian Gen. Ferdinand Ferdinandovich Wintzingerode (1770–1818).
21 Maj.-Gen. Herbert Taylor.
22 The Guards had landed at Helvoetsluis on 6 Dec. and the French had instantly evacuated Willemstadt.
23 Breda had been captured by 300 of Benckendorff's Cossacks who captured 600 of the garrison.
24 Gibb's Brigade.
25 Marshal Jacques Etienne Joseph Alexandre Macdonald, Duc de Tarente.
26 This refers to the French defeat of the Swiss rebellion and the imposition of the 'Mediation Act' of 1803 by which Napoleon gave a new constitution to the Swiss confederation. Karl Friedrich von Steiger (1754–1841) was a member of the legislature, of the Great Council of Berne.This constitution was abandoned in 1815 and an old-style feudal confederation resumed.
27 Cadiz was struck by yellow fever in 1813 and it was this that was possibly carried by the Guards northwards with them.
28 Rumour or hearsay.
29 The 10th is written in the text but is clearly an error.
30 Prussian Gen. Karl Heinrich Leopold Ludwig von Borstel (1773–1844).
31 Prussian Lt-Gen. Heinrich Ludwig August von Thumen (1757–1826).
32 French Marshal Etienne Jacques Joseph Alexandre MacDonald, 1st duc de Taranto (1765–1840)
33 Maj. Werner von dem Bussche, 2nd Hussars KGL.
34 Almost certainly Jan Egbertus van Gorkum who left a memoir of the storming of Bergen op Zoom, *De bestorming der vesting Bergen op Zoom op den 8sten Maart 1814* (Leiden, 1862). This has been in part translated and edited by Geert van Uythoven and put on the internet.
35 The 'lions' was a colloquial term of the time meaning 'the sights'.
36 Col John Macleod, 78th Foot.
37 Karl August, Duke of Saxe-Weimar-Eisenach (1757–1828), was given command of a force of 30,000 men which was to operate in the Netherlands.
38 Lt-Gen. Prince Willem Frederik Karel of Orange, brother to Prince William.
39 Mechelen in Dutch is known as Malines in French.
40 Prussian Field Marshal Gebhard Leberecht von Blucher, Furst von Wahlstatt (1742–1819), hero of Waterloo.
41 Denhorst is now indicated by a restaurant on the outskirts of Schoten.
42 A page has been left for his sketch but was obviously never completed.
43 James was not to know that his sister Lucy had died on 1 March 1814.
44 Lier is southeast of Antwerp.
45 On his march towards Paris.
46 He was a little premature, Napoleon did not abdicate until 6 April.
47 Latikia or Lattique is in Syria.
48 Prince Bernhard Carl of Saxe-Weimar-Eisenach (1792–1862).
49 Now known as Tienen.
50 There have been two major Battles of Neerwinden, the first in 1693 between the French, British and Dutch, which is also called the Battle of Landen, and that of 1793 between the Austrians and the French.
51 French Marshal Jean Baptiste Jules Bernadotte, Count of Ponte Corvo, had been elected Crown Prince of Sweden in 1810 and he fought for the Allies in 1813–14.
52 Now Aachen in Germany.
53 The Count of Wallmoden-Gimborn commanded the newly raised Hanoverian troops.
54 Fortescue in his *History of the British Army* (1920), vol. 10, p. 33, questions James's statement that he also discussed possible withdrawal; based on the fact that Bathurst wrote on this subject on 28 Feb. It is however quite possible that Graham was aware of these issues before the official letter, particularly as James recorded the interview immediately afterwards.
55 This refers to the defeat of corps under Russian Gen. Dmitri Osten, Count Sacken and Prussian Gen. Hans David Ludwig von Yorck at the Battle of Montmirail on 11 Feb.
56 Austrian Field Marshal Karl Philip Prince Schwarzenberg (1771–1820) was in overall command of the Allied forces.
57 Maj. Albert Steiger (captain in the regiment) was an extra aide de camp to Lt-Gen. Sir William Stewart.
58 I believe this to be Henry Thornton, cousin of William Wilberforce and member of the Clapham Group which fought for the abolition of slavery.
59 Swedish Admiral of the Centre Carl Edward Gyllenskold commanded the field train in the campaigns of 1813–14.
60 George Canning MP who was later to become Prime Minister.
61 The Russian Gen. Count Woronzov.
62 Prussian Gen. Johann Adolf Freiherr von Thielmann.
63 The Battle of Dennewitz was fought on 6 Sept. 1813. Marshal Ney on march to Berlin was ambushed by Bulow's Prussians and Bernadotte's Swedes. The Prussians fought hard and won whilst Bernadotte delayed to protect his troops and only arrived in time to chase the French away.

64 Pieces of sod.
65 Lt-Col Charles Morice, 69th Foot, was killed at Quatre Bras.
66 Lt-Col Robert Henry 21st Foot.
67 Lt-Col George Clifton, 1st Guards, was killed.
68 Lt-Col Arthur Macdonald, 3rd Garrison Battalion, was Deputy Adjutant General.
69 A wall built across the ditch of a fortification, with a sluice gate to regulate the height of water in the ditch on both sides of the wall.
70 Lt-Col Sir George Adam Wood, Royal Artillery, who went on to command the artillery in the Waterloo campaign.
71 Lt-Col Frederick Muller, 1st (Royal Scots) Foot.
72 Lt-Col Leslie Grove Jones, 1st Foot Guards.
73 The French Governor was General de Division Guilin Laurent Bizanet.

Chapter 14
1 David William Murray, 3rd Earl of Mansfield (1777–1840), married Frederica Markham on 16 Sept. 1797.
2 Half Moon St runs off Piccadilly, opposite Green Park.
3 These notes to Lady Mansfield are to be found in file C276 at the CFKS.
4 The use of opium to relieve pain had been known since Egyptian times and in Germany in 1806 Merck had developed the ability to extract morphine (the active ingredient) to regulate the dose given. It would appear here, however, that James was receiving opium in its raw state.
5 This nickname crops up a couple of times and refers to someone at headquarters during the Waterloo campaign. I suspect it to be Col Colin Campbell, commandant at headquarters.
6 James Carrick Moore was a surgeon (1762–1860) and a biographer of his famous brother: *The Life of Sir John Moore* (London, 1834).

Chapter 15
1 Hamilton confirms that he is recorded in the Muster Books from the 20th.
2 This confirms Wellington's complaints that few of the officers appointed to his staff in Belgium were his choice.
3 An unknown lady friend.
4 Maj.-Gen. Sir Henry Torrens, military secretary to the commander-in-chief.
5 Gen. Richard Grenville was an unmarried great uncle; therefore who the lady referred to is unclear.
6 On 3 May 1814, Sir Thomas Graham had been raised to the peerage by the title of Baron Lynedoch of Balgowan.
7 Gen. Charles Lennox, 4th Duke of Richmond and Lennox, unfairly most famous for the ball his wife held at Brussels just before the Battle of Waterloo and for his unfortunate death by rabies, having been bitten by a pet fox in Canada. Lennox was majorly involved in the growth of cricket, helping to found the Marylebone Cricket Club.
8 Maj.-Gen. Peregrine Maitland 1st Foot Guards, commanded 1st Brigade of the Guards Division.
9 This would be the meeting at Tirlemont about which historians love to make assumptions, but about which little is actually known. It was probably simply a meeting to discuss the timing of the advance into France and possibly their plans if Napoleon attacked.
10 Lady Charlotte Greville was the eldest daughter of the Duke of Portland and was married to Charles Greville; their eldest son, also Charles Greville, was the famous diarist.
11 Lord and Lady George Seymour of Wellingore, Lincs, were resident at Brussels and went to the famous ball.
12 Lady Charlotte Greville, nee Charlotte Cavendish-Bentinck, was a daughter of the 3rd Duke of Portland, one of her brothers being Lt and Capt. Lord Frederick Cavendish-Bentinck, Coldstream Guards.
13 This presumably refers to William Henry Cavendish-Bendick who became the 4th Duke.
14 The family seat at Scone Palace.
15 Lt-Col the Hon. Sir Frederick Cavendish Ponsonby, 12th Light Dragoons.
16 Lt-Gen. Sir Galbraith Lowry Cole was to wed on 15 June and missed the Battle of Waterloo.
17 *Le Moniteur* was the French state-run newspaper and mouthpiece for Napoleon.
18 He served as an Assistant Quarter Master General reporting to Col Sir William De Lancey.
19 Caen Wood attached to Kenwood House, their London home. It would be of great significance to James in later life.
20 The 14th-century Chateau of Beloeil was home to the Princes de Ligne and is still advertised today as the Versailles of Belgium.
21 Lady Anne Alvanley and the two Miss Ardens.
22 William Arden had served in the Coldstream Guards as a captain but retired from the Army in 1812. He had become 2nd Baron Alvanley in 1804.
23 This almost certainly refers to Lt-Col Otto Baron Trip, a Dutchman who had entered the British Army in 1800 and had served as an ADC to Wellington and Uxbridge at various times. In 1815 he was principal ADC to the Prince of Orange. Rumours of a liaison with Harriet Capel abounded. Harriet certainly loved him but he was less keen. He eventually was called out by Harriet's father, the Hon. John Capel, and in the ensuing duel both fired to kill, much against etiquette. Trip committed suicide in 1816.
24 Charles Stuart, 1st Baron Stuart de Rothesay (1779–1845), was a British diplomat.
25 His old companion Lt-Col Lord George William Russell who had been a fellow ADC of Graham at Cadiz was now in the 102nd Foot but did join Wellington's staff in France.
26 Old Hanoverian denoting the troops of the King's German Legion and New Hanoverian denoting the new levees raised in recently liberated Hanover.

27 Joseph II (Joseph Benedikt Anton Michael Adam, 1741–90) was Holy Roman Emperor 1765–90 and ruler of the Habsburg lands 1780–90. He was the eldest son of Empress Maria Theresa and her husband, Francis I.
28 I suspect this refers to Lady Caroline Paget, wife of the Hon. John Capel.
29 From John Dryden's 'Eleonora – dedicated to the late Countess of Abingdon'.
30 Col Sir Hudson Lowe had been Quarter Master to the Army in Flanders, but was relieved on Wellington's request and in May was given command of the troops at Genoa (about 1,400 British and 3,000 Italians which had been landed by the Royal Navy). Lowe of course went on to become Governor of St Helena whilst Napoleon was held there and was turned into a figure of hate by the Bonapartists.
31 The army was eagerly anticipating the order to advance into France in mid-June.
32 Insurrection had broken out in the Vendee against Napoleon. This was quelled quickly but the troops sent were a drain on Napoleon's army and did miss the Waterloo campaign.
33 Lady Sarah (nee Cavendish) was the second wife of Arthur Annesley, 1st Earl Mountnorris, who died in 1816.
34 Disquisition – a formal discourse.
35 This presumably refers to Maj.-Gen. Sir Edward Barnes who eventually proposed to Maria Capel but was rejected by her, not her sister Harriet who had been with Baron Trip. Barnes did then turn his attention towards Harriet but she was still smitten with Trip.
36 An Irish poet, 1709–65.
37 Col Sir William De Lancey had met Magdalene Hall and married her in Edinburgh on 4 April 1815 after a whirlwind romance. Orders for Belgium reached him on his honeymoon at Dunglass and he arrived in Brussels on 25 May where he was appointed Deputy Quarter Master General. Magdalene followed him and her diary of their time at Brussels, his wounding and death have been published as a very moving read entitled *A Week at Waterloo in June 1815* (London, 1906).
38 Presumably nicknames for her two sons, William and Charles, her third child Emily being born in 1816.
39 Lady Jane Dalrymple Hamilton.
40 Lady Elizabeth Conyngham.
41 This lady was very close to the Duke of Wellington and rumours abounded of an affair; indeed her husband took the editor of the *St James's Chronicle* to court for damages in 1816 and won but was awarded a derisory amount.
42 The various lists which have been prepared of the guests who attended the Duchess of Richmond's Ball all state that James attended, which is clearly incorrect.
43 The United Services Club was launched in 1816 at Albemarle Street with Lord Lynedoch as president.
44 After returning to France in 1814, after twenty years of exile, Marie-Therese-Charlotte, the daughter of Louis XVI and Marie-Antoinette, was contacted by the Sisters of Charity at the Hôpital des Incurables in Paris. One of their patients was Madame Simon, widow of the infamous Simon the cobbler who had brutalized the little Louis XVII in the Temple prison. Widow Simon claimed that the boy king had been smuggled out of the Temple in a basket of laundry, and that he had not died in 1795, but had been replaced by another boy who died in his place.
45 Given that the weather was so poor, it is perhaps surprising that Napoleon did not delay his advance the next day, but certainly the Belgian mud did exert some influence on both sides in the ensuing campaign and was a factor in his eventual defeat.
46 At this time the Prince of Orange did not know of the Prussian retreat from Charleroi towards the area around Ligny although it was their prearranged plan to assemble there if seriously attacked.
47 Note by James Stanhope: The Duke afterwards explained in a conversation where I was present his motives which were *as follows* and nearly in his own words. 'It is impossible to be everywhere. I knew my army was a more manoeuvring one than the Prussian. I left mine so placed that I could collect them on any point of the main road to Brussels. This was of the greatest consequence for I knew I could get to the assistance of the Prussians but I could not so well trust on their being in time to assist me'. Another unlucky circumstance was that part of Lord Hill's Corps had been moved several miles to the front for a field day and had consequently so many more miles to march. On such small circumstances sometimes hangs great events.
48 James is in error here, the Brunswickers arrived just after 3 pm, having marched from Brussels behind the 5th Division.
49 James is in error here again, as Lt-Col Robert Henry Dick was from the 42nd Foot and led the regiment at Waterloo despite his wound.
50 Col the Hon. Alexander Abercromby Coldstream Guards, Assistant Quarter Master General.
51 The I Corps of d'Erlon marched between the battlefields and achieved nothing. Their influence on either of the battlefields of Ligny and Quatre Bras may well have been decisive.
52 Ensign James Lord Hay, 1st Foot Guards, was killed at Quatre Bras.
53 Lt Arthur Gore, 33rd Foot, was killed at Quatre Bras.
54 Capt. and Lt-Col William Miller, 1st Foot Guards, was wounded at Quatre Bras and died at Waterloo village 19 June 1815.
55 Both Fortescue, *History of the British Army*, vol. 10, p. 563, and Hamilton's *History of the First Guards*, vol. 3, p. 82, state that James was on Wellington's staff at Waterloo. This is clearly an error. Indeed Wellington's words during the battle quoted by Fortescue, as recorded by Stanhope, do not appear in either his journal or letters.
56 This is an anachronism, as he served at Waterloo as the Earl of Uxbridge, however James's mistake is understandable as he became the Marquis of Anglesey only five days later.
57 There is quite a good deal of first-hand evidence that Uxbridge was not happy with the actions of some of his cavalry during the battle, but perhaps understandably after the battle only praise was heard from him.

58 Capt. Horace B Seymour, 18th Hussars, aide de camp to the Earl of Uxbridge who was later wounded and temporarily captured.
59 Capt. and Lt-Col Alexander, Lord Saltoun, 1st Foot Guards.
60 There is much circumstantial evidence that initial preparations for retreat were under way on the right wing at this period. Not actual retreat, but preparations made in case of retreat; a sensible precaution given the circumstances.
61 Col Sir John Elley, Royal Horse Guards, Deputy Adjutant General, who was wounded.
62 Capt. and Lt-Col Edward Stables, 1st Foot Guards, died soon after.
63 The Guards initially advanced after the retreating column, but were forced themselves to retreat to the crest as the second column arrived, which was engaged by the 52nd. It is presumably the moment when the guards had advanced when James returned.
64 The 1st Dragoons King's German Legion had recently converted to Light Dragoons.
65 By the end of the battle, only two companies of the Coldstream Guards remained with their colours on the crest, the remainder fighting in Hougoumont. Only these two companies followed the general advance.
66 George Bowles was a lieutenant and captain in the Coldstream Guards at Waterloo, he became a brevet major after the battle. His letters have been published: G. Glover (ed.), *A Guards Officer in the Peninsula and at Waterloo: The Letters of Captain George Bowles, Coldstream Guards 1907–19* (Godmanchester, 2008).
67 Maj.-Gen. Sir John Byng had commanded the 2nd Guards Brigade at the battle but temporarily succeeded to command the 1st Division when Maj.-Gen. Cooke was wounded.
68 Lt-Col Sir Henry Hollis Bradford, 1st Foot Guards, Assistant Quartermaster General.
69 Stanhope's note: Some time afterwards the Prince of Orange asked General Alava at his father's table what the Spaniards would have done in such a battle, unawed by the presence, that gallantest [sic] & honest of men answered 'Like Your Highness's troops, but I think they would have come back again!'
70 A very interesting statement if it can be substantiated.
71 Stanhope's note: The Duke was very anxious for the arrival of the Prussians & said 'He never in his life looked so often at his watch.'
72 This of course refers to d'Erlon's corps which did not consist of Guard troops.
73 Mme Giuseppina Maria Camilla (also Josephina) Grassini (1773–1850) was a noted Italian contralto. She had been Napoleon's lover and seems to have become Wellington's.
74 Lt-Col Ponsonby, 12th Light Dragoons, was seriously wounded by a lance in his back during the great cavalry attack which defeated d'Erlon's corps. His narrative of the hours he spent lying on the field of Waterloo as the battle raged around him is particularly interesting.
75 Stanhope's statement applies to the captains and lieutenant-colonels of the 1st Foot Guards of which 14 were on regimental duty throughout the campaign, 5 others being on various staff duties. Of these 14 officers 5 were killed (Stables, Francis d'Oyly, Thomas, Miller and Milnes), 4 were wounded (Townshend, Cooke, Henry d'Oyly and Fead) and 4 were unharmed (Saltoun, Reeve, Stanhope and Colquitt).
76 The text is clear but I believe this to be an error in writing by James. I believe he meant out of 100 men, i.e. his company, of which 30 remained unwounded. The losses of 3rd Battalion 1st Guards were recorded immediately after the battle as 4 officers and 101 men killed and 12 officers and 487 men wounded, leaving 433 men unwounded in total, an average of 43 per company, therefore James's company clearly suffered more than most.
77 This was the total force available to Napoleon, 30,000 of which had been detached with Grouchy to pursue the Prussians after the Battle of Ligny. This detachment was not known to the British army at this time hence the incorrect assessment of his force. Napoleon had approximately 68,000 troops at Waterloo, but a much superior number of cavalry and artillery than Wellington.
78 The Battle of Leipzig was fought on 16–19 Oct. 1813 and is known as 'The Battle of Nations' because of the numerous armies involved. 600,000 men were involved in this battle and around 100,000 became casualties. Napoleon's defeat signalled the end of his reign of power in Germany.
79 These figures refer to the Guard Division which lost 1,596 killed and wounded from a total of 4,128. Figures from *Battle of Waterloo, By a Near Observer* (London, 1815).
80 Reproduced with the kind permission of the British Library; Add Ms 34703.
81 Capt. and Lt-Col Henry Wyndham, Coldstream Guards, survived and lived to 70 years of age.
82 The Battle of Malplaquet, fought on 11 Sept. 1709, was one of the main battles of the War of the Spanish Succession.
83 Hamilton's description of the assault is at variance with James's; however James was on the spot and fully involved in the operation and I trust his version of events.
84 Almost certainly Private William Wheeler of his company, listed in the Waterloo Medal Roll.
85 His nephew was Ensign William Taylor, 4th Foot, who served at Waterloo, being the son of his sister Lucy and Thomas Taylor of Sevenoaks.
86 Marshal Louis Nicolas Davout, Duc d'Auerstaedt, Prince d'Eckmuhl, was serving as Minister of War.
87 Lady Henrietta Frances Spencer, mother of Lt-Col Sir Frederick Ponsonby.
88 It is interesting to note that the Guards marched over 25 miles and arrived at about 4 pm, in time to influence the Battle of Quatre Bras. Whereas the cavalry, some only a few miles further away, did not reach the battle until after dark. Not enough has been made of the failure of any British cavalry to arrive in time.
89 Unfortunately the sketch is missing.
90 Richard Edgecumbe (ed.), *The Diary of Frances Lady Shelley, 1787–1817* (London, 1912), vol. 1, pp. 139 and 142.
91 James was clearly planning for a leave of absence to travel into Switzerland and probably Italy to meet Hester.

92 The Battle of Waterloo was the first occasion that all British soldiers received a medal, previously only commanding officers had been issued medals. It was made of solid silver.
93 Col Sir Andrew F Barnard who commanded the 1st Battalion 95th Rifles at Waterloo until wounded.
94 Reich Graf Maximilian Friedrich Freiherr von Merveldt was Extraordinary Ambassador for Austria in London and died of natural causes on 5 July 1815.
95 Samuel Whitbread, the famous Whig reformer, committed suicide on 6 July 1815.
96 Thomas Philip Robinson, 3rd Baron Grantham, was married to Lady Henrietta Frances Cole.
97 Ensign the Hon. Thomas Seymour Bathurst, 1st Foot Guards.
98 Henry George Bathurst, Lord Apsley, born at Apsley House, he was the eldest son of Henry Bathurst, 3rd Earl Bathurst, and his wife Lady Georgina, third daughter of Lord George Lennox. He was a Commissioner of the India Board at this time and later became the 4th Earl Bathurst.
99 John Henry Upton, 1st Viscount Templeton in the Irish nobility, had two sons who had both presumably been out to Paris, Henry Montagu (2nd Viscount) and George Frederick (3rd Viscount) who became a general. It is presumably George who has just arrived.
100 Joseph Lancaster (1778–1838) was an English Quaker and public education innovator. In 1798, he founded a free elementary school in Borough Road, Southwark, using a variant of the monitorial system. The method of instruction and delivery is recursive. As one student learns the material he or she is rewarded for successfully passing on that information to the next pupil. Lancaster wrote *Improvements in Education* in 1803 and later travelled to the USA to lecture and promote his ideas. The height of popularity of his system was in the first decade of the 19th century. 1808 saw the creation of the Society for Promoting the Lancasterian System for the Education of the Poor. However, despite initial successes, Lancasterian schools were criticized. The standards were poor and the discipline to which children were subjected was harsh, even by contemporary standards. Lancaster fell out with the Society over a number of issues. While poor financial management was ostensibly the reason for the clash, his colleagues had also discovered that Lancaster had been privately beating a number of the boys with whom he worked. He was forcibly ejected from the Society, which renamed itself the British and Foreign School Society.
101 General Maximilien Sebastien Foy (1775–1825).
102 Charles Angelique François Huchet, Comte de la Bedoyere (1786–1815), had been an aide de camp to Napoleon at Waterloo; he was captured whilst visiting his wife in Paris, tried by a military court and shot on 19 Aug. 1815.
103 A quote from Milton's *Paradise Lost*.
104 From Laurence Sterne, *The Life and Opinions of Tristram Shandy, Gentleman* (1760).
105 This is the first time that their daughter, his future wife, gets a mention in his letters.
106 In fact Davout was not asked, Moncey refused to head the trial of Marshal Ney and was deprived of his marshalate for eight years as a punishment. The marshals who did attend the trial were Jordan, Massena, Augerau and Mortier.
107 'The Doctor' was the nickname of Henry Addington, 1st Viscount Sidmouth (1757–1844), Home Secretary in 1815.
108 During the wars, Napoleon had systematically stolen the great art of Europe and deposited it at the Louvre, making it probably the greatest art collection that will ever be seen in one place. In 1815 the Allies repatriated these works, much to the disgust of the French.
109 Towards the end of the battle the majors and all the senior lieutenant-colonels were wounded or absent on duty. This incident must have occurred whilst Saltoun was still detached at Hougoumont and James had gone to find artillery horses. This would leave John Reeve and Goodwin Colquitt left with the battalion to take command. Reeve in this situation would have been senior, he is not recorded as wounded and Reeve's letter in G. Glover (ed.), *Letters from the Battle of Waterloo* (London, 2004) does not indicate his absence or any reason why he did not command instead.
110 The four horses of Venice had been taken to Paris by Napoleon in 1797. They are bronze sculptures which adorned the Basilica San Marco and are now housed within the church to preserve them.
111 The treaty required the payment of reparations to the Allied countries and to accept a force of occupation for up to five years which were to be fed and paid for by the French government. The French government paid the reparations early and the occupying force left France in 1818.
112 Henri-Benjamin Constant de Rebecque (1767–1830) was a Swiss-born nobleman, thinker, writer and French politician.

Chapter 16
1 Quoted from Olivia Stanhope and G P Gooch, *The Life of Charles, Third Earl Stanhope* (London, 1914), pp. 265–6.
2 Mrs Lackner had come to Chevening as a music teacher but soon took control of the earl and his house, forcing his wife to separate.
3 Mr Samuel Varley of Chevening was a watch and instrument maker. He became an assistant to the Earl.
4 C276/3 CFKS.
5 I have stated the date as 15 Dec. based on James's statement that he died on Sunday and the calendar for 1816, this is confirmed by the tablet at Chevening Church. Ghita Stanhope and Aubrey Newman both incorrectly state that his death occurred on 17 Dec.
6 With kind permission of Cumbria Archive Service, D/Lons L1/2/63.
7 James received a letter from Mahon coldly stating: 'I wrote to my father several weeks ago to assure him that if my presence could afford him comfort or be in any way desirable to him I would hasten to obey his call. I have ordered legal proceedings to be at once begun which will secure from the grasp of legatees the personal property in money as well in goods and clothes.' *The Life of Charles, Third Earl Stanhope*, p. 266.

8 Henry Richard Vassal-Fox, 3rd Baron Holland of Holland and 3rd Baron Holland of Foxley (1773–1840), was a politician and a major figure in Whig politics.
9 William Norton, 2nd Baron Grantley (1742–1822), MP.
10 Joseph Jekyll, MP (1752–1837).
11 Their daughter Lady Anne Lowther married Sir John Beckett, 2nd Baronet, on 20 Jan. 1817.
12 Chile became independent of Spain in 1818, Mexico followed suit in 1821.
13 Anne Louise Germaine de Stael-Holstein (1766–1817), commonly known as Madame de Stael, was a Swiss author living in Paris and abroad. She influenced literary tastes in Europe at the turn of the 19th century.
14 Admiral Sir William Sidney Smith, famous for his defence of Acre against Napoleon.
15 With kind permission of Cumbria Archive Service, D Lons/1/2/63.
16 Sir Robert Liston (1742–1836) was Ambassador to the Ottoman Empire.
17 Sir Robert John Wilmot-Horton MP for Newcastle under Lyme.
18 The 3rd Battalion only left Cambrai on 23 Nov., therefore James must have been at home on leave.
19 With kind permission of the Derbyshire Record Office, D4576/20/15.
20 U1590 C266/3 CFKS.
21 The 15th-century Cathedral of St Michel and Gudule.
22 The Catholic Church of St Joseph of Waterloo.
23 The 'observatory' had been built prior to the campaign by Belgian cartographers and there is no evidence that Napoleon used it.
24 This is of great interest and throws great doubt on the veracity of Decoster's famous statement.
25 Now known as Old St Pancras Church, a new much larger church being completed in 1822.
26 There is a codicil to James's will added in 1824, bequeathing Miss Elizabeth Barrett £10,000 on the death of Lady Banks, when he would inherit Spring Grove, presumably this was his intended.
27 C285 CFKS.
28 His mother.
29 Augustus Bozzi Granville MD, FRS (1783–1872) was a physician, writer, and Italian patriot. Born Augusto Bozzi in Milan, he studied medicine before leaving to avoid being enlisted in Napoleon's army. After practising medicine in Greece, Turkey, Spain and Portugal, he joined the Royal Navy and sailed to the West Indies. There he learnt English and married an Englishwoman. He later moved to London, where he practised as a physician and writer.
30 C473/26 CFKS.
31 The ball and bone splinters had become embedded in the muscles surrounding the spine. This had not caused any paralysis, but the wound would constantly produce a flow of pus. When the wound closed temporarily, it would cause a build up of the sepsis and this severe pressure would cause chronic pain which undoubtedly led to depression and delirium.
32 An error, he was 36 on his death.

Appendices
1 Lt-Gen. the Hon. Charles, Earl of Harrington.
2 Ensign John Patterson is very disparaging of the role of a second major, being a subaltern officer himself, stating 'ever and anon the second major falls back, and, in order to show his consequence and zeal, especially if a general with his Staff should chance to be passing, he calls out, in a most important tone "Gentlemen, get into your places!" "Keep on the flanks!" and other friendly admonitions ... By the by, I know of nothing else that these second majors have to do, unless it be to act the part of moveable pivots for dressing up the line, (in which they are generally very fussy), or in whipping in the young subalterns, whom they endeavour to keep in order.' *The Adventures of Captain John Patterson* (London, 1837), pp. 58–9.
3 Maj. Charles Hill was severely wounded at the Battle of Vimiero.
4 HMS *Africa* of 64 guns under Capt. John Barrett. *The History of the Ships of The Royal Navy* states that the ship had gone to Sweden in April and was later joined by the fleet carrying Moore's force; this is clearly incorrect.
5 Col George Murray 3rd Foot Guards, who was Quarter Master General throughout the Peninsular War, but missed Waterloo, having been sent to America. Murray was returning from a mission to London to clarify the government's views on the demands of King Gustavus.
6 The force had been sent to bolster the Swedish forces, who were threatened by the French in Denmark. However the Swedish King Gustavus did not like the British terms of operation, by which they remained independent of his command. After weeks of fruitless negotiations and and the placing of Moore under arrest, Moore escaped, returned to the fleet and the army sailed for England.
7 HMS *Victory*, flagship of Admiral Saumarez.
8 Strangely, I can find no reference as to how this accident happened, presumably a fall on the ice.
9 HMS *Audacious* of 74 guns.
10 There was a very small action at Obidos on 16 Aug. but here he clearly refers to the Battle of Rolica which took place on 17 Aug.
11 This marks the start of Moore's march into Spain to help support the Spanish forces in repelling the French advance on Madrid.
12 Ensign John Patterson of the 50th states that the bridge had been burnt, so the battalion passed over by means of three small boats.

13 They arrived at 2 pm according to Ensign Patterson.
14 Moore had finally decided to march further into Spain to threaten the flank and rear of Napoleon's army. The 50th marched from Salamanca as part of Lt-Gen. David Baird's Division in Maj.-Gen. Lord Bentinck's Brigade, consisting of 1/4th, 1/42nd, 1/50th.
15 Moore received news that Napoleon had turned his army northward to trap his army and destroy it. He began the long dreadful retreat to Corunna which cost the army so dearly; but Moore now had little alternative.
16 The battalion were quartered in a large convent near to the citadel until the Battle of Corunna was fought on 16 Jan. when Charles was killed at the head of his troops.
17 This must be an error, for it is nearer 22 leagues between Lugo and Corunna.
18 General Burrard took command of the army immediately after the Battle of Vimiero and declined to order a rapid pursuit of the defeated troops. This was the main reason why the heavily criticized Convention of Cintra was finally signed. On his arrival as senior officer, Sir Hew Dalrymple concurred in Burrard's actions.
19 The senior Maj. Charles Napier had been in England with the 2nd Battalion but was on his way out. He was captured at the Battle of Corunna. He was allowed to go to England on parole and was duly exchanged, allowing him to serve again in the Peninsula at Busaco where he was severely wounded, a ball smashing his jaw. He later became a general and became known as the 'Conqueror of Scind'.
20 From file C253 CFKS.
21 It was not realized at this time that Sir Harry Burrard would soon be going home to answer for his role in the Convention of Cintra.
22 This and the following letter to the Duchess of Richmond can be found in the Goodwood Papers, 350 FJL/AV59, West Sussex Record Office.
23 Here he refers to Sir Hew Dalrymple.
24 He refers to Sir Harry Burrard.
25 Col George Townsend Walker, 50th Foot. Despite these uncomplimentary comments on the colonel's organizational skills; it should be noted that he would appear to have been a brave officer. He became a major-general in 1811 and was severely wounded at Badajoz, where he was mentioned in dispatches, and whilst serving on the staff was wounded again at Orthes.
26 The 1st Battalion 3rd (East Kent) Foot was brigaded with the 1st Battalion 6th (1st Warwickshire) Foot and 50th Foot under Lt-Gen. Sir Moore Townsend Disney who had stopped at Lisbon on his way home from Sicily. When the brigade moved into Spain the 3rd were detached to escort a convoy to Guarda.
27 Capt. the Hon. Sir Joceline Percy escorted General Junot and his staff back to La Rochelle on HMS *Nymphe* of 36 guns, a French ship captured in 1780.
28 Capt. the Hon. Henry Percy, 7th (Royal Fusileers) Foot, was an aide de camp to Sir John Moore.
29 For his bravery Patterson claims that Clunes (now a lieutenant) was promoted a major in the 54th (West Norfolk) Foot in July 1809, which is confirmed by the Army List.
30 Patterson, *Adventures*, p. 113. Ensign Robert Moore was wounded but died at Plymouth in March 1809. Ensign William Stewart died at Corunna.
31 Lt-Gen. John Hope succeeded to command of the army on the death of Moore and wrote the Corunna dispatch. He commanded divisions throughout the Peninsular War and eventually became Lord Niddry.
32 Reproduced with the kind permission of the National Library of Scotland, MS 3611 fos 41–4.
33 Gen. Graham had gone home the previous autumn with a serious eye complaint; it would appear that the eyes had already begun to give trouble again in the harsh glare of the Portuguese sun, immediately on his return.
34 The spelling is clear but I can find no officer of this name or similar. Rory Muir has suggested that it could refer to Sodre the Portuguese interpreter at headquarters, the 'great warriors' epithet being given in sarcasm; but this is far from certain.
35 Presumably from Col Sir Hussey Vivian.
36 Lt-Col the Hon. Charles Murray Cathcart, 2nd Earl, Assistant Quarter Master General and 'first assistant' to the cavalry.
37 Lt-Col Henry Frederick Bouverie Coldstream Guards, Assistant Adjutant General to 1st Division.
38 Lt-Col Richard Downes Jackson, Assistant Quarter Master General 2nd Division. I cannot discover the tragedy in his family.
39 Gen. Francisco Xavier Castanos commanded the Fourth Spanish Army.
40 Lt-Gen. Don Juan O'Donoju, Captain General of Andalucia, and Brigadier D. Tomas O'Donoju.
41 Mariscal de Campo Don Luis (Ludwig) Wimpffen (1765–1831), a Swiss by birth.
42 Evidence from the journal of James Stanhope shows this blank to be his penis.
43 Latin 'Being in all respects capable of functioning for sexual pleasure'.
44 Does this suggest the use of prostitutes for medicinal purposes?
45 Maj. William Geddes, Assistant Quarter Master General, ran the Lisbon office 1812–14.
46 This probably refers to the only Hesse in the army who was Capt. Charles Hesse of the 18th Light Dragoons. It is unlikely to refer to Capt. Augustus Heise, 2nd Light Battalion KGL, as records show that he was already in Spain as Deputy Assistant Adjutant General.
47 Capt. Felix Calvert, 29th Foot, had been an Extra ADC to Graham at Cadiz.
48 Gen. Charles William Stewart, Marquess Londonderry, left the Peninsula in April 1812 but did not resign his post as Adjutant General until May 1813.

49 William Prince of Orange was serving on Wellington's staff as an ADC at the time; his father was with the Allies in Germany, hoping soon to launch an insurrection in Holland against the French occupiers.
50 Lt-Col Ulysses Burgh, 92nd Foot, was ADC to Wellington, but Hume seems to indicate that he also acted as assistant military secretary.
51 Lt George Lennox, Earl of March, 9th Light Dragoons, was ADC to Wellington.
52 Lt-Col Richard Henry Sturgeon, Assistant Quarter Master General, was in April 1813 placed in charge of the Corps of Staff Guides and the Post Office vice Scovell.
53 Maj. George Scovell, 57th Foot, was appointed as major commandant of the newly formed Staff Corps of Cavalry in March 1813.
54 U1590 S5 C60/4 CFKS.
55 Perhaps now the most famous of the prisoner of war camps of the Napoleonic period, although others like Dartmoor prison still exist today. The site, a 40 acre field, was purchased by the government in 1796. Five hundred carpenters and labourers erected what were considered at the time to be permanent buildings and some 30 wells were sunk to draw drinking water for the prisoners. The prison barracks were planned to hold 6,000 prisoners.
56 Pitt's house stood on Putney Heath and was known at the time as 'Bowling Green House'.
57 Presumably Lord Hawkesbury (to become Lord Liverpool in 1808), who was Home Secretary.
58 George Rose MP was then joint Paymaster General.
59 It is probable that Pitt was actually suffering from either a duodenal (peptic) ulcer or pancreatic disease and had probably contracted typhoid fever in the later stages. It has been stated that Pitt died of acute liver failure brought on by his heavy drinking. However there is much conjecture over Pitt's death and current medical thinking is that the most likely cause was a duodenal ulcer which had so narrowed the outlet of Pitt's stomach that nothing could get through. He would thus have had pain, vomiting and weight loss; this would be caused by stress, alcohol and diet. Since there was no evidence of jaundice, he probably did not die of hepatic (liver) failure or severe chronic liver disease. His liver function may, nonetheless, have been impaired, as a result of his drinking. One other possibility exists, that he had acute or chronic relapsing pancreatitis – i.e. inflammation of the pancreas, as a consequence of his alcohol excess.
60 Sir Walter Farquhar (1738–1819) was Physician in Ordinary to the Prince Regent.
61 The Earl of Chatham was Master General of the Ordnance.
62 Dr Mathew Baillie (1761–1823) was Assistant Physician to King George III.
63 Dr Henry Reynolds (1745–1811), Assistant Physician to King George III.
64 The Prince Adolphus, Duke of Cambridge, seventh son of George III.
65 The Prince Ernest Augustus, Duke of Cumberland, fifth son of George III. Later he became King of Hanover.
66 William Sturges Brown, a Tory politician, is normally referred to as William Sturges.
67 Thomas Steele MP.
68 Sir George Pretyman Tomline, 5th Baronet, Bishop of Lincoln, had been appointed by Pitt against the wishes of the King.
69 This is an oral infection in debilitated patients with the organism candida albicans.
70 Col Sir Herbert Taylor was Private Secretary to George III.
71 This almost certainly refers to Lord Harrowby, then Chancellor of the Duchy of Lancaster, who had been sent by Pitt on a special mission to the courts of Austria, Russia and Prussia.
72 This refers to a nutritious jelly produced by boiling down stags horn.
73 William Adam, MP.
74 U1590 C269/2 CFKS.
75 Probably Surgeon J W K Parkinson who practised medicine in Hoxton and later in Islington. This was the son of James Parkinson (1755–1824), who wrote a piece on the 'shaking palsy' in 1817, which is known today as Parkinson's disease.
76 Presumably a nurse.
77 Freddy undoubtedly suffered from puerperal sepsis or post delivery fever, whereby the womb became infected and septicaemia set in.
78 Physician Martin Tupper who had learnt his trade at Guy's Hospital.
79 24 ounces of blood equates to approximately 720cc.
80 Each leech was capable of extracting between 20 and 30cc of blood.
81 Could this be the Physician Sir James Clark? He is reputed to have come to London from Edinburgh in 1826, but did he come to London earlier?
82 It is likely that the baby had an inflammation of the bowels and suffered febrile convulsions before succumbing.
83 Becca Hall near Leeds was the home of Archbishop Markham, a great friend of the Earl of Mansfield and who had married James and Frederica.
84 Lord Stormont was the eldest son of the Earl of Mansfield, hence Freddy's brother.
85 Elizabeth Elliott had married Earl and Viscount Cathcart in 1779.
86 Thomas Wilson (1663–1755) was Anglican Bishop of Sodor and Man. Presumably the book mentioned is *A Short and Plain Instruction for the Lord's Supper* (1733).
87 Richard Mead, Earl of Clanwilliam.

Bibliography

Unpublished Archives
Centre for Kentish Studies
U1590 0166A Messina 2 November 1806 by Charles Stanhope
'Exercises for Instruction of Recruits to the 52nd Light Infantry'
U 1590 C264/1 Note of Itinerary in Peninsular War 1808-9 (incorrectly assigned to James Stanhope when it is written by Charles Stanhope: see Appendix A to this volume)
U 1590 C264/2 Private Memoranda and Journal of James Stanhope 1810-12.
U1590 C264/3 Journal of a Campaign by James Stanhope 1812-15.
U1590 C264/5 'Extract of General Orders 1810 & Treatise on tactics etc plus Diary of the Proceedings of the Cortez assembled at the Isle de Leon 24th September 1810' by James Stanhope.
U1590 C266/1 338 Journal of a tour of Belgium, Germany & Italy 1819-20.
U1590 C266/3 325pt Journal of Continental Visit 1819-20.
U 1590 C269/1 331/2 An Account of Lady Frederica's death by James Stanhope.
U1590 C270 329/2 Letters from James Stanhope to his mother 1808-16.
U1590 C271,2 329/1,6 Letters from James Stanhope to his brother the 4th Earl.1803-5 & 1817-23.
U1590 C276/1 344 Letters from James Stanhope to Earl & Lady Mansfield 1815.
U1590 C276/2-6 342,345,349,354,356 Letters from James Stanhope & Frederica Murray to Earl & Lady Mansfield 1815-24.
C279 329/9 Letters from James Stanhope to Lady Hester Stanhope 1810.
C281 351 Letter from Duke of York to James Stanhope 1819.
C284/1-2 341 Letters relating to death of Lady Frederica 1823.
C285 329/5 Letters and newspaper cuttings concerning illness and death of James Stanhope 1825.

Cumbria Archives (The Lowther Archive)
DLons L1/2/60 Letter of James Stanhope to Lord Lonsdale. 1809.
DLons L1/2/63 Letters of James Stanhope to Lord Lonsdale. 1817.

Derbyshire Archives
D4576/20/15 Short note from James Stanhope to Sir Robert John Wilmot-Horton 1818.

Lincolnshire Archive
2 HAWLEY/2/B/63 28 Dec 1819 Deed of Settlement of Sir Joseph Banks.
RA/4/C/1 Last Will and Testament of James Hamilton Stanhope with codicil 1824.

West Sussex Record Office
Goodwood Ms 350 Letters of Charles and James Stanhope to the Duke of Richmond 1808–9.

Published Material
Army Lists, various years.
Anonymous, *The Royal Military Panorama, or Officers Companion*, vol. 4, London, 1814.
Anonymous, *The Royal Military Calendar*, London, 1820.
Aspinall-Oglander Cecil, *Freshly Remembered: The Story of Thomas Graham, Lord Lynedoch*, London, 1956.
Battle of Waterloo, By a Near Observer [anonymous, but now attributed to Miss Charlotte Eaton], London, 1815.
Chandler, David G, *Dictionary of the Napoleonic Wars*, London, 1979.
Cholmondley, R H, *The Heber Letters 1782–1832*, London, 1950.
Gore, John, *The Creevey Papers*, London, 1963.
Dalton, Charles, *The Waterloo Roll Call*, London, 1904.
Edgecumbe, Richard (ed.), *The Diary of Frances Lady Shelley 1787–1817*, London, 1912.
Fortescue, Hon. J W, *A History of the British Army*, London, 1899–1920.
Glover, Gareth, *Letters from the Battle of Waterloo*, London, 2004.
Glover, Gareth (ed.), *The Letters of 2nd Captain Charles Dansey Royal Artillery 1806–1813*, Godmanchester, 2006.

Glover, Gareth (ed.), *From Corunna to Waterloo* (London, 2007).
Glover, Gareth, *A Guards Officer in the Peninsula and at Waterloo: The Letters of Captain George Bowles, Coldstream Guards 1907–19*, Godmanchester, 2008.
Glover, Gareth, *A Young Gentleman at War: The Letters of Captain the Honourable Orlando Bridgeman 1st Foot Guards 1812–15*, Huntingdon, 2008.
Gore, John, *The CreeveyPapers*, London, 1963.
Grehan, John, *The Lines of Torres Vedras*, Staplehurst, 2000.
Gwynn, Stephen, *A Brotherhood of Heroes: Being Memorials of Charles, George and William Napier*, London, 1910.
Hall, John, *A History of the Peninsular War*, vol. 8, London, 1998.
Hamel, Frank, *Lady Hester Lucy Stanhope: A New Light on her Life and Love Affairs*, London, 1913.
Hamilton, Lieutenant-General Sir F W, *Origin and History of the First or Grenadier Guards*, London, 1874.
Hunter, Archie, *Wellington's Scapegoat: The Tragedy of Lieutenant Colonel Charles Bevan*, Barnsley, 2003.
Lodge, Edmund, *The Peerage of The British Empire*, London, 1832.
Meryon, Charles Lewis, *Memoirs of the Lady Hester Stanhope*, London, 1846.
Moore Smith, G C, *The Life of John Colborne Field Marshal Lord Seaton*, London, 1903.
Muir, Rory, *At Wellington's Right Hand*, London, 2003.
Nafziger, G F and Park, S J, *The British Military 1803–15*, Cambridge, Ontario, 1983.
Napier, General W C E, *Passages in the Early Military Life of General Sir George T Napier KCB*, London, 1884.
Napier, William, *History of the Peninsular War*, London, 1835.
Napier, General W C E, *Life of General Sir George Napier*, London, 1884.
Newman, Aubrey, *The Stanhopes of Chevening*, London, 1969.
O'Byrne ,William, *A Naval Biographical Dictionary*, London, 1849.
Oman, Carola, *Sir John Moore*, London, 1953.
Oman, Sir Charles, *Wellington's Army 1809–14*, London, 1913.
Patterson, Captain John, *The Adventures of Captain John Patterson with notices of the officers & of the 50th or Queen's Own Regiment from 1807–21*, London, 1837.
Penny, N B, 'English Church Monuments to Women who Died in Childbed between 1780 and 1835', *Journal of the Warburg and Courtauld Institutes*, 38 (1975), 314–32.
Pool, Bernard, *The Croker Papers*, London, 1884.
Reid, Stuart, *Wellington's Officers*, Leigh on Sea, 2008.
Robertson, Ian, *Wellington at War in the Peninsula*, Barnsley, 2000.
Stanhope, Ghita, and Gooch, G P, *The Life of Charles, Third Earl Stanhope*, London, 1914.
Suarez, Federico, *Las Cortes de Cadiz*, Madrid, 1982.
Veve, Thomas Dwight, *The Duke of Wellington and the British Army of Occupation 1815–18*, Westport, CT, 1997.
Ward, B, *A Week at Waterloo in June 1815 by Lady DeLancey*, London, 1906.
Ward, S G P, *Wellington's Headquarters*, Oxford, 1957.
Warre, William, *Letters from the Peninsula 1808–12*, London, 1909.
Watson, Steven, *The Reign of George III 1760–1815*, Oxford, 1960.

Index